ADVENTURES IN THEATER HISTORY: PHILADELPHIA

Dedicated to

Dr. Joe Lex

With deep gratitude
for his support, his wisdom,
and his friendship.

ADVENTURES IN THEATER HISTORY: PHILADELPHIA

PETER SCHMITZ

BROOKLINE
books
Havertown, Pennsylvania

Brookline Books is an imprint of Casemate Publishers

Published in the United States of America and Great Britain in 2024 by
BROOKLINE BOOKS
1950 Lawrence Road, Havertown, PA 19083, USA
and
47 Church Street, Barnsley, S70 2AS, UK

Copyright © 2024 Peter Schmitz

Hardcover Edition: ISBN 978-1-955041-37-9
Digital Edition: ISBN 978-1-955041-38-6

A CIP record for this book is available from the British Library

All rights reserved. No part of this book may be reproduced or transmitted in any form or by any means, electronic or mechanical including photocopying, recording or by any information storage and retrieval system, without permission from the publisher in writing.

Printed and bound in the United Kingdom by CPI Group (UK) Ltd, Croydon, CR0 4YY
Typeset in India by DiTech Publishing Services

For a complete list of Brookline Books titles, please contact:

CASEMATE PUBLISHERS (US)
Telephone (610) 853-9131
Fax (610) 853-9146
Email: casemate@casematepublishers.com
www.casematepublishers.com

CASEMATE PUBLISHERS (UK)
Telephone (0)1226 734350
Email: casemate@casemateuk.com
www.casemateuk.com

Cover image: "Arch Street Theatre, 'Ranch 10,' Monday, Nov. 26." (1883 lithograph from the Theater Posters Collection of the Historical Society of Pennsylvania, Permanent ID 1071)

Contents

Map	viii
Acknowledgements	xi
Foreword	xiii
List of Images and Illustrations	xvii

Part One: Only in Philadelphia

Durang's Hornpipe	2
36 Indian Chiefs and Warriors at the Olympic	6
"A Young Gentleman of this City"	10
Miss Philadelphia of 1896	15
"Three Cheers for Captain Sigsbee!"	18
Freedom at the Sesqui and *The Miracle* at the Met	21
Shakspere in the Parkway	28
Shakespeare's Birthday at the Edwin Forrest Home	32
Won't You Come Home, Pearl Bailey?	34
The Show Rescued by a Helicopter	37
Philadelphia '76	40
The Return of Lady Day	42

Part Two: The Wicked Stage

William Penn Sees a Play	46
The Friends of Virtue	50
Theater Is Illegal in Philadelphia	55
The Moral Structure of the Academy of Music	58
"Let Us Live to See the Theatres All Deserted"	62
The Battle of *Salome* in the Opera War	64
Let My People Come on South Street	67
Hugh Hefner in Old City	71

Part Three: Playhouses

The Mysterious Case of the Stolen Spikes at the Old Theatre	76
The New Theatre on Chestnut Street	79
Ricketts' Circus, Benedict Arnold, and the Death of Major Andre	81
The Spanish Consul and the New French Circus on Walnut Street	84
Farewell to Old Drury	89
Mrs. John Drew's Arch Street Theatre	91
Opening Night at Hammerstein's Opera House	94
The Adventures of Chlora on Delancey Street	98
Snake Hips at the Lincoln	101
The Invention of the Wilma	103
The Arden in Old City	105
A Great Day on South Broad Street	107

Part Four: Local Heroes

Edwin Forrest Plays Richelieu	112
The Heron Takes Wing	116
The Little Tycoon	119
May Manning Lillie, Quaker Cowgirl	121
Blythe Spirit, or All Them Barrymores	125
Imogene Coca in Manayunk	129
One of the Kelly Boys	131
They All Want Something from Big Bill Tilden	134
"The Girl Who Falls Down"	138
Molly Gets Married	141
Charles Fuller's Inspirations	144

Part Five: Visiting Stars

George Frederick Cooke	150
Edmund Kean Takes a Bow	153
Fanny Kemble Makes a Fateful Debut	155
Rachel Gets a Cold Reception	159
Bunthorne in the Quaker City	163
Sarah Bernhardt and the Mummers	167
Katharine Hepburn's Philadelphia Story	170
Paul Robeson's Hammer	172
Peter Brook Finds the Empty Space	175

Part Six: Disputes, Deaths, and Disasters

Kean's Riot	180
Charlotte Cushman Sends Too Many Flowers	183
The Marble Heart of John Wilkes Booth	186
The Death of Annie Kemp Bowler, the Original Stalacta	190
The Temple Theatre Catches Fire	193
The Fall of Apollo	195
Curtain Time, Minus Zero	198
Zsa Zsa Gabor Gets Fired	202

Part Seven: The Tryout Town

The Marx Brothers Stay for the Summer	206
Mrs. Penfield Backs *Fioretta*	209
Lysistrata—Modern Abdominal Merriment	212
Ayn Rand Writes a Play	215
Brando on Walnut Street	218
World Premiere of *Death of a Salesman*	220
~~Something Wild in the Country~~ *Orpheus Descending*	226
Philadelphia, Here I Come!	229
The King and Oy	231
Muhammad Ali vs. Big Time Buck White	233
The Line of Least Existence—Last Days of the TLA	236
Auntie Mame Leaves Early	239

Part Eight: The Manning Street Theatre

Hamlet in the Rafters	242
The Two Joes	248
The Orphan	254

Epilogues

Ghost Light	262
Love Unpunished	264

Permissions	266
Bibliography	267
Notes and Sources	274
Index	301

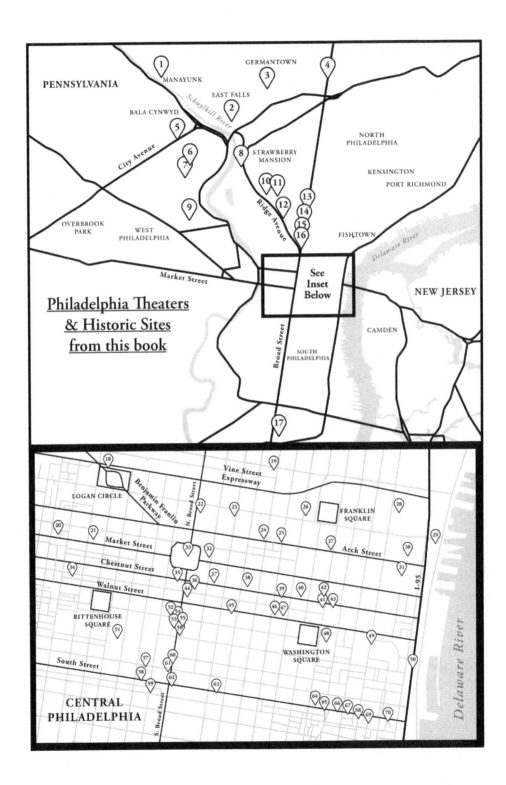

Map Key

1. Empress Theatre
2. George S. Kelly family home
3. William Tilden II home
4. Logan Theatre
5. City Line Dinner Theatre
6. Gentlemen's Driving Park
7. Playhouse in the Park
8. Robin Hood Dell
9. Edwin Forrest Home for Retired Actors
10. James Weldon Johnson Homes (Charles Fuller and Larry Neal childhood homes)
11. Pearl Bailey childhood home
12. Pearl Theatre
13. Grand Opera House
14. 1) Edwin Forrest Mansion, and 2) Freedom Theatre
15. Philadelphia Opera House/Metropolitan Opera House/The Met
16. Park Theatre
17. Sesqui-Centennial Stadium
18. Shakespeare Memorial
19. New National Theatre
20. Erlanger Theatre
21. Mastbaum Theatre
22. Lyric and Adelphi Theatres
23. Barrymore family home
24. Arch Street Opera House/Trocadero Theatre/The Troc
25. Ninth and Arch Dime Museum
26. Bijou Theatre
27. Arch Street Theatre (Mrs. John Drew's Arch Street Theatre, later Blaney's Theatre)
28. Painted Bride Art Center, Callowhill Street
29. FringeArts
30. National Showroom
31. Arden Theatre Company
32. Tivoli Gardens
33. City Hall
34. Adrienne Theatre (originally Wilma Theatre)
35. Prince Music Theatre/Philadelphia Film Center
36. Garrick Theatre
37. (Third) Chestnut Street Theatre
38. Chestnut Street Opera House
39. Welch's National Theatre & Circus
40. Temple Theatre & Egyptian Museum
41. Ricketts' Circus and Art Pantheon
42. 1) New Theatre, and 2) "Chesnut Street Theatre" or "Old Drury"
43. Independence Hall
44. (First) Forrest Theatre, Broad Street
45. Forrest Theatre, Walnut Street
46. Walnut Street Theatre

47. Continental Theatre (later American Theatre, Central Theatre, Gilmore's Auditorium)
48. Prune Street Theatre
49. Edwin Forrest family gravesite
50. Plumsted's Warehouse
51. Little Theatre/Plays & Players Theatre
52. Locust Street Theatre
53. 1) Horticultural Hall 2) Shubert Theatre (later Merriam Theatre, Miller Theater)
54. Academy of Music
55. Kiralfy's Alhambra Theatre (later Broad Street Theatre)
56. Wilma Theater
57. Manning Street Theatre
58. Royal Theatre
59. Emerson's Bar & Grill
60. Suzanne Roberts Theater
61. Dunbar Theatre/Lincoln Theatre
62. Arts Bank Theatre
63. Standard Theatre
64. Painted Bride Gallery South Street
65. Grendel's Lair
66. Old Theatre/Southwark Theater
67. Theatre of The Living Arts
68. Yiddish Theatre Hall (Columbia Theatre), later Theatre Center Philadelphia
69. Edwin Forrest's childhood home
70. Theatre at Society Hill

Acknowledgements

Thank you:

To every newspaper reporter, critic, feature writer, photographer, or editor who has covered Philadelphia theater over the past 250 years. These printed chronicles, as they are preserved in both digital databases and physical archives, have made my work on this book possible.

To Charles Gilbert, for his early support of my work, for his help as my colleague—and his presence as my friend. And for being the guy who, when asked whether I should write a book or do a podcast about Philly theater history, said "Yes!" to both.

To librarian extraordinaire Sara MacDonald, for all her research help; and to my dear cousin Nina Haigney, for her writing advice. Both of you were so important to me, especially in the early stages of this project.

To Karin Suni, at the Rare Book department of the Free Library of Philadelphia, for always being able to point me to real treasures of Philadelphia theater history.

To Pig Iron Theatre, New Paradise Lab, the Wilma Theater, the Arden Theatre, the Paul Robeson House & Museum, the Walnut Street Theatre, Plays & Players Theatre and the Philadelphia Theatre Company, for their kind assistance in obtaining photographs and images. Special thanks in this regard go to Sara Garonzik, Bernard Havard, Whit MacLaughlin, Amy Murphy Nolen, Kristin Finger, Raven Buck, Sid Sachs, Nicole Keegan, Peggy Hartzell, Dan Rothenberg, and Terry Fimiano Guerin.

To Josue Hurtado, and all the wonderful staff of the Temple University Library, the Kislak Center of the Library of the University of Pennsylvania, the Library Company of Philadelphia, and the Historical Society of Pennsylvania.

To Dr. Eric Colleary, Cline Curator of Theater and Performing Arts at the Harry Ransom Center, University of Texas at Austin, for all his invaluable advice and generous research assistance.

To Tom Keels, Philadelphia historian, for all his deep wisdom, scrupulous fact checking, and sage advice. Thanks also to John Cooper, Robert Davis, Paul Gagliardi, Sara Garonzik, Joe Lex, Michael Lueger, and Whit MacLaughlin for reading and fact-checking certain sections and chapters of my manuscript.

To my two wonderful sons, Mack and Tom, who all their lives have patiently let me Explain Things to them.

To Christopher Mark Colucci, the great Philadelphia musician, photographer, composer, sound designer, and my dear friend. The podcast episodes we created together were the essential basis for so much of this work.

To Jennifer Green at Brookline Books, for believing in me, and for asking me if I had ever thought about turning my podcast into a book.

To Lizzy Hammond at Casemate Group for her invaluable editing expertise—and to all the many other editors, publicists, designers and typesetters who helped to make this book a reality.

Above all, to the entire theater community of Philadelphia—performers and audiences, past and present—with admiration for all they have already achieved, and in anticipation of all the amazing things they will do next.

Foreword

For a while now, I have been researching, writing, and hosting a podcast about Philadelphia and its theater history. Back when I first began this labor of love, I decided to call it *Adventures in Theater History: Philadelphia*. It felt like an adventure to me then, and I am pleased to report that it still does.

In fact, the deeper I go in this work, the more I appreciate how theater and the other performing arts have consistently been a strength of Philadelphia. Thousands of American actors, playwrights, dancers, musicians, designers, stage technicians, and other theater artists have made Philadelphia their home—or their starting place. I want their lives and works to be remembered, honored, and enjoyed.

In addition to the podcast, I have also undertaken a regular practice to share daily posts and images about Philadelphia's theater history on various social media platforms. It has become a bit of an obsession, really. Each morning, I take a stroll through my books and online archival sources until I come across something unexpected—or at least until I find a new angle on something familiar. Then I shape a brief narrative, attach relevant photographs and images, and send it off to gather reactions and comments from my online followers. At first, I worried that eventually I'd run out of material, but it seems like there is always more to discover.

After a few years of this daily practice, I have investigated, written, and shared literally hundreds of stories. In fact, between making all the podcast episodes, writing a blog about them for my website, and creating these posts, I have generated thousands of pages of scripts, essays, and online articles, all of which I have carefully copied and kept in my files. Even long after the scripts are broadcast or the pieces have been posted online, I find that I return to these files again and again—to further craft and improve them, as additional information comes to my attention.

A selection of these writings forms the basis of the book you are holding. You'll notice that most chapters begin with a date, as my online posts tend to be short essays that begin: "On this date in theater history. ..." Some of the longer chapters were either adapted from the episodes in the podcast or from my blogs, with lots of new material added. Others are being published for the first time anywhere.

Let me stress that this book is not intended to be a *comprehensive* history of theater in Philadelphia. Instead, this book strives to be a different way of introducing people to the overall topic. Inevitably, many intriguing stories were regretfully laid aside during the writing and editing process, and I confess that I would like to have covered more modern Philadelphia theater. There are fewer stories here from the 1980s, 1990s, and early 2000s than I had originally intended. I can only say that my investigations into those decades are ongoing, and I hope to write more about them—and all the other bypassed topics—in the future. Still, if I've done this right, this book will serve as a reliable resource for historians and scholars as well as an entertaining journey for everyone else. It should feel less like school, and more like—well, an adventure!

A great deal of care and effort has gone into selecting images and illustrations to accompany each chapter. In fact, they often have provided the very basis for the chapter's story. I've made the decision not to place captions and source credits directly next to these images, in order to provide an uncluttered page that focuses the reader's attention on the relation between the image and the text. If you would like to know more about their provenance, please refer to the list of Images and Illustrations at the beginning of the book for all credits and attributions. Similarly, to keep the chapters from looking like an academic treatise, I've intentionally avoided placing numbers indicating endnotes and references in the text itself. Each chapter's sources and notes can be found in the back of the book.

Rather than providing a strictly chronological narrative, I've divided these stories into eight thematic groups. Each of these themes is a different aspect of the history of theater in Philadelphia. Although within each group the stories are presented in chronological order, you don't have to read them in sequence. Feel free to dip in and out, reading the chapters in whatever order you please. I must admit that during the creation of this book some of the stories have jumped back and forth between different groups, as I struggled to herd them into their proper corrals. Their eventual placement in a particular group was sometimes more of an esthetic judgment on my part than an absolute historical necessity.

The eight groups are:

Part One: *Only in Philadelphia*—Stories about theater people and things that were never going to happen anywhere except in this city. In fact, I'm not sure they could exist, or even make sense, anyplace else.

Part Two: *The Wicked Stage*—This is a collection of tales from the long history of *opposition* to theater in Philadelphia (mostly from religious leaders, but from political and social reformers, too). It starts in the early history of the city's foundation—and ends with examples of how some preachers' and politicians' worst fears and direst prophecies became … well, gloriously *true*, in the long run!

Part Three: *Playhouses*—A selection of some of the most consequential buildings that have been used as Philadelphia theaters over the past 250 years. It's also, inevitably, the story of the people that have built, used, and shaped those venues and given performances in them.

Part Four: *Local Heroes*—These are vignettes about theater people, plays and institutions that are "from" Philadelphia. Almost all the subjects were born in the city, or nearby. Some of them started their careers in Philadelphia and moved on, and some never left. Some went away, but then came back in the end. The plays I discuss in this section, for their part, were either written *in* or *about* or *because* of Philadelphia.

Part Five: *Visiting Stars*—Philadelphia has a very long history of receiving visits from important theatrical people from other American cities and elsewhere in the world—not just actors, but directors, designers, composers, and playwrights. Typically, these visitors only stayed for a brief while, usually on tour with plays, operas, vaudeville acts, or other shows. All of them made an impact on the cultural life of the city, and many provided valuable insights about Philadelphia as they passed through.

Part Six: *Disputes, Deaths, and Disasters*—These are mostly sad or disturbing stories. Sometimes things go horribly wrong in the theater, as arguments and misunderstandings occur between artistic collaborators. Sometimes brand-new theaters go up in flames, and other beautiful old venues get torn down. And even worse, sometimes we lose theater people along the way, long before we wanted them to make their final exits.

Part Seven: *The Tryout Town*—Along with other cities (such as Boston, New Haven, Baltimore, Washington, and Chicago), for most of the 20th century Philadelphia was one of the main "tryout towns" for commercial American plays and musicals. Broadway producers would book Philly theaters to get immediate reactions to scripts, jokes, songs, routines, and performers. Sometimes what they learned from Philadelphia audiences led to big overhauls in these shows. Titles were changed, songs rewritten, scenery was thrown out, actors were fired. Sometimes big stars walked out of projects they thought were duds—and were replaced by someone else who became suddenly famous themselves. Other shows were obvious hits right from the start. In fact, because of its large theater-going public and its easy accessibility from New York, Philadelphia was often the *preferred* Tryout Town. This is why many famous plays and musicals had their world premieres on its stages. Some shows, of course, never made it out of Philly at all—and those stories are just as much fun to read about.

Part Eight: *The Manning Street Theatre*—This story is a bit longer than the others in the collection, so I've split it into three parts. In one way, it's really an "Only in Philadelphia" story, about a tiny little-known company of young theater artists. But it's also about a play that was in development here and that everybody hoped would go on to New York. Plus, the narrative involves *both* visiting stars *and* homegrown heroes. In the end, since it seemed to belong to so many categories, I've decided that it gets one all of its own.

I conclude the book with two brief and rather personal *Epilogues*, which take us as far as the resumption of live theater performances in Philadelphia following the COVID-19 pandemic.

Finally, let me say that my purpose in investigating *all* these stories is not to argue that theater in Philadelphia is more interesting, artistic, or consequential than theater in any other city in the world—New York, London, Tehran, Cleveland—anywhere. Of course it isn't. But I insist that, just like the theater of all those places, the story of Philadelphia theater is fascinating when you get up close to it, and not enough people in the world know about it. So, I'm doing what I can to fix that. It has been a marvelous adventure to explore this topic over the past few years, and now it is a pleasure to share so many of the stories I have found with all of you.

Note: Throughout this book, I will consistently employ the modern American spelling of "theater." But whenever a group or venue I'm discussing—or a writer I'm directly quoting—uses "theatre," I will retain their original spelling. Furthermore, numbered streets—which run north–south in Philadelphia, as per William Penn's original plan for the city—were usually written out as "Second Street, Third Street," etc. in the early years of its history. But by the 20th century, when the city's grid of streets stretched all the way into the far reaches of West Philadelphia, it because usual to only use numerals ("54th Street," for example). I have generally retained this numeration for street names for events that take place after the year 1900. The variation is not an error of editing.

List of Images and Illustrations

Page 2: "John Durang in Character of a Hornpipe," by John Durang. (Collection of the York County History Center, York, PA. Used by permission)

Page 6: "Exhibition of Indian Tribal Ceremonies at the Olympic Theatre, Philadelphia," by John Lewis Krimmel. (Collection of the Metropolitan Museum of Art, New York)

Page 10: "Mr. E. Forrest as Rolla." (University of Illinois Theatrical Print Collection)

Page 15: "A Scene from Miss Philadelphia." (*Philadelphia Times*, April 12, 1896)

Page 18: "Captain Charles Dwight Sigsbee, USN." (Wikimedia Commons)

Page 21: "Freedom," advertisement. (*Philadelphia Inquirer*, June 27, 1926)

Page 26: "The Mock Wedding of the Nun and the Prince," by Charles E. Bell (1874–1935). (*Philadelphia Inquirer*, October 1926)

Page 28: "Shakespeare Memorial, Logan Square—1930." (Courtesy of the Free Library of Philadelphia, Print and Picture Collection)

Page 32: "Reviving Years Before the Footlights," (shown: Herbert Duke Fortier, Helen Potter Jackson, and April Duke). *Philadelphia Evening Bulletin*, April 28, 1943. (Courtesy of the Special Collections Research Center. Temple University Libraries. Philadelphia, PA)

Page 34: Cab Calloway as Horace Vandergelder and Pearl Bailey as Mrs. Dolly Gallagher Levi in "Hello, Dolly!" (photographer unknown). (Collection of the Museum of the City of New York. Used by permission)

Page 37: "Isometric Sketch: Playhouse in the Park," *Philadelphia Evening Bulletin*, May 5, 1963. (Courtesy of the Special Collections Research Center. Temple University Libraries. Philadelphia, PA)

Page 40: "Miss Phebe Williamson gives out the free tickets for '1776' at the Municipal Services Building, near City Hall," *Philadelphia Evening Bulletin*, July 27, 1976. (Courtesy of the Special Collections Research Center. Temple University Libraries. Philadelphia, PA)

Page 42: "Billie Holliday under arrest in Philadelphia," 1947. (Smithsonian, National Portrait Gallery. Used by permission)

Page 46: "William Penn in Armor (After Schoff's Steel Engraving from the Original)." (New York Public Library Digital Collections)

Page 50: "Plumstead's Warehouse: the first building used as a theater in America" (artist unknown). (Collection of the Harry Ransom Center, University of Texas at Austin)

Page 54: "Mrs. Hallam (Mrs. Douglas)." (Hutton's *Curiosities of the American Stage*, 1891)

Page 55: Notice of a "concert" placed by the American Company in the *Independent Gazetteer*, July 23, 1788. (The *Independent Gazetteer*)

Page 58: Cover of the pamphlet, *History and Description of the Opera House, or American Academy of Music, in Philadelphia*, 1857. (Collection of the Library of Congress)

Page 61: "Academy of Music, Interior." (*Century After: Picturesque Glimpses of Philadelphia*, 1875)

Page 62: Photo of Rev. John Chambers c. 1873, from the book *John Chambers, Servant of Christ and Master of Hearts, and His Ministry in Philadelphia*, published in 1903. (*John Chambers, Servant of Christ and Master of Hearts, and His Ministry in Philadelphia*)

Page 64: "Mary Garden as Salome," by Giovanni Viafora. (The New York Public Library Digital Collections, Music Division)

Page 67: Production of "Let My People Come" at Grendel's Lair, photo by Frederick A. Meyer for the *Philadelphia Evening Bulletin*, October 16, 1977. (Courtesy of the Special Collections Research Center. Temple University Libraries. Philadelphia, PA)

Page 71: New Paradise Lab company portrait for *Planetary Enzyme Blues* (2006). Photo by Steven H. Begleiter. Counterclockwise from top left: McKenna Kerrigan, Matt Saunders, Lee Ann Etzold, Mary McCool, Jeb Kreager, Aaron Mumaw. (Courtesy Whit MacLaughlin)

Page 76: Detail from a drawing by Edwin F. Durang (1829–1911), based on an earlier drawing by an unknown artist. From Charles Durang, *History of the Philadelphia Stage*. (Penn Libraries, Colenda Digital Repository)

Page 79: "Inside view of the New Theatre, Philadelphia." (Collection of the Cooper-Hewitt Museum, New York)

Page 81: Left: Detail from advertisement for Ricketts' Circus, published in the *Aurora General Advertiser*, February 7, 1799. Right: Detail from "Ricketts' Circus in 1797"—1875 watercolor by David J. Kennedy. (Collection of the Historical Society of Pennsylvania, V. 61)

Page 84: "The Walnut Street Theatre," by Frank Hamilton Taylor. (The Library Company of Philadelphia, Frank H. Taylor Collection)

Page 89: "Chestnut Street Theatre. North East Corner of Sixth and Chestnut Streets, Philadelphia. Drawn and engraved by D.C. Baxter." (The Library Company of Philadelphia)

Page 91: Arch Street Theatre, 1868. (The Library Company of Philadelphia)

Page 94: "Oscar Hammerstein and His New Philadelphia Opera House and Mlle. Labia Noted Prima Donna." (*Billings Gazette*, Montana, December 8, 1908)

Page 98: "Philadelphia's Little Theatre," from *The Theatre Magazine*, August 1913, Vol. 18, No. 150. (Courtesy Plays and Players Theatre)

Page 101: "Southwest Corner of Broad and Lombard Streets, January 11, 1932," Philadelphia City Archives. (Used by permission of PhillyHistory.org)

Page 103: Blanka and Jiri Zizka during renovations of Sansom Street space, 1980. (Courtesy Wilma Theater Company)

Page 105: Terry Nolen, Aaron Posner and Amy Murphy Nolen, March 1998. Photo by Gerald S. Willilams. (Courtesy Arden Theatre Company)

Page 107: Producing Artistic Director Sara Garonzik, during construction of Suzanne Roberts Theatre, 2006. (Courtesy Philadelphia Theatre Company)

Page 112: Edwin Forrest as Richelieu, studio of Matthew Brady, c. 1861. (National Portrait Gallery, Smithsonian)

Page 116: Matilda Heron as Bianca in *Fazio*, c. 1853. (The New York Public Library Digital Collections)

Page 119: Scene from *The Little Tycoon*. (The New York Public Library Digital Collections)

Page 121: May Lillie and Pawnee Bill, c. 1888. (Wikimedia Commons)

Page 125: John, Ethel, and Lionel Barrymore, 1904. (Wikimedia Commons)

Page 129: "Brunette and Blonde: Miss Imogene Coca was photographed with her pure white Persian cat which she will exhibit at the annual show of the Quaker City Persian Society, to be held this week." (*Philadelphia Inquirer*, November 27, 1927)

Page 131: George Kelly. (The New York Public Library Digital Collections, The Miriam and Ira D. Wallach Division of Art, Prints and Photographs)

Page 134: Bill Tilden II. (Collection of the Library of Congress)

Page 138: Joan McCracken as Sylvie in the original Broadway production of *Oklahoma!* Photo by Graphic House, Inc. (The New York Public Library Digital Collections, Billy Rose Theatre Division scrapbooks)

Page 141: Molly Picon in *Mazel Tov, Molly!* 1950. (The New York Public Library Digital Collections)

Page 144: Charles Fuller receiving a citation from Mayor Wilson Goode, 1982 (detail). (Courtesy of the Free Library of Philadelphia, Theatre Collection)

Page 150: Thomas Sully, "George Frederick Cooke as Richard III." (Collection of Pennsylvania Academy of the Fine Arts)

Page 153: Edmund Kean as Richard III. (Wikimedia Commons)

Page 155: Thomas Sully, "Frances Anne Kemble as Bianca." (Collection of Pennsylvania Academy of the Fine Arts)

Page 159: "Mademoiselle Rachel." (*Dramatic Mirror and Literary Companion*, James Rees, editor, (Turner and Fisher: Philadelphia, 1841) vol. 1, no. ix, p. 1)

Page 163: Left: Oscar Wilde, photographed in his lecture outfit by Napoleon Sarony, New York, January 1882. (Wikimedia Commons); right: John Howson as Bunthorne in *Patience*. (The New York Public Library Digital Collections)

Page 167: Sarah Bernhardt in *L'aiglon*, 1900. (The New York Public Library Digital Collections)

Page 168: "The New Years' Mummers on Chestnut Street, Philadelphia." Illustration from *Harper's Weekly*, January 14, 1888. (Hathi Trust)

Page 170: Katharine Hepburn, 1939. (The New York Public Library Digital Collections)

Page 172: Robeson as Othello, *Philadelphia Evening Bulletin*, October 18, 1943. (Courtesy of the Special Collections Research Center. Temple University Libraries. Philadelphia, PA)

Page 175: Audience at the Locust Theatre, Philadelphia. *Evening Bulletin*, March 1967, Tom McCaffery, photographer. (Courtesy of the Special Collections Research Center. Temple University Libraries. Philadelphia, PA)

Page 180: Theodore Lane, "Theatrical Pleasures, Plate 2: Contending for a Seat.," c. 1835. (Collection of the Metropolitan Museum of Art, New York)

Page 183: Thomas Sully, *Charlotte Saunders Cushman "of the Walnut Street Theater"* (1843). (The Library Company of Philadelphia)

Page 186: Arch Street Theatre bill, March 11, 1863. (The Library Company of Philadelphia)

Page 190: "The Black Crook." (Collection of the Harry Ransom Center, University of Texas at Austin)

Page 193: Drawing titled "Scene on Chestnut Street," (accompanying article "The Temple Burned"). (*Philadelphia Times*, December 28, 1886)

Page 195: "Arch Street Theatre Just Prior to Demolition," *Philadelphia Evening Bulletin*, June 1936. (Courtesy of the Special Collections Research Center. Temple University Libraries. Philadelphia, PA)

Page 198: Philip Loeb. (Collection of the New York Public Library)

LIST OF IMAGES AND ILLUSTRATIONS • xxi

Page 200: Friedman-Abeles, "Publicity photo of Zero Mostel for the stage production *The Merchant*, 1977." (Photo by Friedman-Abeles © The New York Public Library for the Performing Arts)

Page 202: "Actress Zsa Zsa Gabor enters the City Line Dinner Theatre in Philadelphia 6/2/1983 carrying one of her dogs with an aide following her." (UPI photo)

Page 206: *I'll Say She Is* with the Marx Brothers, marked "November 17, 1924." (The New York Public Library Digital Collections)

Page 209: Theater program advertisement for *Fioretta* at the Erlanger Theatre, Philadelphia. (*Plays and Players* playbill, January 1929)

Page 212: "Lysistrata, 1930," drawing by Al Hirschfeld. Shown (L to R): Sydney Greenstreet, Ernest Truex, Hope Emerson, Violet Kemble-Cooper, Miriam Hopkins and Hortense Alden. Originally published in *The New York Times*, May 25, 1930. (Copyright © The Al Hirschfeld Foundation, www.AlHirschfeldFoundation.org)

Page 215: Verna Hillie, Marcella Swanson, and Doris Nolan in a publicity photo for *The Night of January 16th*. (The New York Public Library Digital Collections)

Page 218: Karl Malden, Marlon Brando, and Jessica Tandy rehearse for *A Streetcar Named Desire*. (Photo in the *Philadelphia Inquirer*, November 16, 1947)

Page 220: Mildred Dunnock, Lee J. Cobb, Cameron Mitchell and Arthur Kennedy on Lee Mielziner's set for *Death of a Salesman*, 1949. (Billy Rose Theatre Division, The New York Library for the Performing Arts)

Page 226: Advertisement for Orpheus Descending. (*Philadelphia Inquirer*, March 3, 1957)

Page 229: "Black dot marks location of the Walnut, Philadelphia theater where none of the Irish actors in 'Philadelphia, Here I Come!' has ever been. In New York where they are rehearsing, stage manager Mitchell Erickson pinpoints the location to kneeling cast members, Donal Donnelly, Patrick Bedford and Eamon Kelly (from left) and, standing from left, actresses Mairin O'Sullivan and Mavis Villiers, playwright Brian Friel and director Hilton Edwards." *Philadelphia Evening Bulletin*, January 9, 1967. (Courtesy of the Special Collections Research Center. Temple University Libraries. Philadelphia, PA)

Page 231: Playbill for *Chu Chem*, New Locust Theatre, November 1966. From "*Chu Chem* Headed to Broadway." (Posted by Virginia Wing on *Performing Arts Legacy Project*, Research Center for Arts and Culture, Entertainment Community Fund, 2022)

Page 233: Advertisement for *Big Time Buck White*. (*Philadelphia Inquirer*, April 23, 1969)

Page 236: The company and crew of *The Line of Least Existence*, Theatre of the Living Arts, Philadelphia, January 1970. Photo by Bill Watkins. (Courtesy of Tom Bissinger, Nicole Keegan and Peggy Hartzell)

Page 239: Angela Lansbury in *Mame*, 1966. (The New York Public Library Digital Collections)

Page 242: "Manning Street Theatre founders Stuart Finklestein and Mary Kaye Bernardo sit on stage and survey empty house after city blocked opening." *Philadelphia Evening Bulletin*, April 24, 1970. (Courtesy of the Special Collections Research Center. Temple University Libraries. Philadelphia, PA)

Page 248: Photo of Manning Street Theatre, by Frederick A. Meyer for the *Evening Bulletin*. Left to right: Joe Stinson, Marlea (Linda) Evans, Fritz Kupfer, John P. Connolly, Jim Lambert, and Susan Payne. (Courtesy of the Special Collections Research Center. Temple University Libraries. Philadelphia, PA)

Page 254: Photos of David Rabe's *The Orphan* at the Manning Street Theatre by Gene Thomas. Left: Bonnie Cavanaugh and Tom Hulce. Right: The curtain call of the Philadelphia cast of *The Orphan*. (Courtesy Bonnie Cavanaugh and Barnet Kellman)

Page 262: Photo of Walnut Street Theare interior, by Lori Aghazarian, March 15, 2020. (Courtesy of the Aghazarian family)

Page 264: Scene from *Love Unpunished, 2021*. From left: Kyle Vincent Terry, Dito van Reigersberg, Quinn Bauriedel, Jenna Horton, Makoto Hirano, Hinako Arao, Jaime Maseda. (Photo by Mimi Lien, Courtesy of Pig Iron Theatre Company)

PART ONE
Only in Philadelphia

Durang's Hornpipe

Even three decades later, John Durang could still recall the costume he made for himself that night in January 1785:

> My dress was in the character of a sailor, a dark blue round about full of plated buttons, petticoat trousers made with 6 yard of fine linens, black satin small clothes underneath, white silk stockings, a light shoe with a handsome set buckle, a red westcoat, a blue silk handkerchief; my hair curled and black, a small round hat gold lace with a blue ribband, a small rattan.

In his old age he also painted, from memory, a watercolor of himself in his youth, wearing that dark blue sailor's outfit and dancing a hornpipe.

In the painting we can see Durang, poised gracefully on his right leg and lifting his left one lightly into the air. He holds a cane (that "small rattan") behind his back. On the rear wall to his right is a framed portrait of a woman in a red dress, hands on her hips. To his left there is an open window, whose flapping curtains seem to be dancing, too. In the foreground, a blue stage curtain drapes across the top of the picture, framing the scene. Three ranks of square pillars bracket the image, bordering the planks of a wooden stage. True, Durang seems to have freely borrowed elements of an old British print, *The Humours of a Wapping Landlady*, for his painting but he has placed himself, happy in his art, at the center of it. It is one of the first depictions ever made of a performance in a Philadelphia theater.

John Durang had been born farther to the west, out in Pennsylvania Dutch country, where many people still spoke a dialect of German whose origins were from the Rhineland. His parents were immigrants from Alsace, and his father set himself up as a "barber-surgeon" and storekeeper in York, Pennsylvania. As a boy, Durang was sent to a local German language school, but was always more interested in the lessons offered by the occasional traveling performers that found their way to the local tavern. If they were dancers, especially, he quickly made their acquaintance and learned all the steps and acrobatic tricks they could teach him. He was clever with his hands, too, and he picked up some magic tricks, learned to play several musical instruments, and developed skills in sewing, painting, costume design, and puppetry. He was one of the first American-born theater artists of his day. He was also one of the first to set down his life story in a memoir. It is an engagingly written—if roughly spelled—narrative.

In the book, Durang relates how his father, who had served as a soldier during the Revolution, relocated the family to Philadelphia sometime around 1779, after the British occupation of the city had ended. At that point John would have been 10 or 11 years old. Though this was a low period in the theatrical life of Philadelphia, the newly arrived boy from the country voraciously partook of whatever exhibitions or shows there were to be had in what was then the biggest city in America—wire-walking, festivals, fireworks, concerts, and pageants. He even got his first formal dance training, learning the French-style hornpipe from a dancing master named Roussell.

He had an urge to travel, however. At 15, Durang met a man who had a line of business in popular entertainment—mostly magic lantern shows, mechanical devices, and singing ("all bad enough, but anything was thought great in those days"). The entertainer (whose name Durang later claimed he could not remember) invited the teenager to be his assistant on a tour of the newly-formed nation. In 1783 John set off on a journey with this man through New England and New York. His father evidently had his doubts about the whole enterprise, but John was excited to run off on an adventure and begin his career. For the next two years, Durang carefully saved the small wages he received and continued to improve his dancing repertoire whenever he could—even in his sleep. Unable to learn the mystery of the "pigeon wing" (a jaunty combined movement of arms and feet that was derived from African sources) in his daily practices, he went to bed. "I dreamed I was at a ball and did the pigeon wing to admiration of the whole company; in the morning … I was master of the step."

In early 1785, now 17 years old, Durang finally returned to his family's house in Philadelphia. He stepped through the door with some trepidation, but was met with happy cries and open arms. "Our tears [were] our substitute for words; they expressed at once a welcome and reconciliation with my father." He immediately set about offering his hard-won dancing talents around the city, creating a sensation when he showed his skill at the hornpipe during a ball at a wealthy Philadelphia family's house. This success earned him a recommendation to the long-established Hallam theatrical company, who were back in residence at the Old Theatre in Southwark, after a long absence.

Though they called themselves the "Old Americans," the leading players of this company were in fact almost all born and raised in England and had spent the years of the American Revolution in the Caribbean. By London standards, the "Old Americans" were perhaps a third-rate provincial company, but to Durang they seemed like theatrical royalty. Its leader, Lewis Hallam, was evidently very interested in hiring a talented native-born American performer for the troupe. Still, it is charming to note that Durang's first audition, as he recalled it in his memoirs, was just as nerve-wracking for him as it would be for any young performer today:

> When I came on the stage, Mr. Hallam introduced me to Mr. and Mrs. Allen. The presence of them setting in the front of the stage to see me rehearse rob'd me of my best powers. A kind of fright seized me and weaken'd me of my better strength, which will always be the situation of a novice on his first examination, especially when before such sterling old actors; you dread the criticism of their judgment. Mr. Hallam play'd the "Collage Hornpipe" on the violin. I dancet a few steps and made an apology, and hoped he would be satisfy'd by my dancing at night. He encouraged me by assurance that he was already satisfied, with the certainty that I would please. Mrs. Allen gave me a compleat discription of the suitable dress, with the advise to finish every step beating time.

The newspaper *Dunlap and Claypoole's Daily Advertiser* (likely using copy directly supplied to it by Hallam) touted the show in which Durang was to make his debut:

> We hear that the preparations for the exhibition at the Theatre THIS evening, have been attended to with greatest care; particularly the Finale; it is divided into two parts, and consists of dialogue and dumb shew; which are so blended, that with the assistance of Magic, Scenery and Machinery, all entirely new, will place it foremost in the list of entertainments that have been offered to the public this season … It is to be hoped that their endeavors to please will meet with the approbation and encouragement of the public.

Durang's sister Catharine, a singer, had also been added to the troupe, along with other talented young persons from the city—a clear ploy to win favor from the local audience.

That evening, Durang arrived at the theater to do his dance, which was placed in the order of the program so as to be the penultimate act of the show, just before a final pantomime play. He watched from the wings as another local boy made his own debut in a comedy described only as "A Variety of Characters." The house was crowded with supporters of this other young Philadelphian. But Durang, displaying the considerable inventiveness and audacity he would exhibit throughout his subsequent career, knew how to steal the show.

> I had contrived a tramp[oline] behind the wing to enable me to gain the centre of the stage in one spring. When the curtain rose, the cry was "Sit down, hats off!" With the swiftness of Mercury I stood before them, with a general huzza, and dancet in bu[r]sts of applause. When I went off the stage, I was encored. They made such a noise, throwing a bottle in [to] the orchestra; apples, &c on the stage, at last the curtain was raised again and I dancet a second time to the general satisfaction of the audiences and managers, and gained my point.

But as popular as his efforts had been with the Philadelphia crowd in the theater that night, plays and dances of any sort were looked upon as unwelcome by other citizens. This was a common moral sentiment in America at the time, and apparently anti-theatrical forces in Philadelphia were not appeased by all this excellent entertainment. "Great exsertions [were] making at this time through the city to shut up the theatre," wrote Durang. "Some went about with paper to sign against it, and some for it." A particular person who had been in the audience (whom Durang remembered as having the unfortunate name of "Shitz"—and which one hopes was pronounced *Sheetz*—acted as an "informer" against the company and brought them up on charges in local court. Fortunately, when Shitz (or Sheetz) "brought it to trial," he "lost the cause, and was severely handled by the populous crowd outside of the courthouse."

Theater folk, and Durang's hornpipe, had won the day. And what is even more satisfying, John Durang and his family were to play a continuing role in American theater for generations thereafter. He became a featured performer in circuses and pantomimes, and danced in many plays and ballets at the New Theatre on Chestnut Street. In the summers he often rented the Old Theatre on Cedar Street (later renamed South Street) to do his own productions. His children were recruited by him onto the Philadelphia stage, and many of them became dancers and musicians themselves. His sons Ferdinand and Charles were the first to perform the song "The Star-Spangled Banner" while volunteering for the defense of Baltimore against the British in 1812. Charles Durang later became a distinguished dancing master and theater historian of the city. (We will cite his work many times in this book.) John's grandson, Edwin Forrest Durang, became a prominent Philadelphia architect, and designed a theater building that still stands today, the Trocadero on Arch Street. Many generations later, the playwright Christopher Durang (albeit raised in New Jersey) could also cite his deep connection to Philadelphia theater history.

Most of all, as the historian Lynn Matluck Brooks writes, at a time when theater in the new nation was still dominated by transplanted Britons, "Durang himself embodied a new ethnicity in the theatre: that of the *American* performer." On July 4, 1787, the Philadelphia artist Charles Willson Peale helped design and stage a pageant and parade to celebrate the completion of the United States Constitution. John Durang was cast in a small but highly prominent role in the gala: he was to ride on a float atop a printer's press, dressed as Mercury. In fact, Sarah Bache herself, the daughter of Benjamin Franklin and one of the organizers of the procession, made his costume. It was a flesh-colored gown, with a blue sash and a cap with feathered wings. "Dr. Franklin was in the room at the time she fit the cap on my head," Durang recalled happily. He always did like a nice costume.

36 Indian Chiefs and Warriors at the Olympic

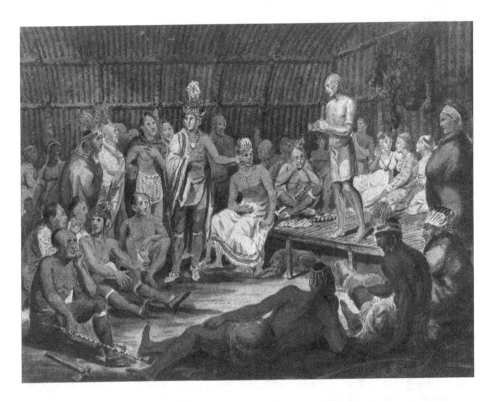

The title of this picture, a watercolor in the collection of the Metropolitan Museum of Art in New York, is *Exhibition of Indian Tribal Ceremonies at the Olympic Theater, Philadelphia*. In the museum's own notes, the work is attributed to the German-American painter John Lewis Krimmel, who was active in Philadelphia in the early 19th century, and is dated as being completed "between 1811 and 1813."

Could this image really depict a theatrical event in early 19th-century Philadelphia? It's certainly plausible. Groups of Native Americans from the Ohio Valley and the Great Lakes were commonly seen in the city during these years, and it was not unknown for them to attend plays at local theaters while they were in town. But their main reason for visiting the city was political, not entertainment. During one visit to Philadelphia in the 1790s, the leaders of several tribal delegations had signed a treaty with the federal government, supposedly permanently settling certain territorial boundaries. In return, the government stipulated that it would give them money and goods at specified locations in the Northwest Territories, including Fort Wayne and Detroit. All too soon, of course, it became clear that the government was not keeping its part of the bargain. Worse, white settlers continued to push into territories that are now called Indiana, Ohio, and Michigan. Violence often broke out; the scourges of alcohol and disease became widespread. Among the leadership of some tribes, new embassies were deemed necessary. It was a matter of survival.

In late 1801 a delegation of allied Indigenous chiefs from the Ohio River Valley made a journey to Washington, which had succeeded Philadelphia as the federal capital, to officially register their complaints with President Thomas Jefferson. There was no direct land route over the Allegheny Mountains to Washington, so they traveled up the Ohio River to Pittsburgh, and then made the journey overland to Philadelphia. Only then did they turn south, through Maryland, toward the District of Columbia. The chiefs met with Jefferson and formally delivered their complaints, which had been translated into English for them by an interpreter named William Wells. "Father," they wrote, "when our white brothers came to this land, our forefathers were numerous and happy; but since their intercourse with the white people, and owing to the introduction of the fatal poison [i.e., alcohol], we have become less numerous and happy."

In early January 1802, their grievances having been delivered, the members of the delegation needed to make their way home. Mostly they traveled on foot, but they utilized wagons and boats where they could hire them. By late February, the group was back in Philadelphia, and they needed funds for the long trek across Pennsylvania to Pittsburgh—where they could once again reach the Ohio River.

They knew, from previous experience, that Philadelphians would pay to see an exhibition of dances, and they knew where white men liked to gather. On Saturday March 6, 1802, a notice appeared in the *Federal Gazette*. "NEW-THEATRE," it read, "Monday evening, March 8, Will be presented (for the last time this season) a Historical Drama, in five acts, called *Deaf and Dumb, or The Orphan Protected*." At the end of play, the notice continued, "for the second and last time, by desire The Shawanese and Delaware Chiefs now in this City, will dance several of their country dances, particularly, the CORN PIECE, the WAR DANCE, etc. The principal Chief will speak an address." Presumably this chief, who was not named, planned to deliver to the Philadelphia public a version of the protest he had just made in Washington.

So how did this evening go? In the memoirs of the Philadelphia actor and theatrical manager William Wood, we find the following account:

> These dancers were (as was said of them) so terribly in earnest, that in their furor piece after piece of their scanty drapery became so unfixed and disarranged, as to occasion the flight of several ladies from the boxes. A villainous punster, hearing some doubts expressed whether these were real Indians, declared it his conviction, at least as far as the "show knees" [Shawnees] were concerned.

What Wood was describing, in a discreet way, was that the dances of the Native Americans had created quite a sensation on the stage when what we nowadays might call a "wardrobe malfunction" occurred. That is, some of the men's loincloths opened, revealing rather more of their anatomy than they likely intended—and not just their knees.

But Wood also tells us that, overall, the show was quite popular with the public, and the ticket sales that evening "brought large receipts to the treasury." The Native American chieftains evidently collected enough to make their journey home to Ohio and Indiana, at any rate. But the story about the flapping loincloths evidently became an item of local popular lore. It even came to the attention of John Lewis Krimmel, who was living and working in the city by 1809. When yet another Native American delegation came through Philadelphia in the late summer of 1812, and again offered a fundraising dance performance—this time billed as "36 Indian Chiefs and Warriors at the Olympic"—his thoughts seemed to have returned to that earlier story. Though it's not clear if Krimmel was present himself that evening, we do have a written description of it by a Russian traveler named Pavel Svin'in. Most historians heavily discount the accuracy of Svin'in's account, however. He also seems to have obtained many of Krimmel's paintings—including this one—and tried to pass them off as his own.

I suggest that we put aside both Svin'in's suspicious appropriations and also the modern title of the painting and look again at Krimmel's watercolor. Like many of the artist's works, it portrays a lively grouping of human figures. In the image, there is a room crowded with people, all Native American, evenly divided between males and females. The room's walls are lined with lashed logs overlaying a square trellis. A bearskin hangs on one wall, with claws extending down. This is clearly *not* the interior of either the New Theatre on Chestnut Street or the Olympic Theatre on Walnut Street, nor does it seem like a representation of any scenery likely to be in either one's stock collection. There is a raised platform at one end of the room—a sort of small stage, to be sure. A couple of sleeping dogs lie beneath it. The humans depicted are not themselves in vigorous motion but are arranged by Krimmel in relaxed or casual poses. (In fact, many of these poses are modeled on the works of well-known painters like Benjamin West, which he has obviously studied closely.) This can't be a representation of an "exhibition." It is not an ongoing performance or ceremony at all.

What is happening, then? Two male figures are the focus of the scene. One, with a tall, feathered headdress, a necklace, a blanket, loincloth, and leggings, stands just left of center, clearly a chief or authority figure. The figure is looking to his right, with a stern expression, sharing his gaze with a group of half a dozen other men who are all either scowling or smiling with evident amusement. This chief gestures to his left, pointing at the other main figure, a man with a shaved head. This man is standing somewhat isolated on the little stage, wearing only a light blue loincloth or kilt. His hands are raised in a gesture of apprehension. Another man sitting nearby puts his hands to his face. Everybody else around them seems a bit embarrassed, and the women in the background are excitedly whispering in each other's ears.

It is essential, I would argue, to notice exactly where the chief at the center of the painting is pointing: directly at the crotch of the man in the blue loincloth. Other art historians who have described the image have missed this gesture's significance, lacking the added context of Wood's theatrical anecdote. Suddenly, the story being told in the image is quite clear. Though executed with admirable attention to detail, the whole picture is a rather silly and smutty joke. This is Krimmel's representation, not of the ceremony, not of a dance, but of the moment after the Indian dancer's "scanty drapery became unfixed and disarranged."

Krimmel's watercolor, therefore, refers to what in 1812 Philadelphia was a well-known theater story, dating from the incident 10 years earlier. Krimmel's watercolor is a sniggering depiction of the shock, titillation, amusement, and embarrassment, not of the Indians, but—by proxy—of the white Philadelphia theater audience.

"A Young Gentleman of this City"

No one looms larger than Edwin Forrest over the history of Philadelphia theater. He wasn't unusually tall, checking in at just about 5 feet 10 inches, but his massive and muscled body, sculpted by years of intense discipline and exercise, made an immediate impact when he strode onto any stage. His costumes were designed to show off his bulging arms and thick legs. His deep voice thundered to the rafters of every house he played. One of his signature moves was to lift another actor—or at least an unfortunate supernumerary—up into the air and fling them into the wings, to the audience's great delight. The theater would erupt in applause and cheers whenever he emerged victorious from another stage fight, or whenever he didn't and instead died gloriously and tragically.

His various characters died at the conclusion of almost every play—Hamlet, Macbeth, Lear, Metamora, Spartacus, Jack Cade—he was a tragedian, and Dying Big was what he did. Sometimes he thudded so hard onto the stage the boards shook. The fans roared madly for him after every death scene, and at every curtain call, for many decades.

He had not started big. At birth Edwin Forrest was a small, frail-looking boy, the seventh of eight children born into the lower-middle-class Philadelphia family of William and Rebecca Forrest. His Scottish immigrant father, a failed shopkeeper who had only a lowly position in a Philadelphia bank, suffered from chronic tuberculosis, and naturally he worried about his youngest boy. "Little Ned," as his family called him, was thin and pale, cried a lot, and had narrow stooping shoulders. Deeply attached to his mother, he clung to her physically and emotionally. Surely Ned would be taken by consumption before he reached adulthood, William said mournfully to Rebecca. Neighbors whispered the same thought to each other and looked at the boy sadly.

But that pale little boy, overhearing the adults talking about his likely early grave, decided then and there to *fight* against his fate. He wanted people to *notice* him, all the time. On Sundays the family went to St. Paul's Episcopal Church on Third Street, where Rev. Joseph Pilmore was the priest. Like most boys, he found it a trial to sit still during lengthy boring sermons, but Little Ned noticed how much attention the preacher got. At home, after church, he would stand on a chair and give his delighted family an exact imitation of Rev. Pilmore, with his glasses perched on his nose. His father thought it was a sign that Ned might someday be educated for the clergy. He was sent off to school for lessons in reading and writing, and even got private lessons with local teachers of elocution, such as Lemuel White and Alexander Wilson, who was also a famous ornithologist. Ned wasn't interested much in birds, though; he wanted to learn how to be an orator—so Wilson taught him the poems of Robert Burns, and Young Norval's speech from the play *Douglas* by John Hone—the one that began: "My name is Norval! On the Grampian hills/ My father feeds his flocks." Apparently, these elocution lessons stood Forrest in good stead for the rest of his life, because he never got any other sort of formal voice training. His three sisters—Henrietta, Caroline, and Eleonora—made their baby brother a harlequin's outfit to wear for recitations in the family home, complete with a mask and a wooden dagger. He would also eagerly show off these speeches for his friends in the neighborhood, earning the local title "The Schoolboy Spouter."

When he was 10 years old, spindly young Ned Forrest became entranced by the physiques of circus acrobats—surely this was the way he could become strong and drive away the fears of the inevitable early death his father had predicted for him! He began to hang around rehearsals at the Olympic Theatre on the corner of Ninth and Walnut Streets, and some kindly circus folk taught the eager kid how to climb ropes, stand on his head, walk on his hands, and do backflips and somersaults. His body began to develop strength and agility, and he acquired a lifelong obsession with physical exercise—hiding the sickly child he once had been under massive shoulders, beefy arms, and thick legs. He also began to develop his acting muscles by performing amateur dramatics with a group of other young Philadelphians called the "Thespian Club" that his older brother William had organized. Inspired by the success of the young American actor John Howard Payne at the city's New Theatre on Chestnut Street, they imagined that they too could play on the stages where normally only British-born actors seemed to tread.

Ned recited to the workers at the tannery where his oldest brother Lorman worked—he used any chance to shine and see that admiring look in people's eyes that he could then run home and tell his doting mother about. People up and down Cedar Street knew about him. A desperate Charles Porter, manager of the ramshackle Old Theatre on Cedar and Apollo Streets, even hastily enlisted the lad for a last-minute substitute as Rosalia, a female role in a melodrama called *Rudolph or the Robbers of Calabria*. There was no stage business to be learned, Porter assured him, and Forrest played the role lying on a sofa in a borrowed dress, an improvised wig on his head, and a script at his side. The engagement went fairly well, all things considered, until one of the local boys in the audience noticed that "Rosalia" was wearing heavy boots and blue Germantown socks. Jeering and raillery issued from the house, and fair Rosalia began yelling that she "would fight and lick them all, as soon as the play was over!" Fortunately, before matters reached that point, Charles Porter hauled the young actor off the stage.

Forrest's father died when he was 13, leaving his mother with many debts and expenses. Times were hard, so his brother Lorman took a ship to South America, hoping to make a fortune—and was never heard from again. His three sisters opened a millinery shop at the family home. Ned had to help out too, so he left school and went to work with his brother William in the print shop of *The Aurora*—a fiercely Jeffersonian newspaper which helped to shape his lifelong political allegiance to the Democratic Party. He got another job working at a ship chandler, where he still doggedly spouted speeches amidst the shelves in the back room, much to his employer's annoyance. He was firmly instructed that this theatrical infatuation would be his ruin, and was warned that "actors never grow rich."

Undeterred, Ned continued to attend plays, circuses, and other entertainments whenever he could, and he was in the audience at the open-air Tivoli Gardens amphitheater, on Market and Thirteenth Streets, one summer evening in 1820. There he watched a public demonstration by a so-called "professor" about the effects of nitrous oxide, or laughing gas. When volunteers were called for, Ned stepped out of the crowd and offered to take several deep whiffs of the stuff. Upon receiving its disinhibiting benefits, he immediately began reciting a speech from Shakespeare's *Richard III* and turning somersaults. The audience roared its approval, and a delighted Philadelphia city alderman who saw the incident, John Swift, was instantly convinced the young lad had something special and told him he could be playing at the Walnut Street Theatre. Years later, when Swift became the Mayor of Philadelphia, he would proudly boast that he had set young Forrest on the path to stardom.

It was not to the New Theatre on Chestnut Street that the alderman directed him, because it had burned down in April 1820. Its managers, William Warren and William Wood, ensconced themselves and their acting company in the old circus hall formerly known as the Olympic. After some hasty renovations, it became, for the first time, the Walnut Street Theatre. Every effort was made to entice their former audience to follow them into this new venue, but when the season opened on November 10, 1820, attendance was merely respectable. Big stars were booked to appear later in the season, but clearly the managers, who were in serious financial straits, needed a box-office boost of some kind in the meantime.

John Swift, the alderman who had been so taken with the Schoolboy Spouter on laughing gas, thought he had just the answer for them. He introduced Edwin to William Wood, claiming the lad was 16 and ready for his debut. Wood, always suspicious of local talent, had seen many a likely young Roscius walk though his door and then out again. Dubious, he did his best to talk the fresh-faced young Philadelphian out of pursuing a career on the stage, he recalled:

> We had been so unfortunate in the numerous "first appearances" of late, that the young aspirant could hope for little encouragement of his wishes, the drooping state of theatricals furnishing

another and stronger reason for our course ... The toils, dangers, and suffering of a young actor were represented with honest earnestness, but, as was soon discovered, in vain. Forrest was at this time a well grown young man, with a noble figure, unusually developed for his age, his features powerfully expressive, and of a determination of purpose which discouraged all further objections.

But since business needed picking up, the managers decided to see if South Philadelphia would turn out to see a neighborhood favorite. Forrest was given the script for the part of Young Norval—a fitting debut role for young leading men—and told to go home and learn it. The self-assured "well-grown young man" immediately stated that he already knew the role, and in rehearsals they saw this was the truth. The play *Douglas* was announced on the bills of the Walnut Street Theatre for November 27, 1820. William Wood was to play Glenalvon, the villain, and William Warren would play his foster father, Old Norval.

It must have been a memorable night, because the playbill from the show still exists, carefully preserved in the scrapbooks of Charles Durang. As was typical of an era, the debutant was billed only as "a Young Gentleman of this City." It was another common custom—a precaution, really. In case things went badly, this discretion would save all parties involved from future embarrassment.

We don't have any reviews or detailed accounts of Edwin Forrest's debut at the Walnut Street Theatre, but it evidently went well enough to warrant a second engagement in the same play, because—on another preserved playbill—we find that he was back again at the Walnut on December 2, "in obedience to the wish of many in the audience." At the end of December, he played the role of Frederick in the melodrama *Lovers' Vows*, a play adapted from a work by August von Kotzebue. But then, when the box office for that night did not prosper, the managers told the ardent and confident young man that they had no further employment for him.

Besides, two famous and important English actors of the day, Thomas Cooper and Edmund Kean, were soon coming to Philadelphia. Warren and Wood needed to rehearse the regular company and concentrate on arrangements for their productions. When Thomas Cooper arrived, Forrest, eager to press his case and get advice, arranged an interview with him. The experienced star, who had been performing in America for more than 20 years by this point, gave the young man the standard advice: to wait his turn, take some smaller roles, and slowly learn his craft.

That was not at all what the young Philadelphian, now 16, wanted to hear. He would never consent to being a supernumerary or a servant, he declared. He wanted to be a leading actor—a star performer—from the beginning. Nothing else would do. So, Edwin Forrest angrily stalked out of the room. For a brief period he tried starting his own theater company in a converted space on Prune Street, but this wasn't going to make him a star, either. And so, like many ambitious young Americans in those days—he went West.

***

Five years later, in 1825, Edwin Forrest came back to Philadelphia. His life's journey in the intervening years had been an amazing campaign, in the literal frontiers of the burgeoning world of American theater. He had played in wooden shacks in Kentucky and palatial theaters in New Orleans. He had befriended a formidable Choctaw chief along the Mississippi and had even acted with Edmund Kean at a theater in Albany beside the Hudson.

Now he was back home, ready to try his luck again with Warren and Wood's company in their reconstructed theater on Chestnut Street, which had been completed while he was away. By this point, the two longtime managing partners were barely speaking to each other and could not agree on much; however, they were obliged to honor the request of a member of the stock company, Charles Porter, regarding his "benefit night"—that is, the time-honored and common practice of the British and professional stage in which, towards the end of the season, each member of an acting company was assigned a performance to which he or she was entitled to most of the box office receipts. It was the most important day of the year for actors, as their weekly salaries were often quite meager. This was the same Charles Porter who had first cast Forrest as Rosalia 10 years before, and he specified that Forrest be allowed to perform with him in Otway's *Venice Preserv'd*. It turned out to be a good decision. Porter's share of the box office was quite impressive, and Forrest's performance was even better, earning him nine rounds of cheers at the curtain.

Forrest was immediately booked again to play Rolla in Sheridan's *Pizzaro*—a play about a young Peruvian rebel leader—another role considered a standard steppingstone for a young actor on the rise. Backstage he was still shy about entering the famously well-regulated Chestnut Street Theatre's Green Room, but onstage he was masterful. One Philadelphia reviewer wrote something especially satisfying for any returning hometown hero: "He left us a boy, and has returned a man." Better yet were the tears of joy his mother and sister shed, when he swept them out of their cramped South Philadelphia lodgings and placed them in a new and spacious home on North Tenth Street.

A print was made of *Mr. E. Forrest as Rolla*—an item his growing legion of fans could collect and share, real proof that he was now a star actor. It is the earliest actual image we have of the young Philadelphian, looking stern and fierce in the beaded necklaces adorning his "Peruvian" costume, a sword hilt clasped firmly in his hand. It would become the first in a long line of images of the great Edwin Forrest—soon to be the most famous actor in America.

Miss Philadelphia of 1896

A SCENE FROM MISS PHILADELPHIA

Miss Philadelphia was not a show about a local beauty queen. Produced at the Park Theatre in the spring of 1896, *Miss Philadelphia* was a show named after the city itself, written and directed by Edgar Smith. It had songs from several composers and songwriters, though the only name we might recognize today was Victor Herbert. Most were pleasant love ballads, though some were peppy up-tempo numbers or vigorous marches.

The producers were the team of Askins and Tyler, the new managers of the Park Theatre on the corner of Broad and Fairmount in North Philadelphia. They had hit upon the idea of producing a play with lots of local Philadelphia settings and references, in hopes of attracting an intensely loyal local crowd who might return to see the show multiple times. Most American musical plays in that era were thinly plotted comedies and were usually either set in New York City or in some exotic foreign locale. There had been no drama staged in a Philadelphia theater whose action was actually set in the city since Mrs. John Drew had staged *The Poor and Proud of Philadelphia* at her Arch Street Theatre back in 1874. But that was an adaptation of a Dion Boucicault script that was originally about New York. *Miss Philadelphia* was an entirely original production.

To drum up the Philadelphia theatergoing public's interest in the show, here's how the *Philadelphia Times* described its plot. Mind you, this was before the show even opened! Back in that day people liked to know exactly what they were going to see in a play; they weren't worried about "spoilers."

> William Penn, Jr., lineal descendant of the original William, is a wealthy young man about town, upon whom devolves the duty of celebrating the birth of his illustrious ancestor. This he decides to do by giving a ball in the family mansion.
>
> Upon the evening of the ball, he falls asleep and is visited in his dreams by the spirit of William Penn. The spirit chides him for his rather rapid mode of life, and after listening to his argument—that several hundred years have made a great alteration in the town and the customs of its inhabitants—the spirit accepts the young man's invitation to make a sight-seeing tour.
>
> In the second act there is portrayed part of Broad and Walnut streets, including the Hotel Bellevue and the Union League. Mayor Warwick reviews the City Troop from the steps of the great Republican organization … The cleverest scene presentation in the play will represent Ninth and Chestnut streets, with the Post Office Building and the Continental and Girard Hotels in view. Along the highway march the New Year's Shooters—typically a Philadelphia institution—and an attempt will be made to portray in the ranks representations of well-known Philadelphians.
>
> The third scene will picture the United States Mint and Wanamaker's store … Strawberry Mansion will figure as another local presentation, displaying children indulging in summer games and a bicycle parade …

In the course of the tour the ancestral Penn begins to discover that he rather likes the modern Philadelphia after all, and getting into the spirit of things, even decides to try one of those new-fangled bicycles himself for a spin around the town. Meanwhile the young Penn realizes his sweetheart, a girl named Ruth, is not too demure and sedate, as he had feared, but that in fact both she and her maiden aunt (who takes a fancy to the older Penn) "possess latent, sporty talent of a high order."

> Just when the excitement is at its height young Penn wakes up, and rushing into the ball room, not yet thoroughly aroused, creates a sensation by treating Ruth, her aunt and the guests generally as he had treated them in his dream. They think he is intoxicated, and the ball is about to break up when it dawns upon him that he has been dreaming—and the play ends.

So, *Miss Philadelphia* was yet another representative of an "And Then I Woke Up" story. This was not only a well-used trope even then, but also, frankly, the show's creators were appropriating the time-traveling idea of the play itself—i.e., a central character from History, marveling at what they had brought about in the present day. It was quite similar to the recent Broadway show *1492 Up to Date, or Very Near It*, which had employed Christopher Columbus in a similar manner.

It was an era when Philadelphia's upper crust was getting a bit obsessed with the city's early history. As hundreds of thousands of immigrants arrived in Philadelphia during the late 19th century, this was an appealing way of reasserting the central narrative of long-time Philadelphia families and groups that had traditionally wielded social and cultural power in town. Over the next decade or so there would be a regular series of historical "pageants" staged in Philadelphia that used Quakers and William Penn as main characters. And, of course, even as this musical was being staged, everyone would have been familiar with the ongoing project of raising the huge statue of William Penn to the summit of the tower of City Hall—a project that would finally be completed in 1897. The costume of the character of "William Penn" (played by actor William Armstrong) in the play would be almost exactly modeled after that of the work of resident sculptor Alexander Milne Calder, which had been standing for a long while in City Hall's courtyard, prior to its eventual elevation.

Miss Philadelphia had a cast of about 80 people. Many of them were actors who had performed in New York shows or national tours. These included John Henshaw, who was playing the young Penn, and Florence Lillian Wickes, who was playing his fiancée. But many of the chorus members and bit parts were recruited locally—including a number of what the newspaper reviewers called "colored youths." They were cast to play bootblacks in a scene in which old William Penn got his shoes shined.

The show premiered at the Park Theatre on April 20, 1896, and unsurprisingly it was a great success. It fit the mood of local pride perfectly. "A veritable triumph!" crowed one reviewer. "A PLAY THAT IS OUR VERY OWN," enthused another. "Bright 'Miss Philadelphia' is the City's Winsome Protege. Its strong local color, plot, scenery and people all represent that which is best known in the City of Brotherly Love, while the lines, music, costumes and dances and troops of pretty girls add a sparkle and dash that are irresistible." And indeed, people were soon flocking to see it repeatedly, as the producers had hoped. Philadelphians especially loved the scenes that showed streetscapes of their dear old city, and the bicycle number always made a hit. And everybody loved the grand scene with "The New Year's Shooters"—i.e., the Mummers Parade.

After a few weeks *Miss Philadelphia* moved to the larger and more prestigious Chestnut Street Opera House, where it ran the rest of the summer. That September, the *Philadelphia Press* published special supplements in its Sunday editions, with sheet music of songs from the show—including "Sweetheart I Love None But You," whose cover showed a courting couple on bicycles in Fairmount Park.

Miss Philadelphia never had any theatrical success outside of the Quaker City, but it was never meant to. Rather, it was there to tell a certain class of Philadelphians a happy story about themselves, and to reassure them that things would always be the same as they ever were.

"Three Cheers for Captain Sigsbee!"

April 20, 1898: The sentiment for war with Spain was reaching a fever pitch in America, so U.S. Navy Captain Charles Dwight Sigsbee decided to relax by taking in a show in Philadelphia. Not wanting to attract public attention, he came in quietly after the lights had gone down and sat in a rear box of the auditorium. Sigsbee was accompanied by William Swett, the manager of the brand-new Hotel Walton at the corner of Broad and Locust.

His reluctance to make his presence known was due to his sudden—and unwanted—celebrity. The commander of the USS *Maine* only two months earlier, Captain Sigsbee had lost his ship. On the night of February 15, it suddenly exploded in Havana Harbor. Three quarters of the ship's crew had perished, but Sigsbee had survived. Accusations were made by many Americans that Spanish agents had blown up the vessel, to prevent the United States from supporting Cuban rebels fighting for their independence. For the next two months, the constant agitation for immediate war with Spain—most notably in the American newspapers controlled by rival publishers William Randolph Hearst and Joseph Pulitzer—was overwhelming. Captain Sigsbee became a national hero, and when the official commission of inquiry cleared him of responsibility for losing the *Maine*, he was given command of the USS *St. Paul*.

The *St. Paul* had originally been launched in 1895 as a civilian passenger liner by William Cramp & Sons, the longtime Philadelphia shipbuilders. Under orders from the Assistant Secretary of the Navy Theodore Roosevelt, Cramp's yard swiftly refitted the vessel as a warship, and it was ready by the end of March. On Wednesday, April 20, Captain Sigsbee had just been through a ceremony at the Navy Yard, taking formal command, and now he wanted to relax for the evening. After all, soon there was likely to be a great deal for him to do. That same afternoon, President William McKinley had signed what was called "The Cuba Resolution," which gave an ultimatum to Spain to either give the island its independence or else face war with America. This news, published in every afternoon newspaper, was buzzing around the city.

The place Sigsbee chose for relaxation was the Chestnut Street Theatre—the third Philadelphia building of that name, constructed during the last big war America had fought, back in 1863. On the Chestnut's boards that night was the newest show from the producer Edward E. Rice, *The Ballet Girl*—whose book had been mostly borrowed and Americanized from a British musical called *The Circus Girl*. Rice was the composer of quite a few shows at that point in his career, including *Evangeline* (which had played the Walnut Street Theatre in 1876) and the Columbus-themed show *1492* (which had been the model for *Miss Philadelphia*). Now primarily a producer of other composers' works, Rice hoped that with *The Ballet Girl* he would have yet another hit. It included such cheerful songs as "A Boom," and sentimental ballads like "Her Mem'ry Brings Me No Regret." Like most light and frothy musicals of the era, it was short on plot and heavy on costumes, sets, and dancing girls. It had done quite well as a light springtime entertainment, and ticket sales were brisk.

Unknown to Captain Sigsbee, however, the managers of the Chestnut Street Theatre had an additional feature on the program that evening. During breaks in the action, they would project stereopticon photographs onto the stage curtain. Since the coming war with Spain was on everyone's minds, a photo of the sunken USS *Maine* was the first image, followed by pictures of Captain Sigsbee, President McKinley, and the American flag.

"When the picture of the *Maine* was shown there was the usual applause," reported the *Inquirer*. "That of Captain Sigsbee was next thrown on the canvas. Then someone who had recognized the Captain made known his identity." Indeed, still wearing his dress uniform from the afternoon's ceremonies, as well as his distinctive handlebar mustache, the hero was hard to miss.

"'Three cheers for Captain Sigsbee!' someone shouted, and then the house went wild," wrote the reporter. "Men stood up and threw their hats into the air. Women's voices swelled the cheering. 'Sigsbee! Sigsbee!' came the cries from all parts of the house, with cheer upon cheer as accompaniment." The cast of *The Ballet Girl*, hearing the uproar, all rushed out upon the stage and joined in the demonstration. "The excitement was at a tremendous pitch. There seemed no likelihood of its coming to an end." Sigsbee bowed several times in thanks. Somewhat flustered, he signaled the crowd to stop, but 15 minutes later, the cheering was still going on. Philadelphia audiences were infamous in those days for demanding curtain speeches from actors, and now they turned their well-practiced demands on the celebrity hero in their midst. "SPEECH! SPEECH!" was the general cry.

Finally, comparative quiet was established, and the embarrassed Sigsbee consented to say a few words to the Philadelphia crowd. Looking like he would much prefer to be on the deck of a ship under fire in battle, he thanked the audience again, but said it would surely be better to have the performance of *The Ballet Girl* continue than to hear him make a speech. This only provoked more applause.

Eventually the uproar subsided, and the second act of the play commenced. But after it ended, most of the audience immediately left their seats and lined the sidewalks of Chestnut Street. Everyone wanted to watch the Captain exit the theater and get into his waiting carriage. As Sigsbee walked the few steps from the doors, wild cheers broke out again. Even once he was seated, men kept tearing open the vehicle's door to shake his hand. Finally, he was allowed to leave, but "cheers for Sigsbee and the United States were heard as the carriage drove away," wrote the reporter.

The next day, Spain refused the United States' ultimatum, and severed diplomatic relations. The U.S. Navy began a blockade of Cuba. On April 23, Spain declared war and the U.S. Congress immediately followed suit. "The country whooped to war," wrote one historian. He was likely not referring directly to the fervent demonstration at the Chestnut that night, of course. But the emotional outpouring by Philadelphia theatergoers illustrates the national mood during that heady springtime of war fever and the rush to begin the era of American imperialism on the stage of the entire world.

Freedom at the Sesqui and *The Miracle* at the Met

July 3, 1926: The biggest theatrical production ever attempted in Philadelphia, entitled *Freedom*, had its opening night performance. Blistering summer temperatures and the constant threat of torrential rain did not seem to discourage attendance at the outdoor show—at least according to some newspapers. "Eighty thousand people packed the Sesqui stadium here tonight," reported the *Kansas City Star*, "to witness the first performance of 'Freedom,' the huge stage spectacle sponsored by the city of Philadelphia as the official celebration commemorating the one hundred and fiftieth year of American independence. The performance was attended by Mayor W. Freeland Kendrick, many members of the state and federal governments and by the official sesquicentennial committee."

Not present, notably, was U.S. President Calvin Coolidge. Despite the repeated entreaties of Mayor Kendrick, his fellow Republican, the ardent Sabbatarian refused to make any trip which would require him to make official appearances on Sunday, July 4. Plus, it was an election year, and Coolidge apparently wished to limit his political association with the City of Philadelphia and its World Fair entirely. The department-store mogul and philanthropist John Wanamaker, who had first championed the project (and who had given it the distinctive spelling of "Sesqui-Centennial") had died in 1922, and his beneficent moral odor had long since dissipated. The stink of graft, corruption, and official incompetence was evident all over the administration of the "Sesqui" (as most people called it). Many of its buildings and exhibition halls were not even finished when the fair opened on Memorial Day, May 31. Even the prospect of seeing *Freedom* was not going to tempt Coolidge to Philly that night.

Unlike the nearby indoor Sesqui-Centennial Auditorium, whose enormous pipe organ was not quite ready to play, the Sesqui-Centennial Stadium was at least actually prepared to receive the crowds. The horseshoe-shaped seating area provided a view of the central field, which would eventually host track and field events and boxing matches. By July, a huge stage was erected across the open north end of the stadium. This was where *Freedom* could be found, and performances were scheduled to occur three times a week. Several smaller stages were also placed on the field to present "historic tableaux," while the main stage was being changed to present yet another one of the "spectacular scenes of outstanding importance."

As composed by Willam W. Matos, the "Chairman of Pageantry" for the Sesqui-Centennial, *Freedom* was supposed to be a dramatic representation of the entire history of the very concept of "freedom" going back deep into the depths of time. It had 50 scenes in all, and employed 4,347 people (75 "principals," 1,500 "extras," a 1,000-member chorus, 250 ballet dancers, 125 musicians, and a veritable army of technicians and stagehands). There were dozens of sets, thousands of costumes, and a musical score culled from the works of Tchaikovsky, Rimsky-Korsakov, Massenet, and John Philip Sousa. It had two stars in the company. Most eminent was the Broadway veteran DeWolf Hopper (a descendant of Philadelphia Quakers, chiefly famous for his vaudeville performances reciting "Casey at the Bat"), who would play the narrator character "History." Paired with him on the bill was the coloratura soprano Belle Story, who would embody "The Spirit of Freedom" and sing patriotic arias. Backing them up, besides all the other actors and extras, were dancing elephants, camels, horses—and several enormous papier-mâché dinosaurs.

The producer of the spectacle was Broadway impresario R. H. Burnside, who for years had created and directed shows at the enormous New York Hippodrome. Burnside hoped to make a killing at the Sesqui, selling 80,000 tickets a night at prices of either a dollar (for the best seats) or 50 cents (for those higher up).

According to Philadelphia historian Thomas H. Keels in his book *Sesqui! Greed, Graft, and the Forgotten World's Fair of 1926*, "the scenario for 'Freedom' traced man's quest for liberty throughout the ages."

> Beginning in pre-history, when cavemen battled for independence from "the icthyosaurui" and "the tyrannosaurui," the pageant followed a convoluted path to the present day. Historical vignettes depicted critical moments, including the assassination of Caesar, Columbus discovering America, and the signing of the Declaration of Independence. Between the vignettes, the mood was lightened by ballets, acrobatics, and four performing elephants. The show concluded with a spectacular "Ballet of the Cities," celebrating the New Declaration of World Peace of 1926, set to music by John Philip Sousa.

The opening night apparently went well, despite the threat of rain. But an enormous storm would batter the fairgrounds the next day, July 4, heavily damaging those buildings and exhibitions which had been completed, and delaying those that were not.

Indeed, Burnside had not counted on the utter brutality of Philadelphia summer weather, which was to plague him throughout July and August. The oppressive heat kept many people from coming out at all, deeply depressing attendance figures. Plus, he had taken out a $125,000 insurance policy for stoppages due to rain—but its coverage kicked in only if the rain started before curtain time. He had not accounted for Philly's infamous late-night summer thunderstorms.

The timing was almost diabolical, Keels writes:

> [T]he first drops inevitably fell once the show was under way. By mid-August the show had been stopped by rain eleven times, and Burnside was $170,000 in the hole. The star, DeWolf Hopper, declared *Freedom* to be the "raining success" of the Sesqui. Its performers grew adept at dashing over to the usually dark Auditorium and staging an impromptu cabaret once the weather stopped the outdoor pageant. Hopper performed Gilbert and Sullivan ditties, the four elephants danced a shimmy, and female lead Belle Story brought down the house with a rousing rendition of "Philadelphia, My Home Town."

Finally Burnside conceded defeat, and September 11 was announced as the final show. Inevitably, it was also rained out. The Sesqui was not over—it would continue into November, but the pageant had completed its ill-starred run.

***

The true candidate for Best Sesqui-Centennial entertainment was not what you might expect. It was not a patriotic show. Instead, it seemed to seize people's emotions and imaginations in a completely different way. It was being staged not in a temporary fair building, but instead in the stunning opera house on North Broad Street that Oscar Hammerstein had built two decades previously. The impresario's control of the huge "Philadelphia Opera House" had not lasted long, however. Now it was referred to as the "Metropolitan Opera House," the name of the rival New York opera company who had wrested control of it away from him, and which had briefly used it to stage their own productions. By 1926 it was only occasionally used for live performances. That fall, due to the efforts of another New York impresario, Morris Gest, it sprung to life again.

In October, Pierre de Rohan, the elegantly named theater critic of the *Camden Courier-Post*, was in ecstasy over the production he had just seen, entitled *The Miracle*. His October 5 column was headlined "When All Superlatives Fail: *The Miracle* Surpasses all Expectations or Dreams for Dramatic Force and Sheer Loveliness."

"When the historian of a hundred years hence sits down to write of the American theatre," de Rohan began, "he must perforce record that a new era began with Morris Gest and *The Miracle*. For never before has the stage witnessed such indescribable richness, such imaginative beauty, such overwhelming emotional demands, such atmospheric loftiness and grandeur, such vividly lovely and spiritually moving scenes as those revealed in *The Miracle* at the Metropolitan Opera House in Philadelphia last night." De Rohan was not alone in his enthusiasm—theater critics in almost every other newspaper in Pennsylvania, New Jersey, Delaware, and Maryland were writing similar paeans to the show.

What had sent de Rohan into such raptures? Well, along with thousands of other people in America, he had been to see one of the most popular theater spectacles of the early 20th century—one that is almost completely forgotten today. Nonetheless, when you read such fulsome praise for anything, you wonder if you haven't missed something along the way. After all, there were several important names in American theater history connected to the show—Norman Bel Geddes and Morris Gest in particular—but the name that really stands out is that of Max Reinhardt.

Reinhardt was one of the most famous directors of the early 20th century—perhaps *the* greatest director of his era. Not only had he been instrumental with starting the worldwide "Little Theatre" movement with his Sound and Smoke Cabaret in Berlin in 1901, but he had also founded the Salzburg Festival in his native Austria in 1920. Reinhardt was famed for his erudition, his scholarship, and his artistry in directing plays of many genres. But for the larger theatergoing public, he was most famous for his huge spectacle productions, such as his massive stagings of Sophocles' *Oedipus the King*, Shakespeare's *A Midsummer Night's Dream*, and Hugo von Hofmannsthal's *Jederman*. And, of course, for *The Miracle*.

The play *The Miracle* by Hans Vollmöller was one of the best-known "art dramas" of its day. A wordless story about a wayward nun, a knight, an evil minstrel, and the Virgin Mary, it was supposedly drawn from a 12th-century Spanish legend, as well as a later German medieval "mystery play." To modern eyes, however, it reads very much like all the many Symbolist and Expressionist dramas that were very much the rage in "artistic" theatrical circles of the early 20th century. It required enormous casts—the production staged at the Olympia Theatre in London supposedly had 1,600 people on the stage. It was not a unique presentation at all—it had been staged by Reinhardt in almost every major city in the world by the time it came to Philadelphia in 1926. It was even made into a film in 1912, and several other times after that. In 1924, it was staged in New York, Chicago, Cleveland, Boston, and St. Louis. After Philadelphia, it was going on to Kansas City and Los Angeles.

The music for the show was written by German composer Engelbert Humperdinck. Now mainly remembered for his children's opera *Hansel and Gretel*, he considered *The Miracle* his late-in-life magnum opus—and, as for Reinhardt, it was a great money-spinner to finance other projects. The designer Norman Bel Geddes was doing both the sets and costumes. One of the great new talents of American design, Bel Geddes was already creating other projects for New York's Metropolitan Opera and Broadway, as well as being a leading industrial designer.

One of the other regular aspects of the play's various international productions was getting aristocratic (or at least very rich) young society ladies to add their glamor to the project. Not only was Lady Diana Manners in this version, but so were several young women from prominent families in New York, Philadelphia, and Chicago. This added an extra note of "class"—literally—to the whole thing, even though it was being produced as an "adjunct" (i.e., not an official part of the fair) of the Sesqui-Centennial Exhibition. However, *The Miracle* did rather better than the Sesqui, at least in terms of profits.

One can find a lot of great photos and original design renderings from a 1926 book *"The Miracle" Edition of Max Reinhardt and His Theatre*, edited by Otto Sayer, which was printed as a companion to the production. (For a play with no words, it's still quite long.) It begins with a detailed description of a young woman who is about to become a nun and is undergoing her commitment to her vows in a huge medieval cathedral, in front of a statue of the Madonna. But let's go back to Mr. de Rohan, who provided his readers in the *Courier-Journal* with a synopsis:

> A young nun, sacristan of a cathedral, is lured away from her vows by the spirit of evil, personified in the Piper. She flees with a handsome young Knight, who is slain by the Robber Count. The terrified girl is seized, and later becomes the property of the Prince, who steals her from the Robber Count. The [Emperor] covets his son's prize and takes her for his own. When the Prince attempts to steal her back, he is slain by his own father, who goes mad when he learns the truth.

Enthroned as the Empress, the girl is seized by revolutionists led by the Piper, and as a mob attacks and breaks into the castle, she escapes death "only to suffer a worse fate"—by which, de Rohan meant rape, torture and martyrdom. "Meanwhile, the Madonna in the cathedral comes to life and steps down from her pedestal to assume the discarded vestments of the faithless Nun. In the end the Nun returns and assumes the vows once more, while the Madonna again becomes a venerated statue." That last bit was "the miracle" of the play. It turns out the Virgin Mary was taking the girl's place—suffering on her behalf the whole time. Then at the end Mary steps back into her niche on the altar, a statue once again, after interceding for Christ's forgiveness on behalf of the wayward protagonist.

On the whole, it was a *very* Christian play, an inspirational religious fable about forgiveness and redemption. But it displayed an obvious horror of revolutionary politics, and a lot of people saw it as a rejection of Bolshevism. Evidently it appealed to others on sheer esthetic grounds too—some of its most ardent supporters in Philadelphia, as we shall see, were prominent Jewish business leaders, like movie theater magnate Jules Mastbaum, as well as secular cultural leaders, such as the conductor Leopold Stokowski.

All of this was accomplished in nine highly detailed action-packed scenes, filled with medieval props, fabulous costumes, and stirring music. Directing this show must have been like conducting a military campaign; there were so many logistics involved. For the audiences, just getting to see the Philadelphia show at the

Met was conducted rather in the spirit of organizing a pilgrimage. Church groups, musical clubs, and other cultural societies all bought huge blocks of tickets—often in conjunction with a visit to the Sesqui-Centennial, too.

In an "Open Letter" published in all the Philly-area newspapers as the run of the show ended, Morris Gest thanked the city:

> Philadelphia can well be proud of the spirit in which it has received *The Miracle*. No other city in America has responded so promptly to its appeal. No other city has observed so faithfully the request to be in their seats by 8 o'clock. No other city has handled so smoothly and effectively the enormous traffic before and after the performance. By its response on this epoch-making occasion, Philadelphia has ranged herself in the appreciation of art alongside the great art centers of the world such as London, Vienna, Berlin, Salzburg, [and] New York.

The last bit, Gest knew, must have really pleased Philadelphia, which was having a bit of an existential crisis in the 1920s. Did it really *matter* as a city anymore? Was its history and culture now totally outweighed by its infamously corrupt politicians and shameless bootleggers? Was it just a "sleepy" town which rolled up the sidewalks on Sundays? Gest—who had gotten his start in showbiz as an assistant to Oscar Hammerstein—assured Philadelphia that it *did* matter.

> When we started to discuss doing *The Miracle* in the Metropolitan Opera House, everyone said: "No one will go there; the place has been closed for years ... [But] convinced of the unique suitability of the Metropolitan Opera House, which was built during my association with Oscar Hammerstein, I made up my mind to do it and to do it there.

Gest then went on to thank many of the civic leaders of Philadelphia for their assistance—including the wealthy financier Edward Stotesbury—but concluded with a huge gesture of thanks to one man in particular:

> Last but not least, I want to thank the little modest man who walked in at the luncheon to which Dr. Stokowski and other prominent citizens were giving me to discuss *The Miracle*. He quietly said to me: "Morrie Gest we want *The Miracle* in Philadelphia. We mean to have it. Look to me for it." Without asking for any personal gain whatsoever, that man made it possible for *The Miracle* to be produced in Philadelphia. It is no other than Jules E. Mastbaum, I want to thank him for all that he did.

Sadly, Jules Mastbaum, the owner of dozens of Philadelphia movie theaters and a great local philanthropist, died shortly thereafter, at the age of only 58. One hopes he felt great satisfaction, in this gift to the city, by sponsoring an enormous spectacle of Art. For that one month, the glories of Hammerstein's former opera house shone once again on North Broad Street. That miracle alone almost redeemed the fiascos down at the far end of South Broad, but in the end even a divine intercession could not save the "Sesqui." It closed in November 1926, leaving the city government with a multimillion-dollar debt, and the lingering reputation of failure and civic embarrassment hung over Philadelphia for years.

Shakspere in the Parkway

April 24, 1930: A group of ladies from The Hathaway and West Philadelphia Shakespeare Clubs, all clad in cloche hats and stylish overcoats, commemorated the 314th anniversary of Shakespeare's birth by hanging a wreath of flowers from the dangling toes of one of the Shakespeare Memorial's allegorical figures.

Philadelphia's tribute to the Bard, installed on the Benjamin Franklin Parkway, in front of the Main Branch of the Free Library of Philadelphia, has always been a striking example of how to honor Shakespeare. Perched atop a dark marble base are two human figures—cast-bronze creations of the sculptor Alexander Stirling Calder. Calder had been born and raised in Philadelphia, where his father, Alexander Milne Calder, had spent decades creating all the statuary that adorns Philadelphia City Hall, including the famous huge figure of William Penn at its very peak.

Without knowing any of its context, it's quite common for casual passersby to think that this dark-hued Shakespeare statue is a somber "Pietà." At first glance, it certainly seems like one figure, head bowed, is mourning over a recumbent companion who is perhaps dying or injured. After all, directly across the street to the south is a memorial to the heroic sacrifices of African American troops in the Spanish–American War, the Philippine Insurrection and World War I.

True, if one looks down, the words "Shakespeare Memorial" are clearly emblazoned in gold letters across the bottom step of the pediment, and with that hint one might finally surmise that the bowed figure seated in the chair is Shakespeare's Prince Hamlet, representing Tragedy. Or perhaps you might not—the name "Hamlet" appears nowhere on the work, after all. Nor is the other figure, the guy with the dangling sleeves and pointed shoes, identified. You definitely might need to do a little research to learn that this is the clown Touchstone, from *As You Like It*. He is not dying, but rather is laughing. Touchstone is there to represent Comedy—though his tautly grinning face and his twisted pose do look somewhat pained, rather than happy.

The figure of Hamlet moodily raises a dagger, no doubt wondering if he should make his quietus with the bare bodkin. Touchstone, for his part, is casually holding a fool's staff, topped by the head of a Punchinello doll. Looked at in a different way, of course, one could also easily imagine that Hamlet is contemplating stabbing the clown, who has impudently slung an arm across the Prince of Denmark's lap, and perhaps just bopped him on the head with Mr. Punch. After all, what else did these two characters have to say to each other? "ALL THE WORLD'S A STAGE, AND ALL THE MEN AND WOMEN MERELY PLAYERS" is carved on the front of the pediment. This is not a line that either Hamlet or Touchstone actually speaks, of course. You might argue that if you're going to quote Jaques, you might as well put him in the scene, too.

Most Shakespeare memorial statues, all over the world, usually attempt to portray the author himself. There's the well-known 17th-century figure of Shakespeare, placed on the wall of Stratford-upon-Avon's church, overlooking the Bard's final resting place; the 19th-century statue in New York's Central Park; the one in London's Leicester Square; the one in Sydney, Australia … they all depict Shakespeare. Or rather, they depict what their artists *imagined* Shakespeare looked like, because we don't really know. There is no authenticated portrait of him made during his lifetime.

Maybe this is why Philadelphia's Shakespeare statue is allegorical—though if that is the case, why is no figure in the assemblage representing the playwright's Histories, or even his late plays (often termed Romances or "problem plays")? Well, a Philadelphia-centric historian might point out that this sculpture is yet *another* in a notable series of theatrical pairings of Comedy and Tragedy in the city. In the previous century, all Philadelphians were familiar with William Rush's carved wooden Comedy and Tragedy, which for decades graced the facade of the first two Chestnut Street Theaters. Such a historian (okay, me) might also point to the rather less well-known cast-iron figures of Comedy and Tragedy (with a bust of Shakespeare in between them) that stood high atop the cornice of the *third* Chestnut Street Theatre—until its demolition in 1917, when they were destroyed. A. S. Calder would have known these Comedy and Tragedy statues well, since they were quite close to where he had created similar crowning statues of great Presbyterian ministers for the Witherspoon Building on Walnut Street.

We should note, however, that this statue was not originally commissioned to have anything to do with "theater." It was nowhere near any of Philadelphia's historic theatrical houses, for one thing. It was more of a civic improvement and beautification project, really. The idea of a proper Shakespeare memorial for Philadelphia in Fairmount Park was proposed as early as 1892, during a period when many wealthy people and social organizations frequently used to donate sculptures in public parks. Figures from history, poetry, and mythology were often suggested, as were other famous authors (Goethe and Schiller, for example, whose bronze statues stand gazing at each other across a lawn in West Fairmount Park).

During the 300th anniversary of Shakespeare's death in 1916, it was noted by some that it was a shame that Philadelphia had no public memorial honoring him. Everyone was aware that other world cities were building substantial Shakespeare monuments—even entire museums and theaters dedicated to the Bard. True, that summer a temporary version of the original Globe Theatre was built on the grounds of the University of Pennsylvania, and his play *The Comedy of Errors* was staged in it. But a *permanent* memorial, not just something as insubstantial as a mere play, was thought more fitting. A Shakespeare Tercentenary Committee was formed, and the Fairmount Park Art Commission pledged $10,000 toward a statue and challenged the committee to match the amount.

The project stalled during World War I and the great influenza epidemic that followed. In 1922, the Philadelphia chapter of the Sons of St. George, a long-existing Anglophilic society that was holding its 150th Anniversary Grand Ball, once again urged that some memorial to England's greatest writer be erected. At this point, yet *another* venerable Philadelphia organization, the Shakspere Society, got involved in the effort. Since the 1850s, this group of amateur and professional Bardolators had dedicated itself to honoring Shakespeare as a literary genius—though it's true they once did admit the actor Edwin Booth into their numbers. Like similar Shakspere societies elsewhere in the world, it *insisted* on spelling his name as their hero himself had actually signed it. They were scholars, after all, and sticklers for accuracy.

The efforts of these two groups to call attention to Shakespeare found a new opportunity for fruition—the enormous expanse of Philadelphia's new Benjamin Franklin Parkway. This was a massive urban project which, in recent years, similar to what Baron Haussman had done in mid-19th-century Paris, opened a huge diagonal swathe between City Hall and the new Art Museum, then rising on a hill to the northeast. The daunting task of suitably ornamenting the vast amount of open space along the Parkway finally got the Shakespeare Memorial back on the agenda of the Fairmount Park Commission. At the midpoint of the parkway, Logan Circle, the Philadelphia architect Wilson Eyre collaborated with A. S. Calder in creating the Swann Memorial Fountain, with its three allegorical figures representing the Schuylkill, Delaware, and Wissahickon Rivers. The critical praise heaped on Calder and Eyre's elegant fountain, right in the center of the Parkway, led to the idea that the pair also ought to undertake that long-delayed Shakespeare project. The memorial was designated for an area of parkland to the northeast of Logan Circle, in front of the new Central Building of the Free Library, and not far from the planned Rodin Museum—itself full of significant sculptures of human forms.

Naturally, A. S. Calder was excited to get yet another Philadelphia commission in such a prominent location. According to his daughter Margaret, the sculptor also truly loved the theater, and *Hamlet* was his "favorite drama." His original proposal was to show an Elizabethan actor performing—that's how the phrase

"All the World's a Stage" made it into the work. But the idea of depicting an actor *performing* Shakespeare evidently did not pass muster with the committee, and so the allegorical duo, with the comic figure sprawling at the tragic figure's feet, was decided upon, instead.

The site near the library led the city's civic leaders to conceive of the memorial statue as a literary homage. Perhaps Calder himself held out for some reference to actual performance—apparently the original design even called for stone benches to be arranged around it, as if waiting for an audience that might someday witness Hamlet and Touchstone rise and speak to them. The rear surface of the pedestal at least strikes a compromise. But rather than saying anything about Shakespeare himself, instead Art, Theater and Literature *each* get a mention. There are three columns of names carved into the marble surface. In the middle column, it says, "Erected by the Shakspere Society and the Fairmount Park Art Association," above the names of Eyre and Calder. (But someone misspelled the middle name of the latter, since it reads "Alexander *Sterling* Calder.")

The left-hand column lists names of famous actors "who brought luster to the Philadelphia stage." Some of these are Philadelphians: Edwin Forrest, Louisa Lane Drew, John Drew, Jr., William B. Wood, Thomas Wignell, James Murdoch. But they've also stuck Joseph Jefferson in there—who, though *born* in Philadelphia, performed very little Shakespeare during his career. And why include the Boston-born E. L. Davenport, when Fanny Kemble, John McCullough, and Edwin Booth (all with deep connections to Philadelphia theater) are left out? And though there are many Hamlets in this list, there are no actors who ever played Touchstone.

On the right side of the pedestal's rear face is another list of distinguished scholars of Shakespeare associated with Philadelphia, including Joseph Dennie and Asa Israel. The name Horace Howard Furness, the longtime editor of *The New Variorum Shakespeare*, is up there twice—because his son Horace Howard Furness, Jr., later took over the great work after the elder's death.

Admittedly, whatever ideological compromises led to its creation, it's quite successful as a work of public art—even though it did get moved over a hundred feet from its original site when the Vine Street Expressway project began to plow across the neighborhood in 1954. This memorial, from its inception, was meant to prove that Philadelphia was a cultivated city. It was a matter of civic pride to place it in front of the elegant Beaux Arts facade of the Free Library—which itself masked the grim bulk of the Baldwin Locomotive Works which once stood to its immediate north. And after all, the statue looked nice out the window of Philadelphians' cars as they motored past, along the Parkway modeled after the elegant boulevards of Paris.

In the final analysis, this memorial to Shakespeare wasn't *representing* theater, or scholarship, or the man himself, but at least it *evoked* all of those, in some way. At any rate, in the photo from April 1930, we can see that the ladies of the Hathaway and West Philadelphia Shakespeare clubs were quite pleased with the whole arrangement.

Shakespeare's Birthday at the Edwin Forrest Home

In his will, the 19th-century Philadelphia actor Edwin Forrest set aside a substantial sum to establish and endow a home for retired actors. A dozen elderly former thespians (chosen by application) would be comfortably supported for the rest of their lives. Originally settled in Forrest's former summer home in the Holmesburg area of Northeast Philadelphia, the institution was moved in the 1920s to a Tudor-style manor on Parkside Avenue in West Philadelphia. There, surrounded by Forrest's lifetime collection of artworks, his library, and rooms full of other memorabilia, a dozen former theatricals (both male and female, all of them white) lived out their final years in a small community, with meals, healthcare, and household servants all provided. On Sunday they were served a glass of wine with dinner, compliments of Mr. Forrest. When they passed away, a large plot in West Laurel Hill Cemetery was reserved for their final resting place.

Edwin Forrest made two additional stipulations in his will: that every year the residents gather to celebrate America's independence on the Fourth of July, and that they also gather to honor William Shakespeare on April 23rd—"when a eulogy upon his character and writings, and one of his plays, shall on that day be presented or read."

While the institution was still located in Holmesburg, the annual Shakespeare celebration was often overseen by the theater owner J. Fred Zimmerman. Sometimes the entire company of New York productions of Shakespeare's plays would be brought to Philadelphia for the occasion. Zimmerman, a founding member of the monopolistic "Theatrical Syndicate," eventually also left a significant sum in his will for the Forrest Home's endowment. This gift, though very generous, was not without its critics: "Zimmerman had squeezed his fortune out of helpless actors who had to do his bidding or starve; now he returned what he had taken," groused Forrest's biographer Richard Moody.

By the mid-20th century, it had become an annual feature of Philadelphia newspapers to record the Shakespeare celebration at the Forrest Home, though by that point the festivities were usually moved to the Sunday nearest the Bard's birthday. Sometimes the residents would put on performances of scenes from Shakespeare, and sometimes they would be joined by other, younger thespians from the local area. Wealthy members of Philadelphia society who were on the Board of the Forrest Home would often put in an appearance, and their presence was duly recorded in the society columns of the newspapers. In 1980 Helen Hayes came by for the occasion and recited Portia's speech from *The Merchant of Venice*: "The quality of mercy is not strained."

It was a nice old Philadelphia tradition, but by 1988 the home was getting structurally outdated. Further, it was judged that income from the home's endowment could be spread more broadly than to care for just 12 people. Everyone, at long last, realized that Forrest's stipulation that all the residents be white was completely unacceptable. The Edwin Forrest Home was finally combined with a Staten Island institution for retired actors, and today the Lillian Booth Actors Home in Englewood, New Jersey, run by the Actors Fund, boasts an "Edwin Forrest Wing." Back in Philadelphia, readings of passages from Shakespeare over Edwin Forrest's grave in Old St. Paul's Episcopal burial ground lasted into the 21st century, but usually on the anniversary of his own birthday, March 9th.

On occasion, ceremonies have even been held in front of Edwin Forrest's massive statue in the lobby of the Walnut Street Theatre. This imposing portrayal of the actor in the character of Coriolanus had once stood guard in the front lobby of the retirement home, and other painted portraits and prints of him hung on almost every wall. Over the years, they all doubtless received many blessings, toasts, and thanks from the grateful residents.

Won't You Come Home, Pearl Bailey?

She was born in 1918, in Newport News, Virginia, to William and Ella Mae Bailey. By that point, the family already had a boy and two girls, and her father had been *sure* it would be another boy—one that he had already decided to name Richard. But little Pearl arrived on the scene instead. Still, for the rest of his life, William Bailey insisted on the excellent joke of calling his youngest daughter "Dick." He was a forceful presence in the family, so the rest of them tended to follow suit.

When Pearl was very young, the Baileys moved to Washington, DC, when her father became a preacher for a Pentecostal "Daddy Grace's House of Prayer" congregation. But he and the family also enjoyed going to shows at local Black theaters, and meeting their casts, and Pearl could recall cast members from a touring production of the show *Shuffle Along* coming over for dinner and teaching her older brother Willie some of the "new steps." But her mother was increasingly unhappy in the marriage, as Bailey later wrote in her published memoir, *The Raw Pearl*. Though she never learned what the problem was, Bailey recalled that after one especially huge spat between her parents on an Easter morning, her mother moved away by herself to Philadelphia. This was understandably traumatic for a little child. "Every Easter morning I wake up the first thing, even this Easter, and I remember that scene."

The Bailey children stayed with their father, but 18-year-old Willie missed his mother so much that he rode his bicycle all the way to Pennsylvania in search of her, even though he did not know her exact address. Amazingly, just by asking around, he found her—living in an apartment in North Philadelphia, now remarried. A few months later, Willie went back to DC and fetched little Pearl, too. "We caught the train and arrived in Philly around noon. Mama didn't know Willie's plan, so what a surprise when she opened the door, and bless him, Willie said, 'Mama, I've got Dick!'"

After her father consented to let her stay in Philadelphia, Pearl attended the Joseph Singerly School on Twenty-Second and Berks Streets. She would also recall the nearby ballpark where she would attend Negro League baseball games, and the long stone wall along Diamond Street, bordering a huge graveyard—where she would hang out with other neighborhood kids, watching traffic go by and "counting cars" until late in the evening. Meanwhile, her brother was building his career as "Bill Bailey" at the Cotton Club in New York and touring with Duke Ellington's band.

After the family had lived in several different apartments, Pearl recalled:

> Mama bought a house on Twenty-third Street … where my career started … Around then, brother Willie was getting a big reputation in show business as a tap dancer, and we were proud of him. The Baileys had a star in the family … He'd bring different performers to the house for dinner; even the neighbors began to look forward to his playing the Pearl Theatre [on 20th and Ridge Ave.] … It was a gay household when Bill brought people home. None of this had any influence on my finally going into the business, because we all had sung and danced from the beginning, with no lessons.

At the age of 15, hearing about an "amateur night" contest at the Pearl, she used her brother's fame to talk her way onto the list of contestants. She performed "The Talk of the Town," danced a bit, and got a huge hand from the audience. She did an encore, singing her favorite song, "Poor Butterfly," as she shaped the air with her expressive hands, and was overwhelmingly voted the winner. "They gave me a five dollar prize and the offer of a week's work." At the end of the week, in lieu of pay she was offered the inducement of an additional week's work with an even higher salary. "The following Wednesday, when I made that dramatic entrance into the alley leading to the stage door, I saw the acts standing there. They were all staring at the beautiful padlock on the gate leading down to the door." The theater was closed, and the management had skipped town with everybody's money. It was a lesson she never forgot: get paid first.

Still in love with showbiz, however, she left home and began making her own way, performing in nightclubs all over Eastern Pennsylvania. By 1945 she was performing with bandleader Cab Calloway. After one performance back home in Philly, a local journalist enthused she was "extraordinary" and in a class by herself. "Gifted with a high-voltage personality, and a pair of fascinating and expressive hands, her songs, despite an apparent minimum of effort, pack a terrific wallop."

While touring with Calloway, she met and married the band's drummer, Louis Bellson, and together they had two children. It was a rare interracial marriage in American showbiz of that day, but Bailey was such a hugely popular performer that it never seemed to matter. She was a sensation in the 1954 Broadway show *House of Flowers* and appeared in the movies *Carmen Jones* and *Porgy and Bess*.

In February 1970, Pearl Bailey was again back in Philadelphia, now a well-established star on Broadway, and in cabarets, movies, and television. She was touring in David Merrick's hit all-Black production of *Hello, Dolly!*, which had been a big hit in New York for her and co-star Cab Calloway.

It was a big hit in her former hometown, too, as the audiences at the Forrest Theatre all went crazy from the minute Pearl walked on the stage. "Triumph is hardly an adequate word for the phenomenon," wrote William Collins in his review in the *Inquirer*.

> It's more of a royal progress than a show. The cheering started the moment the audience first caught sight of Miss Bailey perched on the back of that pretty little street car and, at the end, after her Dolly had been helloed to a fare-thee-well, practically everybody was standing up and hollering. Receptions like that occur only once in a great while for performers in Philadelphia, at least outside of the Spectrum. Let history record that it happened at the Forrest and probably will go on happening there for the next four weeks of the engagement, which is a sell-out.

In her 60s Pearly Bailey went to college, earning a degree in theology from George Washington University. No doubt her father would have been proud. Later, as a loyal Republican Party member, she had been a frequent guest at the White House in the Nixon, Reagan, and Bush administrations. George H. W. Bush even made her a special ambassador to the United Nations—work which had been especially important to her.

On August 17, 1990, while in town for medical treatment at Jefferson University Hospital, Pearl Bailey passed away in Philadelphia, after suffering a heart attack in her hotel room at 4th and Arch Streets. She had not lived in the city for decades, but many others in her family still did. Before his own death in 1978, her brother Bill Bailey had frequently been a preacher in local churches—many of them converted theaters and movie houses in North Philadelphia. It was at just such a building, the Deliverance Evangelistic Church on North Broad Street, that Pearl Bailey's funeral was held on August 23rd. Two thousand people filled the seats at the former Logan Theatre, and it took four hours for mourners to pass by the open casket to pay their respects. She was wearing a blue suit and a string of pearls, and her hands were holding a single red rose. More elaborate arrangements of flowers, including those from singers Lena Horne and Ella Fitzgerald, were displayed nearby.

Cab Calloway was present, acting as a pallbearer. "Pearl was love, pure and simple love," he told the press. "I mean it from my heart and soul that Pearl Bailey was something you'll never see again."

The Show Rescued by a Helicopter

September 10, 1974: Everyone was on edge at the Playhouse in the Park, the city-owned summer theater in the round, set in the parkland above the west bank of the Schuylkill River. The night before, John Lewis Carlino's play *Cages*, the final show of the summer season, had experienced a rocky first preview.

First, the star, Shelley Winters, had picked up a virus and barely made it through the Monday night performance. "Who said 'The show must go on'?" she moaned afterwards to producer Milton Moss. Second, there was an even bigger problem with her co-star Joe Mascolo. Winters thought he was not right for the part.

On Tuesday morning, Mascolo left the show. Either he too had fallen ill, or he just wanted out of his contract, or he was fired due to "artistic differences"—accounts varied. But he was definitely not going to continue the two-week run. There was no understudy. What could Moss do except return every ticket buyer's money and cancel the rest of the season? "Call Nehemiah Persoff," Winters told him.

This seemed like a good idea. After all, Winters and Persoff had just done *Cages* together in August at the Berkshire Playhouse Theatre in Massachusetts, so he already knew all the lines and blocking.

There was one major problem—Persoff was at home in Los Angeles. But after a frantic phone call from Winters, he had immediately rushed to the airport—only to miss the plane. Nevertheless, he had gotten on the next flight to Philadelphia, script in hand, reviewing his lines.

The audience at the Playhouse in the Park arrived for the show that evening, only to be greeted by Executive Director Michael Frazier, who explained that Persoff was on his way, and that the curtain had been moved to 9 pm. Any annoyance or disappointment they felt was mollified by management passing out free coffee, ice cream, and hot dogs. Shelley Winters came out onstage and took questions from the audience to keep them happy.

They were also told to keep their ears tuned for the sound of chopper blades, because Milt Moss had hired a Bell Jet Ranger helicopter to shuttle Persoff right to the theater from the airport, in five minutes flat. Well, this was exciting! The audience buzzed with anticipation when they heard a helicopter's rotors in the distance at about 9 pm. But then it flew away. Rustling and murmurs of discontent were heard throughout the house, which was about three-quarters full.

It was nail-biting time. Persoff's flight from LA was behind schedule, arriving at 8:40 pm. At 8:45 the actor was finally off the plane. There he was met by Milton Moss, press representative Jim McCormick, and *Daily News* reporter Stu Bykovsky. Moss had a floor plan of the Playhouse stage in hand, and immediately started explaining the position of props and cues as they ran to the waiting Bell Jet Ranger. As Bykovsky told the story to his readers the next day:

> Back at the airport, a cool and collected Persoff was seated in the helicopter at 9:09. At 9:16, just as we got clearance to take off, the pilot announced, "The radio's not working." A ground technician fixed it quickly. More precious minutes lost.
>
> Finally, at 9:20, we lifted off. At 9:24 the park came into view. "This looks like Vietnam," the pilot said. "Where do we go?" McCormick pointed him to the lights of the theater and was relieved to note that there were still cars filling its parking lot.
>
> We banked and circled the Playhouse. At the bottom of the [Belmont] Plateau, four police cars were parked in a square, red lights revolving and headlights glaring. This was our landing strip.
>
> We touched down at 9:26. Persoff was hustled into a police car for the quarter mile trip up the hill to the Playhouse.
>
> At 9:37—without makeup or preparation—Persoff stepped into the spotlight and gave a flawless performance.

When interviewed the next day, the actor stated that the whole experience had heightened the theatricality of the show. It didn't matter that he walked onto a stage he had never seen before in his life. "I rather welcomed it. It was interesting ... I'm just sorry the critics weren't there last night. There was an excitement in the air."

What is most amazing is that Philadelphia critics rather heartlessly showed up the very next afternoon to review Persoff, based solely on the subsequent matinee performance. The *Daily News'* Jonathan Takiff called the performances "uneven" and was unimpressed with Carlino's script. In the first half, Persoff played a repressed customer of an over-the-hill prostitute (Winters). In the second half, he had to be wildly uninhibited, as he portrayed an ornithologist who was only sexually aroused by his wife when he acted out the part of a rooster: "At first, this seems a humorous notion, made much more so by Mr. Persoff's straight-faced clucking and strutting, twisting his hair into a cock's crown, attempting to establish 'pecking order' supremacy over his wife, a cool-at-any-cost advertising copywriter... One suspects, however, that the bird man's afflictions are also the author's." Meanwhile, the *Inquirer* made no reference to the last-minute heroics of the previous evening, and rather dismissed the play. Perhaps Moss should have had an actor arrive by helicopter for every show. Expensive, sure, but what an entrance!

Philadelphia '76

The crowds of out-of-town tourists mostly went home after the Fourth of July. It was only then that crowds of Philadelphia theatergoers started showing up to the tent theater on Independence Mall. The musical *1776* played all summer long—not to consistently full houses, true. But at least to a respectable number of occupied seats.

The whole thing had not started well. These were bad years for Philadelphia, times of population decrease and a pervasive sense of civic decline. An ambitious idea that some people had proposed—that the city once again host a World's Fair in 1976, just as it had done in 1876 and 1926—was quietly shelved. There were too many other issues for the city to grapple with: rising crime, failing schools, closing factories, aging infrastructure. It was an all-too-familiar litany of problems, ones faced by so many large American cities.

The production, backed by "Philadelphia '76"—the city's official agency for the Bicentennial celebration—had opened in May at the Playhouse in the Park. In late June the show was scheduled to shift venues, to the lawn in front of the actual building where the drafting and signing of the Declaration of Independence had taken place.

But there was competition. Amazingly, it was not the only production of *1776* in town. In fact, another Philadelphia version of *1776* was already playing at the Riverfront Dinner Theater on Delaware Avenue and Poplar Street. (The buffet, advised the ads, began at 6:30 for an 8:30 curtain.) The Candlelight Dinner Theatre in nearby Delaware was also staging the show that summer. In that Bicentennial year, the rights to composer Sherman Edwards' musical had been widely sold across the nation, and there had been no contractual restrictions placed on regional competition.

The Philadelphia '76 version of the show was supposed to last for 10 weeks and would cost an estimated $40,000 a week to produce. Initial reviews had not been kind. "Bicentennial schlock," said *Inquirer* reviewer Willam B. Collins.

It was a "second-rate production" that belonged in a bus-and-truck tour, he wrote. The staging played to the worst aspects of book writer Peter Stone's "cartoon-strip" version of history, with "toilet jokes and sex jokes [that] seem more than ever like entertainment for rubes." Only the director/actor Don Perkins as John Adams did a creditable job, Collins felt, with Lesley Stewart as his wife Abigail having the best voice in the cast—though that wasn't high praise, he made clear.

Jonathan Takiff, writing in the *Daily News*, was a little more charitable and said the in-the-round staging of the show wasn't bad at all. As for the show's rough aspects, well, maybe that suited the age we were living in. "So the hell with decorum or authenticity—if the public wants a Ben Franklin (Sam Kressen) who's an egocentric buffoon, or a young Tom Jefferson (John Almberg) who's a sex-starved maniac ... then that's what we'll get. In sum, characters just as frail, flaky or fault-ridden as the rest of us."

The production transferred to the big tent near Independence Hall in late June, with much trepidation on the part of Philadelphia '76. Executive Director William Rafsky said the show would break even if 63 percent of the 2,400 seats in the theater were sold, at three bucks apiece, during each of the eight weekly performances. But if the house was only half-sold, it would mean a loss of $8,000 a week. There was an overall budget of 3 million for all the scheduled performance activities—folk dances, puppet plays, costumed storytellers—on the Mall that summer. But the production of *1776* was the central showpiece. It was ruled that it must stay running, no matter what. If losses on it exceeded $75,000, they would simply cut the other events. If it got worse than that, they would close it early.

The turnout for the early weeks of the Bicentennial celebration in Philadelphia had been underwhelming. Local political leadership had not helped. Philadelphia Mayor Frank Rizzo had publicly warned of huge crowds of "radical demonstrators" invading the city in July and had asked for the National Guard to be called out to protect the city from what he claimed were inevitable riots. The producers of the play quietly banged their heads on the table while the subsequent media firestorm played itself out. On July 4 itself, Bicentennial celebrations in New York City (where the "tall ships" paraded up the Hudson River) and Washington, DC (where gala concerts and spectacular fireworks drew huge crowds along the National Mall) were better attended and got better media coverage.

But Philadelphia audiences, true to their long-standing reputation, still reliably *loved* musicals, and as that Bicentennial summer progressed, locals realized that the rush of tourists was mostly over. The city was literally giving away tickets—if you went to the Municipal Services Building near City Hall, there was a nice lady at a card table who would hand them to you for free, so why not? Attendance began to pick up, and *1776* stayed open all summer long. It hadn't been a great run, but at least it hadn't been a disaster. Philadelphia, the city which had learned over the recent difficult years to temper its expectations, would settle for that.

The Return of Lady Day

December 2, 1992: *Lady Day at Emerson's Bar & Grill* opened at the Wilma Theater on Sansom Street. It was not the first time the show had been performed in the Philadelphia area, nor was it even the first play about Billie Holiday to be written and produced in the city. Just like the singer's own relationship with the city where she was technically born (but not raised), it was complicated.

Holiday's horrific early years in Baltimore and her eventual escape to Harlem, where her astounding singing career first blossomed, were of course well documented in *Lady Day*. So were her drug use and her many travails with the criminal justice system.

Philadelphia comes into the story there, too. In May 1947, while she was in town gigging with Louis Armstrong's band at the Earle Theatre on Market Street, Billie had only very narrowly escaped being arrested. A police raid had descended on her manager's room at the Attucks Hotel in South Philadelphia. She was out front in her chauffeured car at the time, but when she saw the cops swarming the hotel's entrance, Holiday quickly exited the car and fled on foot, while her chauffeur tried to speed away from the scene. The car was overtaken and confiscated on Lehigh Avenue after a police chase. Heroin was found during the raid, and Holiday was finally arrested a few days later at her apartment in New York. She was charged with drug trafficking—a federal offense. Despite her protests that she was just a user, not a dealer, the court sentenced her to a year in prison. "I have been arrested all over the country," her character says in *Lady Day*. "But Philly's the only place ever made me a candidate for federal housing."

In fact, Holiday lived for several periods in Philadelphia (there's a historic marker outside her former apartment on Lombard Street), and in the last years of her life she really needed to perform in Philadelphia clubs, because New York City laws would not allow anyone convicted of a felony to perform in cabarets or bars.

One of the places Billie could still sing when she needed a few bucks was at Emerson's Bar & Grill, a gritty establishment at the northwest corner of 15th and Bainbridge Streets in South Philadelphia. The singer died in July 1959 in a Harlem hospital at the age of 44. Many of these sad details would end up in the play, too.

The author of *Lady Day*, Lanie Robertson, had also lived in many places in his life, but he had stayed in Philadelphia after graduating from Temple University. Robertson had been a struggling Philadelphia playwright for many years, and as he used to joke, he had written "more plays than Shakespeare, and none of them nearly as good." There were some successes along the way. Robertson's *The Trials of Mrs. Surratt*, about the woman unjustly convicted and executed for involvement in the murder of President Lincoln, had been produced as a radio play for NPR. His drama about the murder of playwright Joe Orton, *Nasty Little Secrets*, would be staged at the Walnut Street Theatre Studio Five in 1987.

But if Philadelphia theatergoers remembered Robertson, it was probably for *The Insanity of Mary Girard*, which had been produced by Theater Center Philadelphia at The Painted Bride Art Center on South Street in 1976. The play, which detailed the mistreatment of an 18th-century woman who was mentally ill, the wife of Philadelphia iconic businessman Stephen Girard, had been a definite downer during the Bicentennial Celebrations that year.

As he searched for a different subject to write about, there was another Philadelphia story about a woman battling personal demons that Robertson could not get out of his mind. A friend had told him many times that in 1958 he had seen the great Billie Holiday perform at Emerson's. By that point she had been arrested multiple times for heroin possession, and her addiction had ravaged her. "There were about six or seven other people in the place. On the piano was a big glass of liquor, which she never touched," recalled Robertson in an interview. "She came in, stumbled over the microphone cord and she sang. She sang for over an hour and stumbled out."

The idea for dramatizing Billie Holiday's life story, however, was not new. There was the Oscar-nominated 1972 film *Lady Sings the Blues*, which featured Diana Ross. In addition, there was an entirely different show, *Lady Day*, by James McBride and Stephen Stahl, that had already been staged in Philadelphia. Stahl's play was performed at the Walnut Street's Theater Five in 1981, featuring Nora Martin as Billie. That play had gone on to be a success in Paris and London, where Dee Dee Bridgewater had played the doomed singer of "God Bless the Child" and "Strange Fruit."

It was not until 1984 that Robertson started to write his own Billie Holiday play. By that point he had long since left Philadelphia and moved to New York. (An incident where an actress had taken a break from the run of *Mary Girard* to join her family at the Jersey shore for the weekend had convinced him that Philadelphia was not ever going to be a serious theater city.) But as he attempted and then discarded an idea for a play about another singer, Edith Piaf, the story his friend had told him resurfaced, and the framework for the Billie Holiday play took shape in his mind. "If in some way I could get at what was in the performer's mind as she sang, the songs would become an extension of the interior monologue … so the audience would know what she was thinking as she sings, that's the play." The show would be inherently challenging to produce, requiring a highly talented singing actress and a small jazz combo to accompany her. It also needed a small dog to play Pepi, Holiday's beloved chihuahua.

The play, starring Lonette McKee, was first performed at Atlanta's Alliance Theatre, then moved to the Vineyard Theatre in New York in June 1986. It had gotten rave reviews and was an extended-run hit Off-Broadway, giving Robertson the first real financial success of his career. S. Epatha Merkerson, the understudy, eventually took over the role. It was produced many times at smaller regional theaters, as Black actresses seized upon it as an exciting and appealing vehicle for their careers. One of these was the Detroit actress Miche Braden, who teamed up with Harold McKinney, a talented jazz pianist. They had brought their production to People's Light & Theatre in the Philadelphia suburbs, where it had played to enchanted audiences in 1988. It was this production that was being re-staged at the Wilma in 1992, but this time under the direction of Blanka Zizka. McKinney once again accompanied her, as the character Jimmy Powers.

Robertson's *Lady Day at Emerson's Bar & Grill* would finally receive a Broadway production in 2014, directed by Lonny Price. It would win its star, Audra McDonald, an unprecedented sixth Tony Award for her performance. A new production was also staged in April 2023 at the Philadelphia Theatre Company on the corner of Broad and Lombard Streets—just around the corner from Billie Holiday's old apartment building, and a few blocks north of the former site of Emerson's Bar & Grill. Laurin Talese could always count on a reliable laugh every show when her character groused: "I used to tell everybody when I die I don't care if I go to Heaven or Hell long's it ain't in Philly."

PART TWO

The Wicked Stage

William Penn Sees a Play

On Wednesday, January 1, 1662—New Year's Day—Samuel Pepys, London resident and Royal Navy administrator, made the following entry in his diary:

Up and went forth with Sir W. Pen by coach towards Westminster, and in my way seeing that the Spanish Curate was acted today, I light and let him go alone, and I home again and sent to young Mr. Pen and his sister to go anon with my wife and I to the Theatre.

That done, Mr. W. Pen came to me and he and I walked out, and to the Stacioner's, and looked over some pictures and maps for my house, and so home again to dinner, and by and by came the two young Pens, and after we had eat a barrel of oysters we went by coach to the play, and there saw it well acted, and a good play it is, only Diego the Sexton did overdo his part too much.

From thence home, and they sat with us till late at night at cards very merry, but the jest was Mr. W. Pen had left his sword in the coach, and so my boy and he run out after the coach, and by very great chance did at the Exchange meet with the coach and got his sword again.

"Sir. W. Pen[n]," in this passage, was not the man whose statue now stands at the top of Philadelphia's City Hall. This was his father, the wealthy, distinguished and battle-hardened English admiral, whose nimble politics allowed him to support, successively, both the Commonwealth of Oliver Cromwell, and then the Restoration regime of King Charles II. Pepys rather feared and disliked Sir William but needed to maintain his acquaintance for professional reasons—after all, they shared the same rooms at the Navy Office, and their London houses were quite close to each other. In fact, we can note from the diary that they often dined together. Taking the Penn family to the theater may have seemed a fine way for Pepys to remain in Sir William's good graces.

"Young Pen[n]," as Pepys called him, was then just 16. One day he would become Philadelphia's founder, and eventually that enormous statue of him would be lifted high into its skyline. But in early 1662 he was a rather weedy and serious-minded youth, who had spent some time at both Chigwell School and Oxford University, and a lot of time studying with private tutors. He didn't get along well with his irascible father and would soon secretly begin exploring the theology of "non-conforming" (i.e., not Church of England) Protestant sects—an interest that would drive Admiral

Penn to distraction. However, at this point in his life, at least, Young Mr. Penn was not averse to going to the theater. We know from Pepys' diary that four days previously, he and the Penn family had also gone to see *Bussy D'ambois*, an early Jacobean tragedy by George Chapman.

The drama on that New Year's Day was *The Spanish Curate*, a comedy by the duo of John Fletcher and Philip Massinger. First presented in 1622 by Shakespeare's former company, the King's Men, it was being revived on the London stage as a reliable standard work. (Since during the years 1642–60 there had been no theater allowed in London at all by the Puritan-dominated Parliamentary and Commonwealth regimes, there weren't many new "Restoration" plays to stage yet.) *The Spanish Curate* had a very complicated plot that would have required much attention on the part of the audience. We don't have young Penn's direct account of the show. It's possible he had never been to see a play before. Perhaps he was befuddled and confused by the customs of playgoing, which may have accounted for his carelessness in leaving his sword (a necessary item to wear in public if he wanted to be seen as a "gentleman") in the coach.

But unfortunately, neither of these visits to the theatre seemed to have left a pleasant memory in William Penn's mind, and no play he might have seen subsequently ever changed that bad impression. As he continued his education, he may have had later exposure to the theaters of Paris, and when he briefly studied law at Lincoln's Inn he certainly might have read or seen plays. But we do know that once Penn became a full adherent to the principles of the Society of Friends (during a visit to Ireland, of all places), he came to the firm conclusion that the entire practice of theater was indecent and ungodly. It was just this sort of opinion that increasingly got him into trouble with His Majesty's government. In 1668, he was thrown into the Tower of London for allegedly denying the Holy Trinity. While incarcerated there, Penn had a long time to reflect on the ills of society, and to his mind playgoing was one of the worst.

In his subsequent book *No Cross, No Crown*, written while he was confined in the Tower, Penn condemned the habits of a certain sort of Londoner:

> ... [Their] afternoons are as commonly bespoke for visits and plays; where their usual entertainment is some stories fetched from the more approved romances; some strange adventures, some passionate amours, unkind refusals, grand impediments, importunate addresses, miserable disappointments, wonderful surprises, unexpected encounters, castles surprised, imprisoned lovers rescued, and meetings of supposed dead ones; bloody duels, languishing voices echoing from solitary groves, overheard mournful complaints, deep-fetched sighs sent from wild deserts, intrigues managed with unheard-of subtlety ... all their impossibilities reconciled: things that never were, nor are, nor ever shall or can be, they all come to pass!

This scornful description of a typical dramatic plot sounds very much like those of *Bussy D'ambois* and *The Spanish Curate*.

Of course, we shouldn't put too much weight upon that one day. It wasn't just the typical ribald jests and overly complex action of Restoration Era theater that likely offended Penn. We learn from *No Cross, No Crown* that even the clothing worn by audiences and actors revolted him. The men he had seen on stage tended toward effeminacy, and the women dressed to provoke lust, he felt strongly. And the undoubted open presence of prostitutes in the playhouse would have also disturbed him. Furthermore, he and other Quakers objected to the social distinctions on display in theater. Rich and prominent people sat in the best seats to show off their finery—even on the stage itself! If all souls were equal in the sight of a just and loving God, as Quaker doctrine held, such artificial distinctions were an abomination. Most damningly, in Scripture there was no indication that the Early Church had *ever* countenanced attendance at the theater: "How many plays did Jesus Christ and His Apostles recreate themselves at? What poets, romances, comedies, and the like did the Apostles and saints make, or use to pass away their time withal? I know they did redeem their time to avoid foolish talking, vain jesting, profane babblings, and fabulous stories." The Christian reformers of the present day should do the same, he concluded.

When eventually he came to establish the new Commonwealth along the west bank of the Delaware River that would bear his name—and the City of Brotherly Love he intended for its principal town—Penn was not only concerned about the proper shape of its government, but also about its public morality and habits. In the 1682 *Frame of Government of Pennsylvania* that he created, Article 37 states, "That as a careless and corrupt administration of justice draws the wrath of God upon magistrates, so the wildness and looseness of the people provoke the indignation of God against a country." Therefore, along with lying, fornication, and murder being criminalized, it was advisable that "all prizes, stage-plays, cards, dice, May-games, gamesters, masques, revels, bull-battings, cock-fightings, bear-battings, and the like, which excite the people to rudeness, cruelty, looseness, and irreligion, shall be respectively discouraged, and severely punished."

And there was little doubt that most of the new Quaker citizens of Philadelphia agreed wholeheartedly with him. Their religious and moral principles would continue to affect the respectability—indeed the legality—of theater in Philadelphia for many, many years. Indeed, Philadelphia ministers and politicians of all stripes would employ similar arguments and language to condemn theater well into the 19th century.

Penn did not spend many years of his life in Philadelphia—he only came to Pennsylvania twice, and only stayed for a few years each time. On the whole, he found actual administration difficult, and his relations even with other Quakers did not always go smoothly. As events developed, several other revised "Frames of Government" were to follow that first one.

When he departed Pennsylvania for the last time, in 1701, Penn left behind a final Frame of Government that established a representative Assembly for the colony.

It also set forth principles that were important to him, such as trial by jury, and the right of the accused to legal counsel. This time, however, it did not explicitly mention banning stage plays, masques, and revels. It only regulated taverns and public houses, and places of "public entertainment" (places that served people drinks, not plays—though the possibility was always there).

To his eternal credit, Penn wished to establish a spirit of tolerance in his namesake Commonwealth and in its principal town of Philadelphia. The final document he left behind there stated that, "the Happiness of Mankind depends so much upon the Enjoying of Liberty of their Consciences." Even though William Penn clearly did not like theater, to his credit, he endowed Pennsylvania with broad civic principles that would eventually—in the long run—make room for it to grow and evolve there.

The Friends of Virtue

In the first seven decades or so after Philadelphia was founded in the 1680s, it was hardly worthy of being called a city at all. It entered the 18th century with only about 700 houses and a few thousand people. By fits and starts, it kept growing, and eventually achieved a population of about 15,000 by 1750.

Philadelphia magistrates kept a tight lid on things within their jurisdiction—the grid of streets between the Schuylkill and the Delaware Rivers, and the blocks between Vine Street to the north and Cedar Street to the south. If anyone was going to get up to anything that the authorities might not approve of, it usually took place outside of the city limits proper—either to the south or to the north of Philadelphia, where smaller and less regulated townships could tolerate a bit of diversion and fun.

But that didn't mean Philadelphia was not *in* the theater. Back in London, the English dramatist Susanna Centlivre created a Philadelphia "Quaking Preacher" named Simon Pure for her 1718 play *A Bold Stroke for a Wife*. "Oh, the wickedness of the age!" was his best line. Centlivre, therefore, was likely the first playwright to immortalize a Philadelphian for the stage, even though the Quaker City (as it wasn't called yet) had no interest in hosting a production of any play of hers at the time. Though Simon himself entered late in the action of the comedy, his coming was foretold, and for reasons of the plot he had already been impersonated by Colonel Fainwell, the main character. (Subsequently, "simon-pure" was to become a byword with a double meaning: both to signify "the real thing" and also "a censorious person.")

This trope of the Stage Quaker in English drama was to last for quite a while. We can find him again in *The Young Quaker*, a 1784 comedy by Irish writer John O'Keefe. As the play begins, we meet another Philadelphian, Reuben Sadboy, who had been sent to England to look after family business in a responsible manner. But Reuben evidently had soon abandoned the pious and chaste ways of the Society of Friends during his London sojourn. One character describes him as wearing his wide Quaker hat, but not his deep Quaker principles:

> Egad, young Broad Brim ... improves by rapid degrees in to a man of Pleasure—[he] has been already at two Plays, one Opera, three Concerts—nay bespoke his dress for the Masquerade ... engaged a Dancing and a Fencing master—takes off his hat to a noted Demirep—his yea is succeeded by zounds, and his nay is gentleman usher to a damme, ha, ha, ha! Such a Quaker.

At the end of the play his father, Old Sadboy, arrives from Philadelphia, and brings the chastened lad back to the straight and narrow path.

It is important to note that not everyone in Philadelphia was a member of the Society of Friends (as they preferred to be called). From its foundation, the city had an explicit tolerance of other faiths, and in fact there was a large non-Quaker population, including Jews, Catholics and Lutherans. But this tolerance by the Quaker leadership did not extend to the matter of theater. In this they were in agreement with other Protestant denominations, including Presbyterians, Methodists, Baptists, and Mennonites—all of whom generally were not great supporters of the performing arts, either. Theatergoing was usually associated with the city's social elites, who were increasingly parishioners of the Church of England.

These latter Philadelphians considered themselves inheritors of mainstream British intellectual and social traditions—and that included music, dance, and theater. Or, like the most famous Philadelphian of that era, Benjamin Franklin, they aspired to be part of the broad progress of international intellectual and cultural advancement, in which theater played a part. We know that many colonial travelers had seen plays during visits to London, Paris, and Dublin, or even to Barbados, Jamaica, and Virginia, where plays were also occasionally produced and presented. In 1723 some persons set up a small temporary performance stage on Society Hill, to the south of the Philadelphia city limits, advertising that they intended to mount an evening of drollery featuring dancing, jokes, and tricks. Alarmed, the General Assembly tried to get Pennsylvania's colonial lieutenant-governor Sir William Keith to stop the show, but Keith refused, and furthermore declared that he rather fancied going to see the show himself. After that, theatrical activity mostly died down again. But there must have been constant pressure from substantial sections of the Philadelphia populace to see plays and popular entertainments such as puppet shows and wire-walking, or the authorities wouldn't have instituted so many local rules and regulations against them. Interestingly, most laws that the Quaker-dominated legislature of the Commonwealth of Pennsylvania passed prohibiting plays and touring companies were repeatedly overturned and repealed by the parliamentary government back in England. It was regarded as an unacceptable precedent that the colonies should place any restraint on trade from the home country.

However, in 1749, a small group of English players led by two men, Walter Murray and Thomas Kean, arrived in town. What sort of plays did they bring with them? The standard popular 18th-century English repertoire: a few Shakespeare adaptations, some Restoration dramas and farces, ballad operas, and sentimental comedies. Kean and Murray's company, for its part, seems to have had only five main pieces (including Addison's *Cato*) and three afterpieces in their repertoire.

When the actors first arrived, there was some alarm about the moral dangers the actors carried with them, along with their plays. But Murray and Kean assiduously paid calls to the best families of the city, and distributed handbills about taverns and coffeehouses, attracting an audience of the curious to come and see what they had to share. And though many people didn't want them there, since Pennsylvania's laws against theater had once again been overturned, legally they were entitled to put on a show—if only they found somebody to give them a building to perform in.

And they did find one—a converted warehouse down by the docks. Right on the Delaware riverbank, on the corner of Pine Street and Water Street. This warehouse was hardly what London folks would call a proper theater—probably it just had a platform, a curtain, and some wooden benches. It was owned by a merchant named William Plumsted (sometimes spelled "Plumstead")—himself a former Quaker, who, like many other politically and socially ambitious men of the time, had found it more congenial to become a member of the Church of England.

Rather than suffering any consequences for this bold move, William Plumsted would go on to be elected Mayor of Philadelphia, so we can see that by the mid-18th century, many Philadelphians were quite amenable to participation in an active intellectual and cultural life. Rather than setting themselves apart from the rest of the European world; they wanted to share in the Enlightenment and partake in one of the era's most common social activities. Like Reuben Sadboy, they were highly intrigued by the possibility of going to plays, operas, and concerts—if they only got the chance.

In 1754, Franklin's newspaper *The Pennsylvania Gazette* printed an article stating that there had been a re-appearance of live drama. Philadelphians had witnessed the arrival of a company of actors from England, led by the actor Lewis Hallam, and many happily welcomed the performance of stage plays. "On Monday, the 15th of this inst. April, the Company of COMEDIANS from London, opened the New Theatre, in Water-street, when the FAIR PENITENT, and MISS IN HER TEENS, were perform'd before a numerous and polite Audience, with universal Applause."

There had been, of course, stern voices raised as soon as the prospect of yet another theater troupe coming to Philadelphia had been announced. In the *Gazette* back on March 13, a letter from a citizen signing himself "A. B." reminded his fellow Christians that "The Stage is the great Corrupter of the Town."

> Should I pretend to give a View of the Wickedness of the Theatre, I should not know where to begin … For whether I insisted on the Lewdness or Impiety of most of the Plays themselves; on the infamous Characters of the Actors and Actresses; on the scandalous Farces they commonly tag the gravest Plays with, or, above all, on the inhumanly impudent dances and Songs, with which they lard them between the Acts; I say, which soever of these Particulars I insisted on, each of them would furnish Matter for a great many Pages; and much more, if I should enter upon a full View of them All.

Mr. A. B., warming to his topic, indeed went on at length, and in greater and greater detail. In fact, as the letter continued, his warnings increasingly made the theater seem not so much like a den of iniquity, but rather like a fascinating and instructive place! One wonders if Franklin was having a bit of fun by impersonating an anti-theater scold, or, if the letter was in fact from an anti-theater citizen, he printed it as a screed that bordered on self-parody. (In a subsequent issue of the *Gazette*, a "Mr. Y. Z." replied to him and wittily parried all his arguments.) At any rate, A. B.'s warnings were all either ignored by (or secretly intrigued) many Philadelphians, and many showed up to see the plays.

Just as he had done the first time a professional theatrical company came to Philadelphia, William Plumsted offered playgoers the warehouse he owned to be converted into a theater, and Franklin happily supported him in his influential publication. The *Gazette* further reported that before the performance of the plays, a prologue had been spoken by an actor in the company:

> To this new World, from fam'd Britannia's Shore,
> Thro' boisterous Seas, where foaming billows roar,
> The Muse, who Britons charm'd for many an Age,
> Now sends her Servants forth to tread the Stage; …
> The World's a Stage, where Mankind act their Parts,
> The Stage a World, they show their various Arts.

The actor speaking the prologue was pushing on an open stage door, as it were, since moral opinions in the city were clearly shifting. Nevertheless, throughout their stay, a group of Philadelphia magistrates kept a wary eye on the players, lest they show any improper performances.

The Hallam Company eventually moved on, having evidently given pleasure to those Philadelphians who were eager to see them, and left for the even more prosperous islands of the West Indies to try their fortunes there. Unfortunately, Lewis Hallam died in Jamaica in 1756, but his wife Sarah Hallam kept the troupe together. Eventually, she married another actor in the company, David Douglass, who took over its leadership. In 1759 Douglass brought the company—which now included about two dozen actors and even a group of musicians—back to the cities of the Atlantic Seaboard, including Philadelphia.

Now billing themselves "The American Company," in 1759 they built a theater, called the Society Hill, just on the other side of Cedar Street (the modern South Street) in the area that was technically a different township, called Southwark. Southwark had an apt name for the purpose—like its London counterpart on the south bank of the Thames in Shakespeare's day, the area to the south of Philadelphia was where less socially respectable activities generally took place.

The return of the American Company and their construction of actual playhouses naturally got instant attention from the dominant population of Quakers and Presbyterians. A flurry of indignant letters in the newspapers decried "blasphemous spectacles, wanton amours, profane jests and impure passion"—the sort of rhetoric that William Penn had used in the previous century. Their viewpoint still packed some punch, even in townships outside of Philadelphia, because the Society Hill Theatre was shut down in six months, and the structure was eventually made into apartments. The actors left the area to more welcoming places—such as New York.

But over the subsequent years the American Company would return again and again to Philadelphia—even constructing, at last, a permanent playhouse south of the city limits, as we shall see. "Oh, the wickedness of the age!" thought some Philadelphians, no doubt.

MRS HALLAM (MRS. DOUGLAS).

But many more in the city increasingly agreed with the words spoken at Plumsted's warehouse at the conclusion of the play in 1754. When the performances of *The Fair Penitent* and *Miss in Her Teens* were done, the *Gazette* had recorded, Mrs. Hallam ended the evening's entertainment with an epilogue, which concluded:

If then the Soul in Virtue's Cause we move,
Why should the Friends of Virtue disapprove?
We trust they do not, by this Splendid Sight
Of Sparkling Eyes that grace our Scenes To-night;
Then smile ye Fair propitious on the Cause,
And every generous Heart shall beat Applause.

Theater Is Illegal in Philadelphia

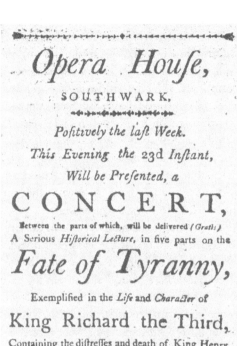

July 1788: A concert was presented at the "Opera-House, in Southwark." Significantly, this was not billed as a *play*, nor was the "comic lecture" that followed it. The coy fiction was obvious, but as a matter of law, neither could be marketed or described as what they plainly were. Indeed, for nearly a decade it had been forbidden to perform plays—not just in the city in 1754, but anywhere in Pennsylvania.

Disputes about the legality and regulation of theater had not stopped with the arrival of the Hallam Company in the city, and they continued during the decades leading up to the Revolution. Indeed, the effort by colonists to regulate theaters without interference is a rather overlooked item in the long list of grievances leading to the break with the Mother Country. In 1774 the Continental Congress forbade "every species of extravagance and dissipation, especially all horse racing, and all kinds of gaming, cock fighting, exhibition of shows and plays, and other expensive diversions and entertainments." This linking of gambling and theater may puzzle us now, but there's no doubt that when the British Army occupied Philadelphia in 1777 its officers did spend rather a lot of time doing exactly those things. By that point, however, the Hallam Company had abandoned the field, and spent the war years in Jamaica.

After the British occupation ended in 1778, many of Philadelphia's wealthy citizens and even U.S. Army officers (including George Washington) began to patronize plays once again. But in their revolutionary fervor, many of their elected representatives thought that "true religion and good morals are the only solid foundation of public liberty." Congress (which was meeting again in Philadelphia) passed an additional resolution sanctioning persons holding official positions who "act, promote, encourage or attend such plays." This anti-theatrical legislation was generally ignored in other states, but Pennsylvania's own legislature, then dominated by a radical egalitarian-minded majority, followed suit. In 1779 it instated a ban on theater in the entire Commonwealth. The Southwark Theatre sat mostly unused.

There matters stood. Even a brief attempt in 1782 by students of a certain M. Quesnay to perform plays in French, as an educational exercise, was stamped out. After the fight for national independence was won and hostilities had ceased, simmering interest in theatrical life began to show itself again. Lewis Hallam Jr., son of the original Lewis Hallam and now the leader of the reconstituted family troupe, brought it back to New York from Jamaica. He renamed it the "Old American Company" and petitioned the Pennsylvania Assembly to repeal the law, so that he could bring plays once again to Philadelphia. The effort was unsuccessful.

But Hallam knew there was still considerable interest from many people in the city to see plays. Some Philadelphia citizens who wished to attend theatrical entertainments crossed the Delaware River by boat to New Jersey, braving the perils of the waters to see touring actors perform in hastily built theater spaces. New York, Baltimore, Virginia, and the Carolinas all had proper legally sanctioned playhouses by that point, but not Philadelphia. "Hostility against the drama was too strong to admit of a visit," wrote the historian and playwright William Dunlap. The Old Americans were forced to stay away, or to cast their Quaker City performances in coy terms, as they did when John Durang danced his Hornpipe during "Instructions" and "lectures" in 1785.

In the summer of 1788, however, Hallam thought he sensed a change in the political climate and brought his troupe once again to the old theater in Southwark—even though, in deference to the strict letter of Pennsylvania law, he could not call it a theater or even a "playhouse" in the advertisements. Concerts, lectures, and operas, crucially, were *not* prohibited, so in all the advertisements and playbills the "OPERA-HOUSE, Southwark" was once again presenting "concerts," "historical lectures," "moral lectures," and even "comic lectures."

In fact, all the titles Hallam devised during this extended sojourn gave pointed reproach to the Pennsylvania legislature. Not only did Shakespeare's *Richard III* become "a lecture on tyranny," but Oliver Goldsmith's *She Stoops to Conquer* was billed as "A Comic Lecture in Five Parts on the Disadvantage of Improper Education, Exemplified in the History of Tony Lumpkin." An advertisement that appeared in newspapers on June 27, 1788, announced, "A Concert; Between the parts of which will be delivered (gratis) A MORAL LECTURE, in Five Parts, called Filial Piety; Exemplified in the History of the Prince of Denmark." (For which, read: *Hamlet*.)

However, despite all the hidden messages, subterfuges, and the obvious ploys, evidently this summer-long attempt to revive local interest in dramatic performance did not go particularly well in terms of box office, or artistic quality.

(Many members of the Old American acting company, fearing arrest, had even refused to accompany Hallam to Philadelphia that summer.) On July 25, 1788, the group ended its run by advertising "A comic lecture in Five Parts on the Pernicious Vice of SCANDAL"—accompanied by a quote from *The School for Scandal* by Richard Brinsley Sheridan, and concluded with another "comic lecture" in two parts, called *The Miller of Mansfield*, but it was unlikely that much profit came from their efforts.

Nevertheless, all these pointedly titled presentations by the company were effective in bringing matters to a head. According to Philadelphia historian Horace Lippincott, a petition signed by 1,900 persons was presented to the legislature asking for a repeal of the law against theater. The anti-theater forces, for their part, pushed back, and "a remonstrance came at once headed by all the Protestant Ministers of the City and several elders of the Society of Friends." But the theater had its *own* Friends, so to speak, and a committee calling itself "The Dramatic Association" was formed. (Its numbers included William Temple Franklin, the grandson of Benjamin Franklin, who had only recently passed away.) In the end, up to 6,000 Philadelphia citizens signed the petition *for* legalizing theatre, while 4,000 others signed one *against* any changes in the law.

There had been a recent shift in power in the Pennsylvania Assembly, and it was clearly feeling considerable pressure to modify the statute. Significantly, Philadelphia was soon to become the national capital of the entire United States, the men of The Dramatic Association argued; if it was going to host statesmen and international diplomats, it had to act like a great city. In the Assembly, other men of great political standing, such as the financier Robert Morris and the war hero General Anthony Wayne, spoke in favor of theater's civilizing and uplifting virtues. True, there were still those members of the legislature that held that theater was not only un-Christian, but it was also an undemocratic art form that only flourished under absolutist tyrannies. According to William Dunlap, one of these doubters, a certain Mr. Smiley, thought the minds of the people would be led to forget their political duties: "Cardinal Mazarine, he said, established the academy of Arts and Sciences in France with this view. He avowed himself 'no friend to the fine arts,' and asserted that 'they only flourished when states were on the decline.'" Nevertheless, the law against theater was finally repealed in March 1789. Licenses for three years of theatrical performances were authorized. They were never to be withdrawn again.

On January 6, 1790, the Old American Company finally reopened the Theatre in Southwark for drama, and presented plays that openly acknowledged that they were, in fact, plays. Sheridan's *The Rivals* and *The Critic* were the first ones performed. Thomas Wignell, the company's leading comedian and its newly appointed local manager, placed a large wooden American eagle above the proscenium of the stage. The figure was holding in its claws a banner with a line from Shakespeare's *Titus Andronicus*, "The Eagle Suffers the Little Birds to Sing"—a triumphant declaration of independence for plays in Philadelphia.

The Moral Structure of the Academy of Music

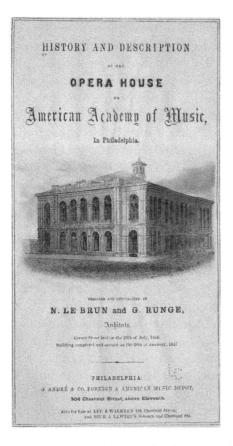

As early as 1839, small groups of wealthy and influential Philadelphians had been meeting to discuss what they regarded as a serious problem. The Chestnut Street Theatre, which was the longstanding favorite house of genteel Philadelphia society, was regarded as too small for truly great opera productions. The Arch Street Theatre, the Walnut Street Theatre, and its neighbor the National Theatre, occasionally hosted operas, but for the most part were also considered unsuitable. This was not only because of their limited size, but also the indelicate matter of the managers of these houses being financially dependent on liquor sales in their saloons and upper galleries—which not only encouraged a rowdy audience culture, but also tended to attract prostitution.

The Musical Fund Hall—a concert space on Locust Street near the Walnut Street Theatre—was also occasionally utilized for opera, but its stage was not really built for theatrical productions. Ambitious plans were discussed to fund and construct a new hall in the traditional theater district near Chestnut and Sixth, but the financial panics and bank failures of the early 1840s put a halt to these plans.

By the mid-19th century, most major American cities were seeking to build theater spaces where general audience behavior could be adequately regulated and high society properly celebrated. The wealthy elite of New York City moved first. The 1,800-seat Astor Place Opera House, built in 1847 at the conjunction of Broadway, the Bowery, and Astor Place, was meant to be this grand civilizing space, but it failed financially in its first year of existence. Then, when it subsequently was converted to be used as a legitimate theater—hosting tours of great Shakespearean actors—another disaster occurred. It was the site of the famous riot of May 1849, when the fans of Philadelphia's Edwin Forrest clashed with the New York militia troop who were protecting the supporters of English actor William Charles Macready inside.

During the riot, not only were dozens of people killed—many of them innocent bystanders—but the opera house was completely ruined. Manhattan's opera lovers decided to try again, and in 1852 the 4,000-seat New York Academy of Music was built, with the specific mission of "advancing musical taste and to secure musical entertainments accessible to the public 'at moderate charge.'" This time they were careful to locate their new grand opera house in a nicer part of town—on Irving Place—farther away from working class areas. Soon the city of Boston was also building an Academy of Music.

The original *Prospectus for an Academy of Music in Philadelphia* specified that the management "would give throughout the whole year a series of Operas, English and Italian, promenade and other concerts, the pure drama, Pantomime and French Vaudeville." Families of all classes, it was stressed, would find it a pleasant resort of superior character.

The designation "Academy" was therefore an assertion of a superior social space; it suggested that a theater was governed by a group of eminently respectable citizens, who would oversee the status and quality of all performances. When the construction of the Academy of Music on Broad Street was completed in 1857, the Board of Directors put out a pamphlet: "History and Description of the Opera House, or American Academy of Music, in Philadelphia." Inside there was a lengthy description of every detail of the newly opened building, from the facade to the restaurants and backstage areas.

But the pamphlet began with a brief discourse on the overall moral basis of the enterprise, and only then moved on to its practical advantages for hosting operas and plays. Interestingly, the writer tended to blame Philadelphia's long Quaker heritage for the situation which made the Academy necessary in the first place. This was his argument:

> The inhabitants of Philadelphia, so long as they have been known to the world, have always borne the reputation of being one of the most conscientious, sober-minded, and plain-thinking communities. Being originally a colony of Quakers, the spirit of these religious philosophers exercises, to the present day, its influence on the minds of citizens in general. Thus it has happened, that, while the city was growing to a considerable size, and was taking its place in the ranks for the first commercial communities, its inhabitants still retained an excessive love for the cultivation of their firesides, and an indisposition to support places of public amusement.
>
> However laudable this may be in one respect, it has certainly been productive of great disadvantages, morally and physically; for it was owing to this circumstance that those places of amusement which existed, and always will exist in a large community, were of an inferior kind, where sensual gratification was in more repute than mental refinement; so that an individual, whose natural inclination was in opposition to a quiet life at home, was placed in much greater danger of becoming demoralized, than if our citizen possessed some really respectable and well conducted public establishments.
>
> It is only of late that a movement in this direction is noticeable; but simultaneous with it, it became apparent to every interested person, that there was not a single theatre in Philadelphia,

worthy to represent the intelligence and refinement of a city of over five hundred thousand inhabitants. All the principal points, viz.: spaciousness of accommodations, free exits, ventilation, etc., were sadly neglected; and it must be said, that up to the present moment, Philadelphia had not a single theatre in which a visitor could find anything equivalent to the comfort, cleanliness, and safety to which he was accustomed at home, to say nothing of the exhibition of those miserable farces, so frequently and impudently brought before the public, to the disgust of every cultivated mind, and the demoralization of youth.

Thereafter, the writer of the pamphlet spent a great deal of space listing all the names of the Board, and describing the challenges and difficulties of construction, and of the rising interest and excitement among the public as they watched the building take shape, and finally, open to the public. "May it stand for ages, a beneficial object and ornament to Philadelphia."

Speaking of ornamentation, the outside of the Academy famously used only red brick to outline its austere and elegantly tall round-topped windows. This exterior fit right in with many other brick buildings in Philadelphia of the era, but even so was regarded as a bit surprising for such an expensive and prominent civic amenity. A local urban legend has often been repeated that the brick exterior was an effort to save money on the part of the building committee, and that a marble facing with showy columns and entablatures were meant to be added later, but never they were. However, as the architectural historian Michael J. Lewis has written, this restrained brick design was entirely intentional, and that architects Napoleon Le Brun and Gustave Runge had revised their initial opulent Venetian design at the request of the director of the building committee, George Pepper. This conformed to the sensibilities of the Quaker-trained local aesthetic, which avoided showy outward display to one's neighbors.

It was the *interior* of the Academy, with its marble lobbies, red velvet seats, glowing gold paint and stunning ceiling frescoes that really had the "civilizing" effect that its founders intended. We can see this demonstrated in an illustration created a quarter-century later for the guidebook entitled *A Century After: Picturesque Glimpses of Philadelphia and* Pennsylvania. It shows a well-attired and well-behaved crowd on the parquet level, drawn away from their domestic firesides into a communal public space, enjoying a performance under a huge and glowing central chandelier—an image quite unlike all the many images showing the rowdy "pit" areas of early 19th-century theaters.

The image also shows a number of other interesting details. For instance, although the audience is not sitting in a darkened auditorium (an innovation that would come with electric lights in the following decades), the stage is evidently lit by some very spectacular effects, including a spotlight picking out the lead singer of the opera being performed that evening. The drawing also shows four sculptures, the allegorical caryatid figures above the stage boxes. Part of the original 1857 interior decorations, they represent Comedy, Tragedy, Music and Dance—the forms of art that were soon

be featured at the Academy. There would be no miserable farces here to demoralize some susceptible Philadelphia youth! Instead, a figure of Apollo, representing Poetry, was placed in a medallion over the middle of the proscenium that arcs across the wide stage, a beneficial object and ornament to the city. May it stand for ages.

"Let Us Live to See the Theatres All Deserted"

June 7, 1875: As they sometimes liked to do, the editors of the *Philadelphia Times* began the week by printing a report of a local clergyman denouncing the theater in his Sunday sermon.

On this particular Monday, the *Times* featured the diatribe delivered the day before by the Rev. John Chambers, minister of the Chambers Presbyterian Church on the northeast corner of Sansom and Broad Streets. Chambers knew why the city's politicians were so prone to corruption! It was because they went to plays and burlesque entertainments.

Reverend Chambers, despite—or perhaps because—of his congregation's proximity to the Academy of Music, was deeply disapproving of any time spent by Christians in Philadelphia's theaters. And when he had been casting about for a topic for his sermon on Sunday, June 6, his eye must have fallen upon a copy of the April edition of the *Penn Monthly* magazine. There Rev. Chambers found an article written by another eminent Philadelphian: William Shannon Peirce, the great abolitionist, jurist, and supporter of women's education.

In an essay entitled "The Relative Morals of City and Country," Judge Peirce had taken a position against the ancient philosophical argument that rural folk were somehow more morally pure than those of the city, with all its dens of temptation and vice. In fact, wrote Peirce, the theaters of a city actually *uplifted* the moral character of men:

> It is said before the theatre was established in San Francisco the town was given to the lowest revelry and debauchery ... The reason was, men had no other resorts for amusement than to the low dens of iniquity with which the town was flooded. When the theatre was established they were attracted to it, were amused and entertained, and the morals of the town rapidly improved.

In effect, argued Peirce, moral speeches from the stage were just as important to civilization as any sermons ever delivered from the pulpit.

This essay, apparently, threw the good Rev. Chambers into a tizzy. In his sermon, he argued that the people of San Francisco had undoubtedly benefited more by the founding of churches there than by the institution of theaters.

> It is the common experience that where the Bible has gone there has been rapid improvement in the moral condition of man … In my long experience of nearly seventy-eight years I have never heard of a man or woman convicted of sin or converted to God by going to a theatre … If a theatre were ever established in Africa, or in the wilderness of our own country, would you be likely to reform Spotted Tail and other Indian Chiefs? You would probably exhibit on the stage the revolting scenes of murder and other horrible sights.

But had the good Reverend ever actually seen a play, or gone to a theater himself? He admitted that he had! "Before professing religion I visited them three times, but since then, blessed be God, I have never darkened the door of such a place. The three occasions I refer to were the most unhappy of my life, because my conscience was lashing me all the while, and was thinking what my mother would say if she knew her son was in a theatre." In conclusion, Dr. Chambers said to his flock: "Jesus Christ, in His earthly pilgrimage, never participated in any of these questionable amusements. He never went to Rome, so that He was never in the Coliseum. He never frequented similar establishments in Greece. Let us live to see the theatres all deserted."

After Chambers' death, his congregation merged with that of the nearby Wylie Presbyterian Church on 312 South Broad. They both sold their respective structures, and in 1900 built a new Neo-Gothic church at 315 South Broad. This imposing structure still stands and acts as the home of the Broad Street Ministry—though it is now dwarfed by the neo-modernist bulk of its neighbor, a 21st-century apartment building called The Arthaus. It is also surrounded by the many other buildings up and down the avenue including the Arts Bank Theatre, the Suzanne Roberts Theatre, the Wilma Theater, The Miller Theater—and the Academy of Music. In fact, that entire stretch of South Broad Street is officially known as The Avenue of the Arts.

It is rather the *churches* of South Broad Street that are deserted these days, though on Sunday mornings some of its theaters regularly host services by Christian congregations without buildings of their own. This ironic reproach to Rev. Chambers aside, the question of whether our morals have been improved by either religion or theater is eternally unresolvable. But before we discard either our hymnals or our playscripts, let us remember the wise words of Judge Peirce, who wrote: "Man is held from evil by employment and amusement, as well as by moral teaching, and each must play its part."

The Battle of *Salome* in the Opera War

February 9, 1909: As Oscar Hammerstein arrived at the Philadelphia train station, accompanied by his son Harry and other members of his opera company, a stranger suddenly rushed up to him on the platform, grabbed him, and hissed in his ear: "You better not give *Salome*!" Startled, the 66-year-old impresario understandably jumped away from the threat, while Harry Hammerstein grabbed the man and dragged him away from his father.

It was an omen of things to come. According to the newspapers, Philadelphia was divided into "two hostile camps." One camp wished to see the Richard Strauss opera *Salome*, with a libretto based upon the scandalous play by Oscar Wilde, as written and staged by the Philadelphia Opera Company at the brand-new theater on North Broad Street. The other camp, led by an organization called The Christian League, wanted Mayor John E. Reyburn to ban it from the stage.

The great Scots-American singer Mary Garden was engaged to sing the title role, as she had just done in New York. Learning of the growing protests by the League, she had defiantly given a concert recital of the work at the Orpheus Club in Philadelphia. If she meant to acquaint and calm the city with the artistic merit of *Salome*, its opponents were not mollified. They had heard all about the "Dance of the Seven Veils," and how Miss Garden, in character, would kiss the severed head of John the Baptist on the mouth, and they wanted it stopped. The Mayor of Boston had already banned it in his city, after all.

The Reverend Floyd W. Tompkins, of Philadelphia's Holy Trinity Episcopal Church, issued a letter condemning the opera. So did Rev. Upjohn, of St. Luke's Protestant Episcopal Church in Germantown. The Lutheran Ministerial Union, in congregation, issued one too. The Rev. William Roberts of the Presbyterian General Assembly wanted the Philadelphia police to raid the theater and stop the show, just as they would any other lewd performance. And some of their congregants were clearly listening—reportedly 60 "society women," who were regular attendees at the opera, wrote to Oscar Hammerstein and said they would NOT be in the audience if he insisted on giving this offensive show.

For her part, Miss Garden was scornful of all the agitation. When she was asked by reporters if she would modify or tone down her performance in some way, she trumpeted scornfully, "Certainly Not! Modify my performance? No indeed. When I am compelled to do that, I'll turn the role over to Tetrazzini." And scores of Letters to the Editor filled the newspapers, with opera lovers supporting her and Hammerstein's production, too.

Feelings were running high. Hammerstein came out to speak to the audience that filled the Philadelphia Opera House on Tuesday, February 9, after the second act of *Pelléas and Mélisande*. A storm of applause hailed the impresario's appearance before the footlights. He commanded silence with a wave of his hand, and then began to speak:

> I regret to be compelled to come before the curtain. But it is a necessity. I have advertised *Salome* for Thursday evening. It has been given five times in New York and there has been no opposition on the part of the press or the pulpit. I must keep my agreement concerning this modern master-piece.
>
> I respect the sentiments of the gentlemen of the church of any denomination ... Their objection and the objections of some of your leading citizens puts me in a very peculiar position ... What am I to do? I owe the audience the productions I have promised. I owe the church the respect that is its due.
>
> Any persons who have tickets to Thursday's performance and who do not choose to come can have their money refunded at the box office. Then I will produce the opera only for those who choose to see it. After that I cannot conscientiously ... produce the opera again unless asked by the public to do so, and if, after the first performance, the clergy sanction it.

That Thursday evening, February 11, all the boxes were filled, except for the pointedly empty seats in three boxes which belonged to the society women who had signed the letter of protest. But there could have been plenty of takers for those chairs, because the box office was a mob scene. Though technically the theater was supposed to hold only 4,100 patrons, the box office had been selling standing room in all the aisles. Some people paid $50 for a five-dollar seat. Perhaps up to 5,000 Philadelphians were there, all waiting to be scandalized, or thrilled—or who knows? Everybody just wanted to say they were there.

When the curtain came down, of course, the crowd went wild. Most people thought they had absolutely gotten their money's worth, or at least wanted to make sure that everybody thought they had. The calls of "Bravo!" and "Hammerstein!" rang out over and over again. There were five curtain calls, in total, for the cast. For the final one, the diminutive but strong and determined Mary Garden literally dragged Hammerstein himself out onto the stage to take his bows and receive his rightful applause, after which he made a hurried retreat.

In the wings, with tears of joy reportedly coursing down his cheeks, Oscar Hammerstein cried out: "Didn't I say so? Didn't I say so? There's nothing immoral in it!" Out in the house, one woman in the audience regretfully agreed that it was less risqué than those of the famous French star of the *Ziegfeld Follies*. "Anna Held's shows are a thousand times more suggestive," she said. Her male companion replied: "Twenty-five dollars for two seats, and there isn't a show in town as moral. I wish I had my money back."

Reverend Floyd Tompkins, back in his pulpit, knew that the opera's audience members were among his parishioners, and he had not spared them in his next sermon:

> Remember, you leaders of society in the pews, that non-Christians are judging Christ today by you and by your actions. You know that there are in our city, in our life today, plays and other things which affect society that are exceedingly corrupt. A great many of you went to an exhibition in our city—yes, a great many of you took your daughters to the spectacle.

One can imagine Tompkins throwing his arms up in exasperation. "And you came home and said that it was entrancing. That it was fine. And when asked how you could go to such an exhibition you said that you couldn't see anything wrong with it. I beg of you, I solemnly warn you, to cultivate your ideals and your moral standards!"

But Hammerstein's production of *Salome*, far from being banned, went on to be presented in Philadelphia four more times over the next few weeks—which is exactly what the wily impresario had planned to do all along, of course. Nothing like a little scandal to drum up publicity and public interest. And no one who was there asked for their money back. They'd all had a fine time.

Let My People Come on South Street

Taking its name from the hideous monster of the Beowulf legend (the bestselling 1971 novel *Grendel*, by John Gardner, was no doubt the inspiration), Grendel's Lair first opened on South Street in 1972. Owner Phil Roy called it a "coffeehouse," competing with The Electric Factory and other venues in the growing Philly music scene. It was on the second floor of a former South Street clothing store, and the converted showroom featured a platform stage which faced an audience area of chairs arranged on stepped seating levels.

Located in the hip South Street/Bainbridge area, Grendel's Lair had joined other edgy and eclectic performance spaces such as The Painted Bride and the Theatre of the Living Arts. Eventually, Roy turned to producing Off-Broadway-type plays such as *Pretzels*, *El Grande de Coca Cola*, and *The World of Lenny Bruce*. The name of the venue became "Grendel's Lair Cabaret"—and then "Grendel's Lair Cabaret Theatre."

In 1976, after failing with a comedy called *The Boston Tea Party* (Philly was not in the mood yet for Bicentennial jokes), the venue had a small hit with the Pocket Playhouse's production of Bruce Jay Friedman's *Steambath*. That show had very racy dialogue and a bit of nudity. Other explicit shows such as *Tubstrip* (at the Manning St. Theatre) and *Hustlers* (at Plays & Players) had done well in Philly recently. Obviously, sex sells, concluded Roy, so he looked around for another show like them.

In October 1977, *Let My People Come: A Sexual Musical* took up residence at Grendel's Lair. With music and lyrics by Earl Wilson, Jr. (the son of a famous Broadway columnist), it was one of those new "franchise" shows. It had been a big hit at the Village Gate in New York and had long-running productions in London, Toronto, and Chicago. It even had a brief Broadway run—but found it could not compete with that other famous sex-positive show of the '70s, *Oh, Calcutta!* (which had also had a brief run at the Walnut Street Theatre earlier in the decade). For the Philly version of *Let My People Come*, talented local musician Ken Ford was hired to be the music director, and a young professional company was engaged, most of them eager to get their first real job in showbiz. ("It was kinda like doing *Godspell* in the nude," said original cast member Gini Staudt.)

As it turned out, the show ran quite successfully at Grendel's Lair. People came to South Street for its "head shops," progressive bookstores, and nightclubs, after all. They were ready to let their hair down, to find some excitement. Over the next three years, Roy estimated, he sold 53,000 tickets—mostly to middle class audiences.

The trouble began in February 1977, when Pennsylvania Liquor Control Board agent George Gill, on the basis of an anonymous complaint, attended *Let My People Come*. A 13-year veteran of the LCB, he had seen his share of bump-and-grind shows at seedy girlie bars, but this—well, this was different. He did not know what to make of it, he stated at an official hearing the next month.

"There was eight people up there on the stage, some of them without a stitch on," he testified. "Sometimes a male and a female, making gestures ..." Here Gill paused and flushed in embarrassment, then continued: "There was a man conducting a choir, and his, um, rear end was completely exposed. They was all running around acting crazy and males was fondling female parts." By that point he had seen quite enough. He walked out after the first act, so disgusted he didn't even need to take notes, he stated. "I made a mental observation that this was a lewd, indecent show."

Nonetheless, the LCB examining officer ruled that this testimony was insufficient evidence. Gill should have seen the whole play, he ruled, and the matter was dismissed. *Let My People Come* continued to run and play to packed houses.

There things stood until February 1978, when somebody made another anonymous complaint, and once again Agent Gill paid a call to Grendel's Lair. This time he could not even get into the first act—the show was sold out—but was able to enter the establishment at intermission and finally take in Act Two. He saw nothing to change his opinion of the entertainment. Afterwards, he issued another citation. After a hearing on June 28, Grendel's Lair was fined $500 for offering "lewd, immoral, or improper entertainment" in violation of its liquor license.

In newspaper interviews, Phil Roy called the decision "outrageous" and said he would appeal. Secretly, of course, he was very pleased. All this publicity was good for business. Already he was running ads in the papers with the words "LEWD, IMMORAL, and IMPROPER ENTERTAINMENT" in all-caps. "SUPPORT LET MY PEOPLE COME & RESIST CENSORSHIP!" it proclaimed.

This had worked pretty well, as Roy had known it would. Philadelphians flocked to the theater every night just to see what all the fuss was about, and to enjoy the sensation of being present at a public display of naughty transgression and righteous fun.

There was another formal LCB hearing. This time around, the author of *Let My People Come*, Earl Wilson, Jr. was present, as was Phil Roy. For the media, Roy had even organized a demonstration on the sidewalk outside the Pennsylvania State Office Building on the corner of Broad and Spring Garden Streets. In addition, Roy had asked *Daily News* columnist Stu Bykovsky to testify as an "expert witness" about the play's artistic merits. But the LCB examiner, Norton A. Freedman, ruled that he would allow no such testimony, nor would he get involved with constitutional issues of freedom of speech and obscenity. He would make a recommendation to the state board in Harrisburg on that basis.

"I have no doubt in my mind that it is art," Freedman said. "That is not the issue. The issue has to do with a possible violation of the liquor code." Even John Webb, the young lawyer who was prosecuting the case, had admitted the real problem was the law, which made no distinction between bars and theater spaces. Theodore Eldridge, LCB district supervisor, stated that, as a professional matter, he just wanted to know where the lines should be drawn. "If they rule against us in Harrisburg on this one, then good. Then as far as I'm concerned, I won't ask my agents to go against nudity in any bar."

Reporter Dorothy Storck of the *Philadelphia Inquirer* approached George Gill, who was leaning against the wall in the back of the hearing room, still slightly flushed. Whether it was art or not, it was a lewd show, he told her, a bit angrily. He knew what he saw. "I'm supposed to be some sort of theater critic?" he complained.

After the LCB decision against him in June, Phil Roy refused to pay the fine, and appealed the decision. The show, after a 10-week summer hiatus, continued to perform at Grendel's Lair. In January 1980, Common Pleas Judge Charles L. Durham overturned the LCB decision and revoked the fine. "Nudity, per se, is not lewd," the judge ruled. Based on the evidence before him, he said, "I don't think the entertainment was lewd and immoral." Durham further stated that he had not himself seen the show. "But now I can go there legally," he quipped.

The show would run for over six more years. On May 20, 1986, after 2,000 performances on South Street, *Let My People Come* finally gave its last show in Philadelphia—but perhaps because absolutely everybody who wanted to see it had already done so. And the zeitgeist was shifting. South Street itself was changing, becoming less loose and raunchy and—to use two new popular words in the American lexicon—more "trendy" and even "upscale" in places. From now on, said Phil Roy, he would only be offering plays where people kept their clothes on.

Hugh Hefner in Old City

August 30, 2001: The Fifth Philadelphia Fringe Festival was ramping up. Nick Stuccio (who founded the festival in 1997, along with Eric Schoeffer), noted that there were fewer shows and venues than the previous year. But he was fine with that, as he felt the overall *quality* of the performances was increasing, and he could certainly point to the increasing demand for tickets.

A visiting Hungarian troupe had brought Chekhov's *The Cherry Orchard* (in Hungarian, with English supertitles), and the local troupe Theatre Exile was presenting *Amputation Nation*, performed by John Lumia. Also popular was dancer Joe Goode's *Transparent Body*, and the dance works of local choreographers Myra Bazell and Moxie attracted much praise. According to the festival's box office, at least 133 scheduled performances were "complete sellouts" (in the good sense of the term).

Drawing particular attention that year was the work of New Paradise Laboratories, the troupe of actors and artists under the leadership of director Whit MacLaughlin. Originally from Kansas City, MacLaughlin had created the group in 1996—recruiting from his fellow students while pursuing an MFA at Virginia Polytechnic Institute in Blacksburg, Virginia. The core company was composed of seven actors: Lee Etzold, Rene Hartl, McKenna Kerrigan, Jeb Kreager, Mary McCool, Aaron Mumaw, and Matt Saunders. They were based in Philadelphia but performed in many other cities. In 2000, they were given an Obie Award for their performances in New York. Together with other experimental, movement-based ensembles in the city, such as Pig Iron Theatre Company and Headlong Dance Ensemble, NPL was now being cited by certain critics as representing a "Philadelphia School" of collaboratively devised, visually striking, and artistically audacious performance pieces.

In previous years' Fringe Festivals, NPL had self-produced their creations *Gold Russian Finger Love* (about James Bond) and *The Fab 4 Reach the Pearly Gates* (about the Beatles). For 2001 they were part of the officially curated or "filtered"

Fringe, and the festival had helped NPL fund and produce its new performance piece. Like many other Fringe shows, this show offered Philadelphia audiences a long, intriguing, and provocative title: *This Mansion is a Hole: Hugh Hefner Throws a Party at the Center of the Universe.*

The work was being staged inside the barren interior of the former National Showroom, an Art Deco building on 2nd Street in the heart of Philadelphia's "Old City" neighborhood, where most Fringe performances took place. The "devised" theater piece purported to enact a party at the famous Los Angeles residence of Hugh Hefner, and it examined "Hef's sexual Utopian vision." Naturally, as with all Utopian visions, said MacLaughlin in an interview, "things go awry."

Though he did not mention it to the reporter, in MacLaughlin's own family there was additional, real-life drama. His wife, the actress Catherine Slusar, had recently given birth two months prematurely to their twin daughters. Her health, as well as that of the infants, was in a perilous state throughout the rehearsal process for *This Mansion*. But due to the efforts of the entire ensemble, things had kept on course for the opening night: September 12, 2001.

Two weeks after the Philadelphia Fringe Festival opened, things suddenly went completely, *horribly* awry, when terrorists struck America on the morning of September 11, 2001. The entire nexus of world history shifted. Geographically halfway between the two major Ground Zeroes (and some 200 miles to the east of Shanksville, PA), Philadelphia, like everywhere else in the world, was transfixed by the overwhelming news. The Philadelphia Fringe Festival, which was scheduled to run through the 18th, temporarily halted.

But only for a day. Most scheduled events, including *This Mansion is a Hole*, should continue their scheduled runs, Stuccio decided. Philadelphia audiences, many of whom had bought tickets in advance, continued to attend Fringe shows. There was nowhere else to go, after all—all airline flights across America were grounded for many weeks. Despite the pall cast over the entire nation, live theater went on—but now, of course, everything had a new context for interpretation.

As people arrived at the National Showroom, the pre-show was already in motion—14 partiers in beautiful clothes, their activities being recorded by one photographer (Matt Saunders) who was clad in nothing but his camera, standing center stage. Then, MacLaughlin came out to make a speech to the audience. Saunders, completely exposed, could only take a knee and wait for the director's speech to end.

Together with the two previous pieces—those about the Beatles and James Bond—MacLaughlin explained that *This Mansion is a Hole: Hugh Hefner Throws a Party at the Center of the Universe* was the culmination of the company's series of works called "The Loverboy Trilogy." All three dealt with, as he termed it, "male pop-cultural figures that managed to endure the American pop culture mill to survive through to the end of the 20th century and beyond." None of them were performed ironically, or as a gesture of tribute. Rather, NPL was attempting to evoke the immediacy and scope of Ancient Greek dramas, by taking popular myths that already existed in the audience's imagination, and then opening "a wide latitude of potential interpretation."

This was eerily immediately evident to both audience and performers, on that day when airplanes and their fateful journeys were on everyone's minds. Indeed, NPL had already placed what they called "flyovers" in the piece. The action was periodically interrupted by the explosive sound of jets going by, while the actors paused and looked to the sky. It resonated uncannily and prophetically.

In a piece he would publish some years later about *The Loverboy Trilogy*, MacLaughlin described the final scene of *This Mansion is a Hole*:

> Seven actors, male and female, with pipes, are dressed in satin dressing gowns in a simulation of a sort of pan-gendered Hugh Hefner. They sit on a wrestling mat to hear a bedtime story—it's Christmas Eve and Bing Crosby is repeatedly singing the looped phrase "Do you hear what I hear?" from the "Little Shepherd Boy" ... This musical scoring is intermingled with riffs from Miles Davis. The bedtime story tells of a man who preserves a strange masochistic propensity for public voyeurism by burying himself in a concrete sidewalk in order that he might feel public footsteps on his body forever. As the story draws to a close, the seven Hefners are tucked into bed by a professional eunuch in a blue monkey head—he covers each Hefner completely with the grey wrestling mat. It is a very tender image ... Then, a nude actress in a Santa hat and beard enters the space through a fifteen-foot-high fireplace in order to place little wrapped gifts/headstones on the individual lumps of bodies under the large mat.

This Mansion is a Hole proved to be one of the most popular pieces of the 2001 Fringe, and it sold out all its performances. Though (like the early writing of William Penn) it certainly had its own very direct critique of wealth and hedonism, it was a play that one imagines might have come right out of the Founder of Philadelphia's worst nightmares. Indeed, fundamentalist theologians of *many* world religions—of which there were many at the turn of the 21st century—surely would have tried to shut it down, too, if they had anything to say about it.

In a recent conversation with me, as he looked back on the early years of New Paradise Labs, MacLaughlin stated that William Penn's original moralistic vision for Philadelphia had been on his mind from the very start. "We came here fascinated by the utopian project of Philadelphia—the Quakers from the Old World. William Penn's idea had a utopian core—it encapsulated both the working class and moneyed people within a grid system of streets." He felt that this vision jibed with his own "moral, ethical, and weirdly abstract idea of what the creative process and theater was." In fact, even the nagging doubts, the fear of provincialism that for so long had pervaded Philadelphians' common cultural air, intrigued him. "When I came to Philadelphia, the weird tenor of it—'Is this the *best* place, or is this the *worst* place?'—resonated. It has great ideas, and they are always failures. Philadelphia was always at the forefront of an idealistic project but it never worked."

But in what was quickly termed by many "the post-9/11 world," Philadelphia theater artists could at least keep on doing their work. In a time when electronic media was filled with nightmarish images of hijackers, airplanes slamming into tall buildings, and humans falling from the sky, by an unintended serendipity, a small group of deeply committed Philadelphia theater artists were providing meaning and guidance for the audience's collective consciousness. Or, as William Penn might have put it, they were shining an Inner Light.

PART THREE
Playhouses

The Mysterious Case of the Stolen Spikes at the Old Theatre

The old South Street Theatre.

To replace the former Theatre on Society Hill, the American Company had commissioned yet another theater on the south side of Cedar Street. Built by local carpenters, it opened in November 1766. It was called, understandably enough, the "New Theatre." Later, when the novelty had worn off, it became "the Theatre in Southwark." And when Cedar Street's name itself was changed, it became known as the "Theater on South Street." Later still, when a much finer home for plays was constructed elsewhere in the city, everyone began referring to it as the "Old Theatre."

Despite its many years of faithful service, there is only one reasonably accurate depiction of this building, made many years later by someone who had never actually seen it. Frankly, it is not a very inspiring drawing. In the image, the Old Theatre rather resembles a schoolhouse, with its tall cupola, topped with one of Benjamin Franklin's "lightning rods." Or maybe like a barn—a barn that had, once upon a time, a brief thought of becoming a church, and then gave up. Like a barn, the upper wooden exterior is even painted red. One hopes that a farmer would have taken better care of his stock, though, because apparently it wasn't well maintained, and on rainy evenings the roof often leaked upon the audience.

We can see there was one set of plain doors on the brick lower level facing the mud of South Street, and another set of doors on the side facing the narrow alley called Apollo Street. There was no ornamentation or statuary. The cupola was meant to let out the heat in the summer, and a brick chimney ran up one wall to serve a solitary stove that was meant to keep the place warm in the winter, but wise patrons seated on the main floor brought along small portable "foot stoves" when it was a cold day. Holding about 500 people if you really packed them in, its sight lines were bad, interrupted by a number of large square pillars holding up the gallery and the roof. The best seats, it was generally agreed, were in the front of the gallery. There was a proscenium stage with boxes for distinguished spectators on either side. Light was provided by oil lamps.

In October 1772, the American Company had once again returned to Philadelphia, opening with a presentation of *School For Libertines, or a Word to the Wise*. There were a lot of 17th- and 18th-century comedies with the word "School" at the beginning of their titles; many readers may be familiar with Sheridan's *School for Scandal*, or perhaps Molière's *School for Wives*. The trope was used by playwrights to suggest that some social instruction would take place during the play's action. It was meant to allay any worries that perhaps these plays might expose folks to immorality or indecency; in this drama, the titles assured, it is precisely what is wrong with society that shall be sent to school!

That December, the ads in the Philadelphia newspapers would promote the American Company's production of *The School for Fathers, or Lionel and Clarissa*, a comic opera by Isaac Bickerstaff. The two lovers' parts were to be performed by Mr. Wools and Miss Storer, and the comic roles of Colonel Oldboy and Sir John Flowerdale by Mr. Goodman and Mr. Douglass. Lewis Hallam would conduct the orchestra. As an after-piece, the troupe would then perform the rollicking farce *High Life Below Stairs*, including a "mock minuet" performed by Mr. and Mrs. Henry.

"The Doors to be opened at FOUR and the PLAY to begin exactly at SIX O'CLOCK," read the notice placed in the *Pennsylvania Packet and General Advertiser*. "No Persons, on any Account whatsoever, can possibly be admitted behind the Scenes. Places in the Boxes may be taken at the Theatre … TICKETS, without which no person can be admitted, are sold at the bar of the Coffee-house." (Evidently everybody in Philadelphia back then knew where the Coffee-house was, so no address needed to be listed.) The sheet music to the songs of the opera *School for Fathers* could also be purchased there.

In another interesting custom of the day, the ad also specified that ladies and gentlemen who wished to send their servants to hold their seats for them could not do so until four o'clock, two hours before curtain time. But the item that might really catch our modern eyes was one additional notice placed by the leader of the American Company David Douglass, in the *Pennsylvania Packet*, directly below the ad for the evening's show:

> TEN POUNDS REWARD. A BURGLARY. Whereas a number of evil disposed persons, in the night between the ninth and tenth instant (December) burglariously and feloniously broke open the gallery door of the Theatre, tore off and carried away the iron spikes which divide the galleries from the upper boxes; and had they not been detected and put to flight by the servants of the Theatre, who dwell in the house, would, there is reason to imagine, have compleated their malicious designs. In order, therefore, that the perpetrators may be brought to justice, the above reward is offered to whoever will discover any of the persons concerned in the said burglary, to be paid on their conviction.

Though the sight of spikes in a theater would certainly startle us today, by placing them on the rails the American Company was not being unusually cruel. They were merely following an accepted practice of the age, one that had come from London and Dublin. In an era when theater riots were all too frequent, it was a common feature of British theaters to have fearsome-looking spikes on the dividing rails, as well as at the edge of the stage. This not only discouraged people who had paid only three shillings to sit in the gallery from moving into any empty seats closer to the stage (which might otherwise cost up to seven shillings), but it also prevented anyone from rushing up onto the stage if they were displeased with the show. (These spikes had perils for performers, too. The dancer John Durang once accidentally fell off the stage and badly injured his legs on them.)

Speaking of crimes of the past, it's also worth noting the "servants of the theater" mentioned in the ad were likely slaves. Many enslaved African Americans (and even low-ranking white employees) often only had rough beds in their masters' places of business. The papers of the era often had notices offering ten-pound rewards for runaway slaves (and lost horses)—a measure, perhaps, of how much those spikes were valued.

From the notice, it seems as if the perpetrators in the Case of the Stolen Spikes were chased off before they could complete the job, and evidently, they were never apprehended. Douglass regularly repeated his notice in the newspaper for the next four weeks, but I can find no record of any evil-disposed persons ever being brought before a magistrate and being well schooled for committing the burglarious crime. The correction of the more systemic crime against the "servants of the theatre" also went—for the present, anyway—uncorrected.

The New Theatre on Chestnut Street

In 1790, the famous political compromise was struck that would make Philadelphia the national capital for 10 years. George Washington, now President Washington, took up residence in the city. His appetite for theater—one that he had formed ever since he saw his first play, on a visit to Barbados—could now be fully indulged. Many residents of Philadelphia were ready to join him in the audience. Newly elected members of the United States Congress looked forward to recreating themselves at plays, after a hard day of speechifying and legislating.

Sensing an opportunity, actor Thomas Wignell left the Old Americans and formed a partnership with the musician Alexander Reinagle. Together they decided to make a principal claim on the renewed prestige of the Philadelphia theatrical market, and had already begun staging plays at the Old Theatre building. As the Congress and the President settled into the new capital city, a group of Philadelphia investors backed Wignell and Reinagle's ambitions. The two men were soon recruiting a company of actors and were also collecting scripts, costumes, and properties. They started construction of a theater, near the northeast corner of Sixth and Chestnut Streets, right near the political hub of the city—the State House where Congress and the Pennsylvania legislature both met was on the next block.

Their designs called for an elegant and commodious building, one that put the shoddy old theater in Southwark to shame. In fact, Wignell and Reinagle pointedly called it the New Theatre. (Historians of American theater, to avoid confusion for their readers, invariably refer to this building as "The First Chestnut Street Theatre."

But no one in Philadelphia did so at the time—you will find it called "The New Theatre" in every document or newspaper from the day.)

The New Theatre was to have three tiers of 15 boxes each that could hold over seven hundred people. Together with benches on the parquet floor in front of the stage, it had a total capacity of over 1,100. There were French-style oil lamps that could be raised or even dimmed, depending on the requirements of the scene. And because it was somewhat smaller than the huge London houses it was modeled after, it reportedly had excellent acoustics, and allowed a more intimate acting style.

The acting company that Wignell assembled had individual dressing rooms (a welcome innovation for American actors) and a green room for receiving their particular fans. The exterior of the Chestnut Street Theatre would eventually feature an elegant classical portico, but for many years the front of the building was not totally complete. Drawings of the building from the 1790s show a rough-looking sloping roof which extended over the sidewalk to the street to protect arriving theater patrons from the rain or snow. Wealthy Philadelphians would follow the fashionable London habit of arriving at the last minute before curtain time, so having easy access for their carriages was essential.

Originally the company had planned to begin performing in 1793, but the deadly yellow fever epidemic of the summer and autumn of that year put everything on hold. As the cold weather of Philadelphia's winter finally put a stop to the disease's ravages, people slowly returned to their houses and businesses. President Washington even returned to his residence on Market Street. Finally, on February 17, 1794, the New Theatre opened its doors with the play *The Castle of Andalusia*, a romantic drama by John O'Keefe which featured striking scenic effects of Spanish castles. It was followed by the comic afterplay *Who's the Dupe?* by Hannah Cowley.

George Washington, once again, was an eager visitor to see the shows, which were only a short journey from his official residence on Market Street. Washington's arrival and presence in the house would have caused considerable notice amongst the crowd. The New Theatre, under various managements and during some the most consequential years of the early Republic, would continue to be a leading social and artistic presence in Philadelphia for the next quarter century.

Ricketts' Circus, Benedict Arnold, and the Death of Major Andre

RIDING IN A CRITICAL SITUATION,
BY Mr. F. RICKETTS.
A NEW, GRAND, ND FFECTING
PANTOMIME.
Called the
DEFECTION OF GENERAL
ARNOLD,
AND THE
DEATH OF MAJOR ANDRE.
CHARACTERS:
COMMANDER IN CHIEF, Mr. TOMPKINS.
GENERAL ARNOLD, Mr. F. RICKETTS.
MAJOR ANDRE, Mr. DURANG.
American Officers, Soldiers, &c. by the rest of the
Company
Country women, Mrs. ROWSON, and Mrs.
McDONALD.
N B. The representation of this piece Mr.
Ricketts hopes to make as near the reality as pos-
sible, having lately visited the scene where the
transaction took place.

February 7, 1799: The equestrian circus on the corner of Sixth and Chestnut staged "A New, Grand, and Affecting PANTOMIME, called *The Defection of General Arnold and the Death of Major Andre.*"

The British equestrian John Bill Ricketts, who had been performing in Philadelphia since 1793, was reaching for new theatrical achievements in the winter of 1799. For several years Ricketts had toured all around the United States with his company, but his new main base was in the capital city of Philadelphia. He had constructed a large circus ring and an adjoining stage directly to the west of where Congress and the Supreme Court met—and across the street from his main rival, the New Theatre on Chestnut Street.

For several years Ricketts had not just been performing the usual display of horsemanship and feats of agility that formed the core of his act. Although his prize horse Cornplanter was still a featured performer, he also offered the public comic dances, songs, clowning—and grand pantomimes that involved his entire company of human and equine performers.

John Bill Ricketts' younger brother, Francis Ricketts, was the author of the pantomime. The ads in the *Aurora General Advertiser* declared that by "the representation of this piece Mr. Ricketts hopes to make as near reality as possible, having lately visited the scene where the transaction took place."

Ricketts' Circus company toured the Hudson River valley in the summers of 1797 and 1798. In his memoirs, John Durang, who was traveling with Ricketts, noted seeing "the very tree where Major Andre was taken," and that "I found an opportunity to see the very house in which Gen'l Arnold and Major Andre held their conference on the W. side of the river; from this the artful Arnold made his escape to a British vessel … and Andre cross'd the river to the New York side [to] meet his fate." But frustratingly, in his recollections Durang shares no description of the subsequent pantomime in Philadelphia. He did note that John Bill Ricketts sometimes doubted whether these big pantomimes were worth all the expense and trouble it took to produce them, and at one point worried aloud that they "would have proved his ruin if he had to keep them long."

Indeed, Ricketts seems to have offered his brother's pantomime for only one week, and it may have been revised after its initial performance and was subsequently abandoned. We have no pictorial representation of the show, but we know from the ads the circus placed in the newspapers that both John Bill and Francis Ricketts portrayed General Arnold during different performances, while Major Andre was played by John Durang. The "Commander in Chief" George Washington (who sent Andre to his execution) was performed by another company member, Mr. Tompkins. There were also female members of the company employed during the entertainment, as it is noted that Mrs. McDonald sang "The Song of the Cottage Maid" and Mrs. J. Rowson danced a hornpipe.

The audience for this entertainment would undoubtedly have included many people very familiar with historical characters being represented. In 1778 Benedict Arnold, after all, had occupied the very house—just one block away from the circus building—where President John Adams resided, as had George Washington before him. (Another even grander mansion that Arnold subsequently occupied still stands in Fairmount Park.) Major Andre had once been a very popular figure in Philadelphia, too, and he even painted backdrops for entertainments that he and other British officers staged at the Southwark Theatre—scenery that remained in the venue's stock collection for many years.

At any rate, the pantomime about Arnold and Andre, even as a comic piece, must be seen as a significant early attempt to dramatize actual events of American history. But it can't have been a money-maker for John Bill Ricketts, because after these few performances it was never offered again.

Continuing the equestrian's run of bad luck, Ricketts' Circus burned down in late December 1799, and soon afterwards the Ricketts brothers left Philadelphia on the schooner *Sally* with 10 of their horses. They attempted to sail to Barbados to try their luck at producing shows for the rich plantation owners there. They even stowed enough lumber on board to build a circus structure once they arrived, a necessary measure for the by then mostly de-forested islands of the Caribbean. Sad to say, Ricketts' string of ill fortune continued, and the schooner was captured by French privateers near the island of Guadeloupe. Amazingly, although all his property and horses were stolen and sold to locals by the privateers, the ever-resourceful Ricketts managed to recover a few horses, and he even staged enough performances on the nearby island of Martinique to make enough money to charter a ship that would take him back to England.

But this ship would prove to be his last. Evidently an old and unreliable vessel, it never arrived in England and was presumed to have sunk in an Atlantic storm, along with all its crew and passengers. John Bill Ricketts had given his last show, and after several years his family would have him declared legally dead. The informal fellowship of English equestrians, clowns, and acrobats mourned him. "The fame of this person excelled all his predecessors, and it is said he has never been surpassed," a London circus performer wrote, with evident deep feeling.

Francis Ricketts, who had stayed behind in the Caribbean, eventually returned to Philadelphia. However, without his more talented and charismatic brother, he never managed to have further success in the business, and he sold off the empty lot where the Pantheon had once stood. Today, there's no historical marker to commemorate it, though there is a metal sign up on Market and 12th Street, where an even shorter-lived earlier "Ricketts' Circus" structure briefly existed.

The Spanish Consul and the New French Circus on Walnut Street

In preparation for the 1876 Centennial Exposition, the managers of the Walnut Street Theatre placed the words "OLDEST IN AMERICA" across the top of its facade. It was all part of the effort to play up the patriotic appeal of the building to audiences, which in the latter decades of the 19th century was looking a bit dowdy compared to all the other bright new theaters elsewhere in the city.

Many times in its long history, the Walnut was either overused and popular or else unused and outdated, and there were not a few times when it came perilously close to being torn down. It managed to avoid the catastrophic fires which destroyed so many of its early competitors. Ensconced in a relatively unfashionable neighborhood, the Walnut would survive the predations of real estate developers, while many other popular Philadelphia theaters would not. (The theater would receive extensive updating and renovations in 1828, 1920, 1970 and 2024.)

In fact, its longevity has become one of the most famous things about it. "The oldest playhouse in continuous use in the English-speaking world" is the boast of the blue metal historical sign on the pavement out front. Which—though true in the broadest sense—rather ignores those renovations, as well as the fact that the original performers in its earliest days were horses, who presumably didn't speak any language at all, let alone English. On top of that, the Walnut Street Theatre owes its very foundation to two young Frenchmen, Victor Pepin and Jean-Baptiste Casmiere Breschard—and a Spanish diplomat.

The story, in brief, is this: During the years 1805 and 1806 Messieurs Pepin and Breschard were running a well-regarded and fairly successful equestrian circus in Madrid. By all accounts, they were supremely talented and enterprising performers. Small and dashing, Pepin excelled in leaps, jumps, and vaults, though he could double as a clown when needed. A tall and elegant man, cutting a fine figure in a Spanish uniform, Breschard was an expert in Roman Riding—standing on top of several barebacked horses at a time and directing them in synchronized jumps. One must assume they were completely unaware of the empty lot at the northeast corner of Ninth and Walnut Streets—over three thousand miles away.

But Victor Pepin knew about Philadelphia, and he spoke English perfectly well. He had been born in Albany, New York, the son of a French-Canadian father who had fought on the side of the Americans during the Revolutionary War. His family relocated to France when he was a boy, and he had evidently been thoroughly trained in cavalry tactics and military horsemanship in one of the many Parisian "riding academies." John-Baptiste Breschard, for his part, seems to have been a product of the training schools of the burgeoning world of French equestrian circuses. At the height of the Napoleonic Wars, the two men had left Paris and struck out on their own, establishing a new venue for international circus in Spain, having collected their own troupe of other ambitious young performers, themselves mostly of French, Italian, or Spanish origin. In Madrid, at least, they were well out of the hostilities that were spreading across most of Europe.

But in 1807, the political winds shifted drastically, and Napoleon's army began rolling through Spain on its way to a war in Portugal. In 1808 *L'empereur* occupied Spain as well, toppling the Spanish monarchy. Pepin and Breschard were undoubtedly alarmed by this turn of events. Both men were married (indeed both their wives were performers in the troupe themselves), and most likely they did not wish to be swept up by a French conscription party and forcibly enlisted into the Imperial cavalry. But with most of continental Europe now under Napoleon's direct control, and the Spanish colonial empire tottering on the brink of revolution, there weren't many places for them to go. Perhaps only one possibility remained: the United States of America.

Just why the partners settled on Philadelphia is a complicated story, but an explicable one. Three years before Napoleon's invasion, the former Spanish ambassador to the United States, Marquis Martínez de Irujo, had brought his American wife home with him to Madrid. The Marquis' wife, as it happened, was the former Sarah McKean, daughter of the Governor of Pennsylvania. This couple had been fond of Ricketts' Circus when they lived in Philadelphia, and when they came to the circus in Madrid, they could probably have told Pepin and Breschard that since Ricketts' departure the "Athens of America" now had a theatrical market that was wide open for equestrians. At any rate, whether they were acting on Irujo's advice or for some other reason, Pepin and Breschard made the bold decision to take their act to new audiences in the New World.

The *élan* and bravery of their gambit still amazes. Even though it was both the middle of winter and the middle of a war, Pepin and Breschard loaded their costumes, their company, their wives, and all their horses (including their prize steed, a black stallion named Conqueror) onto a ship to America, minimizing risk by taking the shortest possible ocean crossing. Their ship headed directly for the outstretched promontory of Cape Cod, and they landed safely at Plymouth, Massachusetts, in December 1807. Resourcefully, Pepin and Breschard and their company quickly built a wooden circus amphitheater outside of Boston in Charlestown. Here they endured a rather meager winter and very meager audiences. They started by offering three shows a week, then reduced that to two a week, then one—after April 1808 they gave up and left Boston, pushing on to New York City, where they built an amphitheater near the tip of Manhattan and played to respectable houses for most of 1808. Then, their fortunes having finally improved, they moved on to their real goal, Philadelphia.

Even before they arrived in the Quaker City, Pepin and Breschard had borrowed a large sum of money from Philadelphia businessmen, and they ordered the construction of a truly ambitious structure at the corner of Ninth and Walnut Streets to house their circus. Both the loan and the location were likely made possible by the good offices of the Spanish consul in the city. Their structure would not be an uncovered amphitheater this time, but a fully enclosed building. Evidently the two Frenchmen's vision was to run this business for a long time. It was not dissimilar to the Cirque Olympique being built by Franconi in Paris at the same time, though the work was done by Philadelphia builders and craftsmen—it is true, however, that there were quite a few French émigrés in the city who could have told them what was expected.

The New Circus (as it was called at first—acknowledging that it was a successor to the vanished Ricketts' Circus), had thick walls of brick and was 80 feet by 100 feet, with a huge domed roof and attached stables on the north side for the horses. The dome was topped by a flagpole rising 96 feet into the air, taller than any church steeple in the city. On the Walnut Street side, three stately doors stood at the top of a series of steps and led to an elegant lobby. The interior was a large riding ring, with three levels of boxes above (admission one dollar), and a raked audience area (admission 75 cents) beside the ring, seated behind a wooden fence. Above that was an open gallery for the cheapest seats (50 cents). An area for musicians was along one side of the ring. Once the building was finished, the company moved inside and began preparations for their first show.

The New Circus made its Philadelphia debut on Thursday, February 2, 1809. The theater historian Charles Durang (writing many years later in his long-running series of feature articles about Philadelphia's theater history in the Philadelphia *Sunday Dispatch*) recalled that "their company was numerous, their stud of horses was thoroughly broken and composed of splendid animals. Their wardrobe was new, costly and indeed the best thing of its kind that had been seen in the country." For a brief period, their shows would become the sensation of Philadelphia, even rivaling the attractions of the New Theatre company a few blocks away. They even presented their first equestrian drama, with scenes adapted from Cervantes' *Don Quixote*. It is beyond question that equestrian drama, and circuses, were a foundational part of the Philadelphia heritage of performing arts.

In many otherwise well-researched and completely reliable theater history books, one can read the assertion that the Spanish diplomat, Don Luis de Onis y González-Vara (1762–1827), was instrumental in arranging for Pepin and Breschard to come to Philadelphia, and that he even helped them in purchasing the lot where the New Circus was built. But that is incorrect. Theater historians have been giving credit to the wrong person for some time now, and this would be a good opportunity to clear up the matter.

Don Luis de Onis is rather infamous—in Spanish history books, anyway—as being the person who negotiated the Adams–Onis Treaty of 1819, ceding Florida to the United States. But—and here is the key point—Don Luis was not even involved in Spanish foreign policy toward the United States until *after* Napoleon's invasion of Spain. He was appointed Ambassador to the U.S. by the *junta* in Seville that was organized to oppose Napoleon in June 1808. Obviously, this was well after Pepin and Breschard had already left Madrid on their voyage to America. In fact, it seems unlikely that under the circumstances Onis would have made the slightest effort to assist any Frenchmen. He was a member of an anti-French government, after all. Nor did de Onis mention the arrival of a French circus to Philadelphia in the memoirs he published at the end of his career. We must conclude that he had nothing to do with it.

The error in identifying de Onis seems to have been first made by Charles Durang 40 years after these events occurred. His mistake is completely understandable: no doubt Durang remembered that "the Spanish Consul in Philadelphia" had somehow facilitated the transaction for purchasing the land for the Walnut Street Theatre, but his memory was faulty about which Spanish diplomat was involved. Credit must be given not to Don Luis de Onis, but instead to Señor Valentín de Foronda y González de Echávarri. De Foronda was the official administering Spanish national interests from 1807 to 1809, after the departure of Martínez de Irujo. Like most European diplomats at that time, he lived in the more settled and pleasant city of Philadelphia, rather than the still unfinished and culturally barren Washington.

The highly erudite De Foronda was even inducted as a member of Philadelphia's famous Philosophical Society. Skilled in finance and what was then termed "political economy," he would have been especially interested if the two entrepreneurs would help him with the plot of Philadelphia land he had invested in—directly across the street from his house on the south side of Ninth and Walnut. A classic liberal of that era, De Foronda would have been quite open to assisting the two Frenchmen, whose nation now seemed to represent the very spirit of the Enlightenment. He even advocated for the independence of Spanish colonies in the Caribbean and South America. Unfortunately, these sorts of opinions were to get Foronda into deep trouble when he returned to Spain. In 1814 he was imprisoned by the conservative Spanish government which came back into power after Napoleon's defeat.

Ironically, Foronda was also one of the few Spanish intellectuals who keenly disliked the towering literary legacy of the famous author Miguel de Cervantes. During his time in Philadelphia, the diplomat even published a book (*Observaciones sobre algunos puntos de la Obra de Don Quijote*) attacking Cervantes' work! So, ironically, the fact that Pepin and Breschard undertook to stage an equestrian version of *Don Quixote* would likely have annoyed him a great deal.

Eventually Pepin and Breschard's business enterprise would fail, and both men would leave the city. By 1820, the circus they built was remodeled and became a more traditional proscenium theater. In fact, the building now known as the Walnut Street Theatre would be rebuilt, both inside and out, so many times that little of the original circus structure remains. It is impossible to speculate, of course, what Foronda would have thought about the musical *Man of La Mancha*, which was staged at the Walnut Street Theatre 200 years later. But at least we've done what we can to finally give him credit for his essential role in helping to bring about the very existence of one of Philadelphia's most famous theaters, now designated a National Historic Landmark.

Farewell to Old Drury

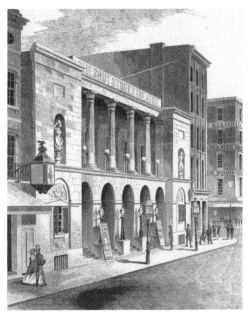

May 2, 1855: The demolition of the Chesnut Street Theatre began. Like many Philadelphia theaters before and since, it had outlived its perceived usefulness. The lot it stood on would soon be occupied by yet another commercial structure in the city's booming central business district.

"Chesnut" is not a typo. As part of wider American orthographic reforms, this was the proper Philadelphia way to spell the name of the street in front of the building in 1855. In fact, a large sign bearing the words "Chesnut Street Theatre" had been recently placed on top of architect William Strickland's classical facade, to try to draw the attention of people passing on the increasingly busy street. (By the 1860s this odd local spelling was dropped, and the silent T was re-inserted into Chestnut Street.) But however you spelled its official name, in truth most people in Philadelphia fondly referred to it as "Old Drury."

Its predecessor, Wignell and Reinagle's New Theatre, had come to a sad end, burning down in April 1820. Its replacement, completed by 1822, became the home of Warren and Wood's company, originally known as the "Philadelphia Theatre." Amongst the city's social and intellectual elites, the rebuilt house represented the best traditions of the city's public buildings. In 1824, it was grandly decorated for a reception and ball for the Marquis de Lafayette. It was in the late 1820s it acquired the moniker of "Old Drury" by right of conquest. The young manager Francis Wemyss, during a trip to London, recruited so many well-regarded English actors to come to Philadelphia that one English correspondent complained that "he will take away the best of the few good performers we have now among us." Throughout the 1830s and '40s the theater on Ches(t)nut Street was the premier home for plays and operas in the city.

But by 1855, the neighborhood was quickly changing, and Old Drury was increasingly deserted by the better sort of theater-going Philadelphian. The "Great Consolidation" of 1854, which hugely expanded the city's boundaries and population, was having enormous effects. The block where Old Drury stood was now shared with billiard parlors, shooting galleries, and dance halls, and there were a lot of competing advertisements, all trying to catch the public's eye. Lately it had only offered second-rate entertainments and even minstrel shows. More people preferred the popular entertainments offered by the nearby National Theatre and the Walnut Street Theatre. Most importantly, in the newly consolidated and expanded city of Philadelphia, the social and cultural elite of the city were preparing to transfer their allegiances to the Academy of Music, which was then rising on Broad Street.

In the last passages of his *History of the Philadelphia Stage*, Charles Durang recounted this final ceremonial performance at the Chesnut. He watched as local actors played short scenes from classic plays from the theater's storied past. Philadelphia critic and author James Rees even penned a long farewell poem to the theater, which an actor read out loud, accompanied by the ringing of Old Drury's famous bell—that instrument that before every performance had summoned the audience to their seats. After each line the bell had been rung once:

> Last night of old Drury! How painful the sound;
> Last night of old Drury! Let the sad words go round.
> Farewell to old Drury! The shadows have pass'd;
> Farewell to old Drury! This night is the last;
> Farewell to old Drury! Thy days once so bright,
> Now close, like thyself, in the gloom of the night.
> Down, down the curtain, thy last act is o'er,
> And echo alone will now answer: encore!

After the last notes of the bell had died away, and the assembled audience had left, Durang made a final tour backstage with Rees. His mind was overwhelmed with decades of memories of performers and performances. He looked at himself one last time in the old dressing room mirror. As he walked down the marble steps, he noted that the bell of nearby Independence Hall was also ringing that evening, to mark the announcement of the final returns of the local elections. "We felt it as sensibly as parting from a dying friend. The scenes of our boyhood associations flitted freely before us in vivid spectres, arousing deep reflections of happy times past and forever gone."

The next day, the workers began taking Old Drury apart. Many of its props, sets, backdrops, and curtains were already sold to the owners of the new Continental Theater—just a couple of blocks away on Walnut Street. All of them would be lost in the fire that destroyed the Continental in 1857. Its bell, however, was saved, and transferred to summon the audiences at the new Academy of Music.

Mrs. John Drew's Arch Street Theatre

Over the summer of 1863 the Arch Street Theatre underwent a major reconstruction, under the leadership of its new manager, Louisa Lane Drew—or rather, "Mrs. John Drew," as she always insisted on being called. Soon "Mrs. John Drew's Arch Street Theatre" would become a byword for excellence in the American theater. The quality of her resident stock company was high and its loyalty was deep. Significantly, the Arch was known as a good place for young actors—a real school where one could learn one's craft from top to bottom and get a wide variety of roles under one's belt.

One of the premier theatrical houses in Philadelphia, it had stood on the north side of Arch Street, just west of Sixth Street, since 1828. It had originally been designed by the architect John Haviland, with a classical facade topped by a triangular pediment featuring a statue of Apollo. The figure was meant to serve as an iconic symbol of the Arch, just as the Chestnut had its statues of Comedy and Tragedy, and the Walnut had a large wooden eagle hung on its facade. Indeed, the Arch's Apollo, carved by the French American sculptor Nicholas Gevelot, was regarded as a remarkable and worthy ornament that the whole city could be proud of. (Gevelot was a major sculptor of that era, and his work *William Penn's Treaty with the Indians* can still be seen at the Capitol building in Washington, DC.)

But for decades the Arch Street Theatre was the only major Philadelphia theater on the north side of Market Street. This was not a fashionable location, but its investors expected that the Arch would rival the Walnut and the Chestnut. However, during the economic downturns of the 1830s and '40s audiences were often quite sparse. (William Wood, the former manager of the Chestnut Street company, was nearly ruined by his tenure there.) But during the good times, and under the control of various other managers, all the great touring actors of the day, including William Macready, Charlotte Cushman, and Edwin Forrest, were featured on its stage.

In the late 1850s, William Wheatley and John Drew successfully took it over, often featuring Drew himself in Irish comic plays, and his wife Louisa in dramatic roles. When Mr. Drew left town on a world tour in the early 1860s, Mrs. Drew was offered the sole management by the trustees of the theater. It was a role she would play for the next four decades.

After her husband's sudden death in May of 1862, the newly widowed Mrs. Drew could immediately see there was now even more local competition for the Arch. The huge new Chestnut Street Theatre was rising near 13th Street, under the management of her former boss William Wheatley. The Walnut Street Theatre was now receiving considerable attention from its new owners, Edwin Booth and John Sleeper Clarke. (No doubt they also saw that the recently fire-ravaged Continental Theatre down the street from them was being rebuilt with much more spacious dimensions.) The Arch would have to keep up, Mrs. Drew decided, and persuaded the owners of the building to invest in an upgrade.

Most of the renovations were to the front of the building. Haviland's triangular pediment was removed, replaced by a rectangular classical facade with two rows of windows. Gevelot's Apollo, however, was carefully preserved and then reinstalled on the new upper level. A bearded face of Dionysus—the other Ancient Greek theater god—was added to the cornice above it. New offices and workrooms with plenty of natural light were made possible by this expansion, and more light was brought into the upstairs lobbies.

Inside the house there was another major change. The infamous "third tier" balcony, where once prostitutes had roamed on a regular basis, was ripped out. This had been a long-standing goal of Mrs. Drew, who wanted to give the theater a much more respectable reputation. This allowed the second balcony level below it to be enlarged, and its rough benches were replaced with sloping rows of fixed chairs. The supporting iron pillars typical of Victorian era theaters continued to impede some people's views of the stage. Importantly, the number of total seats did not really increase, but the prices that could be charged to patrons were adjusted upward. The increased commercial capacity of the house really paid off, and the next five years were the high point of Mrs. Drew's management, both artistically and financially, with a repertory consisting of a few classics, sprinkled into a season mostly of popular comedies and melodramas.

In the collection of the Library Company of Philadelphia, there is a fascinating 1868 photograph of the renovated Arch Street Theatre, taken from the upper floors of a building across the street. Four young people are standing on the steps, looking at the camera. I have no documentation for it, but it certainly seems plausible that these might in fact be Mrs. Drew's four children. They are obviously posing and aware that they are being photographed, wearing nice clothing—as if Mother told them to dress up and stand there for a bit. Indeed, three of the group appear to be teenagers, which would be just right for Louisa, Georgiana, and John Drew, Jr.

There is also the figure of a child standing uncooperatively behind a lamppost to the left of the other three, which might be Mrs. Drew's five-year-old adopted son, little Sidney Drew. (There has been much speculation among historians—and even her own family—that Sidney was in fact her actual son, the product of an extramarital affair with one of her company members. But this has never been definitively proven.)

At any rate, it was summertime when the photo was taken, because we can note that the windows of the theater have been thrown open to let in the breeze. With some difficulty, on the advertising billboard leaning next to the theater's doors one can make out the name "G. L. Fox." This would confirm the date, because Fox's troupe was performing the fanciful pantomime *Jack and Gill* at the Arch in early July 1868, and it would have been just the sort of entertainment the Drew children might have gone to see together.

On a less wholesome note, however, "Bird's Billiard Parlor" can also be seen in the background. As he grew up, young Sidney Drew would spend a lot of time in such billiard halls, which abounded in the increasingly seedy neighborhood surrounding the theater. When he was all grown up, Sidney even became a bit of a pool shark, hustling extra money whenever his allowance from his mother ran low. Known as "Uncle Googan" to his sister Georgie's children, he would sometimes bring little Jack and Lionel Barrymore along with him as lookouts. "Would you like to see Uncle Googan hit the pretty balls?" he would ask them, and then slip out of his mother's view, once again.

Opening Night at Hammerstein's Opera House

April 1, 1908: To accommodate his new Philadelphia opera house, Oscar Hammerstein bought a lot at the corner of Broad and Poplar Streets. It took up the entire end of a city block, with lots of open gardens and with a large building already on it—the gracious Italianate mansion formerly belonging to the late Charles J. Harrah, a Philadelphia steel maker. Of course, the Harrah mansion needed to be immediately demolished, and an enormous hole needed to be dug for the foundations of the new building.

The dynamic New York impresario was in a hurry to open a new front in the "Opera War"—his obsession with wresting away artistic primacy in America from his bitter rival, the Metropolitan Opera Company. For several years, both of them had been bringing their productions down to Philadelphia audiences at the Academy of Music. But Oscar, as was his habit, decided he needed a grand new theater of his very own. Eventually, he hoped to have an entire string of new opera houses, all across the country. The site in North Philadelphia would be the beginning of his campaign.

The city was experiencing an economic downturn, however, and 2,000 unemployed Philadelphia laborers had shown up at this job site, desperately hoping to be hired for the work. Most of these men were African American or Irish. But when they arrived, they soon learned that a special gang of Hammerstein's own crack demolition men from New York had started to do the skilled labor, and an additional 100 Italian immigrant laborers had shown up from South Philly with shovels and pickaxes, offering to do the rough excavation work at very low wages.

There was evidently a history of bad blood between these various groups, and angry shouting and confrontations soon broke out. The Philadelphia police had to call hundreds of officers to the scene, but not before the outnumbered Italians were being chased and assaulted up and down North Broad Street and in the side alleys leading off from it. Anyone who even *looked* Italian was being viciously attacked.

Photographs of the chaotic scene were published in the newspapers the next day, along with the predictable headlines that screamed "RACE RIOT"—because of course, by the journalistic standards of the day, Italians, Irish, and Black people were evidently three different and distinct races. The worst injury reported was suffered by one Italian man who had his head brutally bashed in. He was not expected to live, said the papers. Dozens of other men were arrested before the police finally quieted things down.

Over the next few weeks and months, the Hammerstein crews set to work. The Harrah mansion was rapidly disassembled brick by brick, and its material saved to help form the new structure's walls. Oscar's son Arthur, who was highly talented in the building trades, directed all the work. Astoundingly, by mid-August, the walls of the new theater were already completed.

The design of the opera house was ostensibly executed by the firm of William H. McElfatrick, the most experienced theater architect of the day, and it had filed all the building plans. But everybody knew that Oscar Hammerstein would never entrust his theaters to mere architects. A skilled machinist and inventor, he knew how to create curves and ceilings and railings that embraced the audience and enhanced and amplified sound coming from the stage. From his experience constructing his New York opera houses and vaudeville theaters, he knew how to create sweeping balconies with no pillars, posts, or railings to impede the audience's view. And there were always capacious lounges and promenades for the audience to experience on their way to and from their seats, as well as roof gardens to enjoy after the show, and rehearsal rooms for the cast. There was also, of course, an enormous stage. The proscenium was 52 feet wide and 40 feet high. The backstage area was 120 feet high, 116 feet wide, and 66 feet to the back wall. Plenty of room for huge opera sets to fly around and trundle about—more room than there was at the old Academy of Music on South Broad.

The outside of the new opera house had a cornice 75 feet high, and was faced with cream-colored brick, terra cotta, and marble. Immense cast-iron marquees extended over the sidewalk from the first floor, covering dozens of entrances, all carefully designed to provide easy and quick access to all the various levels and balconies of the house. A line of special boxes extended across the underside of the wide upper balcony section. Red velvet and gold paint gleamed everywhere, lit by chandeliers and surrounded by galleries filled with statuary. It was an era when Grand Opera was still a popular form of entertainment, and the entire city eagerly awaited its completion.

Astonishingly, the whole project was finished exactly when Hammerstein had said it would be: November 17, 1908. He had even already planned, rehearsed, and prepared the opening night performance: George Bizet's *Carmen*, starring Maria Labia. Pictures of Hammerstein, Labia, and the new opera house were printed in newspapers all over the county. The Metropolitan Opera's management, to counter him, offered Philadelphians Puccini's *La Boheme* that very same night, with Enrico

Caruso himself singing the role of Rodolfo and the great Polish soprano Marcella Sembrich as Mimi. What were people to do—especially the wealthy people who held the right to private boxes in the two rival establishments?

According to the historian John Francis Marion, as it turned out, many Philadelphians simply decided to go to both:

> [At first] there seemed no doubt that the Academy had triumphed. When the curtains rose on Rodolfo's attic room, its double horseshoe boxes were three quarters full. Within a short time every seat in the house was filled, and "only the hum of rustling silks and soft satins made gentle accompaniment to the strains of Puccini's music." However, not even Caruso, Scotti and Sembrich could hold certain of the curious. There was a partial exodus throughout the first act, when those who also held boxes in the new opera house left to discover what was happening at Hammerstein's. What was happening at Hammerstein's was pandemonium.

There were 4,000 ticket holders expected in the palatial new theater on North Broad to hear *Carmen*. By 8 pm., many of the audience were already in place, including out-of-town celebrities such as Mr. and Mrs. E. F. Albee and the diva Luisa Tetrazzini, as well as the Mayor of Philadelphia and the Governor of Pennsylvania and their wives. But a sizable portion of the audience—including the most socially prominent ones—were still downtown and miles away on South Broad Street.

Back there, the energy slowly seemed to drop inside the old Academy, as the audience quietly dwindled. Suddenly, things reached the breaking point, and large groups of people started rushing out, climbing into hastily summoned carriages and automobiles, which then all went streaming up Broad Street, circling round the imposing bulk of City Hall in the Center Square in a huge convoy—seven columns of them, in a parade stretching several blocks long. "It was the most wonderful sight I have ever witnessed," said a devoted opera patron, years later.

But when this convoy finally arrived, the carriages and cars were impeded by a crush of gawkers outside the Hammerstein house, all eager to see the swells and richly dressed ladies come and go. Some estimated that there might have been up to 10,000 people gathered on Broad Street. When the huge parade of migrating operagoers from the Academy showed up, there was mass confusion.

Slowly, and with much help from hundreds of policemen holding open a corridor for them through the crowd of onlookers, all the operagoers made their way from the cars to the curbs and sent their cars and carriages away. Due to Hammerstein's numerous and commodious doorways, they quickly got inside, marveling at the glowing and opulent interior decorations. All the Pews, Elkinses, Wideners, Cramps, Clothiers, Cassats, Yarnalls, and Van Rensselaers found their seats. The canny Oscar Hammerstein had held the curtain for them, of course, and then the show finally began. The only last-minute hitch was that someone had mislaid the New York impresario's favorite kitchen chair, the one he used to perch in his accustomed spot in the wings. Fortunately, a suitable replacement was found, and he sat down and drank in the glorious evidence of his total triumph. As the *Public Ledger* wrote the next day:

> It is not often it can be said with genuine verity that an event marks an epoch, but last night's inaugural performance in the beautiful white structure, now one of the city's chief architectural adornments, was actually the beginning of newer, broader, better things in Philadelphia ... [it was as if] some master magician's wand had called the great glowing life-full fabric into being.

At the end of the second act, the stage curtain parted, and there was Hammerstein, bowing modestly to his new Philadelphia patrons, and making one of his patented speeches of thanks and appreciation, while still challenging Philadelphia to continue to support this great new endeavor he had brought to them. "It is for you to decide, and it is for you to make it the greatest opera house in the world. I have done my part. I promised, and I have fulfilled."

The Adventures of Chlora on Delancey Street

Philadelphia's Little Theatre

March 3, 1913: The new little theater company on Philadelphia's Delancey Street staged their first play, *The Adventures of Chlora*, about a young woman exploring her passions and her romantic freedom. The play had been in rehearsal for many weeks, and its opening had been delayed several times by last-minute construction difficulties. "Briefly, the story is formed by a series of five love ventures of an attractive and witty young maid who bears the title name," wrote a Philadelphia reporter in a preview piece. "Mrs. Jay, the director of The Little Theatre, has selected a number of well-known and experienced artists headed by Oza Waldrop, a clever comedienne recently featured in *Speed*, to form the cast. The other members of the company are Hilda Englund, a distinguished Swedish actress; [and] Mabel Wright, who was seen with Dustin Farnum in *The Virginian*."

On the evening of the play's premiere, the audience included prominent supporters of the company, including Dr. S. Weir Mitchell and his family, and Mr. and Mrs. Thomas Shelton. Both of their groups sat in the theater's seats of honor—the two small "boxes" to the right and left of the proscenium. During intermission, all members of the audience were invited to view the lower-level lounge, which was furnished with old prints and decorated "in mission style." Punch was served to the audience by members of the Little Theatre Club.

The newly constructed red brick Little Theatre, with space above for a school for drama and a theater on the lower level, was designed by architect Amos W.

Barnes. Like many historic Philadelphia theaters, it had a signature sculpture on the facade. Barnes placed a terra-cotta frieze of dancing women and animals—all exact copies of figures from the "Singing Gallery" by Luca Della Robbia in Florence, Italy, but combined into one long parade, like that of the Parthenon. There were also handmade Mercer tiles—from the factory in nearby Doylestown, Pennsylvania—set in the brickwork around the frieze. More of the Mercer tiles were embedded in the lobby floor. But unlike other ambitious theaters that were built in the city around the same period—B. F. Keith's vaudeville palace on Chestnut Street, for example, or Hammerstein's opera house on North Broad—it was not a grand temple of Art. The auditorium was only designed for 328 people.

Part of the "Little Theatre" movement which was sweeping elite intellectual and cultural circles in Europe and America in the early 20th century, it was founded by a group of wealthy and well-connected Philadelphians eager to foster artistic theater. Beulah Jay was widely acknowledged as the chief driving force behind the project. A former music student at the Boston Conservatory who had recently become obsessed with theater, she was married to the prominent mechanical engineer Edward G. Jay. (Though not from an old Philadelphia family, he was the scion of an eminent American clan—his ancestors included the first U.S. Supreme Court chief justice, John Jay.)

Mrs. Jay had put $100,000 of the couple's money into the Delancey Street project, an astounding amount for a theater that was intended NOT to make money—though she did hope to at least "meet her expenses," she told the *New York Times*. She had visited every other "little theater" in the world, she claimed, in order to come up with ideas for the perfect theater of her own. She saw everything from the Intima Theatre of Stockholm to the Grand Guignol of Paris. "I know that I am laughed at by many people and that many people think me presumptuous. I don't know why everyone is ready to scoff at the efforts of a newcomer into the field of theater, especially when the aim of that person is wholly artistic." Of course, perhaps one reason for the general skepticism was a salacious story flying around Philadelphia. It was rumored that the money for the whole endeavor had only been coughed up by Mr. Jay as part of an agreement to keep their marriage together. According to the gossips in town, after he had been caught in an extramarital affair, she had demanded money for both the long solo trip to Europe and the construction of her dream theater. But none of that, naturally, was in the papers.

Her first big project, *The Adventures of Chlora*, was billed as "an Austrian comedy." It was a female-centric response to Arthur Schnitzler's 1893 comedy *Anatol*, about the serial escapades of a Viennese playboy. But *Chlora* had no author listed. Many people assumed that Mrs. Jay had written it herself, but this was an allegation that she airily dismissed in an interview in the *New York Times*. It had arrived in the mail, she stated, after she had placed an ad in *The Dramatic Mirror* asking for original American plays. She believed it may have been written by "a New York physician," but that it was a "cream puff, or perhaps I should say, an hors d'oeuvre for the banquet I hoped later to spread." Later in the season she planned to do Ibsen's *Ghosts*. But really, she stated, she wanted to produce more female playwrights.

According to the review in the *Philadelphia Inquirer*, the plot centered around

> Chlora, an oversexed girl, with a longing for "strong and adventurous" male companions, [who] resolves to experience the delights of a chain of flirtations. Her victims are an aviator, who falls through the skylight into her boudoir; a military officer, whom she encounters in a ruined abbey; a Viennese bachelor, a wealthy man, and a summer man, so called. All yield to her frank advances, and the verbal sparring between the men and the woman is spun out to a climax in each one of the episodes.

The scenes evinced considerable laughter from the audience, though one critic wrote that the dialogue was "undistinguished." Whoever wrote the play, said the critic, they were certainly not Austrian. The performance went well on the whole, but he cautioned that "the acting organization has not found its level yet."

Perhaps the theater should have asked for some money for that punch—or at least charged more for tickets. After four seasons, Mrs. Jay's venture foundered, and in July 1917 the Philadelphia sheriff seized the building and all its assets. Though it's not clear why things had reached such a state, evidently Mr. Jay's and Mr. Shelton's pockets were not sufficient to keep things going any longer. Also sold off by the sheriff were the effects of the "Metropolitan Dramatic School" and the "Noyes School of Rhythmic Expression" housed on the building's upper floors. The *Philadelphia Ledger* reported that when the notice to repossess the premises was posted on the front door, Mrs. Jay indignantly tore it down and walked away.

The beautiful jewel box of the theater survived, luckily, and soon became supported and treasured by a new group of backers. Renamed the "Plays & Players Theatre," it still stands on Delancey Street today. After over a century of constant use it is admittedly showing its age in places. Cracks and gaps have opened up in the terra-cotta parade of young ladies on the facade and the neighborhood's birds freely build their nests among them. The plaster walls and ceilings inside need considerable repair work. But the theater continues to be in use year-round, and is a vital and well-beloved local institution. To be fair to Mrs. Jay, her ambitious project was clearly a good idea all along.

Snake Hips at the Lincoln

January 9, 1932: Snake Hips Tucker was in town, in the show *Southland*, billed by its producers as "the fastest, funniest, most elaborate stage production of today."

Earl Tucker always performed in a shiny white shirt and shiny and baggy gold pants, and his amazing gyrations are now considered a precursor to modern hip hop dance. In the group he brought down to Philly with him that week was Wilton Crawley, a clarinetist also known for his amazingly limber acrobatic poses as he played.

The venue was on the southwest corner of Lombard and Broad Streets, in the heart of Philadelphia's African American "Seventh Ward." Built in the 1920s as the Dunbar Theatre, it was always intended as a "legit" venue for African American theater artists and audiences. For a while, it was the home of the Philadelphia branch of the Lafayette Players from Harlem. In the early 1920s it was also called the Gibson Theatre, after its owner, the African American banker John T. Gibson. But he had severe financial setbacks, and lost control of the venue. By the 1930s it had been given a new marquee and was known as the Lincoln Theatre, hosting movies, musical acts, and plays.

The *Philadelphia Tribune*, the leading Black newspaper in city, wrote: "Commencing Saturday, January 9th, at the Lincoln Theatre, Broad and Lombard streets, Southland, featuring the original Earl Tucker (Snakehips) direct from Connie's Inn, New York City, also Dixieland's hottest band, Vernon Andrades' orchestra and such stars as Wilton Crawley, Grace Smith and her four buddies, and the fastest dancing chorus that ever hit Philadelphia." It was all very exciting. Someone even took a photo of all the names on the Lincoln's marquee. That might be some of the musicians standing underneath it, their long overcoats buttoned against the January cold. Meanwhile, a group of young ladies—perhaps those fast-dancing chorines—linger by the corner of the building.

Despite it being the very depths of the Great Depression, African American dancers, musicians, and actors were bringing a lot of New York talent to Philadelphia on almost a daily basis, proclaimed writer Lou Garcia in another article in *The Tribune*. Maybe, he wrote, the next "renaissance" would be here, not Harlem:

> Philadelphia, the new mecca for the theatrical world, opens its arms to colored professional unemployed and the evacuation starts! ... New York City, with Harlem as the melting pot for stage and night club performers looks dead around Lafayette, Alhambra and Connie's Inn ... not because the depression is over; BUT now the panic is on and the BIG TOWN isn't what it used to be and offers nothing in the form of employment.
>
> Just as the Arcadians evacuated their homes and farms in 1755 ... so do the cream of the colored theatrical field, because Philadelphia is now the biggest show town in the country and the theatres are presenting the finest productions in the history of the Negro show world.

Sad to say, this was another journalistic prediction that never came true. Only five years later Earl Tucker passed away at the age of 30—in New York. It was people coming from the South, not from the big cities of the North, that would drive a great deal of the cultural and social energy of the African American community in Philadelphia for much of the 20th century. And the Seventh Ward, as it once had been, was changing. Middle-class families were moving out. The Lincoln Theatre lost much of its regular clientele and served as a venue for Yiddish theater and movies during the 1940s. It was torn down in 1955 to build a city public health center. As I write this passage in the mid-2020s, that building too is now shuttered and closed. The site is about to become the home of soaring luxury high-rise apartments, joining many others that tower above that section of South Broad Street.

Frustratingly, African American urban history has particular challenges and much of the story of the Lincoln Theatre is very difficult to document. That single photograph, now owned by the City of Philadelphia—kept not to honor the presence of some great artists down from New York, but rather to note the details of the subway entrance at Broad and Lombard—has become one of the few records of what the Lincoln Theatre looked like in its heyday.

The Invention of the Wilma

December 29, 1996: The Wilma Theater was about to open its first season at its new home on South Broad Street—though by then the city had begun its rebranding effort to call the central thoroughfare the "Avenue of the Arts."

After spending years in the 99-seat space at 2030 Sansom Street that the two Czech immigrant theater artists had carved out from a former garage, Jiri and Blanka Zizka's company now had a sparkling new home—tucked underneath another garage, the enormous parking ramp for the Doubletree Hotel.

Though it needed to have sturdy interior pillars to support the weight of the cars above, the new space had been constructed to their specifications, with 12 rows of seats along a steep slope. Audience demand for their work was growing, but even though they needed a larger space, they didn't want a house that could hold a thousand people. "A theater changes when you get too large an audience," said Blanka Zizka in an interview. "It becomes something else ... We wanted to stay small." Still, with the fly rail above the stage, an electrical grid for hanging advanced lighting and sound, a modern stage management booth and additional backstage workshops, it was a theater that could support productions of much greater technical ambition than they had ever had before. A two-story-tall lobby at the front of the house could support post-show receptions and even host smaller cabaret performances if need be.

The Wilma's first show, a spectacular production of Tom Stoppard's *Arcadia*, was already almost sold out. When it was performed in the new year of 1997, it was an immediate audience favorite and a critical success. The theater company's future in the new space seemed bright. Productions of *Avenue X* and *Quills* were scheduled for later in the season. Though getting the new space built had been a drama in itself, already Blanka could look down from her office window into the crowds milling about the theater's lobby and declare: "In the end, it was really worth it."

***

Two years later, on February 16, 2000, the Wilma was taking on yet another Tom Stoppard play. *The Invention of Love*, about the late-Victorian poet A. E. Housman, had its "East Coast premiere" in Philadelphia. Blanka Zizka directed.

Preparation for the play, which had already been a sensation in London when first produced in 1997, involved some intense work by Zizka and Stoppard on revising the text, in conjunction with the dramaturg Carrie Ryan. Ryan later detailed the process in an article for *The Journal of Modern Literature*:

> I joined their deliberations in the fall as we approached our first rehearsal in January 2000. It was rather inspiring to work with Stoppard on this often tedious process of going over the play line-by-line in order to assure our audience would have access to a greater part of its tapestry. He came to the table not as the author of a published, fixed text but as a man of the theater who was interested in, and committed to, making the East Coast premiere of his play as immediate and effective for a Philadelphia audience as the original production had been for a British audience.

Zizka and Ryan paid particular attention to removing what they considered obscure Britishisms from the play. In fact, they completely excised the character of Jerome K. Jerome, the Victorian author of the comic book *Three Men and a Boat*, who appears briefly in the scene about rowing across the River Styx, because they felt the Philadelphia audience would not get the reference. Stoppard agreed to most of their changes, including altering a line about "a giraffe at large, wearing twelve styles of celluloid collar." (The Philadelphia production instead went: "a giraffe registered to advertise twelve styles of shirt collar.") Ryan noted, however, that the West Coast premiere of the play in San Francisco performed the joke as written, "and while our new version of the joke was on many nights quite funny, Stoppard more than once let us know that the joke as he had written it got laughs from San Francisco audiences."

The Wilma *The Invention of Love* was a tour-de-force production which received high praise from audiences, and critics and theater artists around the country, many of whom made the journey to Philadelphia just to see it. The moment when Oscar Wilde sailed over the heads of the audience was always remembered by those who were lucky enough to be there. The production would win five Barrymore Awards, including Best Production of a Play for the 1999–2000 Philadelphia theater season. The newest theater on the Avenue of the Arts was well launched.

The Arden in Old City

April 7, 1998: Shakespeare's *A Midsummer Night's Dream* had its opening night at the Arden Theatre Company on North Second Street in Old City. It was the inaugural production for the F. Otto Haas Stage, the larger of the two performance spaces for the dynamic young Philadelphia theater company.

The new production of *Midsummer*, directed by Aaron Posner and designed by David P. Gordon, took full advantage of the new dimensions. "I knew it would fill the space, and I wanted a good piece to show off the space," said Posner in an interview. The director explained that in his vision Shakespeare's play is "about love, it's about sex, it's about dreams, it has people going to sleep all the time. When I thought about sex, and sleeping, beds seemed like a logical scenic device." The audience, seated on the sloping seats surrounding the two-level thrust stage, could even watch the beds fly up into the air.

Impressively, the young company had been founded only 10 years previously, by the trio of Posner, Amy Murphy Nolen, and Terry Nolen. Under a generous arrangement with the Walnut Street Theatre's Bernard Havard, they had been allowed to use a small loft space on the third floor—in exchange for only 10 percent of the box office. "We had no money, no space and no name," recalled Terry Nolen in 1998. "Bernard gave us what we needed most—a place to perform in and a place with name recognition. It was invaluable to our early success."

Like many new theater companies in cities all over America, they had taken advantage of the declining urban churches that needed help filling their historic spaces. In 1990, the company moved to St. Stephen's, the historic Episcopal church that had counted Mrs. John Drew as one of its most faithful parishioners. They had converted the small community building behind the congregation's sanctuary into offices and turned its tiny auditorium into a stage. Five years later, buoyed by some artistic success, a vigorous fundraising campaign, and much assistance from Mayor Ed Rendell, the trio were able to purchase two old industrial structures just north of the historic Christ Church on Second Street, in the "Old City" neighborhood. (Benjamin Franklin had even once run a print shop at the location.)

Of the two adjacent buildings, one was a two-story former U.S. Post Office with large windows. It had been occupied for some years by the PTC Institute, a vocational school which had shuttered in 1994 amidst a storm of allegations of financial impropriety. The rear building was a three-story brick warehouse dating from 1880, which was full of internal vertical columns typical of 19th-century industrial construction.

The second-floor Arcadia Stage was ready by the fall of 1995, and the first production there was Shaw's *Major Barbara*, directed by Posner. Over the next three years, the Arden continued to produce award-winning theater, and its annual attendance rose from 29,000 to 43,000. Its annual budget went from $975,000 to $1.4 million, and its staff went from nine to 25 employees.

Meanwhile, a huge amount of work had to be done to create an envisioned second larger space in the adjoining warehouse building. The interior timber columns, only 18 feet apart, were the biggest challenge. At one point the Arden considered digging out the basement and leaving it at that. Eventually, architects James Timberlake and Richard Maimon came up with the solution of "needling" new steel columns down the exterior walls, removing the interior supports, and then laying 40-foot-long steel trusses across the top to anchor the roof. An enormous 40,000-square-foot flexible performance space was created, with a 36-foot-high ceiling.

For the next quarter century, it would remain a vibrant year-round performing arts venue, and the Arden Theatre Company became one of the most successful non-profit theaters in Philadelphia. The flexible space held up to every demand designers made upon it, and every configuration of seats and stage. Eventually the Arden would have to replace the audience's chairs on the risers, however. They were worn out from so much use.

A Great Day on South Broad Street

October 21, 2007: The Philadelphia Theatre Company inaugurated its new home at the northwest corner of Broad and Lombard. It was just down the street from the Academy of Music, the Wilma Theater, and the Harold Prince Music Theatre. It was also not far from where "The Philadelphia Company"—as it had been known when it was started by Robert Hedley in the 1970s—had found one of its first performance venues in a tiny upstairs 50-seat space in the annex of the Walnut Street Theatre.

A few blocks to the west was the Plays & Players Theatre, which had been the primary home of the non-profit company for 25 years, and where it had produced season after season of new American theater. But the physical limitations of that space—the same ones that had plagued Mrs. Beulah Jay's company when it had first been built—were more evident every year. With both the Wilma Theater and the Arden Theatre Company having already built new homes in the city within the past decade, it was time to make a move.

Two years previously, it was announced that the Philadelphia Theatre Company (PTC) would build a new performance space. The venue would be named "The Suzanne Roberts Theatre." Comcast Corporation co-founder Ralph Roberts had bought the naming rights as a gift to his wife of 63 years, for the theater company they had both long supported. The arrangement included an agreement with developer Carl Dranoff, who wanted the theater to be up and running in time for the opening of his adjacent Symphony House condominium tower. Indeed, the Suzanne Roberts Theatre was constructed as a part of his project, which occupied the entire block. Like the Wilma, the new theater would be placed underneath a massive parking garage.

Along with the construction of the mammoth Kimmel Center's Verizon Hall to the north—the new home of the Philadelphia Orchestra—the Suzanne Roberts Theatre seemed to be a fulfilment of the promise of Philadelphia's rebranding of South Broad Street as the "Avenue of the Arts." The hope was to hearken back to the days a century before, when the street was lined with theaters such as the Forrest, the Shubert, the Garrick, and the Broad. It was as if the earnest little Plays & Players had dressed up and decided to Go Big—and after four years of fundraising and planning and construction for the 25-million-dollar project, it really had.

True, many yawning gaps and eyesores in the streetscape of the "Avenue of the Arts" remained. There were also some architectural ghosts—a lonely blue historical marker on the southwest corner of the intersection commemorated the former Dunbar Theatre (also known as the Lincoln). But in a sign of hope, on the corner of South and Broad was the Arts Bank, a recently converted vacant bank building, which now hosted student productions by the theater division of the University of the Arts.

The first production in the Suzanne Roberts Theatre was Billy Porter's world premiere tribute to Stephen Sondheim, *Being Alive*. Sara Garonzik, a native Philadelphian who had been producing artistic director of the company since 1982, joyfully posed for publicity photos in front of the theater's marquee, and its large sign which honored Roberts—literally, her signature. "It's big," admitted Garonzik, "It's a big honkin' sign, but I think it's beautiful. It's a knock-out." Garonzik also posed for photos in the theater's interior, with its 365-seat auditorium and its proscenium stage that was meant to pay tribute to Plays & Players. There was even a small balcony section, as there had been on Delancey Street. But above that gleamed a modern stage management booth, equipped with up-to-date electronics and communications. Backstage areas were all state-of-the-art, too.

In the front of the house, unlike the cramped intimacy of the Plays & Players' entrance and box office, the architects of the firm KieranTimberlake had designed spacious reception and concessions areas. Reflective materials sparkled in the box office vestibule, and a two-story glass and stainless-steel lobby with large windows along Broad Street gave audiences a place to mingle before and after performances. Enormous photos of productions from the company's history decorated the flat walls of the lobby, but inside the auditorium, rippling gypsum walls painted to look like wood flanked the seats. The entire theater was even underpinned with rubber pads to insulate it from the rumble of the Broad Street subway line, which ran below.

A gala event was held to celebrate the opening, which included theatrical luminaries such as Terrence McNally, Nathan Lane, Edie Falco, Bill Irwin, Richard Thomas, and Doris Roberts. Numerous wealthy benefactors of the company were also in attendance, and the social pages of area newspapers were filled with photos of their proud smiles.

The first season of the PTC in the new space also included the Philadelphia premieres of David Henry Hwang's *M. Butterfly* and Wendy Wasserstein's *Third*, and the world premiere of Bill Irwin's *The Happiness Lecture*. The audience subscription was enthusiastic, and reportedly already over 90 percent of capacity.

Indeed, happiness seemed to be everywhere. "I sat in a tech rehearsal last night, and I felt like I was home," Garonzik told a reporter. "I felt as if I had been there for years."

PART FOUR
Local Heroes

Edwin Forrest Plays Richelieu

The last five nights of September 1839 Edwin Forrest performed the role of Cardinal Richelieu in Edward Bulwer-Lytton's verse drama *Richelieu, or the Conspiracy*. The venue was the former Walnut Street in Philadelphia, whose current manager, Francis Wemyss, had renamed it "The American Theatre" to emphasize that unlike his rival managers in the city, he patriotically featured native-born actors like Forrest.

At the age of 33, the actor was at the peak of his powers. Richelieu was to become—in artistic terms—the greatest role of his career. Forrest had first attempted it, earlier that same month, in New York City at the National Theatre. Up to that point in his career, the actor had been known chiefly for his muscular physique, his powerful voice, and his imposing physical presence on stage. This well suited him in the famous roles from 19th-century plays that were at the core of his repertoire: Metamora, Spartacus, Jack Cade, and Virginius. But Richelieu was an old man, close to his own death. It was a shock for many in the audience to see Forrest using the force of his considerable intellect, to bring the dry humor of the Cardinal's lines and the cunning of his crafty political machinations to the forefront. The famous English actor Charles Kean, who was in the audience, was reported to have turned to his wife Ellen Tree and said, "Ellen, this is the greatest acting we have ever seen or shall see." (Which, coming from the son of Edmund Kean himself, was quite a statement.)

Bulwer-Lytton's play (originally written for Forrest's great rival, William Charles Macready) is completely absent from the modern theatrical repertoire, along with most 19th-century verse dramas. But in its day, *Richelieu* was deeply respected—the only play of Bulwer-Lytton's to be performed more frequently was his wildly popular melodrama *The Lady of Lyons*. Nowadays Bulwer-Lytton is mostly remembered for the opening sentence of his 1830 novel *Paul Clifford* ("It was a dark and stormy night"), but we should perhaps also note that the even more famous adage "The pen is mightier than the sword" first appeared in *Richelieu*.

In terms of box office, *Richelieu* was never Forrest's most profitable of his extensive repertoire of tragic roles, but it was always to be his most highly praised. Part of the impact was due to the visual impact of his costumes for the Cardinal—the 19th-century audience did love to see lavish and "historically accurate" costumes. Forrest's personal costumer, Andrew Jackson ("Dummy") Allen had labored especially hard to produce sumptuous clothes for the whole company in the style of the era of King Louis XIII. Forrest had evidently memorized the massive role in a hurry and was still—as actors say—"finding his way" in the role. But by all accounts, the actor made a true connection with the audience as Richelieu. A New York correspondent, whose account was reprinted in the Philadelphia *National Gazette*, was in ecstasies when he first witnessed it:

> It was as if the mighty statesman were before us ... his indomitable grandeur and pride were portrayed to the life ... In the fourth act, where Richelieu is thought dead, [he] appears before the king and his assembled court, and when cast off by his monarch, yet thunders his threats of excommunication against his successful rival and defies his power, was the climax of a piece of acting, which does honour to Mr. Forrest and to our stage, and drew the acclamations from all parts of the house ... It requires an intellect of great capacity to fill the part as it requires, those who have not seen it filled, have no idea of the power of the character and the redoubled interest it gives the play.

Forrest was naturally pleased by such praise in the newspapers of his home city. He apparently was also especially gratified by the efforts of Francis Wemyss, who had spared no expense to provide the great actor with the finest and most historically accurate sets for *Richelieu*, in order to match the splendor of Allen's costumes. (Wemyss had also performed that night, in the role of the Count de Berighen.)

Wemyss was called to Forrest's dressing room after the show and found him in an excellent mood. The actor complimented the Philadelphia manager and offered him the opportunity to choose any show from his repertoire, as a personal benefit, later in the run. In his memoirs, Wemyss recalled the praise with pleasure "Such a proffer, on such an occasion, from such a man, was a feather in the cap of a manager, which no one has ever been able to pluck away from me." But in monetary terms, of course, Forrest was the clear winner of the entire two-week engagement, netting almost $3,000 as his lion's share of the box office receipts, while Wemyss received a mere $289 from the extra benefit night. (For some reason *Metamora*, the play he requested that Forrest perform, did not draw well.) But this was not an unusual disparity of financial outcome, in terms of the unequal "star system" of 19th-century American theater. In that era, the actor had considerably more power than the producer.

***

In February 1863, Forrest again performed as Richelieu in Philadelphia, this time at the New Chestnut Street Theatre—the third building in the city of that name, which had just been opened west of 13th Street. In the intervening 14 years, most of the events that would make Forrest a lasting name in theater history had transpired—his tours of England and his marriage to the beautiful Catherine Norton Sinclair, his long-running dispute with British critics, the remorseless spite of his campaign against William Charles Macready, the Astor Place Riots in 1849, and his frankly ugly and churlish behavior during his bitter divorce from Catherine. By 1855 he had even left New York and moved back to his native city, buying a mansion on the corner of North Broad and Master Streets, where he lived in solitary splendor. His massive and muscular body was breaking down, and increasingly he was wracked by physical pains caused by the rigors of his long career and his strenuous daily exercise regime. Often Forrest could barely hobble onto the stage, and his battles and leaps as Spartacus and Metamora became rather perfunctory. King Lear and Richelieu were much more appropriate for his body and his spirit, although it was at this point in his career that he added Shakespeare's Coriolanus to his repertoire, and even commissioned a massive marble statue of himself in the role from Boston sculptor Thomas Ball.

Younger theater fans and the intelligentsia now much preferred the more intellectual and sophisticated style of Edwin Booth, who also was performing pretty regularly in Philadelphia those days. Forrest had fallen far in public favor, but still maintained a large loyal following in the city. He performed regularly there, usually starting his annual national tours by giving a week of performances in the fall at the Walnut Street Theatre. But the occasion of the inaugural of the New Chestnut had brought him back home again. For the occasion, he began with Bulwer-Lytton's play, and once again he pulled out his grand robes of the 17th-century churchman. Supporting Forrest was another longtime notable local member of the Philadelphia theatrical world, the actor William Wheatley, as the Chevalier de Maurat. Wheatley was also managing the newly built theater—aside from the Academy of Music, it was now regarded as the finest house in the city.

Wheatley, at 47, was perhaps a trifle old to be playing the young Chevalier (who, as we learn at the opening of the play, has secretly married Julie de Mortemar, Richelieu's young ward). By now Edwin Forrest himself was 56, and he had been playing the part of the wily old French cardinal for over two decades. To many, it seemed his insight into the role had only grown deeper over the years. An admiring Philadelphia journalist wrote:

> His rendition of the part ... is hardly to be excelled. In him we realize our ideas of what constitutes an actor in the true sense of the word. He rises above the petty conventionalities of the common stage ... The author's thoughts burn into his own soul, shake with emotion from his own breast, flash from his own eyes, and leap thunder-clothed from his own lips ... A more splendid performance than that of last evening has not delighted a Philadelphia audience these many days.

For the rest of his career, Edwin Forrest would continue to perform in *Richelieu*—until he was older than the historical character had been in the harrowing death bed scene in Act V. Often, the Cardinal's rattling cough would remain with Forrest long after the show was over, so much so that friends who joined him for a post-show dinner became concerned about his health. In fact, it was to be his last role. The actor's final performance was as Richelieu in April 1871, in Boston. By that point Forrest's health had broken down, and his fans had mostly deserted him. His famous roaring voice of his prime years had become ragged and faint, and those few people present in the seats had to strain to hear him. According to his remaining diehard fans, there was a special poignancy when Forrest delivered the Cardinal's final lines:

> ... Alas!
> Our glories float between the earth and the heaven
> Like clouds which seem pavilions of the sun,
> And are the playthings of the casual wind;
> Still, like the cloud which drops on unseen crags
> The dews the wild flower feed on, our ambition
> May from its airy height drop gladness down
> On unsuspected virtue;—and the flower
> May bless the cloud when it hath passed away!

After Forrest's death in 1872, his longtime friend and admirer, the Philadelphia critic James Rees, had a different line from Richelieu in his mind when he thought of the proud actor in his final years: "I tell thee, scorner of these whitening hairs/ When this snow melteth there shall come a flood!/ Avaunt! My name is Richelieu—I defy thee!" In fact, Rees declared that there was no other actor that ever matched his performance in the role.

Although nowadays we may discount the opinions of Rees—and other rather slavish friends and biographers of Forrest—we also have the opinion of Francis Wemyss. He had seen all the great actors of the era in the part and felt that Forrest's portrayal was superior. "Of Mr. Forrest's performance in this part I can scarcely find words of sufficient praise ... Richelieu will never find a better representative. Macready and Vandenhoff both fall far below Forrest, by comparison." Coming from someone who had nearly gone bankrupt in his attempt to please Forrest, we can perhaps allow the manager's estimation to be the final verdict. Certainly nothing would have pleased the actor more than to beat Macready at the end.

The Heron Takes Wing

February 17, 1851: Matilda Heron, at the age of 20, made her stage debut at the Walnut Street Theatre. She played the role of Bianca in *Fazio* by Henry Hart Milman. Heron made such a sensation with the Philadelphia audience that she was immediately asked back to do the same role a few nights later. It was the beginning of a brief, brilliant—and ultimately truly tragic—career.

Born in County Derry, Ireland, she had come to Philadelphia with her family at the age of 12. Her father quickly found success in the lumber business, but after his death her older brother Alexander took over leadership of the family. Alexander got into the steamship trade and soon was running the Heron Line of transatlantic schooners. His sister Matilda, with whom he was very close, therefore did not have to work. She was sent to a school for young ladies on the southeast corner of Ninth and Walnut and became fluent in French. Her younger sisters, Fanny and Agnes, were also sent to school, but Alexander was often busy, so all three girls were difficult to keep home.

"Tilly," as her family called her, became particularly fascinated with leading the theatrical life that she could see going on directly across the street from her school. Much to the disappointment of her brother, she began taking acting lessons from Peter Richings, who worked at the Walnut. Despite the reluctance of her family to be associated with the socially disreputable world of theater, Tilly "went upon the stage"—first in the Walnut's company, and then in Washington, and then New York. In 1853 she traveled to San Francisco and made a smash hit in the theaters of Gold Rush Era California. (She also made a sudden rash marriage to a San Francisco lawyer, which soon failed.)

Estranged from both her husband and her family, she traveled to Paris in 1854, looking for new roles. She was at the theater to view the highly popular new drama *La Dame aux Camélias* by Alexandre Dumas *fils*. The story goes that she suddenly felt a tap upon her shoulder and turned to find her brother Alexander. Smiling down at her, he said: "Tilly, that's a play that would make your fortune, if you would translate it for America."

Heron did so, and soon was performing her own translation of it, usually known in America as *Camille*, to great acclaim. In October 1855 she brought it back home to Philadelphia, where she played the tragic courtesan Marguerite Gautier to her hometown—at the Walnut, where she had first sought success in acting.

Due to a lack of international copyright in that era, there were already several versions of Dumas' play being performed, but Heron's script was regarded as superior and her performance compellingly definitive. A New York critic wrote: "She exuded the electricity of genius." Another gushed that, every time he returned to the play:

> [I] came away more infatuated than ever. There was no acting—it was all nature; and my heart ached looking at the woman, as I thought all those thousand little evidences of love, those outbursts of passion, could never have been learned, or acted, save by a heart which had gone through a similar fiery ordeal ... "the Heron" must have magnetized, spiritualized or bedeviled me in some way, for I am no longer a free man.

Though she would adapt other French plays for her repertoire, Heron always prospered with *Camille*, and it is estimated that she earned over $100,000 playing the role, all over America. "Other parts she acted, that part she *lived*," wrote the eminent critic William Winter. Indeed, the "realism" that Heron may have injected into the role seems to have been drawn not only from her own tempestuous love life, but that of one of her sisters, who had actually "fallen" in life and become a courtesan.

Matilda Heron's subsequent career and personal life was alternately successful and rocky. She married again, but when her new husband found out about her previous one, as well as her sister's profession, that marriage failed, too. To escape it, she had to settle most of her money on her husband and go back upon the stage. She performed for the last time in Philadelphia, again at the Walnut Street Theatre, on October 14, 1863. "Houses crowded! Hundreds turned away!" said the newspaper ads.

We can surmise that these performances must have been quite stressful for Tilly, because only a month before she had given birth to a daughter, Helene, whom she always called "Bijou." (Later, Bijou Heron would also go onto the stage, first as a child star and later as a mature actress, and would have a long career of her own.) Despite writing, and performing, many other roles for herself, Matilda Heron was always associated in the public mind with Camille. Many other great actresses of the era, such as Helena Modjeska, preferred using her version of the play in their own performances.

Heron was in increasingly poor health, however, and by the age of 47 had turned gray and haggard. She died in New York City in 1877. It is horrifyingly likely that she suffered from syphilitic paresis. One might speculate that she had contracted the disease from her first husband, which would explain her sudden haste to extract herself from the relationship. As is typical of syphilis, after lying dormant for many years the disease may have emerged again, taking a terrible toll. Her obituary in the *New York Times* notes that during her final years: "Now and then ... she herself took part in dramatic representation, eccentric demonstrations and speeches invariably marring the effect of acting sometimes crude and uneven." Her confusing reported last words were "Tilly never did harm to anyone—poor Tilly is so happy."

Despite her lifelong Catholicism, Heron's home church refused to conduct holy rites over her body. Funeral services for Heron were held instead at the Episcopal Church of the Transfiguration, also known as the tolerant "Little Church Around the Corner." She was buried in Brooklyn's Greenwood Cemetery.

"Matilda Heron was one of the most remarkable actresses our stage has ever produced," declared the critic and historian Lawrence Hutton, who had seen her perform in her prime. "She made and held, by force of her own genius—and genius she certainly possessed—a position which few modern actresses have ever reached. Her personal faults were of the head rather than the heart, and may they now rest lightly on her!"

The Little Tycoon

January 4, 1886: Willard Spenser, the Philadelphian who was the author and composer of the operetta *The Little Tycoo*n, rose from his box seat at the Temple Theatre on Chestnut Street and bowed repeatedly in response to the applause of the opening night audience. In a brief speech, he stated the work, "might be known as *The Big Tycoon* by the time it reached Boston, Chicago, New York and the other great cities."

This was a bold assertion, because it had been a long time since Philadelphia had been a force in creating anything interesting or important in American theater. In the newspaper the next day, even the reviewer in the *Philadelphia Times* seemed skeptical of its prospects. "The management mounted the piece in spectacular style," he allowed. "The costuming was gorgeous, particularly in the Japanese attire, and the scenery was equal probably to any ever presented to a Philadelphia audience." Still, he thought, though the production was pleasant and the cast was lively and appealing, the show was long, and needed pruning. Spenser's libretto was "not remarkable for wit," and though "the music as a whole is catchy, it is doubtful if any of the airs will be whistled in the streets or become otherwise very popular."

But, in a phenomenon that was to be repeated again and again, though the reviews were tepid, demand for tickets remained high, and the producers of *The Little Tycoon* kept selling out the house! After all, the kimonos on the 86-member chorus and the hundreds of Japanese lanterns decorating the stage were quite dazzling, and the music was so charming! The run was extended for another week at the Temple Theatre, and then another, and then another. By the end of February, it was still going strong. "Whatever may be thought of it as a work of merit, it is holding public attention."

Part of the appeal of *The Little Tycoon* was the current mania for operettas in general, and those with a Japanese theme in particular. Gilbert and Sullivan's own Japanese operetta, *The Mikado*, was at the peak of its popularity in 1886, with multiple companies performing the show at the same time in New York and Philadelphia.

"Tycoon," though it is used today to describe a successful businessman of great wealth, comes from the Japanese word for military dictator, just as "Mikado" referred to their emperor. No one in America really cared about all this, of course, and the title character wasn't even particularly Japanese—the "prince" in the play could have easily been substituted for all sorts of dispossessed young prince roles in many European operettas of the time.

Unlike *The Mikado*, Spenser's *The Little Tycoon* did not even take place in Japan. The first act was set on a steamship carrying the prince coming *from* Japan, and the second act took place in the drawing room of a New York gentleman named General Knickerbocker, who had undertaken to entertain the visiting Japanese dignitaries. Songs from the show included: "Sham, the Great Tycoon," "The Fatal Step," "Heel and Toe," "Sad Heart of Mine" (a bolero), "Tycoon March," and a waltz entitled "Love Comes Like a Summer Sigh."

The success of the show became a large part of its appeal. People would come to see it just to find out what the fuss was all about. "People like to be amused, and are willing to pay liberally to be amused," wrote the *Inquirer* in February 1886. "There are a million people in and about Philadelphia, and as the majority of them seem to want to see *The Little Tycoon*, it will take at least one entire season to exhaust its attractions."

But that prediction proved to be incorrect as well. Nothing, it seemed, could stop *The Little Tycoon*! And it seems that the success of the show was largely due to the decades-long efforts of American theater managers to make theaters safe and attractive places for middle class women. Prostitutes and the large crowds of drunken men pursuing them were now largely confined to burlesque houses. Most public theaters—which up to then were often seen as places of moral and physical peril for "respectable" women—were now regarded as safe places for them to go, even if they were unescorted by men.

In March 1886, as *The Little Tycoon* was still going strong at the Temple, the *Philadelphia Times* made note of the fact. Mr. Fleishman, the manager of the Walnut Street Theatre was quoted:

> I frequently see ladies in couples and sometimes alone enter the theatre ... At the matinees the ladies are rarely accompanied by escorts. At night performances one can see two lady friends, a mother and daughter or two sisters, come into the theatre without escorts and depart in the same way, after enjoying the performance. Why not? There is nobody to molest them at the theatre.

Mr. Moore, the assistant manager of the Temple Theatre, was also quoted: "Since *The Little Tycoon* has been running hundreds and hundreds of ladies have visited the theatre without escorts. I know of a lady and her daughter who have been here every night except six since the play has been on. They did not come nor go away with escorts. I see no impropriety in it whatsoever." At special benefit matinees for charitable causes, it was reported that Philadelphia women would even pack the aisles and sit on the stairs to see their beloved *Little Tycoon* performed once again. And no man could stop them.

May Manning Lillie, Quaker Cowgirl

July 2, 1888: *Pawnee Bill's Historical Wild West* began performances at Gentlemen's Driving Park at the intersection of Monument and Ford Roads in West Philadelphia.

Among the show's company were its leader Gordon William Lillie ("Pawnee Bill"), his partner "Comanche Bill," and the famous female sharpshooter Annie Oakley. Also among the attractions were trick rider "Mexican Mike," Western orator Captain Harry Horn, and Little Knife (a chief of the Osage tribe, who was said to be 94 years old). All of them were veterans of William Cody's "Buffalo Bill's Wild West," the traveling circus and Western exhibition. They had left Buffalo Bill's employment for the moment, however, and were striking out on their own, forming a new "Wild West" combination.

There was someone in the show, however, who was brand new to show business, and was making her debut in the Wild West genre. The show was a bit of a homecoming for her, in fact, because she was a native Philadelphian: May Manning Lillie, the 19-year-old wife of Pawnee Bill.

May Manning was the daughter of Philadelphia physician Dr. William Manning and his wife Mary. She had two sisters and three half-brothers from her father's earlier marriage. They were a Quaker family, and she had evidently been well educated at schools run by the Society of Friends, because at the age of 14 she went off to study at Smith College in Massachusetts. May was back home from college during the summer of 1884, now just 15, when she and her younger sisters were given permission by their parents to see Buffalo Bill's famous show. The company, which included many members of the Sioux and Pawnee nations (along with "Mexicans and cowboys, all mounted on ponies"), had just arrived in Philadelphia, preceded by the usual showbiz fanfare of publicity and parades.

There were reportedly 5,000 people jamming the exhibition on the first day, but it was May who caught the interest of Gordon William Lillie, then 26. Broad of face and build, the Indiana-born rancher owned a large operation in Kansas. He also had worked with U.S. government agencies in Pawnee territory, before being recruited by Buffalo Bill's outfit as an interpreter and performer, choosing the moniker "Pawnee Bill" for business purposes. Though his hairline was receding a bit, he covered it up with a broad-brimmed hat, with long locks flowing down his neck from beneath. Like many others, he also sported a dramatically drooping mustache, emulating that of his hero. The Wild West cowboy spotted May as she happily led her sisters around the fairground—and she evidently returned his gaze with unconcerned Quaker frankness. In the couple's later account of their meeting, it was love at first sight.

Having been given her name and home address, Gordon began a concerted campaign seeking May's hand, inundating the Manning home with letters expressing his honorable intentions. But her parents, understandably enough, had strong opposition to any association with such an unexpected and unconventional son-in-law. May, for her part, promised her parents that they would not marry until after she graduated from college. Lillie diligently kept providing the Mannings with proof of his earnings from his ranch, and her unswerving devotion to her suitor eventually swayed their feelings about him. Gordon and May finally married, two years after their first meeting, on August 31, 1886.

To celebrate the happy fulfillment of their long courtship, Gordon Lillie's wedding gifts to his bride were a pony and a Marlin .22 target rifle. The couple went off to start their married life in Kansas. As might be expected, May was soon pregnant. Feeling the financial pressures of imminent fatherhood, her new husband left to tour with Buffalo Bill again, and she stayed home to run the cattle ranch. To his credit, Pawnee Bill came hurrying back home when the time came for the baby to arrive. Unfortunately, the delivery was a difficult one, and their child died after only six weeks. Furthermore, the rough frontier-style postpartum medical care May received left her unable to have any more children.

With conventional domesticity out of the question, therefore, it was decided that May would go into the Wild West show business as well. The former Philadelphia Quaker schoolgirl learned how to shoot, how to ride—and soon became quite proficient at both. Much to the annoyance of his former boss, in the spring of 1888 Pawnee Bill joined up with yet another frontiersman named Bill ("Comanche Bill") and decided to organize his own competing Wild West combination. With financial backing from two Philadelphia businessmen (C. M. Southwell and Thomas Ryan), he made his young wife one of the stars of the show. May was billed as the "Princess of the Prairie," and so in July 1888 May found herself right back in Gentlemen's Driving Park, where she and Lillie had first met.

A former part of the fairgrounds for the 1876 Centennial Exhibition, this open field was frequently used for trotting races—hence its name. Now that former open spaces in North and South Philadelphia were filling up as the cities swelled in the last two decades of the century, Gentlemen's Driving Park was a prime venue for many traveling circuses that came through Philadelphia. Special excursion trains would typically bring Philadelphians from the center of the city out to Bala Station.

Or they could take the trolley cars to Belmont Avenue, where fleets of horse-drawn coaches would take them to the park.

To spark public interest, as was the practice of most traveling circuses, *Uncle Tom's Cabin* companies, and Wild West shows, local audiences had been attracted by colorful advertising posters all over town, as well as a parade of the massed Pawnee Bill company that had snaked through the entire city of Philadelphia on July 2. Since it was quite a long and complex procession, the *Times* of Philadelphia reported precisely where the city's residents could view the Pawnee Bill and Comanche Bill Great Wild West parade: "The route will be from Gentlemen's Driving Park to Belmont Avenue, to Lancaster avenue, to Market Street to Thirty-third, to Chestnut, to Third, to Arch, to Ninth, to Ridge avenue, to Broad, to Columbia avenue, to Twentieth street, to Girard avenue, to the Park." When they went by her old home, May waved from horseback to her astonished family.

And what sort of theatrical spectacle was Pawnee Bill and Comanche Bill's Great Wild West? Well, in addition to exhibitions of riding by members of the Pawnee, Comanche, Wichita, and Osage tribes, there was sharpshooting by Annie Oakley, as well as roping and riding stunts by other heavily mustachioed frontiersmen, such as "Donziano," "Mexican Frank," "Happy Jack Sutton," "Cyclone John," and "Texas Desey." There was also "Kansas Lily," a sharpshooter billed as being only two years old.

From the account of the *Philadelphia Times*, again:

> During the show are performed all the most difficult feats of Western life ... catching the trailing lasso, and riding bucking Texas steers and broncos. The show included fancy rifle shooting by Pawnee Bill, May Lillie and Annie Oakley. There is a realistic attack on the Deadwood stage coach by the Indians, who are repulsed by the cow-boys under the leadership of Pawnee Bill, and skillful lassoing of a horse's feet while going at full speed by Mexican Frank, herding real buffaloes and a dozen other attractive features ... Two performances a day are given, the evening performance under the glare of numerous calcium lights.

Later that summer, Pawnee Bill's show evidently had some sort of financial difficulties, and its assets were briefly repossessed by debtors during an engagement near Camden, New Jersey. But there was no doubt in May's mind that her future career was set. May Lillie would remain a Wild West performer for the rest of her life, appearing together with Pawnee Bill all over the country for many years afterwards. Even an accident in 1899 that cost her two fingers did not deter her.

In an era when many "New Women" were asserting their personal, political, and social independence, May had her own fans and admirers, and she certainly knew how to work a crowd. In a speech to a mostly female audience in Chicago in 1907, May said:

> Let any normally healthy woman who is ordinarily strong screw up her courage and tackle a bucking bronco, and she will find the most fascinating pastime in the field of feminine athletic endeavor. There is nothing to compare, to increase the joy of living, and once accomplished, she'll have more real fun than any pink tea or theater party or ballroom ever yielded.

Having proved to her family many times over that she had indeed chosen wisely on that bright summer day in West Philadelphia, in August 1936 May and Gordon Lillie celebrated their 50th wedding anniversary. She died at the age of 67, after an automobile accident in Tulsa, Oklahoma. She is buried in Pawnee, Oklahoma, next to her husband, in the Lillie family mausoleum.

Her reputation never dimmed, at least amongst modern devotees of rodeo and Wild West circus historians. In 2011, May Manning Lillie, the former Philadelphia Quaker schoolgirl, was inducted into The National Cowgirl Hall of Fame.

Blythe Spirit, or All Them Barrymores

March 5, 1906: All three of the Barrymores—Ethel, Lionel, and John (called "Jack" by his two older siblings)—performed together in Philadelphia. The venue was Garrick Theatre on Chestnut Street, between Juniper and Broad Streets. The production was the national tour of *Alice-Sit-by-the-Fire*, a comedy by J. M. Barrie.

The Garrick Theatre was just a few blocks from the house where two of them (Ethel and Lionel) were born, and even closer to their grandmother's home at 140 N. Twelfth St. where all three had lived in early childhood. It would have also been a simple matter to visit Box D of the old Arch Street Theatre nearby to which their grandmother once had the only key, and where on Saturday afternoons they were allowed to come and watch her perform.

"What security [we] could lay claim to resided in Mrs. John Drew," wrote Lionel in his memoirs. "Our affection for her was warm, though tempered sometimes by the kind of respect which one makes his manners to Constitution Hall ... We lived in her home, we went confidently to her for advice—or money; we took her scolding as our due, and we were immeasurably proud of her." But when their "Mummum" died in 1897, "the only home Ethel, Jack and I had ever known, our only link with stability and security disappeared."

When the careers or the whims of their parents, Maurice and Georgie, had seen fit, the three kids were whisked off to London or New York, or on a train ride with yet another theatrical touring company. Sometimes they were in boarding schools, sometimes they were educated fitfully by other actors. Though all three were baptized as infants at their grandmother's St. Stephen's Episcopal Church, Maurice and Georgie re-baptized them as Catholics—at the urging of the charismatic Polish actress Helena Modjeska, to whom they had both become devoted.

It was at a sanitarium in California (near a home belonging to Modjeska) that Georgie, only 36, had died of tuberculosis in 1893. Thirteen-year-old Ethel was the only family member with her at the end, and the girl had to accompany the coffin on the long train ride back to its burial in Philadelphia. Ethel, at least, had found some emotional stability in her religious faith, and spent many happy years in the convent school of the Academy of Notre Dame on Rittenhouse Square. Her brothers, for their part, developed a much less respectful attitude toward any sort of church, to say the least. Unlike Ethel, they initially bucked against joining the family profession, too. "I didn't want to act," wrote Lionel. "I wanted to paint or draw. The theater was not in my blood, I was related to the theater by marriage only; it was merely a kind of in-law of mine I had to live with." John, for his part, was very dedicated to a sort of moody bohemianism, and chasing after beautiful women. But their father's sad decline and death in 1905 (from the long-term effects of alcoholism and syphilis) had made them suddenly feel the need to be more responsible. And because of their last name, the two brothers had found that acting jobs were usually available to them, so they made their way back to the theater. Wherever they were playing, on opening nights, the Barrymore siblings would send each other an apple. It was a longtime family jest, perhaps based on a common enticement to children, that if you sang your song (or spoke your poem) prettily, you would get "a big red apple." The whole family knew all too well the vagaries of their profession, and that such an apple was the only reward you should really ever expect in show business.

By 1906, the Broadway producer Charles Frohman, who had long looked after the career of their uncle, the distinguished actor John Drew, Jr., had finally decided it was time to put all three of the Barrymores together in a single evening. Perhaps because Barrie's play *Peter Pan* was then such a tremendous hit in New York, he chose *Alice-Sit-By-the-Fire*, a play that had originally been written for the actress Ellen Terry. It opened on Christmas Day at the Criterion Theatre to rather startled notices from the press—the part was much more mature than the ingenues Ethel Barrymore had made her reputation in. She was playing the part of Mrs. Grey, an English mother whose daughter wrongfully suspects her of having a flirtation with a young unmarried man. (The young girl knows all about affairs, because she has been to the theater, and every play she saw involved women being unfaithful to their husbands.) As the daughter intervenes to save her mother's reputation, complications and hilarity ensue.

Lionel Barrymore was not in this play, but he was appearing as a clown in *Pantaloon*, the one-act curtain-raiser—another J. M. Barrie work. John Barrymore had been given small roles in both plays. Though he already had a reputation for professional irresponsibility, the producer Charles Frohman had agreed to do Ethel a favor by keeping him in the part. In *Alice-Sit-by-the-Fire*, interestingly, he played the young man, Stephen Rollo, who was supposedly alienating Mrs. Grey's affections. Of the three Barrymores, Jack had inherited more of the startling good looks of their father Maurice, so the role of an alluring young man suited him. However, he was not billed in the ads for the show—and was barely even mentioned in the reviews in his hometown's newspapers. As might be expected, instead they were all about Ethel.

"It is delightful to have Miss Barrymore in Philadelphia again," cooed a local reviewer. "Delightful for a number of reasons. She likes Philadelphia and Philadelphia likes Miss Barrymore. The others can go by the board. After the first act she received four curtain calls, and dear knows how many after the second. They were insistent enough, at any rate, to force from her one of her delightful little hesitating speeches." Ethel was actually a bit shy when not performing, but Quaker City audiences of that era were notorious for demanding that their favorite stars personally address them from the stage during bows, so she complied. But frankly, she did not enjoy doing the show, and neither did her brothers. Not long after the tour left Philadelphia, both of them left the company. Jack joined the cast of another show that was about to tour Australia, and Lionel gave up acting for a while, to finally fulfill his dream of living as an artist in Paris. In April, Ethel developed a case of appendicitis in Boston, and without her presence the rest of the tour was canceled. The visit to the city of their birth had been the last real hurrah for the production.

One might argue, of course, that the Barrymores were *not* Philadelphians, not really. Their father's legal name was either "Blyth" or "'Blythe" (you can find it spelled both ways in records). As a young man, he had slipped away from the legal career his wealthy and respectable parents had in mind for him and impulsively "gone on the stage" at the urging of some friends. Some said he had casually selected the Irish name "Barrymore" from an old theater poster hanging on the wall of London's Haymarket Theatre, though it is worth noting he had used the name even before that, when competing as a successful amateur boxer. He was still using "Barrymore" when he went to New York to join Augustine Daly's troupe—but he was "Mr. Blythe" when his fellow company member, John Drew Jr., brought him home to Philadelphia to meet his delightful and beautiful sister. When Georgiana Drew married him, she too became a Blythe at home, but only used "Barrymore" professionally. (Confusingly, her children Lionel and Ethel had "Barrymore" written on their birth certificates, but John had "Blythe" on his.) Still, legally speaking, "Blythe" was the three siblings' last name the whole time. And when Georgie's body came back east to be interred at the Drew family plot in Mt. Vernon Cemetery, her headstone had "Blythe" carved on it, not Barrymore. It was only when they all eventually went on the stage themselves (however reluctantly) that they used the family professional name "Barrymore." But they never lived in Philadelphia under that name.

So, the *Drews* were most definitely a Philadelphia family—and maybe even the *Blythes*—but not the *Barrymores*. Interestingly, Ethel Barrymore thought both sides of her family were never "true Philadelphians." She knew that her Drew grandparents—wandering actors for most of their lives—had only settled in the Quaker City in the 1850s. "It took far more than three generations to become an old family in Philadelphia, although that appears to be plenty long enough in most other cities." She associated Philadelphia mostly with her beloved grandmother. But she wasn't particularly sentimental about her birthplace—that isn't what either the Blythes or the Drews did, after all.

> It is strange to think of the difference in behavior of my father, coming from the sort of family he did, and the family into which he married. He was, of course, intensely emotional and what is now called uninhibited. So, in a way, are we. But such is the powerful and lingering influence of my grandmother, our deepest feelings are never to be disclosed. They are our own private affairs, never to be paraded in public. Strong emotions—either sad or glad—may be hurled with gusto at an audience, with the footlights in between—and then we are not ourselves, but an author's invention that we leave at the stage door, like the key of our dressing room.

Ethel respected, rather than liked, the city of her birth. "Philadelphia has always seemed to me to have an atmosphere of greatness, perhaps because of Benjamin Franklin and the Continental Congress and the Declaration of Independence. And Philadelphia people always gave one the impression of permanence, of having been there a long time." And deep down she knew that the Barrymores only existed, so to speak, when they performed.

Imogene Coca in Manayunk

December 14, 1919: There was going to be a show that Sunday at the Empress Theatre on Main Street in Manayunk—the industrial neighborhood on the steep hillsides above the Schuylkill River in Northwest Philadelphia. Reverend William B. Forney—a local minister and an ardent Sabbatarian—wanted it shut down.

Coca had been born in 1908 in West Philadelphia and given the name "Emogeane." Her dad was Jose Fernandez ("Joe") de Coca, a local violinist and orchestra conductor. During those days Joe Coca often could be seen leading the bands at the old Forrest Theatre on Broad Street or in various Keith Vaudeville Circuit houses around town. Her mom, Sadie Brady, was a former burlesque dancer and "magician's assistant." It was perhaps inevitable that their daughter (whose odd name was eventually simplified) would go on stage too. All her mom's four sisters were also in showbiz, and they were all married to actors.

Through some family connection, little Imogene was booked to sing a song for the American Legion meeting, along with other vaudeville performers. But would she get her break? What about those blue-nosed Sabbatarians? To the eternal credit of the Legionnaires, the objections of the ministers were brushed aside. "Dr. Forney is a chronic crank who has been telling us how to paint our houses, clean our streets, and keep our milk bottles in the morning," declared J. J. Foran, the local post commander. Manayunk was a rough working-class neighborhood back in those days, and many years later she could still remember that some people were setting off firecrackers in the aisles during her act. But the show went on, and everybody had a fine time, and little Imogene had gotten her first taste of showbiz success at the Empress Theatre.

The family moved around—sometimes they lived in Atlantic City, when there was work to be found there—and little Imogene didn't get much formal schooling. She did get piano and dance lessons, and she sang a lot. The elfin girl with the prominent eyes and big voice made up her own comic plays on subjects such as "Safety First" or "The Evils of Nicotine" or the thoughts of a tree ("Please don't hurt me—I'm a tree"). In 1926, she got her photograph in papers when she took her cat "Lady Luck" to the annual show of the Quaker City Persian Society.

One of her aunts would take Imogene off to New York, and persuaded the producer Sam Harris to put her in the chorus of a show called *When You Smile*. In 1930 she was featured in a topical revue called *The Garrick Gaieties*. By 1936 Imogene Coca was back in her hometown, a featured comedienne in the tour of another revue. This one was called *New Faces of 1936*. It had run for seven months on Broadway, and now was coming down to Philadelphia's new Forrest Theatre on Walnut Street. Coca was in many of the skits, and she had one great bit in particular—as an incompetent burlesque dancer, she would attempt to do a strip tease, but consistently fail to actually remove any item of her clothing. After a great deal of hilarious struggle, by then the end of the act, only a single glove would finally come off—to her amazement and pleasure and to the audience's sustained laughter. One Philadelphia reviewer went into a gleeful rapture about her: "You never heard of her? Well you will from now on, for pint-sized piquant Imogene can do anything."

That's where another local crank comes into the story—only this local crank was also the mayor of Philadelphia, a crusading political maverick named S. Davis Wilson. He liked to call himself "The People's Mayor." He was there on the opening night of *New Faces of 1936*, laughing along with everyone else at Coca's antics. But then, in the second half, a skit by two other comediennes about two First Ladies (Mrs. Lou Hoover and Mrs. Eleanor Roosevelt) instructing a Girl Scout troop in the birds and the bees, got Wilson into one of his theatrical tizzies. He stormed up the aisle and confronted Lawrence Shubert Lawrence, the manager of the Forrest. "It's a damned outrage to poke fun at the President's wife! Either the skit goes, or the show goes!" And despite Lawrence's weak protests, it was the skit that went.

Fortunately, none of Coca's numbers, even the fake "strip tease" bit, had bothered Mayor Wilson that night. But then, the "pint-sized piquant" could do anything, and not even Philadelphia's well-known propensity for censoriousness was going to keep her down. She was soon back in New York, and by the 1950s she could be regularly seen on Philadelphians' TV screens, one of the featured players on Sid Caesar's *Your Show of Shows*.

A hundred years later, the Empress Theatre is still standing in Manayunk—though not as a performance venue. It is currently owned and occupied by the Loring Building Products company. A concrete loading dock had been poured at the back of the old lobby, and inventory shelves and stacks of construction materials are stored all over the former audience seating area. As of this writing, two plaster ornamental cupids stand still guard at the peak of the proscenium arch, and a large moldering curtain still hangs across the stage where little Imogene once sang her song.

One of the Kelly Boys

May 4, 1926: George Edward Kelly won the Pulitzer Prize for Drama. The decision of the three-member committee was unanimous. "*Craig's Wife*, Broadway Success, Written by Philadelphian, Declared Best in 1925" was the headline on the *Inquirer*'s front page.

The paper had evidently gotten an early tip-off from somebody about the award to a local playwright, and they quickly tracked him down. George Kelly usually stayed in New York, but the paper's editors discovered that he was currently visiting his family home on Midvale Avenue in the East Falls neighborhood. They quickly dispatched a man to get a quote. But when the reporter knocked on the front door and told George the happy news, the playwright merely uttered a non-committal "that's nice." "Mrs. Kelly, mother of a rather remarkable trio, was a bit more thrilled, but not much," wrote the reporter, despite his lack of success in securing a vivid quote. So, the newsman made the best of the situation, writing: "He accepted the glory quietly and modestly ... that's typical of the Kelly boys."

Not that the "Kelly boys" needed to be modest; they had plenty to be proud about. George was the ninth of 10 children in the Kelly family. His older brother John B. ("Jack") Kelly was an Olympic rower, businessman, and local politician. His brother Patrick was the builder who was constructing the Free Library on Logan Circle. Brother Charles had made a fortune selling bricks. His oldest brother, Walter Kelly, was a successful vaudevillian, known especially for his character "The Virginia Judge."

George, for his part, had initially trained as a draftsman in the family construction business, but then he also moved into the theater world. But the solo act that Walter was famous for—a racist monologue in which he would perform all of the voices of a Southern courtroom, in which a variety of stereotypically shiftless Black defendants were being summarily dispatched to prison—did not appeal to George. Nor did the constant travel and rough bonhomie of the vaudeville business really suit him.

Being somewhat shy and fastidious by nature, George soon turned to writing rather than performing, churning out vaudeville sketches and comic one-acts. His first successful full-length play was *The Torch-bearers* (1922), which skewered the pretensions of wealthy amateur little theater groups in Philadelphia. The play was based heavily, one suspects, on Beulah E. Jay and her Rittenhouse Square set. He then found real success on Broadway with *The Show-Off* (1924), about a struggling North Philadelphia family whose daughter is courted by an overbearing buffoon named Aubrey Piper (in the end, Aubrey saves the family fortunes, much to everyone's amazement—except his own). Kelly directed the play himself with his usual meticulousness, giving the leading actors Louis John Bartels and Helen Lowell precise and vivid line readings, which seemed to amuse the actors rather than annoy them. Sometimes the actors would deliberately fluff their speeches, just to watch Kelly come on stage and perform them exactly in the manner he wanted.

In 1925, the Pulitzer jury reportedly wanted to give the 1924 prize to *The Show-Off*, but Columbia University overruled them and steered the honor to *Hell-Bent Fer Heaven*, a comedy written by Columbia professor Hatcher Hughes. It's possible that the award to *Craig's Wife* was meant to atone for the previous year's blatant favoritism. (Similarly, the 1926 Pulitzer for an American Novel went to Sinclair Lewis' *Arrowsmith*, when it was widely thought he should have won for his earlier book, *Main Street*.)

Like *The Show-Off*, Kelly's *Craig's Wife* was also satiric, but a more serious play—a theatrical portrait of a possessive and materialistic woman. In the words of one reviewer, Mrs. Craig "allows no speck to tarnish the polished surface of her furniture, hates roses because the petals fall and litter the floor, irks the servants on the ground that they do their work less meticulously than she would do it, [and] worships her home, making it her god." Eventually, she ends up destroying her own marriage. Like *The Show-Off*, it had also been a box office hit, opening in October 1925 at the Morosco Theatre, and running for a solid year. (It would eventually be made into three different motion picture adaptations.) George would write many more Broadway plays—including *Maggie the Magnificent*, which was not a hit, but it did feature a couple of young actors named James Cagney and Joan Blondell when its touring company arrived at the Walnut Street Theatre in late 1929.

All the rest of his life, however, George Kelly did not spend much time in Philadelphia. After winning the prestigious prize, he preferred to stay at his apartment in New York or his house in California. But though the outgoing and gregarious John would run for public office and become a local celebrity, George became known as a bit of an artistically and politically conservative curmudgeon as well as being a social recluse with a trunk full of un-produced and unpublished work. He felt left behind by current theater trends. and resented the influence of left-leaning playwrights like Clifford Odetts and Arthur Miller. He was suspicious of Jews, labor unions, and Franklin Roosevelt's New Deal—though he did allow the WPA Federal Theatre

Project to produce his plays. Sad to say, he was also mostly estranged from his family, who could never deal with his homosexuality or his long-term relationship with his partner William Weagley. To explain his lifelong bachelor status, the Kellys—who like many others of their time and class, were intensely uncomfortable with even the idea of homosexuality—usually said something vague about how "he never got over being rejected by Tallulah Bankhead," and they left it at that. Weagley was often referred to as "his valet."

His niece Grace, John's daughter, would become the most famous of all the Kellys, far eclipsing any of her aunts and uncles. As she made her way into local amateur theater groups in Philadelphia, he was the only one to really take her aspirations to be an actress seriously and encouraged his brother to allow her to do more plays. When her career exploded into worldwide movie stardom, she always treasured his visits and advice about choice of roles and approach to her film characters. He only regretted, he once said with a twinkle, that she hadn't stuck with her stage career. "We would have seen some very fine performances from her."

George died at Bryn Mawr Hospital in the Philadelphia suburbs in June 1974 at the age of 87, the last of his generation of "remarkable Kellys." According to his biographer Donald Spoto, the remaining members of the family did not invite Weagley to the funeral; he had to slip into the back of the church to say goodbye. As he was not part of the cortege, he also could not follow the hearse to see him buried at Westminster Cemetery in Bala Cynwyd. Unfortunately, Princess Grace of Monaco—as she now had become—was not there. If she had been, one hopes she would have spoken up and demanded acceptance and respect.

"To me, he was the most wonderful person," she once said of her Uncle George. "I could sit and listen to him for hours. He introduced me to all kinds of things I never would have been exposed to—classic literature, poetry and great plays. He loved beautiful things and refined language, and these he shared with me in ways I never forgot."

And then, revealingly, Grace remembered that there were occasional conflicts among the Kelly boys: "He was also one of the few people who stood up to my father, disagreed with him, contradicted him. I thought Uncle George was fearless."

They All Want Something from Big Bill Tilden

June 20, 1926: Bill Tilden won two titles in the Middle States tennis tournament at the Philadelphia Cricket Club that Sunday. First, he defeated Manuel Alonso (a formidable Spanish Davis Cup player) for the singles title. Then, he and his partner Sandy Weiner grabbed the doubles title too, playing against Wallace Johnson and Stanley Pearson.

There was no doubt that Tilden was in his usual championship form at Middle States, reported the *Boston Globe*: "His cannonball service scoring needed points at crucial times and his placing and lobbing being of the highest type." Tilden showed no signs of losing his touch at any point in his hard-fought match against Alonso, even though earlier in the day he'd played the semifinals against Johnson. Earlier in the week he had raced through the preliminary rounds, too, hardly losing a set against any opponent he faced.

The local crowds were thrilled to see the famous wizard of the court play. Indeed, the entire tournament schedule had been adjusted to accommodate Tilden, because the organizers knew that on most evenings—and on Wednesday and Saturday afternoons as well—he was required on stage at the Walnut Street Theatre. "Big Bill Tilden" was starring in the new comedy *They All Want Something*.

The production had started its tryout tour in Hartford, earlier that same month. Again, Tilden had balanced his evening spent on the stage with days on the tennis court—this time at the Connecticut State Championships. Admittedly, a bit distracted by rehearsals, Big Bill had lost that final against an opponent he could have easily beaten in normal circumstances. But he didn't seem to care. Tilden was determined to take *They All Want Something* all the way to Broadway, even if it meant missing major summer tournaments.

The play, one of those "Rich Guy Pretends to be Poor" stories that were so popular in the '20s and '30s, was written by his friend Courtenay Savage, adapted from a minor popular novel. Tilden was evidently backing the show with money he had earned from all his many tennis prizes, and he had cast many of his friends in it, including his favorite child actor, "Little Bill" Quinn.

In the script Tilden's character, Wade Rawlins, is the son of a wealthy auto manufacturer, who is enamored of a young lady—but she's engaged to someone else. So, he becomes a wandering hobo in order to play on the well-known charitable sympathies of the girl's mother—and in the manner of such plots, he succeeds in getting invited into the house. Soon he is employed as the family's chauffeur, and later even consents to filling in for a missing Guest of Honor at a costume ball (at one point, somebody asks him "do you play tennis?"—which reliably got the biggest laugh of the show). Eventually Wade's true identity is revealed, and he saves the girl from eloping with the wrong guy, and instead carries her off himself.

Though no one ever was very much convinced by his work in the play's love scenes, by some accounts Tilden did at least a moderately respectable job as a thespian. By other folks' estimation, he was simply a terrible actor. He was one of those types who tended to learn *all* the parts in a play, and he had developed the classic bad habit of silently mouthing the other actors' lines as they spoke. But Tilden didn't care what people thought. He was having a marvelous time.

After the local critics had seen the show at the Walnut that June, most of the show's newspaper reviews were composed in a highly, well, *reserved* vein. "Philadelphia theatre goers can look forward to at least several weeks of good entertainment," wrote the *Camden Courier-Post*, calling it "a comedy without intellectual pretensions … yet providing several hours of amusing entertainment." The *Philadelphia Record* was similarly noncommittal ("The audience found enjoyment in the play"), as was the *Sun* ("an unusually competent cast"), and the *Evening Ledger* ("highly diverting").

Perhaps this reticence was due to an understandable deference Philadelphians wanted to give to a local hero. After all, William Tatem Tilden, Jr. *was* a Philadelphian, the son of a wealthy and socially prominent merchant, William Tatem Tilden, Sr.

Bill Tilden had grown up in the Germantown neighborhood of northwest Philadelphia, and he went to the prestigious prep school Germantown Academy. After his mother's early death, he had moved in with his aunt, and had enrolled at the University of Pennsylvania, supposedly to get a business degree—but he had dropped out during his senior year to work on his tennis game. As a teenager, nobody had ever spotted him as a championship-caliber athlete, but his game suddenly bloomed. He seemed almost to *will* himself into greatness.

But unlike other athletes, he had artistic passions. He loved music and would spend hours in his room listening to records. When he was just 15, he even dared to knock on the dressing room door of soprano Mary Garden at Hammerstein's Opera House on North Broad Street, before a performance of Charpentier's *Louise*. He startled her by saying, "I don't think you sing, Miss Garden, I think you seem to vocalize thought." This observation deeply impressed the great diva, and thereafter they became devoted lifelong friends.

Tilden's other great love was theater, which he had first discovered at the age of 10 at an Adirondacks summer camp, where he was in a play coached by the actress Maude Adams. As he grew older, he loved to be told that he resembled the actor Alfred Lunt, and in November 1923 he even played the title role in the Booth Tarkington comedy *Clarence* (which Lunt had once starred in) at the newly founded Hedgerow Theatre in the suburban enclave of Rose Valley, PA. Evidently Bill had quietly been taking acting lessons at Hedgerow with Sydney Machet, a young leading actor of the company.

As an adult, Tilden had dropped the "Jr." from his name, because he disliked his childhood nickname "June"—from now on, he declared, he would be "William Tilden II." A late bloomer, his complete mastery of tennis did not come until he was 26, but for the next 10 years he dominated the men's game, and he was almost unbeatable. He was playing at a higher level than everyone else in the world, it seemed. Maybe only Mary Garden knew the real reason. "You're a tennis artist," she once told him, "And artists always know better than anyone else when they're right. If you believe in a certain way to play, you play that way no matter what anyone else tells you. Once you lose your faith in your artistic judgment, you're lost. Win or lose, right or wrong, be true to your art." It was a credo that had taken her own career to the greatest heights, and Tilden hewed to it himself, in many areas of his life.

Handsome, lanky, and graceful, Tilden was enormously popular, one of the biggest American sports stars of the 1920s. Even his barely concealed homosexuality did not seriously hinder his fame. He was prone to what sportswriters called "theatrical gestures" during matches. Sometimes he would step onto the court with four tennis balls in his hand, hit three consecutive aces against his befuddled opponent, and then ostentatiously toss the fourth ball away. Other times he would mirror the game of his opponent, imitating their style of play, just to show the fans that he could win any way he wanted. "The player owes the gallery as much as the actor owes the audience," he would say.

In fact, he loved everything about the world of the theater. When he was in New York City he lived at the Algonquin Hotel. There he hobnobbed with the Round Table set, and went to Broadway shows, and was always an easy touch for producers who needed another backer. He made his Broadway debut in a show called *Don Q. Jr.*, which he had, of course, invested in even though it was clear he would never get his money back. Tilden lost a lot of money that way. Eventually, a large part of his tennis winnings would go down the drain in various failed Broadway productions.

That was still ahead of him, of course, and during the rather sad and sordid final period of his life he would no longer have to *pretend* to be poor. Back in that exciting summer of 1926, however, Big Bill was still riding high. The tennis champion didn't even care if being in *They All Want Something* jeopardized his participation in the upcoming Davis Cup and the national singles tournaments that he usually dominated. He began to get interested in acting in movies, and as he continued to tour with his play that summer, he notified the United States Lawn Tennis Association that they would have to accommodate his schedule.

"If I am wanted for the challenge round of the Davis Cup at Philadelphia, I will play with the understanding that I must commute back and forth daily in order to be [in New York] for the evening performance of my show." He could manage the subsequent U.S. Open in August more easily, he figured, since that was in Forrest Hills, Queens—an easy commute to Broadway.

That breezy confidence which had taken him so far in life turned out to be misplaced. For the first time in years, he lost the singles title in the U.S. Open. And in September, he lost in the Davis Cup finals to his great rival Rene Lacoste, in front of a crowd of 2,000 people in Philadelphia.

And when *They All Want Something* opened at Wallack's Theatre in October, it ran for just a few weeks. "He strikes a good many poses and manages to play about half his scenes directly to the audience, enacting the role with none of the vitality he shows on the courts," an exasperated *New York Times* critic wrote. The show closed, taking a lot of Big Bill's money with it.

Tilden's tennis career would thrive for quite a few more years, and he would never lose that breezy confidence. He even thought he could act as his own lawyer, when he was brought up on charges in Los Angeles of "corrupting the morals of a minor"—an Oscar Wilde-like maneuver that also failed to save him from harsh legal consequences. He would die suddenly of a heart attack at the age of 60.

In almost every poll of sportswriters, Bill Tilden was regarded as the greatest tennis player of his era—perhaps of the entire 20th century. But he could not *will* himself into greatness in the theater, as he could on the court. That sort of thing really only works in plays.

"The Girl Who Falls Down"

December 31, 1917: Joan McCracken was born to Mary and Frank McCracken. Her father was a well-known and highly popular sports reporter for the *Philadelphia Daily Ledger*, and the family lived in West Philadelphia—first in a small house on Farragut Terrace, and later a better one on 616 S. 54th Street. Her mother's three sisters all married local sports reporters, too, and the family could always count on getting waved into almost every sports venue—and theater—in the city.

Always bursting with athletic energy, Joan was in dance classes at an early age. She was fortunate to be growing up during a time when Philadelphia had dance instructors all over town, and its many theaters were filled with dance shows. Classes in tap, vaudeville acrobatics, and character dancing were plentiful. At age 14, Joan was already wowing the crowds with exhibitions of acrobatics and "athletic dancing" at YMCA shows. Philadelphia had a deep tradition in ballet, too—more so than New York, really—and it was in ballet class that Joan really found her passion. Key to her development was her studies with the remarkable local dance teacher and choreographer Catherine Littlefield.

Along with several other Littlefield dancers, Joan left West Philadelphia High School and moved to New York. They had been invited to study with George Balanchine himself at the new American Academy of Ballet. She loved her time there and hoped to move up into the regular company. But like several other female dancers whose bodies did not possess the willowy long lines Balanchine preferred, the short, sturdy, and muscular McCracken was not selected. So instead, she returned home to work again with the Littlefield ballet company—soon to be re-christened "The Philadelphia Ballet." And though this new Littlefield company was run strictly on an egalitarian "no stars" policy, somehow it was always Joan's photo that was the one chosen to be featured in the papers (her dad's connections might have had something to do with that).

Most excitingly, Joan and 60 other dancers—almost all of them native Philadelphians—went off on an extensive successful European tour with the company. In London, the British ballet writer Arnold Haskell took particular notice of "a child, Joan McCracken, whose joy in her work was moving and typical of the whole troupe." Over the next two years the Philadelphia Ballet often had long engagements in Chicago, where she again became an audience favorite.

But around that same time, Joan was diagnosed with Type 1 diabetes. It was a serious, life-threatening illness, and she would always struggle to keep her chronic condition to herself, fearing it would damage her career. Fortunately, her closest friends learned to help her find quiet places to do her insulin injections, and they would also learn to carry sugar cubes, oranges, and chocolate in their purses to help Joan, in case her glucose levels suddenly dipped. There were several alarming close calls—once she violently collapsed in the dressing room while putting on her makeup, and only the immediate help of the other girls in the room saved her. Her father's sudden death from a heart attack, in August 1937, also was a horrible blow.

But Joan had recently fallen in love with another dancer in the Littlefield ballet company, Jack Dunphy. Like her, he was a Philly kid, and after two years of dating and working together, in 1939 they finally eloped and moved to New York. It was the perfect time for this step up, as a new breed of American choreographer was looking for dancers with real skills and deep training. Joan, now a mature and highly experienced performer, was soon cast in an exciting new Broadway project by the composer and lyricist team of Rodgers and Hammerstein—Jack got a job in the ensemble, too. The choreographer was Agnes DeMille.

This project, it turned out, was a musical adaptation of the hit play *Green Grow the Lilacs*, originally entitled *Away We Go!* (Eventually, the authors kept the exclamation point but renamed it *Oklahoma!*) The diminutive but exceptionally talented McCracken became a featured member of the dance ensemble. Indeed, Agnes DeMille's innovative and expressive choreography proved to be a perfect outlet for a dancer with McCracken's talents. The repeated comic pratfall DeMille gave her in the number "Many a New Day" drew praise from everyone. Reviewers and audience members who were unable to single out her character's name (Sylvie) in the cast list, usually just called her "The Girl Who Falls Down."

Oklahoma! was the first of many Broadway shows for McCracken, who found that she could explore her talents in acting as well. Many of these shows had tryout runs in Philadelphia before opening in New York. In September 1944, for instance, Joan was at the Forrest Theatre, in a tryout run of *Bloomer Girl*, a new musical about early American feminism, starring Celeste Holm. The *Inquirer*'s drama critic Linton Martin hailed McCracken as a "comedienne of whom this city may justly be proud." In fact, whatever show (like *Billion Dollar Baby*) or movie (like *Good News*) she was appearing in, just as they had always done, local papers ran a photo of Joan, proudly identifying her as a Philly girl.

Known in showbiz circles for being uninhibited and impulsive, her singing voice was loud but rather unsubtle—which perhaps kept her from securing leading roles in musical comedies. But McCracken was determined to develop her abilities and be more than a barnstorming musical theater comedienne. She took acting as seriously as she did dance, and was an early member of the Actors Studio when it was founded in the late 1940s. Impressively, she was soon appearing in such significant Broadway dramas as Charles Laughton's *Galileo*, and *The Big Knife* by Clifford Odets. In what may have been her favorite role ever—so close to her own tomboy personality—she also appeared as Peter Pan in a 1951 Broadway revival of the original J. M. Barrie play.

But as far as her personal life was concerned, well, it often fell down, too. Joan's marriage to Dunphy failed over his infidelities, mostly with other men. (They stayed close friends, however, even after he entered into a committed relationship with the writer Truman Capote.) Her second marriage, to an ambitious dancer and choreographer from the Midwest (a guy whom the Philadelphia papers originally identified as "Robert Foss") went well enough at first, but was also doomed not to last. Even though it was McCracken's recommendation that had gotten Bob Fosse his first big break as a choreographer (for *Pajama Game*), eventually he would wander and leave her too, once he had met his muse (and next wife) Gwen Verdon. But many people—including Verdon—noticed that in Fosse's 1979 film *All That Jazz*, the character of Death, played by Jessica Lange, had a very specific costume. As McCracken's biographer Lisa Jo Sagolla points out, it was identical to the one that Joan had worn in her final professional appearance on stage in 1958, an off-Broadway play called *The Infernal Machine*.

After that last show, the disabling side-effects of her diabetes largely kept her from working, and she understood her own time on earth was likely drawing to an end. Moving to Long Island with her partner, Marc Adams, she made a will, dividing her money between Dunphy, Adams, and her mother. On November 1, 1961, Joan McCracken died in her sleep of a heart attack. Despite her well-known recent health problems, many people were shocked and dismayed at her sudden passing. Some, however, recalled that her father had been felled by the same cause, and at almost the same age. Though the headlines on newspaper obituaries all identified her as being 38, she was in fact 43.

Molly Gets Married

Molly Picon was born in New York in 1898, but when her father proved to be a terrible provider, her mother went back to Philadelphia. They moved back in with her mother's family, the Ostrovskys, who lived on tiny Orianna Street in the Jewish neighborhood along the east end of South Street. Delightfully, for our purposes, this was quite close to where the Old Theatre had once stood, and where both John Durang and Edwin Forrest had lived and first gone on the stage. In the close-packed neighborhood a deep history of popular live entertainment evidently lingered. In fact, the family apartment was just around the block from a hall on S. 3rd Street where a Yiddish-language theater company performed. It was run by Mike Thomashefsky, the brother of the famous Boris Thomashefsky. Her mother got work helping the actresses with their costumes. So, Molly and her sister Helen got used to actors and other show folk coming around.

She had even learned a whole routine of songs and dances from Mamie, a teenage girl who looked after her when Mama was busy sewing. The actress Fanny Thomashefsky, Mike's wife, came by to pick up her costume one day, saw Molly dancing, and said she had promise. Why not try the Saturday night amateur hour at the Bijou, a vaudeville house up on N. 8th Street? The audience always loved to see talented kids there, Fanny assured them. Money was tight, so she and Mama set off to give it a shot. While riding the trolley on the way to the contest, a drunk asked her mother why her kid was "all dressed up like Mrs. Astor's horse." Molly, as she would be for the rest of her life, was up to the challenge:

> In my tiny child's voice, I said, "I'm an actor, and I'm going to sing in the Bijou Theater and win the first prize, a gold dollar piece." And he said, "She's gonna sing? You can't sing!" And Mama said, "Molly, show him." So I got up in the car and did my whole act that Mamie had put together for me. Then the drunk took off his derby and passed it around to the people in the car and collected two dollars in coins, which he gave to me. So I consider that my first professional performance.

When they got to the Bijou, she won the contest. People threw cash on the stage as she took her bows, and she came home and plunked all the money down on the kitchen table in front of Grandma Ostrovsky, who nearly fainted.

In 1907 the Thomashefsky brothers took over management of the old Arch Street Theatre. All the big stars of the day, including the Adlers and the Kesslers, came to perform there. Whenever somebody needed a little girl for their show, they knew they could always count on her. "I watched and I learned and imitated the greats of our theater, and for the first time I began to feel that I wanted to be an actress." And she did, all 4 feet 11 inches of her. She left William Penn High School to join an all-girl vaudeville group called "The Four Seasons." In the act she sang and danced and played the ukulele. They did pretty well, but in the fall of 1918, she found herself out of work, and stranded in Boston. All the vaudeville houses were closed because of the Great Flu Epidemic. Only one group was performing, a traveling Yiddish theater group whose cast included a young Paul Muni (then Muni Weisenfreund) and Menashe Skulnik.

The troupe needed a soubrette, and its manager, a serious and attractive young man named Jacob Kalich, had once seen her perform in Philadelphia. He liked her, so he hired her. He made her laugh, he didn't try to get too fresh with her, and she liked calling him by his Yiddish name, "Yonkel." Molly and Yonkel ended up getting married the next year—in Philadelphia ("because who gets married in Boston?" as she explained in her memoirs)—after he paid the required two dollars for a marriage license at City Hall. They were to spend the next 66 years together.

With Yonkel managing her career, Molly Picon became the unmatched star of the Yiddish stage. At one point there were two theaters in New York named after her. Hundreds of Jewish parents named their daughters "Molly" in her honor. She and Kalich had no children of their own, but over the years they fostered and raised half a dozen kids who needed a home.

She also regularly returned to Philadelphia. In May 1927, for example, she was at the Arch Street Theatre again, this time in the play *Mameleh*. In 1938, she was at the Walnut Street Theatre in the operetta *My Malkele* with Aaron Lebedeff. In 1950, she did *Abi Gezunt* at the Shubert. In 1957, she was back for a week at the Walnut, this time in a show with Jacob—"the American-Yiddish musical comedy" titled *Farblonget Honeymoon*. Some of the shows she did were wonderful—like Jerry Herman's *Milk and Honey*, whose national tour started in Philadelphia. Some, like Mitch Leigh's *Chu Chem*, were—well, meh. But even after that last debacle, Molly Picon soon came back to Philadelphia. The very next fall she was at the Locust's Street Theatre appearing in a pre-Broadway run of *How to Be a Jewish Mother*, a two-hander with the African American actor Godfrey Cambridge. It was all part of a life in show business. "Basically," she said in an interview, "theater is still the same. The same emotions get to an audience. Perhaps plays were a little more melodramatic then, now they're more sophisticated. And productions are more expensively mounted today … But these are the only changes I see."

In the 1970s she and Jacob were invited to be guests on the popular syndicated daytime TV program *The Mike Douglas Show*, which was taped in Philadelphia. On the way to the studio on Walnut Street, the couple drove past the enormous bulk of Philadelphia's City Hall, which was now surrounded by even more enormous modernist office towers. They remembered their wedding, and suddenly realized how much had changed from the days of their youth.

"When we got our license, there had been no skyscrapers, no giant office complexes or luxury hotels. Yonkel looked up at all the new buildings and said, 'My God Molly—look what they did with my two dollars!'"

Charles Fuller's Inspirations

In January 1982 Charles Fuller, Jr.'s career as a playwright was finally taking off. His latest work, *A Soldier's Play*, was one of the hottest Off-Broadway hits, in an extended-run production by the Negro Ensemble Company. (It turned out to be an important turning point in several other careers as well. In the play's cast, which starred Adolph Caesar as tyrannical and conflicted Sgt. Vernon Waters, were Denzel Washington and Samuel L. Jackson, playing two members of the oppressed and doomed all-Black U.S. Army unit.) There was a real chance it would be a major motion picture soon.

"I am really going through the roof," admitted Fuller happily to the theater reporter Nels Nelson in the *Philadelphia Daily News*. But it wasn't just his own success that was bringing him understandable satisfaction. "I am very, very pleased about it because this play was done for reasons no other play of mine was ever done. Every time it's performed it's a reflection of my friend."

The friend Fuller was thinking of was Larry Neal, a companion from his youth in the Strawberry Mansion neighborhood in North Philadelphia. Neal was a poet, a professor, and a leader in the Black Arts Movement during the 1960s and 1970s. He had suddenly and unexpectedly died of a heart attack almost exactly a year previously, at the age of 44.

Fuller had not only dedicated *A Soldier's Play* to his late friend but had put him directly into it. The character of Captain Richard Davenport (the Black army officer who investigates the murder mystery at the heart of the play's plot) was really a personification of Neal, Fuller admitted. He had endowed Davenport with all of Neal's character traits—his intelligence, persistence, and strong moral core.

Fuller felt deeply that he owed Larry Neal almost everything that had gone well with his life:

> If it weren't for him, I don't think I'd have been a writer. He was the first person I ever knew who read literary classics. He introduced me to Kafka. He suggested I read Hemingway. He brought James Baldwin to me—he'd gone into a drugstore and seen Baldwin's photo in a book; he'd never seen a black face on a book before. It was a very exciting moment.

Born in 1939, Fuller spent the earliest years of his life in the Hawthorne neighborhood near 10th and Lombard Streets, until his family moved to the newly opened public housing project, the James Weldon Johnson Homes, along Ridge Avenue. He soon met Neal, who lived just four doors away, and the two bonded almost immediately. They were inseparable friends throughout their years at St. Elizabeth's parochial school and Roman Catholic High, where they both graduated in 1956. They had even had a friendly competition, to see who could first accomplish the feat of reading every book in the school library. Fuller recalled, "You went upstairs in the place, and there was a sort of balcony at the top, and what we tried to do was read our way around it. Though we never got through the whole thing." Still, though the two of them had no particular interest in sports, this reading campaign gave them a certain status among their peers. "We let everybody know about it. You know, the way teenagers do."

He was also a member of a Philadelphia street gang, but Fuller never regarded that as a particularly important aspect of his adolescence. "In those days North Philadelphia was the gangland capital of the world," he had stated in an earlier interview. "It was necessary." But he was not from a broken home, he wanted to stress. "My parents loved me. I was always well taken care of. We weren't rich, but we weren't poor."

But what about theater? That was a different story, and not something either Neal or his parents had ever introduced him to. His very first exposure to live theater, he remembered, was a show he saw as a teenager, when a tryout musical coming through town had sent some free tickets to his school. Though he couldn't quite remember the title, he knew it was at the Walnut Street Theatre, and it starred Molly Picon. To his surprise, the dialogue and the lyrics were all in Yiddish, so naturally he hadn't understood a word of it. But in another way of speaking, he totally got everything. It was a completely wonderful and enjoyable experience—and it sparked a notion that he wanted to become a playwright.

Fuller attended Villanova, a Catholic university out in the suburbs, for a couple of years, commuting back and forth from Philadelphia. After a stint in the Army and study at another local Catholic school—La Salle, in North Philadelphia—Fuller founded the Afro-American Arts Theatre. It was exactly the sort of thing that he and Larry Neal had talked about doing (and to reassure his parents about his financial stability, all this was done while also holding down a day job as a city building inspector). The theater group staged Fuller's first plays and produced local radio and TV dramas featuring his work. Fuller's breakthrough as a playwright came in

1968, when the McCarter Theatre in Princeton staged his *The Village: A Party*—an absurdist drama about a building that houses only inter-racial married couples. Moving to New York, he had several other plays and screenplays produced by the Negro Ensemble Company, including *The Brownsville Raid* and *Zooman and the Sign*. He got married and had kids, and he came back to Philadelphia to a small house in the Northeast section of town. Things were really looking up. "It's ten times easier to work now than it was when I was worrying about the rent and where the food was coming from," he admitted to Nelson.

And then, in 1981, Larry Neal died. After almost four decades of friendship, the loss was painful to Charles Fuller. He found a way to pay tribute to his memory.

> Putting him in the play was my only way of saying thank you. "Richard Davenport" was a character in a play that Larry wrote. So I took him and made him Larry Neal. I put him on the stage and allowed him to do what Larry did best—figuring out things, coming to some kind of conclusion. I have stayed with this play every day because I really wanted it to work exactly the way I saw it, the way it was on the page. And it has come out that way.

Later, in 1982, Fuller's *A Soldier's Play* was awarded the Pulitzer Prize for Drama. Unfortunately, Larry Neal was no longer around to witness his old pal's much-deserved success. But of course, in another sense, he was right there, just like always.

But I'd like to revisit one point in Fuller's story—that Yiddish play that he saw back when he was young. From his description, this can only have been a production of the little-known musical *Farblonjet Honeymoon* (the first half of the title means "mixed up" or "crazy"). This show, written by M. Kalmanowich, had just had a two-year run in Brooklyn (albeit under different spelling of the title). As part of a national tour, it came down for a weeklong run at the Walnut in October 1957, and it did indeed star Molly Picon. It seems the show's producers needed to fill out the audience, so they must have sent some free tickets to Villanova, where Fuller was then a freshman.

According to the local reviewers in the Philly papers, Picon—playing the servant of a widower whom she hoped to nab for herself—was her usual irrepressible and delightful self on stage. Charles Fuller remembered her performance his whole life—he still cited it in interviews shortly before his own passing in 2022. That a future winner of the Pulitzer Prize for Drama from Philadelphia was originally inspired by the performance of another Philadelphian of a much earlier generation, who was performing in a language he did not even speak, depicting a world about as far away from his life as one can imagine—well, it just makes me so happy. Of all the unexpected discoveries I've made digging through the archives of Philadelphia theater, this is my absolute favorite.

As actors in theater often say to psych each other up before a show—especially on days when the prospect of performing the same old play again seems routine and uninspiring: "Hey, you never know who's out there." Usually, this warning is uttered to remind each other that there might be some important director, producer, or agent in the audience—someone who might help one's career. Give your best performance, no matter how you feel today!

But this story about Charles Fuller and Molly Picon goes to show that the person who's "out there" might also be a kid who has never seen a play before in their life. If you do your job right, you might open a whole new world for them—and they could set out to carve a wonderful place for themselves in it.

PART FIVE
Visiting Stars

George Frederick Cooke

March 25, 1811: It was the day of George Frederick Cooke's much-anticipated first performance in Philadelphia at the New Theatre. The great actor, a major star of the London stage, had embarked on a late-career overseas tour. It was widely known that he had left England under a bit of a cloud, and that his American appearances had already made headlines in Boston and New York for their inconsistency. The only question was, would the infamously unreliable star, known for his alcoholic binges, be ready to perform at all? His first appearance in Philadelphia had already been postponed, due to the actor being "indisposed."

Crowds had been mobbing the New Theatre's box office all day, and men had been hired to sleep on the pavement overnight, to be first in line. When the morning's ticket sales began, reported historian Charles Durang:

> ... coats were torn from the backs of those who tried to get near the box office; hats were lost; black eyes and bloody noses were to be seen by the hundreds. The struggle to gain [tickets] ... resembled a tumultuous riot. A certain Dr. B. hit upon the expedient of throwing Scotch snuff into the faces of the crowd. On the first occasion he carried his point by this brutal ruse, [but] ... on the second trial he was most severely handled for the atrocious act. The crowd blocked up Chestnut and Sixth street corners even to the court house.

At 5 pm, Cooke walked from his hotel to the theater. He was perhaps not surprised to see that the street in front of the building was completely thronged with people—that had been the case in New York and Boston, too, but when he attempted to go around the back to the stage door, that was mobbed as well. Since the narrow front doors of the theater were jammed, impatient ticket holders were trying to get in at every possible entrance, ignoring the posted signs that read: "Nobody on any account to be admitted behind the scenes."

Eventually, the crowd consented to clear a lane for the actor to access his dressing room. "Aye," Cooke chuckled to a nervous companion, "they understand their interest now, for as the man said when going to the gallows, there will be no sport without me!"

But Philadelphia's excitement was not misplaced. That evening everyone in the crowded theater's orchestra, boxes, pit, and gallery was treated to the full measure of Cooke's genius. For his opening performance, he presented Shakespeare's villain (as revised by Colley Cibber) "Richard, Duke of Gloster." The curtain rose on Richard's solitary figure pensively gazing into the distance. Cooke never used cheap costuming tricks to show the character's deformity—there was no "mountain on his back," no pronounced limp, no claw-like left hand. The actor's steel-gray hair was covered by a light-brown wig—and a helmet with three black plumes rising from it. He wore the classic red velvet cape, sword, white leggings, and knee boots that most actors of the era used when portraying Richard, but when he began to speak, it was his simplicity, his lack of bombast, that struck everyone in the house.

Philadelphians eagerly took in his performance, from the early spellbinding scene in which Richard woos the angry and mourning Lady Anne, to his seizure of the crown on his brother Edward's death, through the manipulation of Buckingham and the murder of his nephews (by which he finally gains the crown at last). Throughout it all, the Philadelphia audience was glued to their seats, the ladies in the boxes alternately horrified and intrigued, the men in the theater's pit too amazed to even light their usual cigars, the crowd up in the galleries rapt in awe. As the play came to the climactic Battle of Bosworth Field, Richard finally met the character of the Duke of Richmond, offered to exchange his kingdom for a horse, but received only his just and bloody end. No one who saw this performance ever forgot it. Charles Durang, years later, could still describe Cooke in the death scene:

> As he lifted up his left arm over his forehead, and he gave the last withering look at Richmond, the expression of his eyes—as they for a moment vividly rolled, then became fixedly glazed, and then all vision seemed gone... you felt everything he did ... The words that followed riveted your attention and absorbed all attention else. Your mind dwelt on nought beside. You did not see Cooke; you only saw the character. He never lost the feeling of his part. The coloring of the passion was preserved in graphic tints to the end.

George Frederick Cooke continued performing in Philadelphia until the end of April 1811. He played Richard several more times, and on other nights brought out all his other famous roles: Shylock, Lear, Falstaff, Macbeth, Sir Giles Overreach, and the Scotch aristocrat Sir Pertinax MacSycophonat in Charles Macklin's *Man of the World*. By the end of the run, Cooke had brought in over $15,000 in ticket sales—an astonishing total for that era.

Cooke stayed on a rather steady path during his weeks in Philadelphia, and did not go off on many boozy benders. There were more good nights than bad ones. We can attribute this good behavior, perhaps, to two things. First were the assiduous efforts by his minder, William Dunlap, to make it generally known in the city that if anyone wanted to enjoy Cooke's acting, they had to give up the pleasure of his company at the bar. And, to the credit of Philadelphians, everyone mostly cooperated with that unspoken arrangement.

The other thing was that almost every morning the actor walked to the studio of the painter Thomas Sully. There he posed for three separate portraits, which had been commissioned by wealthy benefactors in the city. During these quiet mornings, Cooke was charming and peaceful, engaging in respectful conversations with ladies and children who stopped by to see the great man as the artist sketched and painted away. Cooke always remembered to be on time for Mr. Sully, and he refrained from drinking during these sittings, as if he knew his immortality was somehow at stake.

The Academy of the Fine Arts in Philadelphia possesses the greatest of these portraits. The scene, as composed by Sully, looks as if the actor is standing in the interior of Westminster Cathedral. In the left foreground, the bottom of a pillar anchors the composition with a smooth and solid weight. Cooke's Richard, who had just slid out from behind that pillar, stares directly at the viewer as if we were the virtuous Lady Anne. A slight smile plays on his lips, as he cannily appraises us, and calculates how best to flatter and deceive us to attain his ends. Behind Richard, to the left, a statue of St. Helena stands in an alcove, with a mournful expression. She seems to know all too well that the wolfish villain will soon seduce Anne over the very body of her murdered husband. Although the saint in the alcove is alarmed, we ourselves cannot help thrilling at the prospect of Lady Anne's downfall. We both observe, and are complicit in her fate. The theatricality of the work astonishes, and gives one a sense of what the Philadelphia audience must have experienced watching the great actor perform, all those many years ago.

Edmund Kean Takes a Bow

January 8, 1821: Edmund Kean played his first night in Philadelphia, opening his two-week run in the city with that crowd favorite, *Richard III*. When the show was over, to the astonishment of many, he came out in front of the curtain. As the audience continued to applaud, unexpectedly, he bowed to them. Delighted, they applauded even more.

Kean was the savior and star of Covent Garden Theatre, the first true Shakespearian actor of the Romantic Era. He had been a sensation in London for the last eight years. Though famously small of stature and somewhat eccentric in appearance, his storms of emotion onstage brought forth paroxysms of response from his devoted fans. His Shylock, his Hamlet, his Othello, and especially his Richard III were regarded as amazing revelations. The poet Coleridge had famously declared: "To see Kean act is like reading Shakespeare by flashes of lightning."

Although his star had recently dimmed somewhat in England, due to his scandalous behavior with women and his drinking binges, in 1820 he had easily been able to cross the Atlantic and attract huge audiences in New York's Park Theatre. Next on his itinerary was Philadelphia.

All of Kean's Quaker City performances were at the rather rickety Walnut Street Theatre on the corner of Ninth Street. It was not considered the best house for spoken drama, and had only recently been converted from its original employment as a home for an equestrian circus. But since the New Theatre on Chestnut Street, the usual home for prestigious theater in the city, had burned down the previous year, and its replacement was still under construction, the Walnut would have to do.

But not to worry—Kean's performances, utilizing local actors as his supporting players, had been so well received that he introduced to Philadelphia this new custom: the curtain call.

After his character had offered his kingdom for a horse, and then been dispatched by his nemesis the Duke of Richmond, the final lines of the play were spoken over his dead body. The curtain was lowered, the audience clapped and cheered ... and then were rewarded by the sight of Mr. Kean stepping out *again* to the footlights to bow and smile and receive even more applause!

Not everyone in the Philadelphia theatrical world was well pleased by this practice. "The absurdity of dragging out before the curtain a deceased Hamlet, Macbeth, or Richard in an exhausted state, merely to take a bow, or probably worse, to attempt an asthmatic address in defiance of all good taste, and solely for the gratification of a few unthinking partisans, or a few lovers of noise and tumult, is one we date from this time," groused the actor and manager William Wood, years later. "It has always been a matter of wonder with me that a better part of the audience should tolerate these fooleries."

It was all something imported from the French stage, thought Wood, with its offensive professional claqueurs, and therefore to be greatly deplored. It was even worse when people threw wreaths and bouquets of flowers at the bowing and smiling Kean, still dripping with sweat from his exertions.

Still, allowed Wood, Kean was the great feature of the theater season. And what is more, all his reputation for being a wild man was not in evidence. He "had created no less surprise in the green-room than in the audience. All had read or heard of his wild and irregular habits, his associations with persons most likely to render his manner coarse and offensive." But Kean "appeared among us instead a mild, unassuming and cheerful man, wholly free from every affectation of superiority or dictation." When he suggested a new piece of blocking or staging to the Philadelphia players, reported Wood, they "were always given with a gentleness of manner which secured their immediate adoption." His presence backstage "was always a source of enjoyment … In private society, particularly in the company of ladies, he was distinguished for his modest and unassuming manner as well as conversation."

The only warning sign of future trouble that Wood could see for Kean's continued success was the crowd of hangers-on that met Kean at the stage door afterwards. As has been the case with George Frederick Cooke, some nine years earlier, there were always some fellows ready to party and wanting to take the famous man out with them for some revels. But Kean, Wood was certain, could not hold his liquor as well as Cooke. The manager learned to remain with the visiting star long after the performances had ended, gently but firmly pushing all these well-wishers and would-be partiers out the door. He wasn't going to go through all that again. But as we shall learn in a subsequent chapter, one could never quite tell what kind of surprise—whether innovation or uproar—a touring star actor would bring next.

Fanny Kemble Makes a Fateful Debut

October 12, 1832: She had been the sensation of the London stage for the past two seasons. Now Fanny Kemble was making a grand tour of America. She was accompanied by her father Charles Kemble, and by her mother's sister Adelaide, whom she called "Aunt Dall." Fanny's first American performances had been at the Park Theatre in Manhattan, and though she was supported by what the actress considered an inept American group of actors, audiences were well pleased. A reviewer in the *New York Mirror* had gushed that her large dark eyes and silvery voice had "seduced every heart."

This was enough to whet Philadelphia's appetites for her first appearance there, for which she chose *Fazio*, an 1815 tragedy by Henry Hart Milman. Fanny played Bianca, a young lady bent on revenge for her husband's supposed infidelity.

Philadelphia's Old Drury on Chestnut Streetwas crowded with fashion and beauty that evening, reported Philadelphia stage historian Charles Durang, and people were astounded by what they saw.

> A breathless silence pervaded the entire audience. Miss Kemble came in as a lady would enter into her own parlor, with quiet elegance and polish to receive her guests. The manner was novel, for conventionalities of the stage were entirely absent ... When the progress of the scene brought out the passions of the soul in all their various moods, the fearful energy with which she depicted the emotions of jealousy and rage were intense to a degree that the audience did not anticipate. In her first quiet scenes all was hushed as death ... it was only at each approaching climax ... that the feelings of the excited audience burst forth as ecstasies. She had a flashing black eye; her voice was sweet and musical, well attuned by the elocutionary rules.

But it was the evident depth of her intelligence that filled her every moment on the stage, Durang declared: "It was these intellectual qualities ... that gave birth to Miss Fanny Kemble's school of acting; for she originated a school with her powerful genius. The tone and tendency of Miss Kemble's mind are of the masculine, both in her acting and her very able literary productions, abounding in strength and originality of thought."

After the show, despite nursing a cold that she felt coming on, Fanny went back to her hotel to write in her journal, as she did every night—because she was planning to publish her memoirs of America later on. She was not entirely pleased with the Philadelphia actors she had performed with, or how the evening had gone:

> My Fazio had a pair of false black whiskers on, which distilled a black strip of trickling cement down his cheeks, and kept me in agony every time he had to embrace me. My voice was horrible to hear … [it was] all I could do to utter at all. This audience was the most unapplausive I ever acted to … They were very attentive, certainly, but how they did make me work! … They made noise enough, however, at the end of the play. Came home, supped, and to bed: weary to death and a voice like a cracked bagpipe.

The next day, she had no show to perform. She had hoped to go out riding, but it was raining and she sent the horses away. She tried to write, but "I could not accomplish any thing." She considered going to sit for a portrait by the Philadelphia artist Thomas Sully, who was encouraging her to come to his studio. She decided against it, for the moment. "I will never expend so much useless time again as to sit for my picture; nor will I let any unhappy painter again get abused for painting me as I am." (Fortunately for us, she was to break this resolution, and was to sit for a dozen portraits with Sully—three of them are in the collection of the Pennsylvania Academy for the Fine Arts.)

When Fanny finally came downstairs for tea in the afternoon of October 13, she found "a young gentleman sitting with my father; one Mr. Butler … He was a pretty-spoken, genteel youth enough. He drank tea with us, and offered to ride with me. He is, it seems, [the owner of] a great fortune …" Thus, in her very first week in Philadelphia, she had enacted on stage a rebuttal of a faithless man—and had also met her future husband, Pierce Butler.

Butler was to follow Fanny from city to city as her tour of America continued. He saw every show, his courting was relentless—when he could not secure a ticket, he would sometimes gain admittance to the orchestra pit by offering to play the flute. He was there when she returned to Philadelphia—this time to the Walnut Street Theatre—where the audience's ringing applause led her to write in her journal: "I love the whole city of Philadelphia this time forth for ever more!" He was even there in Boston, when faithful Aunt Dall passed away, and he stood loyally by the family, helping with the funeral arrangements. He always seemed to have funds to pay for everything. By the end of the tour, he and Fanny were engaged.

In April 1834, as the end of her single life approached, Fanny acted in some good-hearted farces that made gleeful light of her situation, with such titles as *The Wedding Day* and *The Day After the Wedding*. On June 7, 1834, an actual wedding took place at Philadelphia's Christ Church, a venerable Episcopal congregation on Second Street. (Her husband's grandfather and namesake, Pierce Butler of South

Carolina, was buried in the churchyard just a few steps away, along with several others among the Founding Fathers.) Interestingly, the ceremony was not a big theatrical production—in those pre-Queen Victoria days, that was not yet a common practice, even among the wealthy and prominent folk in England and America. Nor was there an immediate honeymoon planned; in fact, the wedding was sandwiched between Fanny's two farewell engagements, one in Philadelphia, and one in New York.

Interestingly, the role she was performing in these final shows was not Juliet or Beatrice or any light-hearted comedy, but a tragedy: *The Hunchback*, by James Sheridan Knowles. I don't think I've seen this noted anywhere in any of the many biographies that have been published about Kemble's life, but if you examine the text of *The Hunchback*, there is not much celebration of marriage in it. In fact, Julia has an ominous-sounding soliloquy, after she agrees to marry a man she does not truly love:

> … A wedded bride!
> Is it a dream? Is it a phantasm? 'Tis
> Too horrible for reality! for aught else
> Too palpable! O would it were a dream!
> How would I bless the sun that waked me from it!
> I perish! Like some desperate mariner
> Impatient of a strange and hostile land,
> Who rashly hoists his sail and puts to sea,
> And being fast on reefs and quicksands borne,
> Essays in vain once more to make the land,
> Whence wind and current drive him; I'm wrecked
> By mine own act! What! no escape? no hope?
> None! I must e'en abide these hated nuptials!
>
> …
> He comes! Thou'dst play the lady,—play it now!

In her new role in life, she was about to learn what it really cost to play the lady, and at what price her financial security had been sold for. After she had seen her father off on the boat to England, the realities of her new life suddenly became clear to her. The original Pierce Butler had not only given his name to her new husband, but he had passed along to him and his brother the source of the family's enormous wealth. Just when exactly the truth hit her is uncertain, but within a few months Fanny was writing a frantic note to a trusted friend: "The family into which I have married are large slaveholders. Our present and future fortune depend greatly on plantations in Georgia."

She would rather go back to the toilsome earning of her daily bread in theater, she declared. Acting was a disreputable business, but at least the labor was honest and not drawn from the blood and tears of others. Literally everything around her, she realized, was soiled. She was being fed and clothed by human beings who owned nothing in this world at all, not even their own bodies. No longer Miss

Fanny Kemble, in her role as the new "Mrs. Pierce Butler" she was the wife of a slaveowner. In fact, her husband was one of the largest slaveowners in America. As we will discuss in a later chapter, it would take many years before she could even begin to liberate herself, and the drama would be all too real.

Rachel Gets a Cold Reception

November 19, 1855: The great French actress Rachel played the Walnut Street Theatre. It would be her only performance in Philadelphia, and her time in the city proved to be a dark omen for her future.

Rachel had faced daunting challenges throughout her life. Born in 1821 as Elisa-Rachel Félix, she was a poor girl from a family of Swiss-French Jewish itinerant merchants. She began singing on the streets of Paris at the age of nine, and by 16 she was studying dramatic acting at the Théâtre du Gymnase. She performed in Pierre Corneille's *Horace* at the Théâtre-Français at the age of 17 under the mononym "Rachel," and was such a sensation that by 1841 she was touring London, Berlin, and St. Petersburg.

Word of her fame reached America, and as early as 1841, in the very first edition of the Philadelphia journal *The Dramatic Mirror and Literary Companion* was an engraving of Rachel on the front page. The editor, James Rees, wished to elevate the consciousness of the theatergoing public of Philadelphia, which at that point tended to favor only broadly popular entertainments. The rather crudely cut image showed Rachel in Schiller's *Mary Stuart*.

For 10 years Rachel was the most eminent actress in Paris, known for her elegant and direct classical style. Playwrights wrote plays especially for her—she was the first to take on the title role in Eugène Scribe's *Adrienne Lecouvreur*. Like most actresses of the day, she increased her public stature by taking a succession of notable and influential lovers, among them at least three members of the Bonaparte family—including the future Emperor Napoleon III. But her tempestuous life and many love affairs began to take their toll. She had two children by two different fathers, and she had developed a case of that all-too-common 19th-century health condition—tubercular infection of the lungs, or "consumption." As she aged, and her slender body began to become more and more emaciated by the disease she adamantly refused to acknowledge, her reputation in Paris began to falter.

In the early 1850s, now under the personal management of her brother Raphael, she embarked on another tour of Russia—despite the advent of the Crimean War, which earned much censure back in France. But the money she earned in St.

Petersburg alone seemed worth it to her. Indeed, she felt more than a bit Napoleonic herself, succeeding where the first Bonaparte had failed. Raphael—who seemed to imagine himself a Gallic version of the American exemplar of an empire builder, P. T. Barnum, and that his sister was France's answer to Jenny Lind—organized another grand theatrical campaign, and together with a company that included her sisters in supporting roles, crossed the Atlantic to America. Rachel's troupe played New York to critical success (and even greater box office receipts than she had earned in Russia), and then took a train to Boston. The chilly unheated carriages the actress was forced to ride in were a trial, to be sure, but the reception had at least been warm. Harvard students who had been hired to act as extras all stood enchanted in the wings, only half out of their costumes, admiring her delivery of her final speeches. But the coughing she used in these tragic death scenes was taking on a certain unartistic, even a deeply alarming, reality.

The entire company was glad to head south for what they hoped would be warmer weather, and were booked at the Walnut Street Theatre for a week's run in Philadelphia. Rachel was slated to perform the classic tragedies *Horace*, *Phèdre*, and *Marie Stuart*, as well as the famous new melodrama *Adrienne Lecouvreur*. Tickets to see the exotic star in the supposedly sober Quaker City were set at the extraordinary rate of three dollars for box seats, and a dollar for the balconies—three to four times the usual price of admission. But, as Raphael Félix had suspected, the lure of seeing yet another international celebrity overcame the resistance of Philadelphia theater fans. Special programs were also for sale in the lobby, which provided printed translations of the plays, for those who did not understand French—which was almost everyone, really. Americans, noted the French, always applauded great moments of passion, and didn't care for such things as the delicate subtleties of facial expressions and the metrical exactness of enunciation. Throughout the tour, Rachel learned to pause at moments when the audience needed to turn the page, and the sound of rustling paper filled the air.

Unfortunately, the Pennsylvania winter weather had arrived early that year, and temperatures in Philadelphia were icy. Raphael Félix refused to pay what he considered the exorbitant costs of heating the backstage areas of the Walnut. As the actors glumly entered the freezing dressing rooms, a member of the company, Leon Beauvallet, recalled: "No fire had been lit, and we were thoroughly frozen. Everybody catches a cold." The odor and effluence of the neighboring Herkness Horse Bazaar, directly to the north of the backstage area, did not help. "It is a hideous house, a pitiful theater, this Walnut," sniffed Beauvallet.

The Philadelphia critics, nonetheless, had highly praised Rachel. "She stands at the head of her profession, alongside Fanny Kemble, Ellen Tree, and Charlotte Cushman," gushed the *Public Ledger*. But faced with the icy backstage conditions—after that single *Horace*, the tragedienne had no strength to continue. Beauvallet wrote that Rachel "suffered so terribly that evening from the cold that on the following day she was seriously ill and had to take to her bed." It made no difference that a member of the city's small Jewish community sent a letter begging her to move her scheduled performance of "Adrienne le Courier" to Thursday so that her fellow Jews would not have to break the Sabbath to see it. She was barely able to walk, let alone correct their French. The tragedienne spent the rest of the week in Philadelphia in bed at the Jones Hotel on Chestnut Street, reading translations of the novels of James Fenimore Cooper that Beauvallet had given her. Philadelphia was a beautiful and prosperous city, he allowed, but he could not understand why there were not statues of great authors such as Cooper adorning its public squares. "Americans do not read—they count," he concluded.

Meanwhile, the remaining company members desperately tried to cobble together a repertoire to salvage the run at the Walnut. They lowered ticket prices, and frantically rehearsed with the Walnut's resident stock company of American actors. Rachel's three sisters, Mademoiselles Sarah, Lia, and Dinah Félix, were sent on stage in *Les Droits de l'Homme*, while the Walnut's resident company performed a comedy titled *The Debutante*. But the result was not encouraging, and audiences were thin. While the tiny expatriate French community in Philadelphia applauded from the orchestra seats, the lower-class "gallery gods" in the upper balconies did not. They quickly realized that much of the evening would be in incomprehensible French—and since many could not read English either, they ignored the proffered translations. Instead, to entertain themselves, they resorted to abusing the actors and dancing on the benches with "girls in low-cut dresses, whose demeanor was by no means staid," wrote the exasperated Beauvallet. "During *Les Droits de l'Homme* these madmen made so much noise in the gallery with their imitation of animals that it was quite impossible to make ourselves heard. The French downstairs swore at the Americans, who threw down nutshells and apple peelings on their heads. It was complete pandemonium."

Resigning to reality at last, the company thereafter canceled all further performances in Philadelphia. The Walnut's management, "due to the indisposition of M'lle Rachel," quickly booked the "distinguished Irish comedian and vocalist Mr. Collins" instead, whom they promised would appear in *The Irish Ambassador* and *Teddy the Tiler*. The French actors, finding themselves unemployed for a few days, walked around Philadelphia and amused themselves as best they could. They dutifully visited both the Fairmount Waterworks and Girard College, but were more astounded by the squirrels of Franklin Square. The tiny animals, who were protected by local ordinance, boldly climbed up their backs, demanding to be fed. As they left the park, they were also struck by many prominent advertisements for the city's newspapers, which were plastered on every wall, it seemed. One of these posters screamed in bold type about a recent "ATROCIOUS MURDER!" in which a Philadelphia mother and her nine children had been killed and thrown into the Delaware River. Intrigued, they rushed to buy a copy of this exciting daily journal—only to discover that the victims were merely a local cat and her kittens. The Philadelphia press had learned the pleasant trick of *le canard*, Beauvallet dryly noted.

But Rachel could not join these diversions, and she never really recovered from the experience of the Walnut's freezing dressing rooms. At the end of the week she was carried out of the Jones Hotel to her coach, and at midnight they boarded yet another uncomfortable train. The company wearily made its way to Charleston, South Carolina, hoping for something more like "Italian weather" in which her health might recover, but she was only able to summon enough strength to give one show. Even a subsequent trip to the balmy climate of Cuba did not help. Finally acknowledging the seriousness of her underlying illness, the great actress would never perform again.

Bunthorne in the Quaker City

January 17, 1882: Oscar Wilde was in Philadelphia, and everybody wanted to know what he thought of the wallpaper—and the china—in every room that he entered.

At the age of 27, the Irish-born and Oxford-educated Wilde was becoming a worldwide celebrity, though he had only published one book of poetry, and written one (unproduced) play. It was really his *manner* of living, even as an undergraduate at Oxford, that drew attention, surrounded by carefully selected furniture and decorations. "I find it harder and harder every day to live up to my blue china," he famously once said—or if he didn't say it, he was glad to let everyone *think* he said it. He had already exceeded the reputations of his famous faculty tutors, the art historians and scholars John Ruskin and Walter Pater. In an age when the British Empire was expanding inexorably throughout the world by dint of trade and conquest, Wilde held that Art and Good Taste were even more powerful.

Stories were already appearing regularly in the London press about Oscar's scholarly brilliance, his wit, his views on art. Even his clothes, his way with words, his celebrity circle of acquaintances, and his aesthetics were discussed almost daily, in newspapers around the world. He befriended a young beauty named Lillie Langtry, and he cultivated the hostesses of dinner parties at all the best houses in London.

His conversation was filled with opinions on poetry, painting, music, and, well ... wallpaper. "Life imitates art" was his oft-repeated view. We see things and feel things *because* great art has taught us to appreciate them in the first place.

Wilde had arrived in America on January 2, landing in New York. Officially he was on a lecture tour sponsored by British impresario Richard D'Oyly Carte. The tour was meant to draw further attention and publicity to *Patience*, the Gilbert and Sullivan operetta, which also had a traveling company that D'Oyly Carte was dispatching across the Atlantic. Produced at the brand-new Savoy Theatre in 1881, the show was already the hit of the London season. American audiences eagerly awaited its arrival on their shores, as they did with all new Gilbert and Sullivan shows. However, due to the lack of international copyright protection in those days, American producers would stage their own lavish unauthorized productions of G&S operettas, using pilfered scores and scripts, even before official British touring companies could be organized. It was all maddening, outrageous, and revenue-draining, from the original creators' point of view. Wilde's trip was part of a campaign to get American audiences to demand The Real Thing, and to reject cheap imitations.

When he arrived in Philadelphia on January 16, his reputation had literally preceded him—because his persona was already appearing on multiple Philadelphia stages in *Patience*. An unauthorized American version, produced by "Gorman's Church Choir Company" out of Boston, had been mounted at the Lyceum Theatre near Franklin Square in November 1881, and thereafter moved to the Dime Museum on Ninth and Arch. Soon there was another pirated production playing, in German, at the Concordia Operette Theatre on Callowhill Street. And in what was then a sure-fire sign of cultural popularity, Carncross' Minstrels were soon staging a parody version of *Patience* at their Eleventh Street Opera House, entitled *Four Wilde Oscars*, complete with blackface protagonists.

But the "official" and "authorized" (that is, duly licensed by D'Oyly Carte) American version of *Patience*, mounted by the Ideal Patience Company out of Booth's Theatre in New York, arrived at the Academy of Music in late December, with a cast of more than a hundred performers, including most of the original New York cast. It played throughout the New Year holiday week, ending with a matinee on Monday, January 2. Overall, though, many Philadelphians did not seem to care which one was "authentic," and gladly went to see them all.

There were *two* "Aesthetic" characters in *Patience*, Grosvenor and Bunthorne, that seemed to emulate Oscar Wilde. Though in truth W. S. Gilbert had in mind other figures in British art—such as Dante Gabriel Rossetti and Algernon Charles Swinburne (as well as Pater and Ruskin)—when lampooning young men who lounged about and talked of poetry and flowers, it was Wilde whom everyone associated with them. Bunthorne, especially, was thought to be modeled after Wilde, and indeed the costumes the actor playing Bunthorne was given did seem to mock those outfits that he affected during his public lectures: silk knee breeches, loose soft collars, and flowing long hair.

But perhaps the most amazing public demonstration of the fad for All Things Oscar could be seen in the audience of the Academy of Music on the New Year's Eve matinee. In a parody of the social practice of "young ladies' opera parties," in which dozens of girls from the socially prominent Philadelphia families would go see operas in chaperoned groups, "twenty young unmarried gentlemen, in full dress, accompanied by two married gentlemen" filled two of the boxes at the Academy. All of the young men were playing the "aesthetic" attitude to the hilt. Reported one newspaper:

> They entered with all the listless, abstracted air which young ladies assume on such occasions and seated themselves, like Grosvenor among the maidens, with an air that seemed to say: "Oh, why are we so beautiful?" Each young gentleman had a little buttonhole bouquet, which they arranged in a row on the front of the box, as young ladies do ... When an occasional good thing happened on the stage some young gentlemen threw on the tiny buds, to the amusement of both the actors and the audience. The married gentlemen in the background kept a sharp lookout on their tender charges and escorted them out at last with a great flourish.

Throughout all this, in a reversal of the usual social practices, noted the reporter, interested young ladies elsewhere in the house excitedly scanned the group of eligible young men with their opera glasses, "playing the part of 'Love-sick maidens, we.'"

A few weeks later, now that the Original Aesthete himself had made his appearance on the scene, Philadelphia journalists happily supplied their readers with details about him—even if, perhaps, they had to make some of them up. "When Oscar Wilde, the aesthetic poet, arrived at the Aldine Hotel yesterday evening one of the first things he did was ring for wax candles," reported the *Philadelphia Times*:

> As he threw aside his cloak of sable with silver clasps he cast a glance of disgust at the plain wall paper in the room and heaved a sigh that expressed far more plainly than words his disappointment at not having dados or Japanese figures with borders of Peacock tails. The candles were brought and the gas turned out, and, throwing his cloak over the sofa and putting on his short embroidered jacket, with ruby silk cuffs and facings, the poet lit a cigarette, adjusted his nether limbs, encased in black cloth knickerbockers and silk stocking, and, with his enthusiastic Irish blue eyes directed away from the horrid wall paper towards the fire place, he looked contented and happy and seemed for the moment quite at ease.

Wilde's lecture at Horticultural Hall, next to the Academy of Music, was attended by members of the best Philadelphia families—many, perhaps who had been present at the reception for him the previous night, at the elegantly decorated home of journalist Robert Stewart Davis on Spruce and 18th Street. "The people who entered ... belonged to the opera-going, art-loving class, who live in nice houses, ride in their carriages, give nice entertainments, wear the best clothes and mix among people whom they regard ... as nearly as nice as themselves," wrote the *Times*. However, "there were some plain, unpretending people present, who try to keep abreast of the times, and, having heard so much about Oscar Wilde, want to see him and hear what he had to say." Wilde's lecture itself was long and discursive, cautioned the reporter, but he did appreciate that the poet had stated that "It is possible to reach a closer kinship of humanity through the union of art and sympathy. The bitterest national prejudice exists among the least cultured … art never strengthens itself by isolation, and is never more forcible of feeling than when dealing with the simplest and commonest life."

Having now done his duty to Philadelphia society and to D'Oyly Carte, Oscar Wilde made a point of meeting two famous local residents. He visited the home of Dr. Samuel Gross, the eminent Philadelphia surgeon who had already been immortalized in the Thomas Eakins painting. On January 18, he took the ferry across the Delaware River to meet privately with the poet Walt Whitman, for whom—like many other British poets—he had the deepest admiration. Wilde then left the Quaker City and continued the rest of his American tour, which was to prove so financially successful that he would happily travel throughout the country giving lectures for the rest of the year.

Wilde's tour brought him to Philadelphia again in May, when he lectured upon the principles of home decoration, and in the summer he dined at the Bingham House Hotel, though not in his full public persona. But local theatergoers, at least, were already well satisfied. Another version of *Patience*, from the Comley-Barton Opera Company, was soon playing at the Chestnut Street Theatre in February 1882, presenting "The Original London Version." It had a successful run, and in the ads it was announced that the actor John Howson, who was playing Bunthorne, would even "impersonate and recite an original poem by Mr. Oscar Wilde." When the unauthorized Boston company of *Patience* came back to the Lyceum, it received full houses once again. After all, as a Philadelphia newspaperman stated: "Having seen a real, live Bunthorne, we can return to the Bunthorne of the stage with more satisfaction." Wilde would have replied that it was exactly the other way around, of course, and that both were true works of Art.

Sarah Bernhardt and the Mummers

December 31, 1900: Two of the greatest actors of the French stage, Sarah Bernhardt and Benoît-Constant Coquelin, performed at the Chestnut Street Opera House in Philadelphia, as part of their ongoing tour of the United States. Bernhardt had incurred a massive personal debt opening up a huge theater in Paris and was hoping to make up the deficit on an extended series of performances in American cities and then London. The play was Edmond Rostand's *L'Aiglon* ("The Eaglet"), a six-act verse drama about the son of Emperor Napoleon Bonaparte (aka Napoleon II, aka "le Duc de Reichstadt").

Bernhardt, who was then 56 years old, played the role of the historic character who died at the age of 21. The Duke's stage mother, Marie-Louise of Austria, was played by Maria Legault, an actress 14 years younger than Bernhardt. In the play, the Duke was confined within a palace in Vienna by his unloving mother, and the drama ended with a memorable scene in which Bernhardt theatrically expired "as dying angels would die if they were allowed to," as one critic wrote.

Rostand, fresh off the massive success of his *Cyrano de Bergerac*, in which Coquelin had played the title character, had written *L'Aiglon* particularly for Bernhardt. She added it to her touring repertoire when she brought the company to America, along with *Joan of Arc*, *Tosca*, *Hamlet*, and *Phèdre*. Coquelin played the supporting role of the courtier, Flambeau. (On other nights she would play Roxanne to his Cyrano, and when she performed *Hamlet*, he would play the comic role of the Gravedigger.) Reviews for her December 1900 performances in New York had been full of praise, to say the least. "SARAH BERNHARDT IN L'AIGLON MAKES GREATEST TRIUMPH OF GREAT CAREER," proclaimed one enthusiastic headline.

After Christmas, her troupe moved to Philadelphia. A critic for the *Philadelphia Times* was similarly ecstatic over the famous duo's performances in *L'Aiglon*, and declared it even better than *Cyrano*. However, he sadly noted that the previous evening's seats for her New Year's Eve show had not been filled to capacity. Part of the problem, of course, was the holiday parades of Philadelphia Mummers and "New Year's Shooters" out in the street, dressed in outlandish costumes (many in blackface minstrel costume). Besides their competitive appeal as entertainment, their marching bands made a great deal of noise outside the theater, as did the noise of all the tipsy revelers.

However, the *Times* wrote, perhaps the most charitable reason to explain the lack of an audience to support Mme. Bernhardt was "to suppose that the crowds in the street were of such a size and violence as to render theatre-going an unlovely manner of spending an evening by folk of the kind to whom such an artistic appeal as that made by Bernhardt, Coquelin, and Rostand would be likely to appeal." Furthermore, it finally admitted: "The most popular reason seems to be that Philadelphians do not love the theatre, even its best and grandest estate, sufficiently to pay the tribute in material money demanded by the purveyors." (It should also perhaps be noted that the play was done entirely in French, which only a very limited number of Philadelphians could understand.)

However, concluded the reviewer for the *Times*: "Those who were in attendance were privileged to witness a performance of poetic drama that has not been surpassed in quality, so far as American theatre is concerned, within the memory of any living being … There will be nobody to cavill because of the form or manner of *L'Aiglon*. It is a drama that will endure … the play will take its place on the library shelves with our Shakespeare, our Molière, and our Hugo."

One hates to think what the reviewer would have felt if you told him then that his confident prediction was rather misplaced. In American theater, Rostand's play would soon be entirely neglected, and Bernhardt's performance in it almost forgotten, save for historians and her most ardent devotees.

The Mummers, however, though by law they've been officially forbidden from parading about on December 31, still own the city's streets once New Year's Day arrives, in an annual staged city-sponsored parade. January 1, 1901, was in fact the very first of these parades, and they remain one of Philadelphia's longest running and proudly flaunted traditions. That day, reported the *Public Ledger*: "Three thousand men and boys in outlandish garb frolicked, cavorted, grimaced and whooped, while the Mayor and the members of the Councils, Judges, and other officials looked on."

Katharine Hepburn's Philadelphia Story

February 20, 1939: Katharine Hepburn, whose Hollywood movies had been declared "box-office poison" in 1938, returned to the theater in Philip Barry's play *The Philadelphia Story*. Also in the cast were Joseph Cotten, Van Heflin, and Shirley Booth.

Van Heflin certainly knew the city, having studied acting at the Hedgerow Theatre Company out in its suburbs, and Hepburn had attended nearby Bryn Mawr College, right in the heart of the tony townships to the west of Philadelphia. (Their location along the principal railroad route to Harrisburg had given rise to the social designation of the "Main Line"). But Philip Barry, the playwright, had never lived in Philadelphia at all. However, his good friend was Edgar Scott, a wealthy young Main Line gent who had taken George Pierce Baker's playwriting class with him at Harvard. Scott had married Helen Hope Montgomery, whom *Vanity Fair* termed the "unofficial queen of Philadelphia's WASP oligarchy," and Barry had based the character of Tracy Lord on her. Scott was later the longtime head of the Devon Horse Show, a premiere social event on the Main Line.

Philip Barry was also a founding member of the Theatre Guild, and so before it went to Broadway, the play was given an out-of-town tryout at the old Chestnut Street Opera House as part of the Theatre Guild's series of plays there. The Guild was having its own monetary issues at the time, so ironically the dowdy old theater was one of the cheapest venues the play about *very* wealthy people could find in Philadelphia. (It was torn down the very next year.)

But, after all, there was that title—and the decision to play to a hometown crowd, as it were, turned out to be a wise one. *The Philadelphia Story* was joyfully hailed by Philadelphia critics, and then went on to have a year-long run in New York. Hepburn would also star in the delightful 1940 movie version, with Cary Grant and Jimmy Stewart. It completely restored Hepburn's reputation at the box office.

***

October 1981: "Kate's here!" read the caption on a photo in the *Inquirer*. The image was of a woman in her 70s crossing Walnut Street, her hair in a bit of a mess, holding an umbrella against the falling rain. Despite the cloudy weather, she had large sunglasses on. But everyone could immediately spot who she was. Katharine Hepburn was back in Philadelphia.

Six years after appearing at the Forrest Theatre in a forgettable tryout of the play *A Matter of Gravity*, 42 years after *The Philadelphia Story* at the Chestnut Street Opera House, and over 50 years after her first Philadelphia-area forays onto the stage in such Bryn Mawr College student productions as John Lyly's pastoral *The Woman in the Moon*—Hepburn was back again at the Forrest, in a pre-Broadway tryout of *The West Side Waltz*.

The play was by Ernest Thompson, who had also written the hit *On Golden Pond*—which Hepburn had recently filmed, and the movie was due to be released later that same year. Like that script, *West Side Waltz* was also about a bittersweet relationship between the younger and the older generations. Hepburn played a crotchety widowed pianist living in New York, whose neighbor (played by Dorothy Louden) occasionally comes by to play duets, but mostly gets on her nerves. She eventually softens when a younger woman (Regina Baff) answers an ad to become her roommate.

West Side Waltz was one of the biggest Philadelphia hits ever for the Shubert Organization. Though Philadelphia audiences were famous for showing up mostly for big musicals, they also turned out for big stars. The show was sold out throughout its three-and-a-half-week run, and it grossed over $350,000 in its final week.

This lifelong success would have certainly been a shock to the "sharp sort of girl" back at Bryn Mawr in 1924 who, during rehearsals, had stood next to her in the chorus line of the freshman musical. As Hepburn later recalled, she had impulsively blurted out to her neighbor a new-found ambition: "If I could only be an actress!"

"She looked me up and down and said, 'An actress! You?' I was painfully shy, so I just shriveled up. I vowed to myself that I would never, never mention my idea to anybody—but just the same, I would be an actress."

Paul Robeson's Hammer

December 11, 1939: Paul Robeson appeared in the world premiere of the musical *John Henry* at the Erlanger Theatre. Robeson starred in the title role of the mythical railroad worker who "died with his hammer in his hand," along with the actress Ruby Elzy playing Julie Anne. Other members of the cast included Joseph Attles, Myra Johnson, James Lightfoot, and Musa Williams. The only white member in the company was Alexander Gray, a Philadelphia-born actor. It is interesting to note that both the future folk singer Josh White and the budding political activist Bayard Rustin were in the 50-member-strong chorus of the show during its tryout run.

John Henry was based on the 1931 novel by a white Mississippi writer, Roark Bradford. The libretto was written by Bradford, and the music by New York composer Jacques Wolfe. Wolfe had dedicated much of his career to transcribing African American spirituals. He had worked with singers like Robeson and poets such as Langston Hughes for years. The entire show was meant to highlight American folk music.

In a backstage interview at the Erlanger, Robeson told a reporter he had turned down 10 scripts in favor of Bradford and Wolfe's musical. "It is the sort of thing that will pave the way for a Negro theatre that some day will rank with the greatest in the world—one just as truly a part of a nation as the Comedie Francaise or the Moscow Art Theatre."

The performances of *John Henry* in Philadelphia met with an encouraging reception. Reported the *Wilmington Morning News*: "The audience, stirred by the tragic finale in which John Henry dies in a struggle to roust more cotton than a steam engine, cheered for numerous curtain calls." Later that same month, Robeson was given a silver cup by the student council at Northeast High School and was hailed in a special ceremony as "a splendid exponent of virile Americanism" at the ceremony attended by 5,000 people.

However, when *John Henry* opened at the 44th Street Theatre on January 10, 1940, it was not well received by New York critics. "Robeson is a perfect choice for this role," wrote Burns Mantle in the *Daily News*. "He could have sung until midnight and the crowd would have still demanded more … But there's still work to do on *John Henry.*" In the end, the production ran only five nights on Broadway. Robeson's wife Eslanda always had doubts about the play, and felt the character emphasized the Black man's physical life over his intellectual development. She may have been secretly relieved when it closed.

***

October 16, 1943: The Theatre Guild's production of *Othello*, starring Paul Robeson, had the final performance of its run at the Locust Street Theatre in Philadelphia, in preparation for an eventual Broadway production. Reviewers and audiences alike all realized that they were witnessing a significant landmark in American theater. Robeson was an Othello "unsurpassed for the eye and ear," the critic Linton Martin had written in the *Philadelphia Inquirer*, "[w]ith his stalwart physique and his rich resonant baritone voice to give full value to the Bard's lines."

For almost all African American leading men today, Othello has become an aspirational role, a capstone achievement. But from Shakespeare's day until the middle of the 19th century it was a part that was entirely performed by white actors in blackface. Other Black actors had undertaken the role, true, but (with the notable exception of Ira Aldridge) they were always in all-Black companies, and in front of audiences who were mostly their own race. Even long after Aldridge had blazed the trail in performances in England and Germany (not without some controversy), the prospect of a Black actor onstage with a white Desdemona had been a barrier very few white producers wanted to cross.

But from early on, many people saw the possibilities of Robeson in the role. When he was a teenager, his high school English teacher in Somerville, New Jersey, had even cast him in the part in a student production. And as soon as Robeson began acting professionally, many immediately saw his Othello as an inevitability. Indeed, wrote the *New York World* in 1924, one could imagine that Shakespeare must have had Robeson in mind all along.

In 1930 Robeson had finally played Othello in England—the first Black actor to do so there since Aldridge's day. The West End production, with producer Maurice Brown as Iago, Sybil Thorndike as Emilia, and Peggy Ashcroft as Desdemona, did not go entirely to the critics' satisfaction. Robeson's typically American and psychological (what today we might call "Method") approach to the role clashed with the performances of the British cast, who had been strictly trained in how to properly speak their roles rather than to "live inside" them. Still, back home in America many took notice. The actress Lillian Gish was quoted as saying, "If Robeson is, as one hears, the greatest Othello in the world, I should be glad to play opposite him." But in Philadelphia, it was not as if white society had grown any more at ease with Black male sexuality. That same year the Philadelphia Art

Alliance refused to exhibit a nude sculpture of Robeson by Antonio Salemme at their annual show.

It wasn't until 1942 that Robeson's portrayal of Othello finally was seen in America. First there was a summer production at Harvard University's theater in Cambridge, Massachusetts, directed by Margaret Webster, and then another at the McCarter Theatre in Princeton, New Jersey. Princeton, which was Robeson's birthplace, after all, welcomed the performance warmly, and many Philadelphians made the trip to see it. Extra matinee performances were added to meet the demand. It was a great achievement, wrote a Philadelphia reviewer. "Hero of the evening was Paul Robeson, whose powerful build, resonant voice and intelligent acting made the Moor a figure of noble and moving tragedy." (Princeton graduate José Ferrer, as Iago, also got excellent notices.) Plans were already being made for Broadway.

But due to Robeson's previously booked concert commitments, this *Othello*—again featuring José Ferrer as Iago, Uta Hagen as Desdemona, James Monks as Cassio, and Margaret Webster as Emilia—would take another year. The Theatre Guild signed on as producers, and their favorite designer Robert Edmond Jones, who had first worked with Robeson back in 1924 on Eugene O'Neill's *The Emperor Jones*, was brought in to design the costumes, sets, and lights.

After an initial run in New Haven, Connecticut (yet another Ivy League town), the production went on to Philadelphia in October 1943 for a final tryout before going to New York. The Locust Street Theatre was packed for every show, and praise for the lead actor was plentiful. "Paul Robeson measures up in every sense of the word in his superb acting," wrote the *Philadelphia Tribune*. "In appearance, diction and voice, he projects the picture of the Moorish general."

The *Tribune* also noted in another article that Robeson was not letting his personal onstage success distract him from what he considered even more important causes. As usual, Robeson never hesitated to combine his artistic work with his political passions. At a reception at the home of Mr. and Mrs. Edward Davis at 6336 Overbrook Avenue, sponsored by the Philadelphia School of Social Sciences, Robeson made a speech in which he stressed that despite America's current involvement in war against fascist powers, there was a "seething undercurrent of fascism" right here at home, and that "the rights of minority groups must be recognized and respected, before true democracy can be realized in the United States." And then he sang for the guests at the reception—but not all night. Just one song. There was still work to do.

Peter Brook Finds the Empty Space

May 11, 1964: The Royal Shakespeare Company production of *King Lear*, starring Paul Scofield and Irene Worth, came to the Shubert Theatre in Philadelphia.

The director of *Lear* was Peter Brook. He had even designed the set and props for the production, with rusty iron panels walling in the mostly bare stage, which was decorated only with battered tankards, swords, and wooden stools.

For the week-long run, the company did the great tragedy in rotation with one of the Bard's lighter works, *The Comedy of Errors*, directed by Clifford Williams. Scofield and Worth rested on these nights, but the rest of the company, including Diana Rigg, Ian Richardson, Alec McCowen, Brian Murray, Barry MacGregor, and Julie Christie, pitched in.

The RSC's next stop was New York, so one could say the Brits were reiterating the classic itinerary of taking their shows for a "tryout" in Philly before going to Broadway. Philadelphia reviewers were suitably ecstatic about *King Lear*, and they highly praised both Scofield's acting and Brook's direction, terming them "majestic," as well as "magnificent" and "electrifying." Run, don't walk, to the box office to catch the one-week engagement, advised *Inquirer* reviewer Henry Murdock, giving Scofield credit for "providing one of those experiences which restore a reverence for the craft of the player."

But though *Comedy of Errors* had been a reliable crowd-pleaser, many Philadelphia audience members had found *Lear* a bit of a trial. As Brook had directed it, the first intermission did not come for almost two hours, and the second half of the evening was almost as long. *Daily News* reviewer Jerry Gaghan noted that many in the audience strained to understand the British accents.

One night, a squalling baby had even interrupted the show. The mother attempted to mollify him with a bottle, but it did not work. Eventually, the embarrassed mother left her seat and took the baby home, explaining to the Shubert's house manager that she could not find a sitter for the evening. Other people left, sleepy and yawning, at the intermission. The show was simply too long, they said, and they were going home to bed.

Brook later wrote about that dispiriting 1964 experience in his famous and influential book about modern theater, *The Empty Space*. He compared the performances of *Lear* at the Shubert to the enthusiastic reception the production had previously gotten from European audiences—who did not even quite understand the Early Modern English of the text:

> In Philadelphia, the audience understood English all right, but this audience was composed largely of people who were not interested in the play; people who came for all the conventional reasons—because their wives insisted, and so on. Undoubtedly, a way existed to involve this particular audience in *King Lear*, but it was not our way. The austerity of the production which had seemed so right for Europe no longer made sense. Seeing people yawn, I felt guilty, realizing something else was demanded from us all. I knew, were I doing a production of *King Lear* for the people of Philadelphia, I would without condescension stress everything differently—and in immediate terms, I would get it to work better.

It's important to note that Brook used the story not to disparage or judge Philadelphia theatergoers, but rather to illustrate his point that the theatrical event is composed of fragile, changeable elements, not the least of which is the audience. In the future, he wanted to "unite cast and audience in a universal 'yes.'"

One can say that this was achieved in May 1971, when a work of Brook's next returned to the Shubert Theatre. The famous RSC production of *A Midsummer Night's Dream*—already an international sensation—came to Philadelphia, even though it would have been easy for the company to have just spent three months in Manhattan. The RSC's run at the Billy Rose Theatre at Lincoln Center had been entirely sold out and wildly applauded. But with a kind of missionary zeal, the RSC had also traveled to Brooklyn, Boston, Chicago, Toronto—and then finally Philadelphia, where the tour would finish.

This time, just as had happened everywhere else the groundbreaking production of the play had traveled, the reception was rapturous. For years afterwards, many people who saw it would say it had changed their life.

Unfortunately, Brook had not accompanied the RSC's 1971 trip to Philly, because if he had he would have witnessed the joyful standing ovation at the bows, as the company generously mixed and interacted with the people in the auditorium of the old Shubert. Philadelphia theater audiences had evolved in the intervening years, according to *Inquirer* review William Collins. "The old Theater Guild subscription crowd was there, but so were a lot of people, many of them young, who go to the theater, when they have heard something special is in store for them."

Brook's *Midsummer* had "gotten it to work better" in Philadelphia. Clearly, if the troupe's visit seven years earlier had failed to please, the consensus now was that all was mended. "Those trapezes and slings and colored streamers, that phenomenal knockabout style of performance, the audacious revelations of things in the play we never imagined were there—all are part of a new set of terms in which live theater can regain its power over our imaginations," continued Collins.

"Add to this Brook's conviction that the old illusionist trappings of stagecraft must give way to a stagecraft of utter candor—'We must open our empty hands and show that really there is nothing up our sleeves'—and you have the miracle of his 'A Midsummer Night's Dream.'"

PART SIX
Disputes, Deaths, and Disasters

Kean's Riot

Contending for a Seat.

April 18, 1821: Just a few months after his much-applauded debut at the Walnut, Edmund Kean was driven off its stage, receiving a hail of abuse from the Philadelphia audience. His performance as the main character of Jaffier in the Thomas Otway revenge tragedy *Venice Preserv'd* at the Walnut Street Theatre was so objectionable that the audience rioted, hurling abuse (and items of fresh produce) at the stage, even long after he had left.

Since his successful performances in Philadelphia the previous winter, Kean had been continuing his lucrative tour of American cities. The famously mercurial and impulsive actor had sometimes been hailed by audiences, and at other times he had been reviled. In the spring, he returned to what he hoped would be the friendlier city of Philadelphia, where he had bathed in repeated curtain calls a few months earlier.

For a week he had brought out the most famous roles in his repertoire, such as Hamlet and Richard III. But on the final night of his engagement, which was also the final night of the Warren and Wood's entire season, it all went horribly wrong. That all-too-common event in early 19th-century theatergoing, a "violent audience demonstration"—a theater riot—broke out. The chronicler of the evening's events was an eyewitness, Charles Durang. As he wrote in his *History of the Philadelphia Stage*:

> The theatre was to have closed on Wednesday, April 18th, with the revived tragedy of *The Distressed Mother*. [But] the tragedy of *Venice Preserv'd* was substituted ... Kean played Jaffier, and it must be confessed, in a queer manner. His dress, we recollect, was very beautiful ... His hair was neatly curled. He looked a perfect picture.
>
> He commenced Jaffier in a very impressive manner, but soon fell into eccentric contrasts, doing strange things, so palpably nonsensical, that the audience, especially the box portion began to wince, and at length, to express disapprobation most decidedly.

Completely changing his blocking, his gestures, and even his manner of speaking was a tactic that Kean sometimes employed, especially if he felt things were not going well on a particular evening. He was always an instinctive performer, and strove for emotional impact, and prided himself on never giving a routine, predictable performance. In the distant future, this approach to acting might perhaps be excused as being "Method." But to his fellow actors of that era, this was really the most alarming sort of stage behavior. Typically plays were only rehearsed once, usually on the morning preceding a show. All memorization was done outside of rehearsals. Everyone in the company depended on the star's decisions about blocking (or "business") to remain the same. The Philadelphia company of actors who were performing with Kean were most distressed, recorded Durang:

> Mr. [William] Wood played Pierre, for the first time, on this unfortunate occasion. He became so much annoyed with Kean's freaky mode of acting, and the uneasy demonstrations from the audience in the early parts of the play, that he was perfectly disconcerted and with difficulty proceeded. Mrs. [Juliana Westray] Wood was the Belvidera, an excellent actress, perfectly conversant with her stage business, and letter-perfect in the language of her parts. She also became alarmed and worried to a painful extent. Having all her principal scenes with Jaffier, she was unable to comprehend Mr. Kean's movements, which were more like those of a mysterious mountebank than an intellectual tragedian of incomparable Shakesperian illustration … The cobweb mazes wove in his own brain caused him to assume certain antics that really had no meaning.

However, Edmund Kean did have enough wit to perceive both the confusion of his fellow actors, and he also certainly heard the rebukes of the Philadelphia audience. But this only made things worse.

> He changed his freaks, and attempted hauteur—that is, he left Jaffier and assumed plain Mr. Kean, with an exhibition of ridiculous private feeling … At length hisses came from the boxes, and groans, with "Off!" "Off!" from every part of the house came tumbling down like an avalanche … After some time, the gale lulled, and in pauses of the blast, Kean gained a hearing, and most rudely addressed them. He called them "cowards" &c., with other very strong epithets, so that he was soon compelled to seek safety in a hasty exit. He was certainly not a sane man at that moment.

A wealthy young member of the audience, a dandy named William Bingham, made the unwise choice to defend Kean to people around him. "This interference ended in Bingham and his companions being thrown over the stage box onto the stage."

With the famous star of the evening having deserted the field, the Philadelphia company gave up *Venice Preserv'd* and attempted to mollify the house with the afterpiece, *The Deaf Lover*. But by that point the audience was in no mood for anything.

> The performers were literally hissed and pelted off with apples, oranges and other light missiles … This riotous behavior brought the performance to a sudden close, and the melee in the front was brought to an end by the presence of mind of the lamplighter, in blowing out the lights, which drove out the belligerents who were now fully sated with their caterwauling, groans, hisses, and other horrible demonstrations of savage conduct.

"This disastrous and disgraceful ending of the season of 1821 at the Walnut Street Theatre could have easily been avoided if the least prudence and discretion had ruled," concluded Durang. "Kean's nonsense—for it deserves no better term—was without imaginable cause … and if the cause had been rightly conceived by the public, the actor would have only merited their contempt, instead of the riotous expression which was made."

Kean's antics and misadventures, both on and offstage, would continue. His impulsive behavior in Philadelphia was certainly not unique, and similar incidents throughout the remainder of his North American tour—as well as during his final years in England—eventually would fill the pages of many theatrical memoirs and biographies. But this was part of the excitement of going to see Kean perform in the first place. Indeed, the riots and uproar of 1821 were forgiven, if not forgotten, when the actor returned to yet another packed house in Philadelphia on his second tour of America five years later. Even the street outside the theater was crowded. "On his entrance he was greeted with a loud welcome," reported the *United States Gazette*. This time, at least, there was no improper conduct—on either side of the footlights.

Charlotte Cushman Sends Too Many Flowers

September 22, 1842: It was an important night at the Walnut Street Theatre. "This establishment opens this evening for its winter season, under the management of that excellent actress, Miss Cushman," wrote the *Public Ledger*. "The company is a strong one, and the campaign will, no doubt, be conducted with spirit, and the entertainments be novel and gratifying."

Though only 26 years old, the new manager might have been expected to feature herself in her first presentation. Instead, Charlotte Cushman chose to take the minor role of a widow in *The Belle's Stratagem*, the 1780 comedy by Hannah Cowley. As a prologue, however, she did make an "Original Address" to the crowd, "written expressly for the occasion by a gentleman of the city." It wasn't until later in the season that Cushman would pull out her big attractions for Philadelphia audiences, including her performance as Nancy Sykes in *Oliver Twist*, as Lady Macbeth (opposite Edwin Forrest), and as Meg Merrilies the witch in *Guy Mannering*.

Originally from Boston, after a sudden rise to fame in the theaters of New Orleans, she had become a star of the New York stage, receiving great acclaim for her performances at the Park Theatre. Finally released from her New York contract, she was ready to strike out on her own.

By coincidence, Fanny Kemble Butler, another person from elsewhere who had ended up in Philadelphia, was living quite close to the Walnut Street Theatre. In the autumn of 1842 Fanny was at the absolute low point of her marriage; her husband Pierce was openly having affairs with other women, and he had moved the entire family away from their beautiful house in Germantown to a low boarding house in the heart of the city, just off Washington Square. Knowing that Fanny wanted a divorce, to gain advantage, he strictly limited her access to her own children. To console herself, Fanny often was riding about the city, dressed in her usual outfit of male riding attire, which she preferred to skirts.

It's not surprising that Fanny and Charlotte happened to meet—in fact, Charlotte was a bit obsessed with the famous actress, who had been such a star during her youth, and had sought her out. Cushman, seeing both her riding costume and her misery, thought she knew the answer to the problem.

She flooded Fanny's room with flowers almost daily, and sent her many letters, all stuffed with poetry. Writes historian Lisa Merrill: "Charlotte enjoyed being the savior, and here was a chance to right a great wrong against a woman she adored and render herself indispensable. She offered to help Fanny amass proof of Pierce Butler's infidelities so that Fanny could divorce him and retain custody of her children." But none of Charlotte's zealous attempts to help were successful, perhaps because he acted more like a suitor than a colleague. Charlotte continued to inundate Fanny with flowers, and Fanny was puzzled and overwhelmed rather than consoled by Charlotte's intensity. She certainly didn't care for Charlotte's plan, which was to hire a prostitute who would deliberately entice Pierce Butler into bed—and then have lawyers burst in and catch him in the act. Aghast at such low intrigues, Fanny had to tell Charlotte firmly that her schemes would never do. In the long run, we can note the Englishwoman would find her own way out of her situation, and would eventually even resume her career on the stage. But Cushman was stung by the rebuff and the flood of flowers ceased. She would harbor mixed emotions about Fanny Kemble thereafter.

But if she needed intrigue and drama Charlotte now had a theater to run. True, the company was often alarmed at her lack of financial discipline, which didn't seem to be at all her forte, but artistically, at least, she was still doing very interesting work. In March 1843 Cushman finally gave Philadelphia her performance as Romeo, opposite her sister Susan as Juliet. That the two Cushmans were sisters playing lovers again did not cause any comment. After all, Fanny Kemble had once played Juliet to the Romeo of actress Ellen Tree, back in London. Fanny, in fact, had played romantic scenes with her *father* Charles Kemble at the Walnut a decade earlier, and no one thought anything of it. Indeed, it was rather reassuring to early Victorian audiences that there was no possibility of real sexual activity going on between actors when they were offstage. It made things more respectable.

But what audience members certainly did *not* know is that Cushman was in fact having many affairs in her private life. Just not with men. She was always very aggressive in these matters—as she had done with Kemble, her typical approach was to impulsively test the waters, as it were, with any woman that attracted her. Her magnetic personality was quite enticing, and the tactic often worked. Someone who was definitely attracted to her was a young woman she met that same year while a portrait of the Cushman sisters as Romeo and Juliet was being painted: Thomas Sully's daughter Rosalie.

Another 1843 portrait of the actress, made during this period by Thomas Sully, is now in the collection of the Library Company of Philadelphia under the title "Charlotte Cushman of the Walnut Street Theatre." (He made a copy which is at the Folger Library in Washington, DC.) It's a very flattering picture, possibly showing the actress in a costume for a play, with a red head scarf and green dress. Her eyes stare out with startling force. Sully's characteristic warm and flattering approach to his subjects did much to soften and feminize Cushman's appearance in this painting. But in the 1840s it was rather the double portrait of her and Susan, in which her strong and athletic legs were featured, that was destined to be widely engraved and reproduced.

Charlotte would have a passionate affair with Rosalie Sully, who also painted her in a miniature that also focused on the actress' expressive eyes—though the intention behind them was now decidedly erotic. (Oddly, Rosalie also gave Charlotte a miniature of Fanny Kemble, attached to a braided bracelet made of Fanny's hair, as a love token.) The relationship did not last, however, and when Thomas Sully realized what was the cause of his daughter's distress, he sent all his paintings of Cushman out of the house.

But Charlotte had already followed her overwhelming ambition to establish her career in London, where in 1844 she appeared onstage again with Edwin Forrest. To the actor's extreme annoyance, while his performance as Macbeth was roundly panned by English critics, Cushman's Lady Macbeth received particular praise. Even worse, she was soon acting in the company of his rival Macready! Indeed, she became one of the biggest stars on British and American stages for the next 30 years, rivaling Forrest's own fame. She would play in many Philadelphia theaters during her national tours, including the Walnut, the Arch, and the Academy of Music.

Back in Philadelphia, however, Rosalie Sully never really recovered from the sudden end of her brief love affair with Cushman. She sank into a severe depression and died in July 1847.

The Marble Heart of John Wilkes Booth

March 1863: John Wilkes Booth, a member of the most famous family of actors in America, was performing for two weeks at Mrs. John Drew's Arch Street Theatre in Philadelphia. During his engagement he appeared in a great number of classical roles, including Richard III, Shylock, and Petruchio—as well as *The Apostate* by Richard Lalor Sheil. Booth also performed the part of Phidias in *The Marble Heart* by Charles Selby, a modern drama about a sculpture of a woman that comes to life.

At the age of 24, the handsome John Wilkes Booth was now a certified star, and much in demand. Audiences could book seats up to six days in advance to see his performances, and he commanded a salary of $500 a week for his engagement in Philadelphia. In fact, as he traveled around the country in 1863 to many American theaters, he would earn about $20,000 that year. That was quite a nice sum—only $5,000 less than President Lincoln's salary.

When he had first appeared at the Arch Street Theatre in 1858, however, John Wilkes Booth was but a lowly member of the stock company. He was not regarded as a very good actor when he was younger, and often forgot his lines. But now that he had matured and become a star, all was forgiven. The Philadelphia audience was enthusiastic, the ladies especially joining in the applause.

Booth's family was well known in Philadelphia, of course. The father, the late Junius Brutus Booth, Sr., had been one of most famous actors in the country and had played on Quaker City stages many times. His older brother Edwin Booth, who was already regarded by many as the best actor in the country, had recently bought the Walnut Street Theatre along with their brother-in-law, John Sleeper Clarke. Clarke, a well-known comedian, had been a neighbor and acquaintance of all the Booth brothers since his childhood in Maryland—though Edwin was his particular friend. Like most of the Booth family, he had also gone into show business.

Originally, his name was "John Clarke Sleeper," but he had reversed his middle and last name, because it looked better on theater posters. He had even married their sister Asia in 1859, and had moved with her to Philadelphia, accompanied by their mother, Mary Ann Booth.

But the most important difference between John Wilkes Booth's last stay in Philadelphia and his return appearance was that the Arch Street Theatre was now under the control of new management: the formidable Louisa Lane Drew. A leading actress since her childhood, and still only in her mid-40s, Mrs. Drew performed in most of the shows at the Arch, and was a great favorite of loyal Philadelphia audiences. Booth would have to share the stage with her—she was slated to play Catherine to his Petruchio and Portia to his Shylock. During rehearsals, she pretended to defer to his choices of blocking, since he was nominally the star.

"Where do you want me to stand, Mr. Booth?" she asked him, according to the account of an actor in her company. "Mr. Forrest used to want me to stand here, but not all great actors agree, Mr. Booth." Booth could only stammer out a confused reply. Frankly, he was terrified of Mrs. Drew and treated her with cautious respect throughout the engagement.

After this two-week run at the Arch that spring, John Wilkes Booth never again played in Philadelphia. But he did get an engagement at Ford's Theatre in Washington, DC, on November 9, 1863. President Lincoln, ever an enthusiastic theatergoer, had even gone to see him perform in *The Marble Heart*. The President and his party all sat in a lower box at Ford's, right next to the stage.

As the Civil War raged elsewhere in the country, Edwin had settled in New York City, where in 1864 he, John Wilkes, and their eldest brother Junius Jr. performed together in a special benefit performance of Shakespeare's *Julius Caesar*—enacting the most famous political assassination in world history. By the spring of 1865, as the war was clearly winding down, and the Union victory was assured, the Booth family's fortune seemed secure. Edwin still frequently performed at the Walnut, as did Clarke, and Asia was pregnant and expecting the birth of their twins in a few months.

True, Edwin and John Wilkes were not getting along. They disagreed vehemently about which side to support in the ongoing Civil War, for one thing. After one particularly bad argument between the brothers on the subject, Edwin threw John out of his New York City townhouse.

On April 14, 1865, in the box directly above the one Lincoln had once occupied to watch him perform in a minor play, the younger Booth brother would play his utterly disagreeable but inarguably major role in American history. When the actor strode into the upper stage left box at Ford's Theatre, a small "Philadelphia Deringer" pistol in his hand, he changed the course of the nation in a most horrible and consequential way.

As the news of Lincoln's death reached Philadelphia, the Walnut Street Theatre, where Sleeper Clarke had been slated to perform the play *The Streets of Philadelphia*, was closed. At this point John Wilkes Booth was still at large, and was believed to be fleeing towards the lines of the Confederate Army.

The Arch Street Theatre, where the assassin had performed only two years previously, was also shuttered. So was the newly built Chestnut Street Theatre where Edwin had quite recently appeared. The manager of the Chestnut, William E. Sinn, publicly promised the reward of 500 dollars to anyone who captured John Wilkes Booth alive.

Meanwhile, the body of the murdered President went on a national tour, as it were, on its way to its eventual burial in Illinois. On the afternoon of April 22, a train from Harrisburg arrived in Philadelphia carrying Lincoln's coffin. It was stored overnight at a funeral home on the corner of Tenth and Green Streets in Northern Liberties. A public funeral was scheduled to be held at Independence Hall the next day. An official delegation of Philadelphia actors, managers and stagehands marched in the procession, trying to repair the tarnished public reputation of the entire theatrical profession.

The assassination had certainly destroyed the happiness of the Booth family. John Sleeper Clarke was in federal custody and unable to join the public gestures of loyalty by Philadelphia theatricals wrote desperately to a fellow actor: "The affliction under which I am suffering, worse than death, prevents my personal attendance; proclaim my entire concurrence with any measures of sympathy for the loss of our lamented President, loyalty to our government, or any other steps the wisdom of the meeting may think proper to take." His home and those of the rest of the Booth family were all searched. By April 27 Junius Brutus Booth, Jr., was also locked up in the Capitol Prison in Washington, DC.

That very same day, the fugitive John Wilkes Booth was cornered in a barn in Virginia by federal troops. During the stand-off the barn was set on fire, and in the subsequent blaze he was killed—either by his own pistol, or by lucky shot from one of the soldiers outside. News reports in all the papers were breathless and full of alarm. It was also reported that John Sleeper Clarke had handed over to authorities a letter from Edwin Booth to Asia that detailed in advance his plans to attack the President and other members of his administration. Under deep suspicion of being somehow involved in a widespread plot, Clarke joined Junius, Jr. in the Capitol Prison and would remain there for a month, under intense questioning.

John Sleeper Clarke never got over the trauma of being arrested and accused. When he was eventually released from prison, he told Asia their marriage was over; he wanted a divorce, and he never wanted to be associated with the Booths again. Eventually, the couple agreed to live together in the same house, for the sake of their children, but they moved to London and seldom returned to America. However, John Sleeper Clarke and Edwin Booth were still tied together financially through their joint investment in Philadelphia real estate. Edwin, after a brief retirement, had returned to the stage after successfully begging forgiveness from the theatergoing public for his wicked brother's great crime. Three years later, on April 27, 1868, he was even back at the reopened Walnut Street Theatre—playing another great assassin, Macbeth. On the bill with him, as Lady Macbeth, was his future wife Mary McVicker.

But in England, John Sleeper Clarke still burned with resentment. "The Booths get all the notoriety without suffering," he wrote in a letter to a friend. "Look at me—I was dragged to jail by the neck—literally dragged to prison—and Edwin goes scot-free gets all the fame—sympathy—who thinks what I endured?" The aggrieved comedian nonetheless went on to have a successful career in London, retiring comfortably in 1889 and dying 10 years later at the age of 66. Remarkably, having bought out Edwin Booth's share of the Walnut in 1871, at his death he still owned the theater back in Philadelphia. It wasn't until 1920 that Clarke's heirs—the nephews and nieces of John Wilkes Booth—finally sold the property.

The Death of Annie Kemp Bowler, the Original Stalacta

August 21, 1876: A sudden pall was cast over the theatrical world in Philadelphia during the Centennial Exhibition. The singer and actress Annie Kemp Bowler had died after a backstage accident during a performance of *The Black Crook* at the New National Theatre.

Annie Kemp was born in Boston in 1836. When she was still in her teens, the family moved to New York, and she began training as a singer for the concert stage. Soon the tall, statuesque contralto was giving concerts across America. In the late 1850s she joined Cooper's English Opera Company and fell in love with a fellow company member, the English tenor Brookhouse Bowler. They married in 1860. The next year, she and Brookhouse were both performing in *Rob Roy* at Niblo's Garden in New York, Interestingly, they shared the stage on alternate nights with Edwin Forrest, who was still doing his tried-and-true repertoire of roles, including Metamora. On the days that *Rob Roy* was performing, Forrest did not stay in New York, but commuted back and forth by train to Philadelphia.

When the Civil War broke out in 1861, Annie and Brookhouse, like many American musicians and actors, feared theatrical and concert work would mostly dry up, and thought it best to go to England for the duration. Crossing the Atlantic, by November she was singing in a concert—sharing the bill with the great Adelina Patti—in Liverpool's St. George's Hall. But, as matters turned out, the popular stage seemed to have more regular employment for her, and she made her London debut in 1863 in a spectacular fantasy of *Acis and Galatea—or, the Nimble Nymph and the Terrible Troglodyte* at the Royal Olympic Theatre. (Caves and grottoes filled with nymphs and female sprites were a common theatrical trope of the time.) Annie apparently had developed her comedic talents too, for often when her opera company toured the English provinces, she would appear in a farcical afterpiece entitled *The Yankee Gal*.

Returning to America in 1866, Annie was soon back in a cave again. She had been cast as the original "Stalacta" in the very first production of *The Black Crook*—hailed by some scholars as perhaps the first true American musical.

Annie had played the entire run of 474 nights in the original production of *The Black Crook*, which had been a tremendous sensation when first mounted at Niblo's Garden in New York City. The show took about five hours, and its plot (freely borrowing elements from *Faust* and *Die Freischütz*) was wildly convoluted. Besides the title character (a dark crook-backed magician named Hertzog) and his assistant (the comic Greppo), The cast of characters included young heroes (such as the impoverished artist Rodolphe and his fiancée Amina), and dastardly villains (including the evil Count Wolfenstein and the Arch-Fiend Zamiel). There was also additional comic relief from the servants von Puffengruntz and the soubrette Carline—who sang the flirty song "You Naughty, Naughty Men!" But despite all the names the audiences had to keep track of, the piece had been wildly successful, not the least because of the huge number of female dancers and singers on display in revealing costumes—and because of all the magical stage effects. Behind the scenes, this female chorus was expected to mount all sorts of rickety ladders and stairways as they made their way to their various entrances. Some safety measures were present, but in that era, both falls and fires remained an ever-present danger.

As for Annie Kemp's part, one could summarize Stalacta's contribution to the action in this way: Wolfenstein waylays Rodolphe and attempts to trick him into sacrificing his soul to Zamiel. But along the way Rodolphe discovers a buried treasure and saves the life of a dove. By this act he breaks a spell that has been placed on the bird by Hertzog, and the dove transforms into Stalacta, Fairy Queen of the Golden Realm. The magical queen rewards Rodolphe for this rescue by bringing him to Fairyland with her, where she reunites him with his beloved Amina. Her army of Amazons defeat the Count and his evil forces, and Zamiel's demons drag Hertzog into hell. Amina and Rodolphe live happily ever after, with Stalacta's blessing. At the very end of the show, a final chorus number gave the dancing girls one last chance to show off their legs.

During the 11 years since its initial success, *The Black Crook* had been re-staged again and again, by various producers in New York, Philadelphia, and elsewhere. By this point Annie had moved on to more artistically prestigious projects, joining the Richings English Opera Troupe on a tour of America. In the late 1860s and early '70s she had often sung at Philadelphia's Academy of Music in such operas as *Fra Diavolo* and *Il Trovatore*. But in the Centennial year of 1876, she was induced to return to *The Black Crook*, which was receiving a grand production at the New National Theatre on 10th and Callowhill. Bowler, billed as "the original Stalacta," was engaged to reprise her role, descending from the heights of the stage as she transformed from a dove into the Queen of the Golden Realm, as she had so many times before.

However, on the second night of performances, as Annie prepared for her first entrance, an accident occurred. According to the *Philadelphia Times*: "In the transformation scene she became dizzy, lost her hold upon the supporting rod, and fell to the stage, a distance of fifteen feet, dislocating her shoulder blade and breaking her collar bone." (It was not noted whether the show was stopped at that point, but it's more than likely that her understudy was quickly sent on, and the performance continued.)

However, related the *Times*, the end was near for the unfortunate Miss Kemp. "She was removed to her boarding place and was doing nicely. Her speedy recovery was anticipated, when … she was suddenly taken with an affection [sic] of the heart and expired in five minutes.

"She was a fair, handsome lady, and had a sweet, well-cultivated voice. She had many friends, who knew her as a very estimable lady."

However, neither Annie nor her husband seems to have amassed much of a personal fortune during their careers. Who would pay for the expenses of her funeral and burial? Fortunately, the charitable and fraternal organization of the Actors' Order of Friendship was on hand, and stepped in as it had done before for others of the theatrical world who were in need.

A few days later, the *Times* reported how the theatrical community of Philadelphia had rallied to give her a fitting send-off:

"The funeral services of Annie Kemp Bowler … took place on August 23d at Grace Episcopal Church … There were present an unusually large number of members of the Theatrical Profession and friends." Indeed, the entire company of *The Black Crook* were present—and had made evident their grief for their departed cast mate. "The coffin, which was placed at the centre aisle of the church, was entirely covered in flowers." There were also large floral tributes by Ransom Rogers, the proprietor of the New National, Mrs. John Drew of the Arch Street Theatre, and the company of Kiralfy's Alhambra Palace on Broad Street.

> As the pallbearers were carrying the remains out of the church Madame Salvotti sang "Rock of Ages" and the New National Theatre orchestra (Professor C. Kaufman, leader) performed a solemn dirge.
>
> The remains were taken to Mount Moriah Cemetery, the grave being in the lot of the Actors' Order of Friendship, the permit therefore being kindly granted by Mr. W. H. Turner, the secretary of the excellent Order.

The grave of Annie Kemp Bowler is still visible at Mount Moriah today, surrounded by other actors and performers of the era who met their ends in Philadelphia, and whose families needed some charitable assistance in their time of mourning.

The Temple Theatre Catches Fire

December 25, 1886: The Temple Theatre was packed with audiences eager to witness that great Philadelphia favorite, *The Little Tycoon*.

The Temple was a spectacular place to see a show. A grand Gothic Revival palace built as a Masonic hall in 1855, it had only been converted a few years previously to a commercial theater building, after the Order of the Masons had moved to their new home on North Broad Street near City Hall. One would think by this point, nearly a full year after its initial premiere on January 4, there would hardly be any people left in Philadelphia who hadn't seen *The Little Tycoon*. But apparently it didn't matter. The production, billed as "a Japanese-American operetta," was sold out almost every night, and had made the fortune of its manager, Mr. George C. Brotherton.

As we have previously detailed, when the operetta first opened at the Temple Theatre, many predicted it would not succeed. Lucrative theatrical productions did not originate in Philadelphia anymore, after all.

But, despite all the doubters, Philadelphians kept flocking to the show, the sheet music sales of the score flew off the shelves, and *The Little Tycoon* just kept running and running. Its engagement kept being extended—first by two weeks, then three, then another month. Then it became an open-ended booking—there had never been anything like it in the history of Philadelphia theater.

By the end of March 1886, Brotherton had brought in a replacement company—because he was taking the original cast to New York's Standard Theatre. The New York critics, however, utterly dismissed *The Little Tycoon*. "There is not much pleasure in writing about such a thoroughly miserable and unmitigaging [*sic*] mass of rot as *The Little Tycoon*, but it is certainly interesting as showing the extraordinary difference between the judgment and liking of New York and Philadelphia," groused the *Brooklyn Daily Eagle*. Despite this rough reception in New York, Brotherton kept the show on a relentless tour schedule. It was a big success in Buffalo, Boston, and even Washington, DC. In November it had come back home to Philadelphia, and it was packing in the crowds again—people who had already attended dozens of times before were happily coming back to see it.

And for the holiday season of 1886, there was yet another new attraction added to the Temple Theatre: in other parts of the building, the former club rooms and assembly halls of the Masons had been converted into a "Musee Egyptian"—a wax museum. There were almost 400 figures in all, depicting historical tableaux and scenes from the Bible (the setting of the Crucifixion was especially impressive). There were also depictions of contemporary political figures, such as the Mayor of Philadelphia, and even one of U.S. President Grover Cleveland. People would come to see the wax museum and stay to see the show afterwards. "Now that the Egyptian Musee has been opened in the same building with the Temple Theatre," wrote the *Times*, "Manager Brotherton seems to have arrogated to himself a sort of amusement monopoly."

But as it turned out, the Christmas Day show would be the last day anyone would see the insides of the Temple Theatre. At 11:30 am on Monday, December 27, the supposedly safe new electrical wiring in the Temple Theatre had sparked somewhere in the museum section, and soon the whole building was ablaze. The resulting fire destroyed the theater, and the tragedy was compounded—two Philadelphia firefighters lost their lives when a wall collapsed on them.

The very next day, the story also flew around that city about a Christmas miracle! Amazingly, the wax tableau of the Crucifixion in the museum section was not melted or consumed by the fire; as the walls around it collapsed, it was revealed to public view, hanging in the cold winter air about Chestnut Street. Some people thought it was a sign of something, though no one was quite sure what it signified. To some, the figure of Christ seemed to mourn the ruins of the edifice that had once stood all around Him, and He was blessing the souls of the two lost heroes. Brotherton, sensing an opportunity, moved the Crucifixion scene to a building down the block and charged admission to see it and other items rescued from the fire.

On December 30, 1886, the producer arranged a special fundraising concert at the Academy of Music—all proceeds supposedly going to the families of the dead firefighters. A combined gathering of the touring company and the Philadelphia cast of *The Little Tycoon* sang to yet another packed house. The next day Brotherton took this combined company on a train to Erie, Pennsylvania, where new audiences awaited them.

The salvaged relics of the theater went on a tour of their own. By March 1888, Philadelphians could find them advertised as being on display at C. A. Bradenburgh's Dime Museum on the corner of Ninth and Arch streets. During this Easter season, the wax image of Christ was particularly featured. "Burning beams, joists, and timbers fell around it, but, as if protected by a Supreme Power, it remained unharmed." Nearby in the museum were other exhibits, such Baby Bunting, "the smallest horse ever exhibited," as well as "a statue of stone turning to life."

The Temple Theater would never rise again—but *The Little Tycoon* would be resurrected in theaters all over the country. Eventually, Brotherton's various companies would give over 2,000 performances of the show.

The Fall of Apollo

Summer 1936: The demolition of the Arch Street Theatre began. The scaffolding covering the sidewalk was already up, and the workmen were hauling away all the furniture, curtains, and backstage detritus they could find. Everything had to go.

When it had been built over a hundred years before, and even when Mrs. Drew renovated it in the 1860s, the surrounding neighborhood had been the home to many of the city's Quakers. But though their meeting houses remained, most of their congregants had moved elsewhere. In the last decades of the 19th century, the neighborhood had slowly changed—and not for the better.

The theater business had changed as well. Mrs. Drew dispersed her stock company in the late 1870s. The Arch mostly was rented to touring combination companies—operettas, melodramas, and so forth. But slowly those dried up, too. The old theater now stood in what became dubbed "The Tenderloin," an area full of bars and brothels. It was perilously close to "Skid Row" in the blocks to the east. But despite all this, in the early 20th century the Arch became the host of many vibrant Yiddish theatre companies. It had seen performances by both Boris Thomashefsky and the great Jacob Adler. In its very last years, as "Blaney's Arch Street Theatre," it had also shown movies, booked vaudeville shows, and then finally low burlesque.

Finally, in the depths of the Great Depression, the old theater sat disused and vacant, and developers quickly sprung. Many other Philly theaters were going down in those years, and nobody made much of a fuss about this one. There was no question of preservation. The owners only knew they wanted to get more revenue out of the land it stood on. It was now the era of the automobile, and after the completion of the Benjamin Franklin Bridge in 1926, spanning the Delaware River and linking the city's roads with those of New Jersey, a constant stream of cars and trucks crowded the neighborhood. Arch Street became infamous among motorists for its slow traffic. Businesses all along it suffered because most on-street parking was banned, and the trolley lines were eliminated. There was every financial incentive for many building owners simply to level their structures for a parking lot. In June, the ominous scaffolding suddenly rose around the old theater. In the newspapers, a notice was posted by the Integrity Wrecking Company, listing "All the Equipment and Materials for Sale Including Theatre Seats, Fire Extinguishers, Fans, Chandeliers, Drop Curtain, Asbestos Curtain, Plushes, Velours, Fire Hose, Etc."

June was a busy news month that year—in the runup to the 1936 Presidential election, *both* the Republican and Democratic parties were holding their national conventions in Philadelphia. Some editors sent no reporters at all to cover what must have seemed a minor real estate story. A *Philadelphia Evening Bulletin*'s photographer came by, and at least made some record of the Arch Street Theatre during its last days. In an exterior shot, we can see two automobiles, waiting right against the scaffolding, already hungry for a better parking space.

The *Evening Public Ledger* also dispatched a photographer, who went inside and documented for the last time the woodwork details of the theater's lobby and the painted domed ceiling covering the vacant chairs in the empty auditorium. The *Ledger*'s Henry Murdock, who was apparently assigned to write a feature article about the theater's history, at least thought to poke around the soon-to-be-demolished building. He discovered that up to the very last minute before demolition its stage was being used by painters and craftsmen to create scenery for other local theaters. But even as they continued this final act of creative work in the old Arch, other men labored to remove the backstage dressing room mirrors, desks, curtains—everything moveable was being hauled out. But it wasn't like the place was falling down around them. As he walked out the old stage door, wrote Murdock, "the theater's old watchman, with glum emphasis remarked: 'This old place could outlast a damn theater I could mention. But I won't.'"

Unfortunately, Murdock did not inform his readers what would happen to the statue of Apollo on the theater's facade. In fact, no report I've come across even mentions it. On those final photos of the exterior taken by the *Bulletin*, now in the archives of Temple University Library, the figure of the god can still be seen, rather blackened by years of exposure to the city's air pollution, looking rather forlorn amidst the surrounding fire escape and demolition scaffolding. To a modern-day preservationist and theater historian, so many questions immediately arise. But didn't anyone think to *save* Gevelot's iconic work? Surely somebody at least asked around before breaking it up and throwing it into the dumpster? Perhaps somebody salvaged it, if only for sentimental reasons? Was it sold to some collector? Sadly, as of this writing, I have no evidence at all of its survival. In all likelihood the figure of the ancient god was just toppled to the ground or smashed by someone attempting to move it. Perhaps it was the very first target for the grim operator of a remorseless wrecking ball.

Of course, it would have been even better to have saved both the god *and* the historic stage for which he had served so long as the silent guardian. But in the end, Apollo was powerless to help the theater, or even himself. There were cars to park, and everybody wanted to drive.

Curtain Time, Minus Zero

September 1, 1955: Philip Loeb was found dead at the Taft Hotel in Manhattan. The cause of death was ruled a suicide, by an overdose of sleeping pills. He was 64 years old.

A native Philadelphian, Philip Loeb was a graduate of the city's Central High School and the University of Pennsylvania. He was an avid participant in student drama at both institutions, and had won the Oratorical Prize at Central. After leaving college, Loeb briefly attended law school, but then started a career in journalism, reporting for the *Evening Times* and the *Public Ledger*. But his success in amateur performances at the Young Men's Hebrew Association (and the urging of his college English professor, Thomas O'Bolger) had inspired him to leave Philadelphia and try his luck as an actor in New York. At the age of 25, he started studying with Franklin Sargent at the Academy of Dramatic Art in the evening, and making the rounds of producers' offices by day.

In 1916, the young man had gotten his first big break supporting the aging star actor E. H. Sothern in the play *If I Were King*. Loeb played Colin de Cayeulx, "a rogue of the 15th-century Parisian underworld," to Sothern's Francois Villon. Becoming a well-known character actor with the Theatre Guild, Loeb was seldom out of work thereafter. In 1937 he appeared in the successful farce *Room Service* on Broadway, which ran for 500 performances, and then he co-wrote and appeared in the 1938 Marx Brothers screen adaptation of the same name. He frequently worked at the Bucks County Playhouse, including those seasons during World War II that the suburban theater produced shows inside the Bellevue-Stratford Hotel on Broad Street. He even helped to organize the National Entertainment Industry Council to mobilize show business in support of the national war effort.

In 1948, Loeb was cast in the role of Jake Goldberg in Gertrude Berg's play *Molly and Me*, which was based on her long-running hit radio show, *The Goldbergs*. The production came through Philadelphia in February of that year, playing the Locust Street Theatre before going on to success on Broadway.

The next year *The Goldbergs* was picked up by CBS, the first TV comedy to portray an American Jewish family, with its everyday scenes of simple and heartwarming domestic comedy. As she had always done, Berg continued to write all the episodes. But because of the ominous political climate of the era, and the deepening suspicion of anything that smacked of leftist politics, she said she was careful never to include any material in the show "that will bother people ... unions, fund raising, Zionism, socialism, intergroup relations ... I keep things average. I don't want to lose friends." Philip Loeb again played the role of Jake Goldberg—a role usually described as a lovable nebbish and "meekly philosophical family man"—to her strong matriarch Molly. In 1950 both Berg and Loeb starred in a movie version of the show.

However, in June of that year, Philip Loeb's name suddenly appeared on the list of supposed "Secret Communists" in the infamous right-wing publication *Red Channels*—an allegation apparently based only upon his organizational work for Actors' Equity Association. In that era, any such accusation inevitably meant immediate blacklisting for any unfortunate actor, however unjust and unfair the accusation was. Loeb vociferously denied being a Communist, but the show's sponsor, General Foods, insisted he be dropped from the show. To her credit, Gertrude Berg initially resisted the pressure but eventually gave in—though she paid Loeb a large cash settlement and quietly continued to send him a weekly salary. Still, the show continued to go on without him, and another actor was now playing the role.

Like other actors blacklisted by film and television studios, Loeb did manage to find some work on stage. His last show was *Time Out for Ginger* in 1953–54. But by 1955 he was losing his eyesight, and fearing he would never work again, was deeply depressed. His marriage to Jeanne LaGue had ended in 1940, and he was estranged from their only son. On August 31, he checked into the Taft Hotel, claiming to be "Fred Lang of Philadelphia." The next day his dead body was found by the hotel staff; a mostly empty bottle of pills was on the dresser beside him. He left no note. His pockets contained only a handful of loose change and some papers indicating he lived at 225 W. 86th St.—which was actually the home of his longtime friend, comedian Zero Mostel and his wife Kate. (Also a native Philadelphian, she and Zero had only been charging the struggling Loeb $60 a month to live with them, and tried their best to keep up his spirits.) Loeb was quietly buried by his family at Mount Sinai Cemetery in Philadelphia.

In 1976, the Martin Ritt movie *The Front* attempted to tell the story of writers and actors whose lives had been blighted by the anti-Communist hysteria of the early 1950s. Loeb's friend Zero Mostel portrayed a blacklisted comedian, Hecky Brown, who commits suicide in a midtown New York hotel room. Reportedly, it was a very painful scene for Mostel to play, because he knew it was based on his friend Phil Loeb, even though the method of death was not the same. In the movie, Hecky toasts himself with champagne in a mirror, and walks offscreen. We hear the sound of a window opening, and then the camera pans to the curtains blowing in the sudden wind, and he is gone.

***

September 8, 1977: The English playwright Arnold Wesker's re-imagining and rewriting of the Shylock story, entitled *The Merchant*, was booked into the Forrest Theatre in Philadelphia. The famous comic actor Zero Mostel would play the title role, supported by Sam Levene and John Clements.

John Dexter, who had recently had a smash hit with the play *Equus*, was hired as director. Wesker, the left-wing writer who had made his early reputation in the 1950s with such gritty dramas as *The Kitchen* and *Roots*, had worked closely with Dexter over the years. He had had a string of bad luck, however, and several of Wesker's early promising projects had gone awry over recent years, for one reason or another. He was more than ready for a big mid-life commercial success. This ambitious project could be it, he hoped. Bernard Jacobs, the head of the Shubert Organization who was co-producing the play, described *The Merchant* as a play that reworked Shakespeare, and that examined "what it meant to be a Jew."

The Shubert Organization, which had built and managed the Forrest Theatre since 1927, had recently invested a lot of money in renovating and improving their prime property in Philadelphia. The Philadelphia tryout market was still one of their main conduits for developing shows out of town before bringing them to Broadway, and one of the first places to send successful Broadway shows, as they began national tours. (*A Chorus Line* was already announced for later that year.) Bringing big stars like Mostel to town, in a prestigious production like *The Merchant*, was an encouraging sign of how much the Philadelphia market was still valued by New York producers. The city of Philadelphia was floundering in so many ways in the 1970s, and it wanted to rebuild its reputation as a good town for prestigious theater. The *Inquirer* dispatched two of its main theater journalists, William Collins and Al Haas, to do a flurry of preview articles on both Mostel and Wesker.

Zero Mostel, who often quipped that "success didn't go to my head, it went to my waistline," was a large man—both in body and in personality. But since the role of Shylock was going to be a demanding one, he had gone on a near-starvation diet to slim down to a healthy weight. At the age of 62 he had suddenly dropped from 304 to 215 pounds. With the same determination, he threw himself into the play, arriving at rehearsals with all his lines already memorized.

Perhaps because of the strain he was putting on his body during the week of the show's first previews, Mostel suddenly fell ill. He collapsed backstage and was taken to nearby Jefferson Hospital with what was termed an upper-respiratory infection—or perhaps the Coxsackie virus. In his hospital room on September 8, he complained of dizziness and suddenly lost consciousness. Despite the intense efforts of Jefferson's doctors and staff, he died of what was later determined to be an aortic aneurysm.

While the company mourned the loss, the producers of *The Merchant* canceled its run at the Forrest Theatre. Ticket buyers were told to ask for a refund. Still, Wesker and the creative team hoped for the long-term survival of the project. "In times like this, people in the theater tend to rally and be marvelous … I only know that the spirit is that it must go on. The backers seem to have enormous confidence in the play." Meanwhile, local writers Haas and Collins turned out heartfelt tributes to Mostel that were published in the *Inquirer*—along with news of the show's closing.

The Merchant would later be re-mounted in New York with another actor in the lead role (in tribute, Joseph Leon wore Mostel's costume yarmulke, with his name tag still sewn inside it), but the production would never achieve the hoped-for success. Zero Mostel's remains were cremated, and according to his expressed wishes, no funeral or memorial service was ever held. His ashes were quietly interred with no ceremony by the Oliver Bair Funeral Home on Chestnut Street. Following Zero's instructions, his wife Kathryn Mostel left the final location of the ashes up to them. One hopes, at least, that someone thought to take them up to Mount Sinai Cemetery.

Zsa Zsa Gabor Gets Fired

June 1983: Zsa Zsa was not happy. The role of Ann Stanley in *Forty Carats*, at Philadelphia's City Line Dinner Theatre, had been a rocky engagement for the Hungarian-born actress/socialite/celebrity from the very beginning. Her first leading man, who played what she described as "the young stud" part, was fired for not being what she considered sufficiently "mannish."

"They hired a nice little boy," Gabor told a reporter. "He got $200 a week. He was the little friend of the stage manager." That stage manager, understandably, had immediately quit. But Zsa Zsa was also not happy with the stage manager's replacement, Robert Brandenburg. She held him responsible for an incident where she fell off the stage during rehearsals and bruised her arm.

Not that anyone in the cast was really upset when Gabor suffered that accident. In fact, an ever-growing number of "Zsa Zsa stories" were now being bitterly shared among the Philadelphia cast members of the show. It didn't help that most of them were making the same paltry $200 salary that the fired actor had been earning, while she was reportedly being paid $10,000 a week.

The show had opened on May 26, in preparation for a run that would last till early July. Sales were brisk, and Zsa Zsa's friends President Reagan and Mrs. Reagan had called the theater to congratulate her. Zsa Zsa Gabor was a major celebrity in those days, after all. Her guest appearances on *The Merv Griffin Show*, during which she played to the hilt her persona as a sexy, gossipy, empty-headed, aging gold-digger, were especially famous. Sometimes she would rattle on about her jewels, sometimes she would talk about her many husbands, sometimes she would discuss the similarly gold-digging careers of her equally famous sisters: Magda and Eva. Among the three of them, they had had a total of 17 wealthy husbands. (Or maybe it was 16, because she and Magda had each married the same man, the British actor George Sanders—though after a decent interval of a couple decades, of course.)

All of this drew a lot of attention to her appearance in *Forty Carats*, and many Philadelphians were more than happy to see her in all the splendor of her bejeweled flesh, as it were. Among these fans were the residents of the Woods School and Residential Treatment Center in Langhorne, Bucks County, who had carefully saved up for weeks to buy their tickets. Woods was a long-term facility that specialized in care for people with traumatic brain injuries. Many of its residents were in wheelchairs, and some were cognitively impaired.

The Woods group had come in special buses, along with staff members and caregivers, to see Gabor on the evening of Tuesday, May 31. Following the standard procedure of the theater, the house manager Fred Gaehring had seated the group down front, close to the stage. Because of their disabilities, the reactions to the comedy were often out of step with the rest of the audience. During the first act, their laughter had sometimes burst out at odd moments, and other involuntary noises could occasionally be heard from that section of the audience. This did not go unnoticed by the star they had come to see, and it clearly unnerved her.

At intermission, Miss Gabor had summoned stage manager Brandenburg, and demanded that six wheelchair-bound disabled people be shifted away from their tables near the stage. She had been disturbed and distracted, she said, and she refused to go on for the second act unless they were moved. "She said it was very sad," Brandenburg said later, "but they must be moved or she would not go on."

According to reports, Fred Gaehring refused to carry out Gabor's orders. The unenviable task was finally given to the head waiter of the dinner theater. But when he relayed Gabor's orders to the group from the Woods School, they did not meekly move to the back; they indignantly left the theater entirely. "She made me feel so ashamed," said Beverly Stabler, 44, who suffered from brain damage after being hit by a car three decades previously. "We can't help being in wheelchairs. It's just by the grace of God we have them to get around." The group was soon on its chartered buses and heading back to Bucks County, crestfallen and angry.

As the story broke on Wednesday, June 1, a storm of indignation rose throughout the Philadelphia area. Columnists and TV pundits and editorial pages thundered away, and the *Daily News* even printed a cartoon comparing Gabor to a wicked witch. According to the school's president Harold S. Barber, Gabor had called the school around midnight and "wanted to know how many chocolates to bring"—apparently as a gesture of apology, which he refused. The Woods School staff and residents were still very upset days later. A worker at the facility who had accompanied them to the theater told the papers that "they have been walking around the past two days in tears." National media outlets began picking up the story, and American public sentiment swung heavily against Zsa Zsa.

Local communities of handicapped activists and their supporters soon joined in. Beginning at 4:30 pm on Wednesday, June 2, a crowd of disabled persons and many others were in front of the City Line Dinner Theater, chanting to ticket holders: "Don't Pay! Don't Go In! Discrimination Will Not Win!" Some protestors held handmade signs with such messages as: "ZSA ZSA, YOU GO TO THE REAR" and "FRONT ROWS ARE FOR EVERYONE!" and (perhaps most cuttingly) "ZSA ZSA, THINK!" The theater staff did its best to placate the demonstrators, offering them free tickets to the show, and handing out food and soft drinks.

On Friday, June 3, the news was splashed in headlines across the country: Zsa Zsa Gabor had been fired. Producer John Kinnamon had told Miss Gabor before the Thursday night show that he was sending on her understudy instead.

The owner of the City Line Dinner Theatre, Daniel M. Tabas, was not available for comment. Nor was there any comment from Mickey Rooney, a co-investor and the public face of the Tabas line of theaters and hotels. Rooney, a long-time friend of Gabor's, had apparently persuaded her to take the role in the first place.

But Gabor was not as reticent. She was glad to go, she told a reporter. "I was treated like dirt here. Mr. Tabas does not know how to run a theater." Although she felt kindly toward the city of Philadelphia because of her "best friend" Grace Kelly, Princess of Monaco, she said, she had no regrets about leaving town. After six failed marriages, she was experienced at walking out of bad situations, after all. "I was twenty years old when I left Conrad Hilton. I don't need this theater."

For her part, Gabor maintained to anyone who would listen that not only was she completely innocent; she was the real victim. "When you are famous, everyone wants to attack you. Look at what they do to the Reagans. Zsa Zsa became Zsa Zsa because of hard work." Nonetheless, she soon left town and returned to California, along with her dogs—although she was loudly threatening to sue the theater for her mistreatment.

Tabas and Mickey Rooney apparently approached other stars to take over the role, including Raquel Welch—who reportedly said she was not available. Eventually Terry Moore, another celebrity actress famous for her many failed marriages, finished up the run. Moore always made a point of meeting with audience members, signing autographs and posing for pictures with them.

Almost two years later, on April 12, 1985, the Philadelphia City Commission on Human Relations found the City Line Dinner Theater guilty of discrimination. The commission acknowledged the theater's previous history of accommodating handicapped persons, but nonetheless ordered it to "cease and desist from refusing, withholding from, or denying any person because of his physical handicap, any of its accommodations or facilities."

The *Philadelphia Daily News* reported that the attorney for the theater called the decision "outrageous," saying, "we're being punished for something we never did," and that the responsibility lay solely with Gabor. He blamed the bad publicity over the incident for the theater losing business and going dark over the previous few months.

Asked why the star herself was not cited by the panel, Commissioner Anthony E. Jackson, who chaired the panel that investigated the matter, said that, unlike the theater, "She isn't a public accommodation."

PART SEVEN
The Tryout Town

The Marx Brothers Stay for the Summer

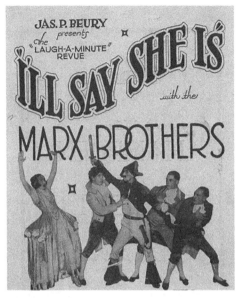

June 4, 1923: The Marx Brothers brought their new musical revue *I'll Say She Is* to the Walnut Street Theatre. They would stay the rest of the summer in the Quaker City.

The comic quartet had long been stars of the Keith-Albee vaudeville circuit. But they had somehow run afoul of E. F. Albee, the powerful head of the company, and the vengeful magnate, who loved to punish unruly performers, had them blacklisted from all his many theaters. The Marxes began to look for a Broadway vehicle to start them in a "legit" show—in any theatrical venue that Albee did not control

They found a low-end theater producer, Joseph "Minimum" Gates, who teamed them with an old script of a show about a millionairess looking for adventure called *Love for Sale*, by Will and Tom Johnstone (who had written a hit show called *Up in the Clouds* the previous year). In May 1923, the team cobbled together the script with skits from the brothers' vaudeville act, and they gathered a large assortment of miscellaneous set pieces from other shows.

With an ensemble that included the leading lady Muriel Hudson, the comic dancers Gertrude O'Connor and Florence Hedges, a couple of "sister act" duos, and a large assortment of chorus girls, they first took the show to the Lyric Theatre in Allentown, PA. But where would they go from there? The long hot summer stretched ahead, and the show needed to be held together until the next Broadway season. It turned out that Joseph Beury, owner of the Walnut, who was looking to keep his air-conditioned theater in Philadelphia open, had the answer.

At first, their audiences were meager. "June Philadelphia weather featured suffocating heat," wrote the Marx Brothers biographer Kyle Crichton. "Only Quakers and sailors from the Philadelphia Navy Yard could be imagined going to a theatre in such weather." Ads placed by producer Joe Gates mainly featured the scantily dressed girls in the chorus. But then the reviews began to pour in.

"It breaks all the speed limits of a conventional summer review," wrote the *North American*. "The chorus numbers, comedy scenes and specialties succeed each other with such bewildering rapidity that constant hustling is required to keep up with the performance." The reviewer for the *Philadelphia Record* returned to see it again and again—and proclaimed it was getting better every time. "It's the perfect summer show," crowed the *Public Ledger*. "Pretty girls, dancing ensembles that touch the top-most type of theatrical beauty, and the Four Marx Brothers, who submit an unusual quality of fun, follow on the long program in a delightful manner that spells cool and invigorating pleasure." Only the *Inquirer* remained lukewarm to the zany quartet's charms. "Interesting and entertaining" was all that its critic would say. It might last the summer, it allowed, praising each of the men not by their character names (Groucho, Harpo, Chico, and Zeppo) but by their actual names: Julius, Arthur, Leonard, and Herbert.

I'll Say She Is did indeed last the whole summer—pausing only for one night, August 9, to mark the passing of President Warren G. Harding. It played for a full 13 weeks before again going on tour.

Changes to the routines and additions to the cast had been occurring all summer long, too, as the comedians prepared to eventually take the show to New York. But the basic plot structure, such as it was, had remained the same.

At the top of the show, four vaudevillians besiege the office of a talent agent, looking for a break in showbiz. The agent declares he has no jobs for them, but tells them that if they want to seek their fortunes, he knows of "a wealthy young lady who claims she will give her heart, her hand, and her fortune to the man who gives her the greatest thrill." At the agent's further suggestion, the brothers variously assume the fairy-tale personas of "Beggarman, Thief, Doctor, Lawyer, Merchant, Chief," and the young lady, known thereafter as "The Beauty," becomes the object of their quest. On this thin structure the rest of the revue proceeded, interspersed with frequent dancing chorus numbers.

In Act Two, Groucho, dressed in long underwear and a tutu, entered as a Fairy Godmother. The Beauty tells Groucho that having been rich all her life, now she wants to be Cinderella and experience the thrill of being poor. He promises to be back at midnight. The Beauty decides to call her Rolls-Royce. Groucho tells her that if she wants to really experience being poor, there's a simple solution:

> **Groucho:** No Rolls-Royce, no taxi, no street car, no roller skates, not even a Chevrolet, you'll walk!
> **Beauty:** Marvelous, it's the first time in all my life I've ever walked!
> **Groucho:** Ah, then you have never been automobile riding?

One evening in August, as the run neared its end, while riffing on the general theme of automobiles and the pursuit of romance, Groucho turned to the Philadelphia audience. With devilish slyness, he confided: "Of all sad words, that from lips have parted/ The saddest are these—I can't get started." Then, waggling his thick painted eyebrows, he remarked he was "in the market for a new car" himself.

Rather missing the risque double entendre of the joke, a rumor that Groucho wanted a new car immediately caused a flurry of interest among Philadelphia auto dealers. As he wrote in a brief humor piece for the *Inquirer*: "The very next day various automobile concerns started calling me up on the phone. One more ambitious than the rest called at my hotel with his demonstration car." Groucho, liking the looks of the flashy new car, admiring the salesman's pluck as much as his pronounced portliness ("the most rotund individual that I ever clapped eyes upon"), agreed to go for a test drive.

> We turned into Broad Street and right in the middle of a highly illuminating speech on the part of my obese friend as to the advantage of four-wheel brakes … why, this bright and shiny bus stopped.
>
> The salesman stepped on the starter. But nothing started … He then did other things that usually spur a motionless car into motion, But nothing happened. A crowd began to gather and offer helpful advice to the embarrassed salesman and his famous passenger, including the classic joke: Get A Horse. "The suggestions from those assembled didn't seem to help. Every minute became more uncomfortable. Finally a traffic cop pushed through the throng. "Shove'er over t' th' curb," said he.
>
> But before any shoving was done, the auto finally responded to the starter's urging and moved along.

Nonetheless, Groucho got out at the next corner, telling the salesman he'd maybe stick with his old car. True, it was dented and needed a little paint, but "the darn thing doesn't collect crowds on Broad Street." Like the "Beauty," he'd just have to walk from here.

I'll Say She Is ended its run at the Walnut just before Labor Day, having reliably collected crowds its entire run in Philadelphia. Still produced by Beury, it moved on to Boston, and then for a long tour of the rest of the country. It landed back at the Walnut in late April 1924 for one final week, before finally opening at the Casino Theatre in New York in May. The Marx Brothers were on the verge of stardom, but it was always a matter of local pride to Philadelphians that they Saw It Here First. It was a boast that the city would continue to make, for many other shows and stars, throughout the next six decades of the city's Tryout Town era.

Mrs. Penfield Backs *Fioretta*

January 14, 1929: Earl Carroll's newest musical comedy, a "Venetian romance" entitled *Fioretta*, arrived for a pre-Broadway tryout run at the Erlanger Theatre on Market Street. Possibly the most expensive musical ever produced in America, it was financed by one woman, a Philadelphia heiress named Anne Weightman Penfield.

The show starred Lionel Atwill, a great leading man of his day, as well as Dorothy Knapp, regarded as one of the most beautiful women in America. Also in the cast was the comedian Leon Errol and the comedienne Fanny Brice, who had often worked together in the annual *Follies* of the producer Florenz Ziegfeld. Overall, there were 150 people in the company, including 56 chorines and a male chorus of 60. Earl Carroll, the famous producer of *Earl Carroll's Vanities*, meant for the show to rival those of Ziegfeld, and to surpass his *Follies* in box office success.

Properly referred to as "Mrs. Frederic Courtland Penfield" in the society pages of the newspapers, the show's backer was the richest woman in America, and possibly the world. The sole heir of her father, William Weightman "The Quinine King," she had also inherited the estates of her two late husbands, Robert J. C. Walker and F. C. Penfield. Now the sole owner of significant holdings in Philadelphia real estate, including a mansion near Rittenhouse Square and the Ravenhill estate in East Falls, Mrs. Penfield regularly paid the highest property taxes in the city. (In fact, back in the days when they used to publish federal income tax returns in the papers, she would be among the top names there, too.)

Mrs. Penfield, now 85, had taken a fancy to two young men, George Bagby and Romilly Johnson (aka "G. Romilly"), who had written the score for the lightly plotted operetta. She contacted Earl Carroll and over lunch informed him that she would finance the show entirely alone, sparing no expense. Twenty-one sets were required, as well as a full orchestra, and costumes that included enormous capes of real fur for the leading ladies, and real metal suits of armor for the male chorus.

Leon Errol, Lionel Atwill, and Dorothy Knapp were quickly engaged at top salaries. Knapp had been in a relationship with Carroll for five years and got the job—at a salary of $1,000 a week—even though she couldn't sing a note. Fanny Brice, supposedly playing "the great-great-granddaughter of the Merchant of Venice," was given a song entitled "The Wicked Old Village of Venice"—which she insisted on singing as "The Wicked Old Willage of *Wenice*."

After previews in Baltimore, Washington, and Philadelphia, the show eventually opened at Earl Carroll's own theater on Seventh Avenue. It was one of the most stellar social events of the season. Dorothy Knapp made her entrance in a sheet of ermine furs, covered in real diamond jewelry—Mrs. Penfield had insisted on no stage jewelry. Fanny Brice sang about Wenice, and the 56 chorines showed plenty of legs. The 60 chorus men even got some baritone notes in, without "straining too hard," said one reviewer, cattily. As for the comic Leon Errol, who was frequently utilizing his trademark bit where his left knee would suddenly fail him on stage, the critic remarked that it was funny the first 150 times, but not so much after that.

But despite many other fawning reviews (mostly by critics on Carroll's payroll), the top-heavy show was a crashing failure with the theatergoing public. Eventually, Dorothy Knapp was fired after being discovered *in flagrante delicto* with Atwill in a gondola backstage. Brice proved to be quite correct about the Wicked Old Willage, it turned out, and foreseeing the coming disaster she left the show in mid-April. Knapp, much to her fury, was replaced with Carroll's *new* girlfriend Beryl Wallace. But after the opening week Carroll was unable to fill the seats, and soon the elaborately produced show folded—as just about everybody in the show had always predicted it would.

Fioretta's choreographer, LeRoy Prinz, later said in an interview with the author Ken Murray: "It was one of the most horrendous experiences I've ever gone through. If I live to be 100 I'll never forget it. God almighty, the show was beautiful, but no matter what happened it didn't have a chance." On the night the show closed for good, the cast and crew all ran to cut up the expensive drapery and curtains in the set—all real silks, satins, and velvet—to make into bedspreads and drapes for their apartments.

Mrs. Penfield lost the $500,000 she had invested in *Fioretta*—this would be roughly the equivalent of $8.5 million today. Knapp, angry about being fired, as well as being cast off by Carroll, sued him and Mrs. Penfield for an additional $250,000 for breach of contract and defamation of character. (Romilly Johnson had originally been named in the lawsuit as well, but despondent over the humiliating failure of his show, the young composer had committed suicide.) After a lengthy trial, the judge found in Knapp's favor, but unconvinced that she had been uncompensated for her losses, awarded her just six cents. A few weeks later Mrs. Penfield passed away, her immense fortune largely intact.

Lysistrata—Modern Abdominal Merriment

April 28, 1930: Aristophanes' 2,500-year-old anti-war sex-comedy *Lysistrata* opened at the Walnut Street Theatre, produced by the Philadelphia Theatre Association. The text was adapted by the writer Gilbert Seldes and was directed by Norman Bel Geddes.

The racy old play had been written in the waning months of the Peloponnesian War, as the Athenian empire lay in ruins. And despite being on the winning side of the Great War, America itself was now in the early months of the Great Depression, when a lot of its world economic power seemed to be crumbling, too. Many of the hard-won achievements of its own international policy lay in tatters. Maybe a lot of outdated social rules needed to be tossed out, in such a situation. Paradoxically, the Athenian "Old Comedy" suddenly had an air of modernity. The ancient play had already been seen in the city four years earlier, in a touring production by the students of the Moscow Art Studio—followers of the great Stanislavsky.

The star-studded American cast of the 1930 production included Fay Bainter as Lysistrata, the leader of the sex strike and political revolt by the women of Athens against the constant war of the city's male leadership. Also in the cast were Hortense Alden as Myrrhina, Mary Blair as First Old Woman, Miriam Hopkins as Kalonika, Sydney Greenstreet as Probulous, the head of the Athenian senate, and Ernest Truex as Kinesias, the comically frustrated Athenian soldier whose wife withholds sex until he agrees to advocate for a peace treaty with Sparta. "There are enough first-rate actors in this cast for a dozen plays," marveled the *Camden Evening Courier*. The chorus of the 70-member ensemble was filled out by the Humphrey-Weidman Dancers.

Amazingly, given the Quaker City's often-demonstrated propensity to censor bawdy shows, the production went completely unhindered by the local authorities. This was likely due to the influence of the wealthy and eminent scholar Horace Howard Furness, Jr., editor of *The New Variorum Shakespeare* and a professor at the University of Pennsylvania. Furness, a regular attendee at the artistic productions of the Plays & Players Theatre on Delancey Street, had developed a late-in-life fascination with Ancient Greek classical drama. He had largely subsidized Gilbert Seldes' work on the translation. *Lysistrata* also had help from the Philadelphia Theatre Association, a group of wealthy and influential Philadelphians. This gave it an air of respectable scholarship and high culture. Additionally, Furness was a member of the Philadelphia Board of Theatrical Censors and could easily hinder any attempt by authorities to stop the show before it opened. However, Dr. Furness had not lived to see his long-planned project come to fruition, because he died of pneumonia just two weeks before the show opened.

As memorial tributes to the great man poured in, nobody in a position of authority in Philadelphia was going to challenge his final project. A local theater critic spotted one of the Board of Censors' most notoriously assiduous members, Reverend Frederick Poole, in the audience on opening night. The reporter asked if he was going to demand that the show be cut or banned (a penalty that Poole had imposed on several shows that had played Philadelphia lately). "I wouldn't if I could," replied Poole with a smile. "It is a beautiful play, but you see it was written about 400 B.C. And B.C. means in this case 'Before Censors.'"

Philadelphia critics and audiences were feeling similarly giddy. The show was "Buoyant, racy and irrepressibly candid," wrote H. T. Craven in the *Record*. "The audience rocked with laughter." Even the most blasé and unsophisticated people in the seats "roared and chucked over the disarmingly frank and spontaneously funny scenes," reported the *Ledger*. The *Bulletin* thought it was a "comical, beautiful and engaging spectacle that should not be missed."

Theater critic Brooks Atkinson of the *New York Times* even came down to Philadelphia to join the fun. Atkinson gave *Lysistrata* a glowing review, and he especially praised Norman Bel Geddes' direction. Furthermore, wrote Atkinson:

> Such free cartooning as Aristophanes was drawing in broad strokes in 411 B.C. is still amenable to several styles of interpretation—as feminist propaganda, as satire on the stupidity of war and peace and government by oratory, or as burlesque of love between the sexes. Describing it as indelicate is putting a fine edge on words. For "Lysistrata" is frankly bawdy. It does not wink at the facts of life. It ogles them with goat-song relish. It roars with delight over the discomfiture of soldiers who, like the men in Socrates' banquet, have returned home to their wives with the briskest resolutions possible. So Mr. Seldes and the current performance interpret it as abdominal merriment, unblushing and unrefined.

Fay Bainter left the lead role after three weeks and was replaced by Violet Kemble-Cooper. The production then went on to New York, where Blanche Yurka starred in an extended and successful run. But New York was experiencing its own struggles between local censors and theater artists. Amazingly, when Brooks Atkinson went to see the Broadway opening, though he still thought the show was delightful, he found it rather toned down from the Philadelphia production.

Ayn Rand Writes a Play

Ayn Rand had written a stage play before, called *Ideal*. But despite living in Hollywood, and having loose connections to the film business, she didn't really know how to craft a compelling script. *Ideal* was sort of a philosophical manifesto, crudely wrapped in a courtroom drama, about how all religion was inherently hypocritical, and by encouraging personal sacrifice it destroyed personal achievement and individual integrity.

What she *really* wanted to do was develop her idea for a movie about a heroic architect who builds skyscrapers. So *Ideal* went back into her desk drawer. Still, the 28-year-old Russian emigre writer was desperate for some sort of financial success. True, a screenplay of hers, *Red Pawn*, had been bought by Universal Studios, but they never produced it. Her agent could not sell her first novel, *We The Living*, to a publisher. Her husband Frank, a rarely employed actor, an amateur gardener, and a would-be artist, was bringing in very little income.

So, Rand quickly cranked out another courtroom drama. This one's plot devices were based upon a 1928 Broadway melodrama called *The Trial of Mary Dugan*. To change it up a bit, she mixed in some actual details from the recent downfall and death of Swedish millionaire Ivar Krueger ("The Match King"). From *Mary Dugan*, Rand also openly borrowed a staging stunt:—the "jury" for the play would be drawn from 12 volunteers from the audience, every night. Depending on the verdict these jurors arrived at, there could be three endings to the play: Guilty, Not Guilty, or Hung Jury. The rest of the audience would be in suspense. They might come back to the theater more than once to see—or help create—a different result the next time around. It could work! It had to work. An initial staging in a Los Angeles theater in late 1934, under the title *Woman on Trial*, went well—well enough to attract the attention of Al Woods, the original Broadway producer of *The Trial of Mary Dugan*.

Woods, who claimed to have produced over 250 shows in his career, was a colorful Broadway character who began every letter with "Hello, Sweetheart," and always signed off "With Love and Kisses." But Woods had also fallen on hard times during the Depression years, and he too was desperate for a money-making project. He regularly read six scripts a day from a pile on his desk, looking for hidden gems. For some reason he became intrigued with Rand's play, especially because she kept refusing to work with him. ("Hello Sweetheart" was not a good way to start a letter to Ayn Rand, apparently.)

Eventually she was persuaded when Woods announced that he had found financing for an actual production, now with the title *The Night of January 16th*. He had even gone ahead and booked the Chestnut Street Opera House in Philadelphia for rehearsals and a weeklong tryout run.. Still, Rand frequently tangled with Woods over other business decisions and his frequent attempts to rewrite her script. To her mind, Woods wanted to make it more of what she considered a "mere conventional drama."

Philadelphia seems to have been chosen for *The Night of January 16th* because the city had lately developed a reputation as a reliable proving ground for Broadway shows. The other inducement was that the Chestnut Street Opera House, a very old and unfashionable theater, was cheap to rent. After holding auditions, Woods cast 19-year-old Doris Nolan in the *femme fatale* role of Karen Andre—the character who is accused of murdering her boss. The actor Walter Pidgeon was cast as "Guts" Reagan, a gangster, and Verna Hillie as the widow. Woods also agreed to cast Marcella Swanson, the longtime girlfriend of powerful New York theater owner Lee Shubert, in the role of an "exotic dancer" who testifies in the second act (this was the favor that had been rewarded with additional backing for the show from Shubert). A Broadway theater was tentatively booked for the future—but the arrangement would be final only if the premiere in Philly went well.

With the help of what seems to have been a good cast, the play's first night—September 9, 1935—went well. In the first act, when the judge in the play asked for a "jury," he was overwhelmed with audience volunteers. Indeed, most of the chosen ones who trooped into the stage jury box were apparently aware that they would be asked to serve and were happy to take the nominal pay they would be given at the end of the night—it was the middle of a Depression, after all. Even those Philadelphians who stayed in their seats in the house got caught up in the murder story, in which every character seemed to have some motive for murdering the millionaire Bjorn Faulkner.

In his review the next day, Philadelphia theater critic Linton Martin wrote:

> Many "stunt" plays happen to be so long on novelty that they turn out to be woefully short on interest and entertainment. This murder mystery melodrama is neither. The novelty of drawing the jurors from among definitely known local lights—who last night responded to their names with such alacrity that they might have been "plants" or ghoulishly interested in the three dollars that had been announced as their cash reward—turned out to be just one adroit detail in a play that mounted constantly in suspense and surprise at the very end ... It is ably written and excellently acted, and the audience applauded spontaneously as the courtroom traffic surged

freely back and forth across the footlights, or, more accurately, up and down ladders leading from the stage to the auditorium.

But what Rand had not counted on was the rigors of that the out-of-town tryout process would demand of her. The producer was keenly observing the Philadelphia audience response, and based on their reactions instructed her to make changes after almost every show. She argued that these changes were damaging to her vision of the play. "One day in Philadelphia, she later recalled, "I was walking along the street ... and I started to cry... I felt like the whole thing was blind experimentation." She compared her play to a child confronted by a surgeon who was "trying to decide what organs to take out." It was an experience that many other playwrights who had accompanied a hopeful Broadway play to Philadelphia could surely identify with. To her additional horror, at one point Woods brought in a professional "play doctor" named Louis Weitzenkorn. Not only was he a self-avowed Marxist, which was bad enough, but his sole contribution was to suggest the insertion of two words (*You bastard!*) motivated by the theory that people were thrilled by a little rough language. To her relief, the line was later taken out.

Still, just as Al Woods had hoped, *The Night of January 16th* left its Philadelphia tryout run with a lot of momentum, and it thereafter became a hit on Broadway. It ran for seven full months, despite not always receiving positive reviews from New York critics. Many raved about it, but in the *New York Times* Brooks Atkinson called it "routine theatre with the usual brew of hokum." Subsequent productions in London and elsewhere did less well. But nonetheless, Ayn Rand had her first big success as a writer.

Rand later claimed that the play was not just a potboiler but a parable of her "Objectivist" philosophy, giving the audience a "sense of life." She considered that the role of the accused murderess Karen Andre epitomized a confident non-conformism and individual achievement, while the prosecution witnesses against her represented unimaginative conformity and the "envy of success." In her autobiography, she wrote that she wanted the play to convey the viewpoint that "Your life, your achievement, your happiness, your person are of paramount importance. Live up to your highest vision of yourself no matter what the circumstances you might encounter. An exalted view of self-esteem is man's most admirable quality."

Most modern critics regard *The Night of January 16th* as having aged quite badly, with stilted dialogue and stereotypical characters. As the writer Jennifer Burns put it, Rand intended the victim, Bjorn Faulkner, to embody heroic individualism, "but in the play he comes off as little more than an unscrupulous businessman with a taste for rough sex." It's been re-staged and re-titled several times, but the gimmick in the show, after years of many other "audience participation" plays being produced, no longer seems original or innovative. Even the underlying Randian philosophical elements now seem like, well, the usual brew of hokum.

Brando on Walnut Street

November 17, 1947: Tennessee Williams' *A Streetcar Named Desire* opened at the Walnut Street Theatre. Blanche DuBois and Stanley Kowalski were in town.

The Broadway-bound production, directed by Elia Kazan, which had already done tryout runs at the Shubert Theatre in New Haven and Plymouth in Boston, was staying for two weeks in Philadelphia before its New York premiere. Like many shows on shakedown tours, it was having issues—in previous towns there had been a bit of a technical shambles. And it didn't help that Tennessee Williams' relationship with his lover Pancho Rodriguez was noisily coming apart during the New England portion of the tour. Pancho would break out into a violent rage against the playwright in their hotel rooms some nights, and Williams would have to flee to Kazan's room to sleep.

Within the cast, Marlon Brando and the other actors were often at odds. To them he often seemed to have a deliberate lack of discipline. His constant shifting of approaches to a scene offended the long-engrained theatrical professionalism that Jessica Tandy, playing Blanche, cared about. Even the easygoing Karl Malden, who was playing Stanley's buddy Mitch, found rehearsing with Brando challenging. The company was looking forward to a steadier couple of weeks at the Walnut.

The play had plenty of competition for audiences in Philadelphia. Ironically, a touring production of *I Remember Mama*—the sweet nostalgia play that had given Brando his first small part in New York—was playing at the Locust to receptive houses. A revival of the musical *Show Boat* was packing them in at the Shubert. In fact, during the mid-20th century, Philadelphia's playgoers had gotten a bit spoiled by the wealth of theatrical fare that regularly showed up in the local theaters. If you missed a show that was previewing in Philly on its way to Broadway—well, you could always catch it again on its post-Broadway national tour, no problem.

Nevertheless, interest in seeing *Streetcar* was very high amongst those who were regular and avid attendees of Philadelphia theaters. Tennessee Williams was regarded as perhaps the most important playwright in the country, and Jessica Tandy was a big name on Broadway. The Society Pages reporter for the *Inquirer* complained:

"It resembled a football crush in the lobby of the Walnut … It was virtually impossible to see what was worn by the audience, as only the tops of heads were visible." Many in the audience were so struck with Brando's magnetism that they sided with Stanley over Blanche—which wasn't what Kazan wanted. Tennessee Williams told the director not to worry. "Marlon is a genius, but she's a worker and she will get better, and better."

After seeing the play, the *Inquirer*'s drama critic Edwin Schloss wrote the next day that it was "a moving and absorbing story," but that the production "showed some symptoms of growing pains." Designer Jo Mielziner's complicated lighting plot was not working well on opening night, for instance, and though Schloss felt that Kazan's direction had a "savage sincerity," he also declared that Williams' writing "did not cross the footlights." In fact, few Philly critics spent much space on assessing the performance of Marlon Brando or other actors. This proved to be the case when the show finally hit New York, too—reviewers gave most of their attention to Tandy, and very little to the rest of the cast. She was a star, after all, and Williams had been right that her steady approach to creating the unstable psychology and dark secrets of her character were beginning to pay off.

Visiting the show later in its Philadelphia run, critic Linton Martin predicted that "this play is bound to linger long in the memory, vividly and vitally, after most of the facile and ephemeral footlight offerings that predominate in every theater season have been forgotten." However, he did carp about Mielziner's set design: "No apparent point or purpose … is served by the device of making the walls transparent, so that outside action may be seen. If such incidental outside action played any integral part or was dramatically significant, it might have a meaning."

So, both Mielziner's designs and Brando's performance, now both regarded as monumental achievements of American theater, received rather short shrift in Philadelphia—at least from the press. But between the beauty of Williams' text, and the quality of *Streetcar*'s design and acting company, Elia Kazan could see what was about to burst onto the American stage—most especially Marlon Brando. "A performance miracle was in the making. What was there to be but grateful?"

World Premiere of *Death of a Salesman*

On Tuesday morning, January 18, 1949, the company of Arthur Miller's *Death of a Salesman* met at Pennsylvania Station in Manhattan and took the train down to Philadelphia. There was quiet excitement amongst the group. The project they were embarked upon seemed to be something quite special, they all felt. Maybe even historic. Their final run-through in the rehearsal space above the New Amsterdam Theatre on Monday had amazed even themselves with the power of drama. A small group of friends, mostly fellow actors, who had watched all leapt to their feet and cheered enthusiastically afterwards.

On Wednesday, January 19, at 10 am, the actors assembled at the Locust Street Theatre, a 1,500-seat house with Gothic-style decor, half a block west of Broad Street. Originally designed to be a legitimate theater, the Locust had been converted to a movie theater almost immediately after it opened, only becoming a home for live theater again in the 1930s. Though it had a large seating capacity, the Locust's small stage, its lack of air conditioning, and its odd location had meant it was never a favorite for Broadway producers looking for Philadelphia tryout run bookings. It certainly wasn't really suited for big musicals. But as a result, it was a relatively inexpensive theater to rent, and touring productions learned to cope with its challenges.

The stage crew and the designer Jo Mielziner were already there, struggling to fit his innovative set and lighting equipment inside. One of the dressing rooms backstage was converted into a sound studio for the musicians who would perform Alex North's incidental music underneath the constantly shifting landscape of the drama. Even more depended on the flow of Mielziner's intricate lighting cues on the extended forestage. There was also the rising section of scenery to the rear—showing the interior of the Lomans' house below, and their sons' bedrooms on view above, outlined by the suggestion of a roof. Due to the shallowness of the Locust's stage, there would be no room for a rear "crossover." The actors would just have to take a narrow passage underneath the stage floor to get from one side to the other, without being seen by the audience.

The cast included such talented and experienced actors as Arthur Kennedy, Cameron Mitchell, and Mildred Dunnock. But everyone—including Miller, director Elia Kazan, and producer Kermit Bloomgarden—knew that the success of the whole play depended on the performance of that large and brilliant Lee J. Cobb, who held the role of the title character. As soon as the actor had read the script, "I knew there was no living unless I played Willy Loman's part," he told an interviewer. "The play says something that has needed saying for a long time." Like many of the actors Kazan liked to work with, Cobb was also a former member of the Group Theatre. They had once been close friends, when they had been together on a tour of Clifford Odets' *Golden Boy*, but they had lately become more distant from each other. Ever since his massive success with *A Streetcar Named Desire*, Kazan had become one of the most respected and powerful directors in America, and he recommended Cobb strongly for the role to the other members of the team. The role was right there in the man himself, Kazan felt, just waiting to be drawn out.

"I knew him for a mass of contradictions," wrote Kazan in his 1988 memoir, *A Life*. "Loving and hateful, anxious yet still supremely pleased with himself, smug but full of doubt, guilty and arrogant, fiercely competitive but very withdrawn … boastful but with a modest air, begging for total acceptance no matter what he did to others. In other words, the part was him." But the actor had worried Miller during the first weeks of rehearsal, saying his words in a low rumble, seemingly so aware of how huge the task was that he had taken on that he needed to conserve his resources for the journey he would have to take every night. In the last week or so the show had really begun to come together. The final run-through rehearsals in New York had been so magnificent that members of the technical and creative team had held onto the sides of their heads and cried. "I began to weep myself," wrote Miller in his own memoir, *Timebends*. "It was as much, I think, out of pride in our art, in Lee's magical capacity to imagine, to collect within himself every mote of life since Genesis and to let it pour forth. He stood up there like a giant moving the Rocky Mountains into position." It is worth noting, however, that Miller's recollection of Cobb's late emergence during rehearsals is not confirmed by the recollections of others present. Alan Hewitt, another member of the company, did not remember Cobb ever "holding back."

The first full day in Philadelphia, most of the available time was taken up with technical rehearsals, as the actors accustomed themselves to working on the actual set. The initial run-through was mostly what is known as a "cue to cue," jumping from place to place in the script, as the needs of the light crew and the prop men running the set's elevator platforms required. The next day, Thursday the 20th, was a dress rehearsal, and the actors finally were given their full costumes and had a chance to try out their makeup. Many scenes were run multiple times, and the rehearsal did not end until midnight. Under Actors' Equity rules, there had to be at least a 12-hour break before the company could be called again. No full run-through was scheduled for the following afternoon, just individual work sessions on those scenes that Kazan or the actors felt needed some attention. Mildred Dunnock, for example, was worried about Linda Loman's final speech over Willy's grave during the play's epilogue. Kazan promised to have a private rehearsal with her that afternoon, before the first audience arrived.

The first public performance—an invited dress rehearsal, really—was on Friday evening on January 21. One can only imagine being one of those lucky Philadelphians who had been given a free ticket distributed by the show's publicists. Meanwhile, perhaps because Mielziner was still working on his multitudes of cues (he had even gotten stage manager Del Hughes to recruit local drama students to be stand-ins for the actors while he focused lights), Miller and Kazan suddenly decided it was very important to take Lee J. Cobb to a concert. Kazan, who had directed other shows at the Locust in recent seasons, was likely aware of the Philadelphia Orchestra's Friday matinees, which were a longstanding local tradition at the Academy of Music. They left word for Dunnock to meet them there, instead.

There is a famous description of this concert in Miller's *Timebends*:

> Across the street the Philadelphia Orchestra was playing Beethoven's Seventh Symphony that afternoon, and Kazan thought Cobb ought to hear some of it, wanting, I suppose, to prime the great hulk on whom all our hopes depended. The three of us were in a conspiracy to make absolutely every moment of every scene cohere to what preceded and followed it; we were aware that Willy's part was among the longest in dramatic literature, and Lee was showing signs of wearying. We sat on either side of him in a box [at the Academy], inviting him, as it were, to drink of the heroism of that music, to fling himself into his role tonight without holding back. We thought of ourselves, still, as a kind of continuation of a long and undying past.

Meanwhile, Mildred Dunnock had been searching for a way to get into the Academy of Music. She finally talked her way through a back entrance and found the three men upstairs, seated together in their box. The concert was just ending, with "every instrument playing full blast," she later recalled. "We came downstairs after it was over, and Kazan said, 'that's just what we're going to do tomorrow.' It was all very exciting." Kazan even showed up for the next day's rehearsal carrying a conductor's baton, ordering Dunnock to give that final speech *fortissimo*.

Crucially, Dunnock did not note exactly what music was being played that afternoon. It is Miller's version of the concert at the Academy that we depend on, and it has been reprinted in many collections of theatrical anecdotes, both popular and scholarly. The consensus has long been that Beethoven, as played by the Philadelphia Orchestra that afternoon, provided Lee J. Cobb with the necessary emotional and psychological boost for *Death of a Salesman*. Miller himself repeated the anecdote when he wrote the liner notes for a 1999 Philadelphia Orchestra recording of Beethoven's *Seventh Symphony*, conducted by Vladmir Ashkenazy.

But memories, even of great artists, are faulty. And theater historians, even great ones, have failed to note a crucial fact: the Philadelphia Orchestra was not performing the *Seventh Symphony* that Friday afternoon. They weren't even playing Beethoven. This can easily be verified by checking the Symphony's ads printed in Philadelphia newspapers for that week. The Orchestra was performing Mozart's *Overture to Don Giovanni*, Samuel Barber's *Symphony Number Two*, and Tchaikovsky's *Violin Concerto*—but not Beethoven. The reviews for these concerts were printed in all the Sunday editions—again, no mention at all of Beethoven. Looking ahead, one can note that the "Fabulous Philadelphians" did perform a work by Beethoven the following week, on Friday, January 28—but it was the composer's *Prometheus Overture*, not his *Seventh Symphony*.

Miller's error of recollection is completely forgivable, of course. *Timebends* is a memoir, not a work of history. Many of us have had the experience of recounting to others a strong and clear memory about our own past, only to discover later that we had gotten a key detail wrong. The character of Willy Loman, in *Death of a Salesman*, does *precisely* this same sort of thing, throughout the play. In fact, the whole dramatic structure of *Death of a Salesman* is based upon the desperate fictions of an unreliable mind—or rather, as the playwright himself once described them: "imaginings torn from the web of forgetting." Miller's original title for the play had even been *The Inside of His Head*.

So, it's unclear if Miller, Kazan, and Cobb were inspired by Mozart or by Tchaikovsky. More likely, the three men were moved by Samuel Barber's *Second Symphony*, a remarkable work that had been recently revised by the Philadelphia-area composer. Barber's darkly shifting tonalities in this piece have much in common with Miller's play, and are consonant with Alex North's music, too.

It's without dispute that Cobb's performances that weekend and throughout the following week stunned the Philadelphia audience. Certainly, we should never discount the major truth everyone who was present felt about this astounding play, which was revealed in another memory Miller shared about that first Philadelphia performance of *Salesman*. It's a fact that is confirmed by other accounts from people in that invited preview on Friday: when the play ended, there was no applause, just a stunned silence. Wrote Miller:

> Strange things began to go on in the audience. When the curtain came down, some people stood to put their coats on and sat down again, some, especially men, were bent forward covering their faces, and others were openly weeping. People crossed the theatre to stand quietly talking with one another. It seemed forever before someone remembered to applaud, and then there was no end to it.

Miller also remembered that as the audience slowly made its way out, from the back of the house he could see "a distinguished-looking elderly man" being led up the aisle, talking to his assistant, very urgently and excitedly. "This I learned, was Bernard Gimbel, head of the department store chain, who that night gave an order that no one in his stores was to be fired for being over age."

On Saturday, January 22, 1949, *Death of a Salesman* had its first official paying audience. As was typical for an important Philadelphia tryout premiere, "New York people" came down to see it. These included many of Miller's friends, such as the composer Kurt Weill and his wife Lotte Lenya, along with the actress Mab Anthony. They all went out together afterwards to a nearby coffee shop and Weill couldn't speak, but just kept shaking his head in amazement at the playwright. Miller recalled that Mab found her voice at last and told him something he would hear over and over again during the next few months: "It's the best play ever written."

There were no Sunday performances in Philadelphia back then, so the next day everyone rested. The first reviews were scheduled to appear in the Philadelphia newspapers on Monday the 24th. However, Alan Hewitt, who was playing the role of Howard, later remembered that the company was called to the theater at 4 pm on Sunday the 23rd, to hear early versions of the reviews that would be coming out the next day. They were all raves.

"*Death of a Salesman* is a truly great play, admirably acted," said the *Evening Bulletin*. "It is theater at its best." The *Camden Courier-Press* termed the play "THE dramatic hit of the year" and called Cobb's performance "the finest of his career." (The critic did suggest that the final scene of the play might perhaps be cut.) *Inquirer* reviewer Edwin H. Schloss, more than anyone else, seemed to understand the significance of what he had just witnessed: "*Death of a Salesman* is not 'entertainment' in the lightsome sense of the word," he wrote. "It is something bigger and better than that. It is an infinitely moving and bitterly splendid play—a triumph of the craft and magic of the theater, and a first rate work of dramatic art."

When these notices hit the streets on Monday, Philadelphians quickly mobbed the Locust's small ticket office. Every night the supposedly staid Quaker City audiences were "tremendously enthusiastic," remembered Mielziner. The entire two-week run was sold out—Lee J. Cobb couldn't even get tickets that he'd promised to an old friend for the final weekend without resorting to scalpers. Mail orders were soon flowing into Bloomgarden's office in New York for the previews at the Morosco Theatre in early February. And when the show had that second opening—the one in New York on February 10, the one most historians cite—once again the theatrical universe seemed to shift, and the critics raved. Miller, Kazan, and Cobb were the new gods of the American theater.

Yet, reflecting years later, amazingly Kazan was somewhat disappointed with Cobb's performances in New York. "When he received his fabulous notices, Lee awarded himself a status even higher than any the theatre world gave him. He was great as Willy Loman until he was told he was great and believed it—then he was less great." On the whole, Kazan thought Cobb had done his best work during the last week of the tryout run in Philadelphia.

It is worth noting that 25 years later, Arthur Miller took over the direction of a production of *Death of Salesman* at the Philadelphia Drama Guild—then the leading non-profit theater in Philadelphia—for a production at the Walnut Street Theatre starring Martin Balsam. (The original director, George C. Scott, had left town suddenly after an argument with Miller.) It is perhaps significant that on February 23, 1974—that very same week—the Philadelphia Orchestra was playing Beethoven's *Seventh Symphony* at the Academy of Music, under the baton of Zubin Mehta. Could this be perhaps the answer to the mystery as to why Miller mentally associated Beethoven's music with *Salesman*? We may never know. Because the answer, of course, was inside of his head.

Something Wild in the Country
Orpheus Descending

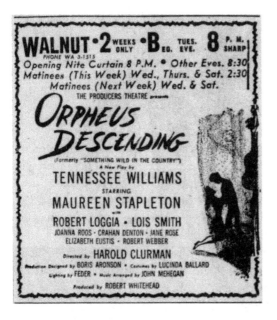

March 5, 1957: The latest Tennessee Williams drama opened at the Walnut Street Theatre. The title and the date of its first public performance had already been changed. Soon it would have a new leading man, too.

Williams had been rewriting the script, a Southern Gothic version of the Orpheus myth set in small-town Mississippi, for years now. An aging Italian beauty named Lady, caught in a marriage to a sick and tyrannical husband, yearns for a handsome young drifter, a musician passing through town. Tragedy ensues. It was one of his first plays ever fully produced when he was a struggling young playwright. Then called *Battle of Angels*, it had failed in Boston back in 1940—but on its reputation he had managed to get a job as a Hollywood screenwriter.

Williams, a compulsive re-writer of his own material, had picked it up again in 1951 after it had spent 11 years in his desk drawer. He kept working on it, on and off, for the next six years. Now one of the best-known playwrights in the world, he had such hits as *The Glass Menagerie*, *A Streetcar Named Desire*, and *Cat on a Hot Tin Roof* to his credit. His film *Baby Doll* had just been released in movie theaters, and other films of his plays had either been great box office and critical successes or were about to made into major Hollywood movies. So, theater producers were very open to backing his next project for the stage, whatever it was.

They were also aware that he'd had his share of commercial failures, too, like *Camino Real*. When *Camino* had come to Philadelphia in 1953 for a pre-Broadway tryout, it had played at the much grander Forrest Theatre, a few blocks up the street from the Walnut. But it did not go well. Philadelphia's reaction was perhaps best summed up by one of its regular playgoers, Mary Louise Graham. While watching a matinee performance, Mrs. Graham found herself befuddled after the first act.

None of the other Philadelphia "society" ladies seemed to know how to make head or tail of it either. During intermission she spotted a lone man thoughtfully pacing around the theater's lobby and approached him. "This play's completely over my head! What do you make of it?" she inquired.

"All you need to do is have a tender heart—and wait until the third act," Tennessee Williams advised her.

Four years later, once again searching for a new play to offer the public, Williams dusted off and rewrote his old work, now calling it *Something Wild in the Country*. His own description of the current version of the play went like this:

> On the surface it was and still is the tale of a wild-spirited boy who wanders into a conventional community of the South and creates the commotion of a fox in a chicken coop. But beneath that now familiar surface it is a play about unanswered questions that haunt the hearts of people and the difference between continuing to ask them … and the acceptance of prescribed answers that are not answers at all.

Like almost all of William's work, the play focused on the fate of delicate and vulnerable artistic souls, sensitive and damaged people that are harshly and violently treated by the cruelties of others. He told everyone he wanted his friend, the Italian actress Anna Magnani, to star in it, along with Marlon Brando, who had been such a sensation both the move and film of *A Streetcar Named Desire*. But Magnani, unsure of her English, turned it down, and Brando (now a movie star) refused to book any project that kept him longer than two months—which meant, essentially, no live plays.

Still, the great Harold Clurman signed on as the director, even though he was not known as being a fan of Williams' work. Clurman and the producers assembled a cast that included Maureen Stapleton and Robert Loggia in the two leading roles, and a young Lois Smith in the character of "Carol Cutrere," a lewd vagrant girl. Boris Aronson designed a set for the play, with long curving staircases leading to a dark and mysterious room.

The show arrived for its developmental run at the Walnut (after a week in Washington, DC) in some state of disarray, however. The producers were having their doubts about both their leading man and their title. The first performance was delayed from March 4 to March 5, and the title was changed back to *Orpheus Descending*.

Always willing to be the public face for his art, just before the show opened, on Sunday, March 3, Williams appeared on the NBC Sunday afternoon show *Wide Wide World*, hosted by Dave Garroway. The live television feed was set up directly from the Walnut Street Theatre. The show's theme that week was "A Man's Story," highlighting some stories of "America's outstanding men of achievement." (Also on the show that week: William O. Douglas, Mickey Mantle, psychiatrists Karl and William Menninger, and Gene Kelly.) In the interview, however, Williams mostly had to field questions about *Baby Doll*. Was it filled with too much sex and violence? Gamely, Williams defended his work, saying it was yet another of his pleas for empathy and understanding that would help improve the human situation. "I believe I can find something to love in any man if I know enough about him."

Still, he was anxious about how the current play at the Walnut would be received. Three days later, after the show's local premiere under the new title, critics in Philly were generally supportive. "Even with his predestined plot, *Orpheus Descending* has emotional vigor, the whisper of poetic expression, and a fascinating gallery of characters," wrote the *Inquirer*. "Head and shoulders above most plays that appear and pass for living theater," said the *Evening Bulletin*. But others were less impressed. Producer Robert Whitehead gamely plucked only the most positive sentences from all the reviews and put them in ads.

The re-titled play spent two weeks performing at the Walnut, but the creative team decided to make even more changes before going to New York. During the run, Loggia was informed that he was being replaced by Cliff Robertson, who would play Val on Broadway. But even though Robertson reportedly rose to the task, the show itself was mostly panned by New York critics and only ran for 68 performances. For several reasons, it marked the beginning of a long and difficult period in the playwright's life. "With *Orpheus Descending*," he told the *New York Herald-Tribune* in an interview, "I felt I was no longer acceptable to the theater public. Maybe, I thought, they'd had too much of a certain dish, and maybe they didn't want to eat any more."

Williams continued to work on the play, nonetheless, as was his habit. Hollywood, at least, was still quite welcoming to him. The drama was eventually rewritten yet again, this time as a film script for the 1960 movie *The Fugitive Kind*—directed by Sidney Lumet and starring both Anna Magnani and Marlon Brando as Lady and Val, just as Williams had wanted. Maureen Stapleton was in it, too—though this time in the role of the gentle housewife Vee, and the part was now quite smaller than in the original play. In the *New York Times*, critic Bosley Crowther wrote approvingly that "the skill with which it is performed sets one's senses to throbbing and feeling staggered and spent at the end." But many other reviewers treated the film quite harshly, and it died at the box office. Even Brando's take on Val has been described as one of his "least interesting performances" and the entire movie as "an unhappy marriage of Greek myth and Southern Gothic."

Williams' own life was soon to spin out of control, as his dependence on alcohol and various other drugs began to rule his life. Ominously, when *The Fugitive Kind* was released, he often escaped the unfriendly critical reception by retreating into drunken binges in the company of the actress Diana Barrymore. The scion of the famous Philadelphia acting family (though she herself had never lived there) was herself alarmingly similar to one of his own damaged and vulnerable characters. Both the writer and the actress, it turned out, had many despairing and fatal questions about prescribed answers—ones that were not answers at all.

Philadelphia, Here I Come!

January 17, 1966: The Irish company of Brian Friel's tragicomedy *Philadelphia, Here I Come!* opened in Philadelphia—where exactly none of them had ever been before. They knew at least that Philadelphia was real, while "Ballybeg" was a fictional place—a typical provincial small town in Ireland, where Friel was to set most of his plays.

The story of the play centers around a 25-year-old named Gareth O'Donnell, who is about to leave Ballybeg for America. The play splits the main character into two roles, the "Private" and the "Public" Gar, though Public Gar is the only one seen by the other characters. Both of the Gars quail at the thought of confronting the cold and uncommunicative father, S. B. O'Donnell, who himself is secretly devastated at his son's imminent departure from the family home, but just can't say the words asking him to stay. "Screwballs," the son calls him, inside his own head.

The city of Philadelphia represents a whole new world of possibility and opportunity for Gareth—as, historically speaking, it had for so many Irish immigrants over the years. As they contemplate their future, both parts of Gareth happily warble the refrain "Philadelphia, here I come!"—substituting the Pennsylvania city's name for "California" in the song Al Jolson had once made famous. The irony is that his destination was just as far from California as it was from Ireland, and Gareth's vision of glorious future will be quickly disillusioned when he finds himself working a dull job in a Philadelphia hotel. He will never come home rich, and the girl he loves will not be back home waiting for him to return, as she has already married. The prospect for Gareth is clear to the family's longtime housekeeper, Madge. He will likely end up full of sad regrets he can never speak about, just like Screwballs.

> When the boss was his age, he was the very same as him: leppin, and eejitin' about and actin' the clown; as like as two peas. And when he's the age the boss is now, he'll turn out just the same. And although I won't be here to see it, you'll find that he's learned nothin' in-between times. That's people for you—they'd put you astray in the head if you thought long enough about them.

Friel's work premiered in 1964 at the Dublin Theatre Festival, where it was hailed as the best play of the year. It was revived in 1965 at the Gaiety Theatre, also in Dublin, and the American producer David Merrick quickly bought the American rights and brought five of the original company to New York for rehearsals. Merrick was famous for the zany stunts he often staged to publicize his productions, but in this case the candidate for the proper city for the traditional out-of-town pre-Broadway tryout was quite obvious.

A staged photo was taken, showing the supposedly puzzled company gazing at a map of Philadelphia, while stage manager Mitchell Erickson pointed at the black dot showing the location of the Walnut Street Theatre. Irish cast members Donal Donnelly, Patrick Bedford (the two Gars) and Eamon Kelly (S.B.) were kneeling. Behind them stood Mairin O'Sullivan (Madge), Mavis Villiers (Lizzy), and director Hilton Edwards puffing on his pipe. At the very rear of the group was Friel himself.

After its Philadelphia opening, local critics were full of praise for the production, which went on to have a 326-performance run on Broadway and helped to establish Friel as a major world playwright. But the irony of its title struck many in the audience of the Walnut Street Theatre, even that first week. Reviewer Jerry Gaghan, writing in the *Daily News*, compared it to *Death of a Salesman*. The emptiness that Arthur Miller had already revealed in the American Dream, over at the Locust Street Theatre 17 years earlier, to his mind, was now even more evident. You could even see it from Ballybeg.

The King and Oy

November 11, 1966: Molly Picon quit the show *Chu Chem*, then in previews at the Locust Theatre. It was an ambitious musical about an actual historical event—the movement of a population of the "Kaifeng Jews" into China during the Middle Ages. But she smelled disaster and wanted out.

It wasn't self-evident to others that it would be a flop. Pre-show sales in Philadelphia had been brisk. True, the book and lyrics were by the relatively unknown trio of Ted Allen, Jim Haines, and Jack Wohl. But overall, *Chu Chem* (which means "wise man") had an impressive creative team: composer Mitch Leigh, director Albert Marre, and choreographer Jack Cole, all fresh off their success with the hit *Man of La Mancha*. The producer was the eminent Cheryl Crawford. The talented Willa Kim designed the costumes.

Coincidentally, a highly regarded touring production of *Man of La Mancha*, starring José Ferrer, was playing a few blocks away, at the Erlanger Theatre. It was hard to find seats for that show, so the synchronicity of yet another Mitch Leigh show in town helped drive ticket sales for *Chu Chem*. But the biggest draw was the cast, including two big names of Yiddish-language theater: Menasha Skulnik and Picon. Several rising Asian American actors were also in the cast: James Shigeta, Virginia Wing, and Tisa Chang. Jack Cole himself was performing the role of a Mongol warrior—rather unfortunately named "Lord Hoo Hah." The story was crafted as a play-within-a-play, as a mixed group of Asian and Western actors attempted to tell the story of a Jewish scholar (Skulnik) who travels into the Orient with his wife (Picon) and daughter (Marcia Rodd).

Picon and Skulnik were long acquainted with each other in the world of Yiddish-speaking performers, but her old friend was never really at home in English, let alone in Chinese theater techniques. "He was forever saying to me: 'What does it mean?' He was completely lost. It was the most vague, muddled script we had ever seen. Yonkel called our first run-through 'Amateur night in Dixie.'" Picon was especially furious with Marre, who had promised her top billing and a role as substantial as the one she had had in her recent hit show *Milk and Honey*. Unsatisfied with her part and frustrated by constant revisions to the script, Picon quit the show just before opening—something she had never done before. But she was glad she did it. "I was unemployed and happy … For the first time in months."

Her understudy, Henrietta Jacobson, took over the role, but the opening night was predictably rocky. At one point Jacobson, muddled, turned to the audience and philosophically announced, "There was a song here, but you'll be better off without it." A long sumo-style wrestling match that Marre had placed at the end of Act One, with two actors playing enormous Mongolians, did nothing to improve the dramatic action, most agreed. Lacking his former *Man of La Mancha* collaborators Dale Wasserman and Joe Darion, Mitch Leigh's songs were nowhere near as appealing to the audience, or the critics.

The reviews in the Philadelphia papers were scathing. Ernest Schier of the *Evening Bulletin* suggested "a better title might be *The King and Oy*." The production closed before the end of its scheduled tryout run, and disappointed—or perhaps relieved—Philadelphia ticket holders were left to scramble for refunds.

Muhammad Ali vs. Big Time Buck White

Muhammad Ali was in town, and as always in those days, he was the center of attention. "I came to Philadelphia looking for Frazier," he told a cheering crowd. "I'm going to his house and snatch him out and chew him up." But Ali wasn't going to fight Frazier—after all, he had a scheduled bout with *Big Time Buck White* at the Walnut Street Theatre.

Although never defeated in the ring, in 1969 Muhammad Ali was technically no longer a world champion. Two years previously, he had refused to be inducted into the Selective Service draft due to his religious convictions. The athlete was convicted in New York City by an all-white jury of dodging the draft under his former name of "Cassius Clay," and was sentenced to five years' jail time and a $10,000 fine. Ali was subsequently stripped of all his titles and lost his boxing license in every state in America. (Joe Frazier, the pride of North Philadelphia, was awarded the Heavyweight Championship instead.) Ali couldn't travel to another country—his American passport was withdrawn by the State Department. To top it all off, he was in a heated dispute with the Nation of Islam, too, as his religious beliefs evolved. The NOI had recently even taken away his right to preach to its congregations.

The U.S. Supreme court would eventually overturn Ali's conviction in June 1971, but while his case was making its way through the system, he looked for ways to keep busy and stay involved in matters important to him. Though he had a home outside Detroit, he often traveled restlessly around the country, preaching and making public appearances. Frequently he went to American universities and colleges and gave speeches. Sometimes he gave sparring matches and promoted the careers of other young Black fighters.

On April 30, 1969, Muhammad Ali was out and about in the streets of West Philly "to visit some of my millionaire friends," he joked to the reporters who were following him. He even conducted a brief sparring round on the street with local middleweight boxer Pigeon Smith. Though he seemed not to have lost his form, Ali quickly broke off the mock fight, theatrically gasping for breath, claiming he was overweight. A story in the *Philadelphia Daily News* read:

> Wearing a black, form-fitting Edwardian jacket and pointed Italian shoes, the fastest heavyweight champion of all time literally caused a traffic jam at a used car lot at 46th and Chestnut Sts. yesterday afternoon.
>
> The defrocked champion was not granting interviews during his Philadelphia visit. "But," he said, "anything you hear you can print." Ali said he's "through with boxing … [And] now that I'm suspended from preaching, I'm a 100 percent college lecturer. I'm leaving tonight for Albuquerque, to lecture at the University of New Mexico. I'm just like a professor."

But as it turned out, this announcement was a bit of rope-a-dope, too. Ali was not leaving town at all. He was staying in Philadelphia—and going to the theater.

Big Time Buck White was not a Philly project, true. The play by the author Dolan Tuotti had been developed in Los Angeles at the Watts Writers' Workshop. It ran for six months in a Hollywood theater, and then moved Off-Broadway at the Village South Theater in New York City. The show's producers wanted to develop it into a Broadway show, and were taking it on the road, hoping to attract a big-name star. In the press they dropped the names of well-known charismatic athletes of the day, such as Bill Russell, Rosie Greer—and Muhammad Ali.

A loose conglomeration of skits and scenes and musical numbers, the show was set during a supposed meeting of a group called B.A.D. ("Beautiful Alleluia Days"). There were characters named Hunter, Honey Man, Weasel, Rubber Band, and Jive. They were all waiting for the arrival of Buck White, a champion debater and public speaker. Meanwhile, there were a lot of interactions with the audience and musical numbers. When Buck White eventually arrived, striding to the podium with his big Afro hairdo proudly on display, things got even more interesting. He began by singing a number called "We Came in Chains." He even took a lot of questions from the audience, such as "Do you hate White People?"—but apparently most of the questioners were "plants." "I see y'all came," Buck White told the crowd. "But that's where you made your mistake. We're gonna be blowing your mind with a whole lot of soul." For the moment the role of Buck White was played by the actor Dick Williams, who also was the director.

This would be the last show staged in the Walnut Street Theatre under the auspices of the Shubert Organization. It had long owned the old house but were now eager to offload it to a non-profit organization that was even then being formed. To the Shuberts' amazement, *Buck White* was doing something that had not often happened lately—bringing large numbers of African Americans to the Walnut. "It's a very controversial play but everybody should see it," wrote columnist Eve-Lyn in the *Philadelphia Tribune*. "It is in tune with life today and has a message and a plot that tells a real true story of what is going on in the ghettos, where an impatient frustrated group cry out for freedom for which we have been hearing for years."

The show had originally been slated for a two-week run at the Walnut, but the enthusiastic audience response had resulted in it being held over again and again. In late April, the cast visited the offices of the *Philadelphia Tribune*—where they "turned on" the staff of the paper (in the positive 1960s sense of the term). "Everyone in Philadelphia knows at least one self-righteous 'militant' who goes through the antics portrayed on the stage when confronted by the white man's money," wrote the paper afterwards. "The play is an uproarious, albeit uncomfortable for some Negroes, way to spend the evening."

On Sunday, May 4, Ali caught the final show of *Big Time Buck White*. Evidently, he liked what he saw, because he agreed to be in it. Now featuring Ali, the show ran on Broadway in December 1969 at the George Abbot Theatre on 54th Street. Some reporters still insisted on calling him "Clay" in their reviews. As had been the case with Big Bill Tilden's appearance in a Broadway show over 40 years earlier, the sports metaphors flew thick and fast. The United Press International critic decreed that the boxer had "won the decision." But the show was not a knock-out. It closed after only one week.

In March 1971, his right to fight restored, Muhammad Ali was back in the boxing ring with Philadelphia's hometown champ. Ali lost to Joe Frazier by unanimous decision—his first ever professional defeat.

The Line of Least Existence—Last Days of the TLA

January 24, 1970: *The Line of Least Existence*, a rock opera with a book by painter and novelist Rosalyn Drexler and music by 21-year-old John Hall, opened at the Theatre of the Living Arts. Tom Bissinger, the artistic director of the TLA, helmed the project, for which he had received a $22,000 grant from the National Endowment of the Arts. It had also received a pilot production at Judson Poets' Theatre in New York the preceding year. Rosalyn Drexler stated to an interviewer that *The Line of Least Existence* was inspired by a story she had once heard about "a half-crazy, paranoiac old man who hung around the court area of Manhattan, giving out handbills about his missing daughter."

Notably, the actor Judd Hirsch, who had starred in several other successful and well-received recent TLA shows (including *Harry, Noon and Night* and *The Recruiting Officer*) led the cast in the role of a "lunatic doctor" named Toloon Fraak. Other cast members included the playwright's daughter Rachel Drexler, who along with Patti Perkins and Stacey Jones played the chorus referred to collectively as "Plastic Masters." Amy Taubin was the key role of Ibolya, the runaway chick out to experience the world.

By all accounts, the most endearing member of the company was a young New York actor named Danny DeVito, who played a talking and singing lapdog named Andy, a sort of hippie puppy who wore sneakers, gloves, and sunglasses. The dog also had a definite sexual affinity for its owner, Mrs. Toloon Fraak, played by Gretel Cummings. One of Andy's crowd-pleasing songs went: "I'm no mutt/ In a rut/ 'Cause I've learned a few tricks in my day!/ It's not smut/ If some slut/ Wants to throw some affection my way!"

Like other avant-garde 1960s shows, *Line of Least Existence* had a loose plot structure and highly colloquial and explicit dialogue. Drexler was a well-regarded writer, and her script had recently made waves in a downtown New York workshop production. So, if its creators' open ambitions were that it could be "the next *Hair*," that was not a crazy idea. Like *Hair*, the show's rights had once belonged to the Public Theater's Joe Papp. Now that it was his project, Bissinger clearly hoped that this musical might save the TLA's fortunes. He was willing to try, anyway, and everyone at TLA did their best to raise local interest in the show. Like *Hair*, there *might* even be onstage nudity, the theater's pre-show publicity hinted slyly.

The stage of the TLA was covered with Eugene Lee's set, which included lighted boxes, a catwalk, projection screens, a psychiatrist's couch, a doghouse, and a ramp extending into the house on which the rock band musicians were seated. It was very reminiscent, in fact, of Lee's previous work (along with John Conklin) on the set of Rochelle Owens' *Beclch*, which two years earlier had also attempted to radically transform the TLA's thrust stage and traditional rows of audience seating.

In the five years since its founding, the TLA had staged plays by Samuel Beckett and Jean Anouilh. But recently, according to *Philadelphia Daily News* reviewer Charles Petzold, the organization was "rapidly moving away from the Theater of the Absurd toward the Theater of the Ridiculous." He declared *The Line of Least Existence* was "an abortive escape from reality." The TLA space, before being converted in the mid-1960s, was a local movie theater and still had a working projector. At the top of the show the credits for the production were rapidly scrolled across a screen. At the end of the first act, a huge inflatable erect penis spewed foam all over the stage. Actual paper programs were not handed out until the show was over.

Petzold described his visit to South Street on the opening night of *Least Existence* for his Philadelphia readers:

> Entrance to the fantasyland is single file through a revolving wooden door which serves no apparent purpose other than instantaneous introduction to the total environment within. Seating, for the most part, is on wooden bleachers erected over the regular seats. They are about as comfortable as the cheapest seats at Connie Mack Stadium. There is a plot, of sorts. It concerns a Hungarian refugee trying to find his daughter. He later locates her in the company of a lunatic doctor. And that's about it.

It all called to mind the recent RSC production of *Marat/Sade* to Petzold:

> The actors seem more like the inmates of the Asylum of Charenton than performers in a play. The asylum feeling is particularly evident during the climactic "Wow Me Now" number in which the performers wear white gowns, cavort in a hospital-like setting and dance in a sea of foam. The nudity hinted at in the pre-show publicity fails to come off.

Overall, declared Petzold, the show was a two-hour-long cartoon which could have ended after the first act. Other reviewers were just as harsh, and not just in the stodgy big publications. The headline in the free weekly paper *Philadelphia After Dark* was: "A poor excuse for a musical." (Everybody admitted they liked Andy the Dog, though.)

The Line of Least Existence also met with little favor from other reviewers and Philadelphia audiences. Even Bissinger would admit he saw how badly it was going. "The script that was funny when I first read it now came across as obvious and puerile ... There was no way to stop the impending crash. I got stoned just to come to rehearsals. It didn't improve anything."

Crucially, the show was also the last straw for the TLA's Board of Directors, who had ejected former artistic director André Gregory over similar excesses in 1967. Box office returns for *The Line of Least Existence* were meager. There was clearly going to be no repeat of the commercial success of *Hair*. The hope that this show would save the theater, that it would go on to have a New York run—it popped like a soap bubble on opening night.

Despite many last-ditch efforts, including selling off parts of the musical's expensive set at a fundraising auction, the non-profit's funders pulled the plug and canceled the rest of the season. Later that summer, the company filed for bankruptcy. The Theatre of the Living Arts—the first real candidate for Philadelphia's ambitions to have its own thriving non-profit regional theater company—had found its own line of nonexistence.

However, eight years later, Judd Hirsch and Danny DeVito found themselves together again in the cast of the hit TV sitcom *Taxi*, which also featured a bunch of wildly eccentric characters. The success of the show would quickly serve to propel both men to greater stardom. And several decades after that, DeVito (who can be seen elbow-to-elbow with Tom Bissinger in one of the last cast photos ever taken at the Theatre of the Living Arts, lying on his back and wearing sunglasses), would learn that no matter what happens, it's always sunny in Philadelphia.

Auntie Mame Leaves Early

April 4, 1966: The Jerry Herman musical *Mame*, starring Angela Lansbury, had its world premiere opening performance at the Shubert Theatre in Philadelphia. Though there would still be some changes to be made, admitted director Gene Saks, Philadelphia had seemed like the natural place to develop and refine the show before taking it to New York the following month.

In his review the next day, *Inquirer* critic Henry Murdock called it "a rollicking raucous and rhythmic musical comedy." The Shubert had been jam-packed for the occasion, he reported, and "with not the slightest dissent from this reviewer, [everyone] seemed to think it was the opening of a hit." The Philadelphia audience was so raucous and appreciative in its guffaws, it sounded like it was working for a TV laugh track, wrote the *Daily News*. Other influential reviewers on local TV stations lavished praise on Lansbury. The *Courier-Press* and the *Evening Bulletin* happily agreed that, though like many shows they had seen in development over the years, *Mame* needed a little trimming, it had every sign of being a winner.

And once the show got to Broadway, it was a hit exactly as everyone had predicted—running for over 1,500 performances over four seasons. It was one of the greatest commercial successes ever developed in Philadelphia during the Tryout Era.

***

July 1983: Auntie Mame was back! Seventeen years after her initial blockbuster tryout, Angela Lansbury headlined a revival production of *Mame*. Also in the cast was one of Philadelphia's own, the actress and singer Anne Francine, as the character Vera Charles.

But there was a markedly different feeling in Philadelphia this time around. The Shubert Theatre, which originally hosted the show, was now called the Merriam Theatre and was used mostly for student productions at the University of the Arts. The revival's producers chose to book the cavernous Academy of Music stage instead, which was vacant during the summer months when the Philadelphia Orchestra was not in residence. The Forrest Theatre, which might have better held the show, was already booked for the pre-Broadway run of *Private Lives* starring Elizabeth Taylor and Richard Burton.

This was nothing like the earlier triumph. Critical response by Philadelphia's reviewers was muted. Individual performers, such as Lansbury and Francine, were highly praised. But still, as the saying went, the show did not come across the footlights. "In the vastness of the Academy of Music stage, the show did not seem to be reaching into the audience as effortlessly as it should at least give the impression of doing," wrote William Collins in the *Inquirer*. "There was some ragged and loud playing in the pit orchestra and the dancing lacked sharpness and verve. The scenery often had a dull, neutral look." In the *Daily News*, reviewer Nels Nelson stated it was difficult to hear the dialogue.

Mame left its Academy of Music run earlier than planned that July. Not, said the producers, because of the lukewarm reviews in Philadelphia, but because the Gershwin Theatre in New York had suddenly become available, and they needed to grab it. Still, once again Philadelphia's verdict had been proved right. The show ran from July 24 to the end of summer, and then closed after only 41 performances.

Notably, this version of *Mame* would be the last Broadway production booked into the Academy of Music for 20 years. It would not be until after significant renovations were completed in the late 1990s and early 2000s that big musicals began being booked there—and then, only in post-Broadway tours. The long Tryout Town era of Philadelphia theater history was effectively over.

Significantly, something else had developed in Philadelphia—a trend which had gotten off to a rocky start in the '60s, but which slowly gathered energy throughout the '70s and '80s. The city's performing arts community had opened a new window, as it were, and now absolutely nothing was the same. Over the next five decades the city developed dozens of professional non-profit theater companies. These were where most new plays were to be found and developed.

PART EIGHT
The Manning Street Theatre

Hamlet in the Rafters

In 1969, two young former employees of the Theatre of the Living Arts on South Street, Stuart Finkelstein and Mary Kay Bernardo, decided to replicate the excitement and the intensely focused energy that had once been the hallmark of André Gregory's TLA by organizing their own theater group. They envisioned starting a "cafe theater"—a combination of a coffee house and cabaret.

The place they found was several blocks north of the TLA, in a building that fronted on 12th Street. The location was on the fringes of Philadelphia's lively and lurid "Locust Strip," an area full of dive bars and after-hours illegal activity. The Midway, a bar that catered to a mostly gay clientele, took up the first floor. Around the corner, on the side of the building, off the narrow alleyway called Manning Street, a small door led to a narrow and steep flight of steps that ascended to the top floor. Finkelstein and Bernardo, using small grants (and writing a few small checks they didn't quite have the funds to cover yet), the pair made arrangements to rent this upstairs area as a performance space.

In March of that year, the *Evening Bulletin*'s theater critic Ernest Schier, wanting to be supportive, climbed the flight of steps and paid a visit to the young organization. He was bemused by the red walls and gilt mirror decor, the free coffee and exotic sandwich menu, and also by the hippie waitress "with a thick, for real pony tail, braided beneath her hips." Nevertheless, Schier was interested and intrigued by the nascent Philadelphia experimental theater scene and wrote an encouraging article for the paper. He also generously reviewed their first few productions (which included plays by both Jules Pfeiffer and Samuel Beckett), something which helped bring in enough crowds to make the shows moderately successful and attract the interest of a base of financial supporters.

Some wealthy Philadelphians proved particularly helpful to the youthful theater makers. A prominent art collector and a former board member at TLA, Daniel Dietrich, helped them find an empty church building at 1520 Lombard Street, in a blighted urban corridor formerly slated for demolition to build a highway. Now the highway project, like the church, had been abandoned, so Dietrich confidently also donated funds for renovation and remodeling. But there was also crucial support from other Philadelphians who were not members of the social elite. Barry Sandrow, the owner of Doc Watson's Bar on 11th Street, provided not only financial support, but his establishment also offered a reliable gathering place for the company—and he loyally came to see every show.

The old church building on Lombard, in the middle of the block between 15th and 16th Streets, was a testament of the deep history of the neighborhood. Unlike the large and elaborate Wesley A. M. E. Zion Church a few steps to the east, it was mostly unornamented. A modest structure with no steeple, it had a narrow A-frame design with tall plain windows facing the street. The double front doors led to a small lobby, with stairs climbing up to a high second-floor worship area. It had been constructed in the late 19th century for a Black congregation organized under the Union American Methodist Episcopal Church. After its congregation had dwindled, the building had functioned as a place for community gatherings. During the 1930s and '40s it was known as "Valyric Hall," available for use by public speakers. But as the Seventh Ward neighborhood had largely emptied out under threat from the highway project, the building had become completely abandoned.

By 1970, as the neighborhood was at the beginning stages of gentrification, it belonged to an adjacent nursing home, which agreed to rent it to the Manning Street group for $50 a month—but only if they would agree to do all repairs and renovations themselves. They took it. For pragmatic reasons the group decided to keep "Manning Street Theatre" instead of renaming itself after the new street address. The realities of running a small non-profit had certain limits, and the relationships that they had already built with local grant givers were too important to risk confusing them with a different name.

To help with the renovation of the new space, Dietrich put Finkelstein and Bernardo in touch with an architect, a Louis Kahn protege named Frank Weise, who lived nearby. Weise's plan for the church space was radical but simple and effective: remove the ceiling and expose the rafter beams to allow the installation of catwalks and a lighting grid, eliminate all the pews and build a series of angled risers for the audience, and construct a dressing room area underneath the stage. There were no seats, but 120 large pillows and cushions were to be scattered about on the risers for the audience to recline upon as they wished.

The construction work, hastily begun and with limited funding, would end up taking the better part of two years—during which the company struggled to continue to produce plays when and where they could. Labor was mostly done by a group of about 30 friends and volunteers. Young actors in the company also joined in. Linda Evans, who had grown up in Oklahoma and arrived in Philadelphia when her husband was assigned to duty in the Philadelphia Navy Yard, impulsively auditioned for the company when she read an ad in the newspaper. She soon became an enthusiastic member of the company.

> It was like a movie: *Hey kids let's make a theater out of a barn!* Heading up to the theater on Lombard Street every day to paint, or nail down carpet on the risers, [or] watch the local architect talk to Stuart and Mary Kaye was exciting. Listening to Stuart fund-raising and arm-twisting on the phone in the new lobby. It was a do-it-yourself effort, and we all loved it.

Still, the Philadelphia Department of Licenses and Inspections proved to be a significant obstacle, and it several times refused to certify the building for occupancy. The first planned production, Peter Nichols' *A Day in the Death of Joe Egg*, had to be postponed repeatedly over the course of the next year, and multiple last-minute cancellation notices were placed in the papers. Finkelstein was darkly suspicious of L&I's motives. He groused openly that perhaps Jay Kogan from the rival Society Hill Playhouse (who also worked for the Department) was behind the trouble with the inspectors. But this was no doubt unfair to Kogan. "I think it was mostly a question of us being young and inexperienced," Finkelstein admitted years later. Eventually he and Bernardo were forced to borrow the space of their former employer, the Theatre of the Living Arts, to get the play in front of an audience. Subsequent productions at 1520 Lombard—intellectually demanding plays by Joe Orton, Harold Pinter, and Samuel Beckett—although well reviewed, also met with trouble from building inspectors, and often played to limited audiences. "I remember playing one matinee to three ladies with cherries in their hats," recalls Evans. "My parents came from Oklahoma to see if I had lost my mind, and after seeing me in Pinter, and my sixth-floor walk-up on Pine Street, went home being quite sure that I had."

By the end of 1971, things were beginning to take a turn for the better. The building inspectors had at last been satisfied. A cabaret show, *The Decline and Fall of the Whole World as Seen Through the Eyes of Cole Porter*, became a surprisingly popular hit for the young troupe, which was forming a core company of local actors, including Evans, Don Kersey, Patrick Cronin, Kate Macauley, and Judith Cohen. The designer Douglas Ensign created simple and imaginative sets, as he would for most of the company's productions over the next four years. The musician Ken Ford, universally described later by all fellow company members as having an immense talent, provided the piano accompaniment and musical direction. The *Porter* show was followed by Molière's *The Misanthrope*—a production in which Finkelstein and Bernardo made a virtue of the company's small finances. Seventeenth-century wigs were fashioned from cardboard and placed on the actors' heads, and at the top of the show the whole ensemble was arrayed onstage as if they were cardboard cutouts, holding a sustained tableau as the delighted audience entered the theater.

Additionally, the troupe was beginning to discover a reliable form of income by staging and marketing shows for young audiences that could be booked by local schools. Ken Ford had written a musical play for children about Robin Hood, and Finkelstein began to actively recruit new company members from Philadelphia area colleges to fill out the cast. In the late 1960s there had been a significant expansion of many Philadelphia area university theater programs and there were a lot of eager young performers to choose from. John Connolly, a student at La Salle College, had only recently turned to theater as a fun and therapeutic break from his anti-war political activism. He was playing Hamlet in an undergraduate production, when Stuart Finkelstein came backstage and offered him a job in *Robin Hood*. "It was one of the moments when you can feel your life changing," recalled Connolly. "I really loved being in that company."

The awareness of national events would shape the choices of the young company, as it developed projects to perform in the space on Lombard Street. In March 1972 the U.S. presidential election campaign began to heat up, and the war in Vietnam continued to rage. Actor and Temple University faculty member Patrick Cronin directed and starred in a documentary play *The Trial of the Catonsville Nine* by Saul Levitt, based upon the recent arrest and trial of anti-Vietnam War draft protestors, including Father Daniel Berrigan. To follow this, the Manning Street group staged a radically rewritten version of Shakespeare's *Hamlet*, in the manner of Charles Marowitz, which also questioned all aspects of authority, and in which the character of the traditionally reliable Horatio would turn out to be the villain of the play. The coveted role of Hamlet would be played by an actor who was still fairly new to the company, Joseph Stinson.

Stinson was a Philly guy through and through, having grown up in the Society Hill neighborhood and having gotten involved with theater at St. Joseph's Prep. He then had studied theater at St. Joseph's College and had also spent some time in the Temple University graduate acting program. He was a dynamic actor, with a drive and ambition that was as evident as the bristling dark facial hair that he often let grow to an impressive extent. Stinson had already auditioned for the few professional-level theaters there were in Philadelphia, including Manning Street, but like many actors he had eventually left town to try his luck in New York. He was honing his craft in Manhattan in the program of Circle in the Square Theatre, and hoping to move on quickly to bigger things. Nevertheless, recalls Stinson, when famous actors would stop by the school to help out, "Never turn down a job" was the advice he would remember most clearly: "Work is work." So, when he got a call from Finkelstein early in 1972, offering him a job if he would go back to Philadelphia to do the title character in the children's theater production of *Robin Hood*, Stinson took it.

Stinson found that the energetic group of a dozen or so youthful Philadelphians now working regularly in the Manning Street company were warm and welcoming. Furthermore, to Stinson, the flexible ramshackle performance space on Lombard Street was everything he wanted and held only possibilities. Finkelstein and his new young company were already working in a style of highly physicalized theater, and that suited the energetic and restless Stinson just fine. As rehearsals for the May 1972 production of *Hamlet* got underway, he realized he could crawl out of the lighting booth at the back of the audience area and get up onto the rafters of the old church. The speech "To be, or not to be …" was delivered as Stinson worked his way precariously along the wooden beams, dangling his feet over the audience's heads—the prince's suicidal thoughts all-too imminent and threateningly real. "We were all just spellbound," remembered his director. "Every night the audience would have a sense of shock." Stinson's bravery and talent quickly made him a leading actor in the company, who would be featured in most of its subsequent productions.

In the fall of 1972, as Richard Nixon (who had been endorsed by the new Democratic Mayor of Philadelphia, the larger-than-life controversial former police commissioner Frank Rizzo) was cruising toward a landslide reelection to the presidency, the group presented *Ubu Roi* by Alfred Jarry in a new English translation by a Temple undergraduate, Jacques Houis. In the Manning Street version, the famously bawdy and juvenile absurdist farce from the late 19th century was played on a stage covered with old mattresses by set designer Doug Ensign. Stinson played Pere Ubu, John Connolly was Ma Ubu, and the rest of the company, including Maureen Garrett, Fritz Kupfer, Linda Evans, and others, took on multiple roles. Trap doors, fart jokes, and an onstage banquet were all part of the show. It was this highly anti-establishment aspect of the play, with plenty of references to both Nixon and Rizzo thrown in, that paradoxically began to draw even more interest from local Philadelphia philanthropists and major newspaper reviewers. "It is all enormously entertaining," wrote Walter Naedele in the *Evening Bulletin*, who approved of the banquet scene, in which the audience was invited to share a messy meal of fruit slices and Philly soft pretzels. "How to dress for your first Ubu banquet: PANTS," advised Susan Walker in the alternative paper *WELCOMAT*. "You will have to sit on cushions and you will find that dancing on mattresses is enormously unbalancing. But it must be the funniest play to hit Philadelphia in some time."

To follow this success, Finkelstein then staged a version of the Hans Christian Andersen story *The Emperor's Nightingale*, with music by Ken Ford, which impressed the *Evening Bulletin* critic enormously: "Area theatergoers whose activities have been confined to the more conventional settings of the Forrest, the Walnut or the Locust, etc. should be certain to do one thing. They should dig themselves up at least one juvenile and make a Saturday afternoon journey down to Lombard Street." But one of the best of all validations, as far as the youthful management team and its board were concerned, was that due to the success of these shows a $5,000 grant had arrived from a local arts foundation.

With some tenuous financial stability achieved, a January production of Bertolt Brecht's play *Baal* was the next project. Although once again the production was well received by critics and the loyal Manning Street audience, there were some signs that personal and professional tensions were beginning to surface among the company. These difficult feelings and other underlying issues all came to a head when Finkelstein decided to stage a classic Greek tragedy, Euripides' *The Women of Trachis*, using an adaptation by Ezra Pound, in February and March of 1973. It was not a popular choice—either with the actors or the audience. A grim, lesser-known

Greek tragedy adapted by a notoriously right-wing poet was a very hard sell, and ticket sales were meager. An important additional complication was that the personal relationship between Bernardo and Finkelstein had come to an end, bringing with it all the awkwardness and emotional repercussions amongst fellow members of the organization that might be expected. (Soon, Bernardo would walk away from involvement with the organization altogether.)

Increasingly, much of the company began to chafe under Finkelstein's highly intellectual leadership. A long and demanding experimental workshop was conducted with the company on the subject of the clown character of Pierrot, inspired by the French movie *The Children of Paradise*. The improvisations and exercises, conducted along the lines of a Grotowski "investigation," however, left the actors of the company rather more resentful than artistically fulfilled. Moreover, there was a general feeling among the actors that their own careers and financial needs were not being considered in an atmosphere that seemed to adhere to a rigorous artistic ideology. Finkelstein and the actors he had gathered were increasingly at odds—and both sides began looking for a way out. "It wasn't what I wanted" Finkelstein told a reporter. "It was getting like commercial theater. Cultural politics—the necessity of raising funds and then pleasing the donors—was forcing us to sell out."

The discontented company members eventually staged what they would later generally call, amongst themselves, a "revolt." They told the board they could no longer work with Finkelstein. "It was both fortunate and unfortunate," the ousted artistic director admitted years later, with the benefit of hindsight. "It was always hard work and hand to mouth, but we had a lot of people who were really talented. Really special and courageous actors who were ready to do a lot of things. I was ready to leave, and I was probably exhausted." The board of the theater cut ties with its founder and handed over creative control to Joe Stinson.

The Two Joes

The actors would run the theater, Stinson told the board. A core group of performers, who had gelled doing a workshop sponsored and hosted by the Walnut Street Theatre earlier in the year, would do all the administrative jobs of the organization, as well as the artistic work of putting on the plays. Stinson would be the nominal artistic director, and Jim Lambert would keep the books. Others would run the box office, apply for grants, set the production schedule, build the sets, and so forth. The board, to Stinson's surprise, quickly agreed with the plan, and the reconstituted company set about planning a new organizational and artistic paradigm. Instead of being rigorously idealistic, it should be pragmatic, flexible, and run on a cooperative basis. Instead of trying to make its way mostly alone, the group would try to form bonds with other Philadelphia and even New York theaters. In a moment of what-the-hell bravado, Stinson even reached out to Joseph Papp and the New York Shakespeare Festival's Public Theatre.

This was highly ambitious, especially for an obscure regional company that had just nearly collapsed. But they had certainly picked a worthwhile aspirational goal. Under the leadership of Joseph Papp, the NYSF was showing the way that an American theater could be run—not only staging classic plays, but also developing new writers and challenging all previous expectations about what material was commercially viable. Productions of *Hair*, free Shakespeare productions in Central Park, and new plays by playwright David Rabe—*The Basic Training of Pavlo Hummel* and *In the Boom Boom Room*—had rocked the American theater world and had often had Broadway as well as critical triumphs. "At the time he was everything, Lincoln Center, the Delacorte, everything," recalled Stinson. He also knew that Joe Papp himself had started out in a similar type of shoestring operation theater in his younger days. And Papp had been down to Philly several times, recently, mentioning in interviews that he thought the city would be a good place for developing theater projects which could then be produced at the Public.

Stinson wrote a few brash letters to the famous New York producer, proposing that since Manning Street currently did not have any new scripts, if he had "any extra projects lying around maybe you could pass them along to us for development." It seemed worth a shot, anyway, and in all the other frantic activity of reforming the Manning Street company he hardly noticed that he received no immediate reply to his offer. There was so much to do. First, the Lombard Street space needed significant repair and cleaning up. The dressing room area needed basic amenities like insulation and showers. But the most pressing problem, according to Jim Lambert: there was no cash coming in to support operations.

Stinson and Lambert proposed to the rest of the company a new financial plan:

> Whatever money we could get from grants or corporate donations should go into production, publicity and advertising. I proposed to the actors that we assemble as a co-op and that we would split equally the box office. And anything we could raise we would put into the production budget. So everyone agreed. Motivation, for an actor: your salary is the box office. Let's make the theater never dark. We would tour, we did puppets and kids shows. We went everywhere you could go. We did a Shakespeare program, doing scenes in high schools with a truck.

It was a risky path, but it proved to be a move in the right direction for the young company.

The initial season announcement by the group about their plans to stage Yukio Mishima's *Madame de Sade*, Shakespeare's *Winter's Tale*, and Tennessee Williams' *Camino Real*—astoundingly ambitious and difficult texts—was quietly dropped. Instead, they decided on a Beckett play, a holiday show, Dürrenmatt's *The Physicists*, *Brecht on Brecht*, and *The Happy Haven* by John Arden. It was an achievable plan, and evidently the board felt reassured—especially when a generous grant was secured from the Haas Foundation. With this new financial support, the board and company could confidently begin the new season. A flurry of solicitation letters went out to local high schools, offering to perform programs of Shakespeare—or any other author the teachers might want to have their classes experience. A veteran member of the famous Bread and Puppet Theater, Martha Kearns, was recruited to bring her skills to their programming for student audiences. She quickly helped craft both puppets and sets for a version of Hans Christian Andersen's *The Snow Queen*, complete with a dozen large-headed puppets typical of the Bread and Puppet style.

As bookings for the school shows came in, a donated ramshackle truck was found to carry sets and props around the area. Items of office furniture, including desks, were salvaged from a touring company of the musical *How to Succeed in Business Without Really Trying*. ("They each had only one working drawer," remembers Lambert, "but you could dance on 'em all day long!") Showers for actors were even installed in the dressing room. Recalled Stinson: "The days were incredibly busy. It was like a high. Working in school in the mornings, grab some coffee, rehearse afternoons and then do shows in the evenings. Like being in heaven. We needed a director, and I had directed a one-act play, so I directed the first and second shows. We just started to work." Interviews with numerous company members from this period of the theater's history all have a similar quality of fond reminiscence. They were young, and they were all doing work they found rewarding and exciting. As Martha Kearns put it: "It was a fantastic time of life."

As the company had agreed, all foundation money that came in was put toward production costs and operating expenses. But everything that came into the box office was divided evenly among the company, as little as it may have been (tickets for shows were only three dollars). One week the checks distributed to the actors were for a mere $12 each. But by October, the invigorated new group was staging a compendium of Beckett plays called *Sam, as in Beckett* (a combination of Beckett's plays *Act Without Words II* and *Endgame*).

The evening of Beckett plays had met with gratifying attention and praise from leaders of influential Philadelphia charitable foundations, who were increasingly eager to revive the Philadelphia performing arts. Some of the philanthropists had their own ideas of how to best perform the play ("You know what this show needs? A pie fight!" were the post-show comments of William Kohler, the Secretary of the Haas Community Fund). But most were highly supportive of the new organizational plan. Grant money began to flow in again. Soon after the opening night of the Beckett show, however, Stinson received some other, more dispiriting news. A sympathetic local journalist had taken him aside and told him that the local zoning board had given permission to their landlord to tear the old church building down in eight months' time. The theater had less than a year to go, at least at their current location. Stinson couldn't bear to tell the company, but eventually the word got out, and everyone in the young company knew that the performance space, offices, and classrooms that had been created with such great effort were not going to exist much longer.

Nonetheless, their work continued. A holiday show, a sure-fire cash cow for any ambitious non-profit theater company, was thrown together and constructed out of spare bits of Dickens and Christmas poems, along with servings of wassail and plenty of Morris dancing. One afternoon, while this project was in process, the Manning Street office received an unexpected phone call. "I'm upstairs rehearsing, and Jim Lambert the business manager comes running in and says 'C'mere, quick! Get on the phone! It's Joe Papp!'" remembered Stinson. "I said 'Fuck you.'" The frantic Lambert hustled him out of the rehearsal and into the office and put the phone in his hand. And it was true: on the other end of the line was Papp. It was every ambitious young American theater artist's dream come true.

Evidently, the long-shot letters Lambert and Stinson had sent a few months before had found their mark after all. The young Philadelphia company had intrigued him, but he needed to further assess the situation. "I want to meet your actors. I want to see your theater," he told Stinson. In January, said Papp, he and his wife, Gail Merrifield Papp, would be coming down by train to visit.

In the frantic period that inevitably followed this bolt out of the blue, it was decided that Steve Stephenson, the company's production manager, would meet the Papps at 30th Street Station when they arrived. The reason, says Stephenson: "I had just gotten a new used car, it was the nicest car anybody in the company had—a big Oldsmobile Delta 88." To avoid any associations with wealth and prosperity, he had been carefully instructed by Stinson not to take the direct route to the theater through the ritzy neighborhood around Rittenhouse Square.

Instead, Stephenson drove the visitors across the South Street bridge over the Schuylkill River, and then along the depressed and dilapidated South Street itself. Papp evidently liked the scruffiness of the view, which reminded him of his own early years when he was managing a shoestring operation theater company out of an old church on the Lower East Side. Reaching the Lombard Street church site, he stepped into the lobby where the company had installed a thick indoor/outdoor carpet only the day before. (They knew they weren't supposed to look prosperous, but they wanted to look at least competent.) Photographs of past productions had been hurriedly pasted on every wall. The only two regulation fire extinguishers the company possessed were surreptitiously passed from room to room as Papp moved about the place. At the end of the tour, Papp slyly acknowledged he saw exactly what the eager young Philadelphians were doing. "A new carpet, eh? Did wonders for us at Lincoln Center. Did you just put that in yesterday?" But suitably impressed, and apparently touched by all the effort, he wrote the Manning Street Theatre a check for $2,000. And along with the check, Papp presented a plan for his new collaborators: he wanted them to stage a production of a play—*The Orphan*, by David Rabe.

David Rabe was one of several promising new American playwrights whom Papp had been developing and supporting. Rabe, a veteran of an Army medical unit who had seen combat in Southeast Asia, had already had enormous professional success with his Vietnam War-themed award-winning plays *Sticks and Bones* and *The Basic Training of Pavlo Hummel*. Papp and Rabe's increasingly intense personal and professional relationship had been on full display recently. Rabe's play *In the Boom Boom Room* (set in a seedy nightclub in Philadelphia's Manayunk neighborhood), starring Madeline Kahn and Charles Durning, had just opened at Vivian Beaumont Theater at Lincoln Center. There had been quite a dust-up when Papp had fired the original director, Julie Bovassao, and taken over the production himself. "It was like the takeover of two jocks. Two pigs," the dismissed director Julie Bovasso angrily groused. "Their relationship is symbiotic. They're on the phone constantly to each other when they're not together. Joe thinks of David as his little Shakespeare." Since Rabe had both studied and taught in the theater department at Villanova University and lived in the Philadelphia suburbs, all this was well known in the small Philadelphia theater community. In fact, Manning Street company member Alkis Papoutsis had been one of Rabe's students.

A play that Rabe had been developing for many years was *The Orphan*, a structurally complex and poetic work based on Ancient Greek plays. An exploration of the cycle of violence in human societies, the power dynamics of language, and the nature of fate, the play used both classical locutions ("Through the flesh of the father to the hand of the son falls the sword") and contemporary speech patterns ("… sending us off to that goddam war. After a couple of months, I was deranged, man"). The stories of the House of Atreus (including the sacrifice of Iphigenia, the murder of Agamemnon, and the revenge of Orestes on Clytemnestra and her lover) were intertwined with the stories of the recent massacre by American soldiers of villagers in My Lai and also the horrific "Manson Family" murders in California. The script required two actresses to play Clytemnestra, had many songs, and specified a highly challenging series of stage actions.

The play had been rushed into production by Papp in April 1973, before Rabe had felt it was really finished, after a planned CBS television broadcast of *Sticks and Bones* had been abruptly canceled by the network. *The Orphan* had a brief run at the Public Theatre, closing after receiving a savage and disappointed response from New York critics. Clive Barnes, in *The New York Times*, though he praised the cast, design, and direction, wrote: "It is not my intention to be negative about Mr. Rabe as such, for he is a playwright of shining promise and talent, but I think at times his dramatic ideas outrun his dramatic language." Even some cast members had lost faith in the text as the run continued. At one performance the actor Cliff De Young, as Orestes, shouted after audience members who were departing in the middle of the show: "Come on, gimme a break! I gotta stay here and say it, you might as well stay here and listen." Papp, for his part, had apparently lost confidence in both the director Jeff Bleckner and in the ability of David Rabe to take his notes and suggestions. He had wanted the second act of the play rewritten, and Rabe had balked at making changes.

But after the show closed Rabe was heartened when the young director Barnet Kellman reached out to him. Kellman wrote in a letter that he had liked the play and proposed that they continue to develop *The Orphan* together, including the problematic second act, outside of the hothouse pressures of New York. A new faculty member at the North Carolina School of the Arts, Kellman approached the play in a manner that emphasized its physicality, restaging it in a production that utilized his most promising student actors. Both he and Rabe were highly encouraged with the results of the student production. Rabe even told Papp that the play was shaping up in the way that he had always wanted it to. He asked him to support one more production of the play, still away from New York but somewhat closer to Villanova, so he could help supervise as well. Perhaps, thought Rabe, this new version could convince Papp to mount the play again, but this time properly conceived and performed. "The objective was to get back to New York," remembers Kellman.

This was why Joe Papp was standing in the offices of an obscure Philadelphia theater company in December 1973, checkbook in hand. Would they like to stage *The Orphan*, he asked, with Kellman again directing, and using many of the cast and design team from North Carolina? He would give them $2,000 right away to get things rolling, if they would match it with local funding. The Manning Street company swiftly agreed, amazed but grateful for this sudden touch of grace from an almost godlike figure of the American theater scene. The Papps returned to New York, and Stinson made a happy announcement to the Philadelphia media about the project, which was slated to begin next March: "Papp put us under scrutiny, financially and administratively. Hopefully this is just the beginning of our association. But Joe Papp made it clear that this is our game. We make it or we blow it."

The Orphan

The year 1974 began on the encouraging note of Papp's support for Manning Street, as they strove to make their cooperative model work. The company, which now counted in its core membership 15 people, had already started offering acting classes to the community led by Alkis Papoutsis, and for the most promising students initiated an apprentice program for young actors. The announcement of this program had indeed served to draw several young Philadelphians eager to start work in professional theater. Among them was the youngest son of Edmund Bacon, the prominent Philadelphia architect and city planner.

"In our little world in Philadelphia, I had a famous father," Kevin Bacon would later recall. At 16, he was not interested in urban design. He had already decided to embark on an acting career. His mother, Ruth, was a teacher and a champion of the arts. "My parents—particularly my mother—didn't give a shit about making money, or even getting great grades or getting into a fancy college. The arts were what was put on a pedestal in our house. It was about what you could create. My mother would say, 'Don't buy a toy; make a toy. Don't watch television; put on a show.'" Without mentioning who his dad was, Bacon enrolled in acting classes that the Manning Street actors offered, and his talent was soon evident. His energy and sense of fun—along with his devotion to Joe Stinson—was a welcome addition to the overworked older company. Both Bacon and another talented and popular apprentice, Dave Calla, were given roles in the company's January production, *The Physicists*.

The Physicists, Durrenmatt's 1962 farce about scientists in a madhouse, was directed by Papoutsis. A simple set was constructed with a series of shadow screens. Again, the entire company was frozen like statues as the audience entered and took their seats. Stinson played the eminent physicist Mobius, while Lambert played Sir Isaac Newton and Connolly was Albert Einstein. Reviews were mixed, but word of mouth was strong, and soon lines of ticket buyers were snaking down Lombard Street for the Saturday night show. But despite all this activity, the finances of the "actor's cooperative" were still shaky. It was not at all certain the theater would be able to stay open long enough to meet the commitment to *The Orphan* project, even though they had arranged to rehearse in a rented room at the University of Pennsylvania in West Philadelphia. How would they pay the 15 actors during the rehearsals, with only Papp's checks and the few additional grants they had garnered?

The answer, as it turned out, was a show about naked men in a hot tub. *Tubstrip*, authored by A. J. Kronengold, billed itself as a "New Play with an All Male Cast" that was "Better than *Boys in the Band*." It was a gay-themed play with onstage nudity, and its explicit publicity flyers promised plenty of "bitchy" banter. It was backed by New York producer and director Doug Richards, who was eager to capitalize on the post-Stonewall permissiveness of theater at the height of the Sexual Revolution. The action of the play featured an onstage tub with real water in it. Familiar with Philadelphia's longstanding tradition as a tryout town, Richards approached Manning Street with an offer: Could he rent their space for two weeks? It was a welcome windfall for the hard-pressed group, and the profits from the rental were soon shared out among the struggling actors.

The Manning Street company, which was now busy with rehearsals for the upcoming project *The Orphan*, could only watch in amazement as a New York crew arrived and started installing the set in the old church sanctuary. The rickety church floors had to be reinforced to support the weight of the water. The production itself (with sales driven by a remarkably explicit poster of its highly attractive and physically uninhibited cast) proved to be extremely popular, selling out every night. "We had guys sitting in the front rows with binoculars," recalled Stinson. The New York cast performed with evident panache for an enthusiastic Philadelphia crowd. Best of all, the producer's checks for the rental of the space all cleared, noted Stinson and Lambert with satisfaction and relief. They could report back to Joe Papp that they had matched the money he had sent them to mount *The Orphan*.

Preparations for that project, the biggest the Manning Street Actors' Theatre had ever attempted, were now well under way. Kellman was rehearsing the company in a space provided by the Christian Association on the campus of the University of Pennsylvania in West Philadelphia. The North Carolina School of the Arts contingent included Tom Hulce as Orestes and Nancy Mette as "The Girl," as well as set designer Debe Hale, and costume designer Christina Ciannini. Philadelphian Jim Leitner, who was quite familiar with the theater's rather primitive and clumsy dimmer system, would design the lights. Kellman had chosen Mark McGovern, Bonnie Cavanaugh, Maureen McFadden, Susan Payne, and Alkis Papoutsis from the Manning Street company members to be in the cast. Significantly, the usual

Manning Street stalwarts Linda Evans and Joe Stinson were not in the cast, but New York actor Richard Fancy had been recruited to play the crucial role of Agamemnon. Other regular Manning Street company members such as John Connolly, Jerry Maher, and Thom Shafer were in the production crew. Two of the young company apprentices, Kevin Bacon and Darrell Rogers, were dressed in gray outfits to help with set changes and onstage technical effects. (Bacon did have one line: "... a little bit of Buxtehude.")

Local journalist Richard Fuller sat in on rehearsals one day, watching Kellman quietly and efficiently reconstruct the staging that had been so revelatory in his North Carolina production. Plans called for an elaborate mesh of ropes and cargo nets to be hung on the set's scaffolding, and a rolling bathtub unit would serve for the murder of the king. The actors moved through the scenes again and again, responding well to Kellman's direction. Fuller marveled at the ease with which the two groups of actors merged themselves together for the task, as well as the extra duties the Philadelphia actors were undertaking to make the show happen at all. "Commitment is, I think, the right word to describe the Manning Company," decided Fuller. For his part, Kellman knew precisely what it was he was trying to achieve with the challenging text. At his urging, Rabe had rewritten a good deal of the second act to solve issues that had been raised by the New York production. Using younger actors and increasing the physical component of the action had proved to be key to unlocking the contemporary and urgent meaning of the piece, Kellman had discovered.

It was as if the very things that had always been the central identity of the Manning Street Actors' Theatre—its youth, its energy, its passionate commitment to theater during a time of political and social upheaval for the nation—had finally found expression in a profound text that was about those very subjects. As opening night approached, despite the enormity of the task, the excitement of the entire company increased. David Rabe was often present at rehearsals, befriending and mentoring the youthful members of the cast. Papp himself continued to check on its progress. It seemed that something important, something that would have a national impact not seen since the Theatre of the Living Arts closed, was finally happening again in Philadelphia. Many of the young cast were sure this was their big break. After all, they were working on a new play by a major American playwright—and Joe Papp, who was supporting the production, *would be coming down to see their work*. If all went well, the entire production might be going back to New York with him.

Joe and Gail Merrifield Papp arrived in Philadelphia for the opening night on Thursday March 14 and settled in to watch the first act. Backstage, David Rabe was nervously nursing a bottle of Haven Hill bourbon in a brown paper bag. To pass the time, he was challenging Stinson and others in the cast and crew to arm-wrestling contests. It was Papp's presence more than any potential newspaper reviews that worried him. There were no critics in the audience—they had already seen the show in previews. (A number of high-prestige shows were also opening in the city around then, including Martin Balsam in the Philadelphia Drama Guild's *Death of a Salesman* at the Walnut Street Theatre, and Henry Fonda in *Clarence Darrow* at the Locust Street Theatre.) As the first act finished and the intermission began, there was only one person in the audience that people's eyes turned to, eagerly hoping to catch his initial reaction. But when the house lights came up, what they saw was Joe Papp bolting out of his seat. Together with his wife, he started to walk through the lobby, heading out toward Lombard Street.

Frantically, David Rabe intercepted the couple at the theater's door. Joe Papp had a history of impulsively walking out of workshops and opening nights if he felt the work reflected badly on him in any way, and Rabe was determined not to let it happen in Philadelphia.

> The actors were all young. They were ecstatic about being in this play in front of Joe Papp—they thought this was going to be their big break ... I saw by the way Joe was leaving that he wasn't coming back in. I was really upset. I felt responsible for these kids and all their work and their feelings about being seen by Joe. I thought leaving like that was rude and insensitive.

The ever-combative Papp, for his part, loudly rejected Rabe's heated accusations of not truly supporting the production, and that he had undermined the earlier one staged at the Public. Standing on the steps outside the church building on Lombard, he declared he had every right to leave the show, since he thought it was not half as good as the version he had done in New York. "We got into kind of a row, yelling 'you son of a bitch' at each other," Papp admitted. All the pent-up history and emotional baggage that the two men had built up over the past few years erupted and poured out.

Gail Merrifield Papp, for her part, remembered that the confrontation was alarmingly close to violence: "David was crab-red in the face, looking like the Golem and getting larger and more puffed up and red moment by moment. And I'm thinking, 'Well, if these two men really come to blows, I myself will step in and do something.'" The Manning Street technical crew soon became aware of the altercation, because the sound was traveling up into the back of the house, "like a roar that came up the stairwell from the downstairs lobby," said Connolly, who was the show's stage manager. "Smoke was coming out of their ears," recalled Stinson.

Director Barnet Kellman attempted to join the heated discussion, but he was quickly waved away by Rabe, who was apparently determined to have this out with Papp alone. Worst of all, the argument continued as the second act began; the two men were still yelling at each other as much of the acting company passed through the lobby as they made their entrance from the back of the theater. It was plain to everyone that things had taken a very bad turn. "It exploded there," said Kellman. "Joe never actually saw the second act that he had wanted re-written, the one that was a payoff for all the changes." Papp would later claim that it was not because he did not care about the play—or that he felt disrespect for the work—it was about the relationship between him and Rabe. "It was because we both cared a lot. I was like his father, and he would have killed his father, but he couldn't do it. Maybe we were acting out the play. It had the same conflict in it." One thing was clear to all involved: after that night, Joe Papp was never going to bring this Philadelphia production to New York.

David Rabe, for his part, tried to make up for the disappointment that the young cast was feeling, and to apologize to them for letting his own anger show in a way that had likely killed any prospect of their production having a further life. He consoled Papoutsis and Kellman at a local bar afterwards, assuring them that this was all about him and Papp, not their work on the play. Later in the run, to restore a sense of fun, Rabe even paid a young apprentice five dollars to get naked and briefly "streak" across the stage during a set change. But a certain spark had gone out of the show, and the reviews from local critics who came to subsequent performances were mixed.

When the limited run of *The Orphan* had at last been completed, and with the deadline for the Lombard Street building's demolition fast approaching, the Manning Street group now had to face the inevitable. Their hope that they could continue to work with Papp as a developmental workshop for new American plays seemed impossible, nor could they continue as a repertory company. "Our whole theater had been conceived and constructed upon a resident theater model," Stinson admitted, but as exciting and challenging as it had been for the members of the company, that had not proved to be sustainable artistically or financially. They had certainly never approached becoming a major player in the Philadelphia cultural scene, and the entire operating budget for the 1973–74 season had been only $45,000. After a final goodbye in May to its loyal audience members and supporters with a presentation of speeches, scenes, and songs from Shakespeare, the Manning Street Actors' Theatre moved away from Lombard Street and became a more mobile and fluid organization without a permanent home, much like every other Philadelphia theater and arts organizations struggling to survive and prosper.

In fact, throughout the Philadelphia region, there was an increasing amount of theater at all levels—amateur, experimental, and professional. Many new theater groups were being formed, and though some would flourish for a brief period and then dissolve, others (like the Wilma, the Philadelphia Company, and the Freedom Theatre) would end up having significant impacts on the subsequent dynamic Philadelphia theater scene. The story of the next four decades would be the story of these companies.

Over the years, some of the Manning Street people stayed in Philly. Jim Leitner and Steve Stephenson, for their part, would become stalwarts of the tech crews of Philly non-profit theaters for many decades. But others of the original group moved on.

Stuart Finkelstein would change his name to Firestein, finally get his undergraduate degree at the University of San Francisco, and become the Chair of Biological Sciences at Columbia University. Maureen Garrett moved to New York and became a longtime cast member of the CBS soap opera *Guiding Light*, as the character Holly Norris. John Connolly, besides continuing his acting career, served in union positions as the head of both AFTRA (the American Federation of Television and Radio Artists) and the Actors' Equity Association. Joe Stinson became a screenwriter, including several hit Clint Eastwood movies. Barnet Kellman became a successful director in Hollywood, including the TV shows *Mad About You* and *Murphy Brown*. Tom Hulce and Kevin Bacon, of course, would both end up having major movie careers, and by 1978 appeared together in the film *Animal House*.

And when the celebrity association game "Six Degrees of Kevin Bacon" became a popular fad in the 1990s, *all* of the former members of the Manning Street Theatre company could easily claim a connection to him—in just one round.

Epilogues

Ghost Light

March 15, 2020: The Walnut Street Theatre halted production, due to the COVID-19 pandemic. It was the very last of Philadelphia's local theater companies to bow to the dispiriting reality of the rising public health emergency.

A production of the Gore Vidal play *The Best Man* was in dress rehearsals, all ready for its first preview performance, when the decision was made. The acting company was sent home, and the stagehands placed the ghost light in the middle of the stage—a standard safety procedure. Then they went home as well.

Before she too left, stage manager Lori Aghazarian got her camera and took one last photo of the dark red rows of the Walnut's empty seats. Lori was actually a bit shorter than the light pole, so she didn't have to step back too far to put it in the proper perspective. Behind it, the red velvet seats glowed under the remaining house lights; the back doors opened onto an empty lobby. The vacant stage management booth, where on so many nights she had called the cues for so many shows, was just visible in the shot, in the upper right-hand corner.

It's an image that could have been taken any night, of course, after that evening's performance was over and the actors, stage crew, and wardrobe staff had left. Stage managers are often the last to leave a theater on a normal night, since they must type up and distribute a highly detailed performance report—as well as post the next day's call times for the cast and crew. There's really nothing in the photo she took that denotes its date or significance.

But once the context for this photo is known, it takes on an extra poignancy—and an air of reassurance. Lori, who was well known among her friends and colleagues for having a keen photographer's eye, simply noticed the possibilities of the image, and captured the moment. "You will come back," the ghost light says. "I'll just wait here and keep things safe till then. Don't want anybody stumbling around in the dark. I'm on it. You go home, hon." In my mind's ear, the ghost light's voice is hers—practical, and with that certain Philadelphia style of mordant dry humor.

That light stood there for quite a while. It wasn't until over a year later, in September 2021, that the Walnut Street Theatre finally opened for performances again. But by then Lori, like a lot of other theater people, had moved on to another job. The big problem was now she required a motorized cart to get around, due to the side effects of a recurring and remorseless cancer. It was a battle that she had been fighting for years. In July of 2022, Lori moved on again. She didn't need the cart to get where she was going, this time.

I remember a somber group of friends, family, and colleagues standing around in a mournful crowd, as a small urn containing Lori's ashes was interred at West Laurel Hill Cemetery, in the rolling landscape along the Schuylkill River. Though it was a bright afternoon, we all felt a bit lost. Many of us had been sitting at home for so long, and nobody quite knew the proper protocol anymore—should we wear masks, even here? Long passages of Armenian Church liturgy were intoned. Beautiful stories about her were shared, and many hugs were given—embraces that were more meaningful after so much isolation.

Afterwards, somehow, we were no longer in danger of stumbling in the dark. Around us were innumerable other gravestones, memorials, and monuments, and their order of placement seemed random and incomprehensible. But we were all strengthened by the experience of simply gathering and remembering why we cared so deeply about each other. We all found our way home. We were grateful for the light she left behind.

Love Unpunished

September 11, 2021: It was my first foray to see live theater indoors in 18 months. That night, everyone in the audience at the Prince Theatre on Chestnut Street wore face masks and had to show proof of their vaccination against COVID at the door. The play I was seeing, originally created in the aftermath of one great national emergency, now had different resonances in the aftermath of another one.

In 2006, Philadelphia's Pig Iron Theatre Company first created and performed their piece *Love Unpunished* at the Philadelphia Fringe Festival. Founded in 1995 by a group of graduates of Swarthmore College as "an interdisciplinary ensemble," Pig Iron Theatre Company has been a driving force in Philadelphia theater ever since. They describe themselves as "dedicated to the creation of new and exuberant performance works that defy easy categorization."

Love Unpunished—according to their own website—was "a hypnotic dance-theater piece about the moments just before the collapse of the World Trade Center ... Set on twenty feet of escape stairs, this mostly wordless hour-long piece asks audiences to contemplate the ordinariness and confusion of evacuees who wonder: Is this an emergency or is this a drill?"

I missed seeing the first production of the piece in 2006. But that night, along with about 200 other folks, I was fortunate to be able to witness the restaging and recreation of this extraordinary piece on the 20th anniversary of the destruction of the World Trade Center in New York. We all witnessed people walking down the stairs to safety or trudging upstairs to their doom—or to bring salvation. Variations of the same actions were repeated many times. The effect was hypnotic, horrible, and hopeful in equal measures.

In his published notes about the production, director Dan Rothenberg wrote:

> In 2005 I confessed to my collaborators that I had been haunted by this image in my head for years. I imagined people descending stairway after stairway: 40 flights, 50 flights, even 70 flights. I imagined them seeing firemen walking up the stairways. I imagined how little they could have known about what was happening, how in every evacuation there is a question: is this a drill? How much are we supposed to panic right now? I imagined the people going down making eye contact with the people going up. Then some people exit the building. Then the building collapses.

Rothenberg continued: "In the weeks following 9/11, skyscrapers around the world conducted evacuation drills, some for the first time. What had once been a pain in the ass that no sane person would take seriously, now it was an insult to take it lightly."

As we all gathered to witness *Love Unpunished* return, 20 years to the day after the horrible events that inspired it, we were all observing strictures (masks, IDs, social distancing) that were a pain in the ass, just so we could be there. Behind all our masks, we were hungry to experience community again. To watch great theater together, despite the surrounding darkness. I can personally attest that nobody in that room—not one—took it lightly.

Permissions

Free for All: The Papps, The Public, and the Greatest Theatre Story Ever Told by Kenneth Turan and Joseph Papp. Copyright © 2009 the Estate of Joseph Papp and the New York Shakespeare Festival. Published by Anchor Books, a division of Random House. Used by permission of Penguin Random House.

Lady Day at Emerson's Bar & Grill. Copyright © 1989 by Lanie Robertson. Published by Samuel French. Used by permission of Concord Theatricals.

Molly! Copyright © 1980 by Molly Picon. Published by Simon & Schuster.

Philadelphia, Here I Come! Copyright © 1964 by Brian Friel. Published by Faber and Faber.

Sesqui!: Greed, Graft, and the Forgotten World's Fair of 1926. Copyright © 2007 by Temple University—of the Commonwealth System of Pennsylvania. Used by permission of the author.

The Empty Space Copyright © 1968 by Peter Brook. Published by Atheneum, New York.

The Fun House Copyright © 2013 by Tom Bissinger. Published by Xlibris. Used by permission of the author.

The Line of Least Existence Copyright © 1970 by Rosalyn Drexler. Lyrics used by permission of the author.

The Orphan Copyright © 1970 and "Afterword 1992" Copyright © 1993 by David Rabe. Published in *The Vietnam Plays: Volume Two* by David Rabe. Published by Grove Press.

The Raw Pearl Copyright © 1968 by Pearl Bailey. Published by Harcourt, Brace & World.

Timebends: A Life © 1987, 1995 by Arthur Miller. Published by Penguin Books. Used by permission of Penguin Random House.

Bibliography

General sources on Philadelphia history and theater

Armstrong, W. G. 1884. *A Record of the Opera in Philadelphia*. Philadelphia: Porter & Coates.
Brede, Charles Frederic. 1918. *The German Drama in English on the Philadelphia Stage from 1794 to 1830*. Philadelphia: Americana Germanica Press.
Davis, Andrew. 2010. *America's Longest Run: A History of the Walnut Street Theatre*. University Park, PA: The Pennsylvania State University Press.
Dunlap, William. 1832. *A History of the American Theatre*. New York: J. & J. Harper. http://books.google.com/books?id=4hRAAAAAYAAJ.
Durang, Charles. 1868. *History of the Philadelphia Stage, Between the Years 1749 and 1855*. Volumes 1–6. Arranged and illustrated by Thompson Westcott. (Penn Libraries, Colenda Digital Repository)
Encyclopedia of Greater Philadelphia, The (website). Mid-Atlantic Center for the Humanities, Rutgers University Press. https://philadelphiaencyclopedia.org/.
Federal Writers' Project, Works Progress Administration, E. Digby Baltzell, and Richard J. Webster. 1988. *The WPA guide to Philadelphia: a guide to the nation's birthplace*. https://doi.org/10.9783/9781512819458.
Finkel, Kenneth. 2018. *Insight Philadelphia: Historical Essays Illustrated*. New Brunswick: Rutgers University Press.
Frame of the Government of Pennsylvania, The Avalon Project: Documents in Law, History and Diplomacy, Yale Law School Library. https://avalon.law.yale.edu/17th_century/pa04.asp.
Glazer, Irvin R. 1986. *Philadelphia Theatres, A–Z: A Comprehensive, Descriptive Record of 813 Theatres Constructed since 1724*. Westport, CT: Greenwood Press.
Glazer, Irvin R. 1994. *Philadelphia Theatres: A Pictorial Architectural History*. New York: The Athenaeum of Philadelphia and Dover Publications, Inc.
Greater Philadelphia GeoHistory Network (website). The Athenaeum of Philadelphia. https://www.philageohistory.org/geohistory/Harvard, Bernard, and Mark D. Sylvester. 2008. *Walnut Street Theatre*. Charleston, SC: Arcadia Publishing.
Hornblow, Arthur. 1919. *A History of the Theatre in America, From Its Beginnings to the Present Time*, vols. 1 & 2. Philadelphia: J. B. Lippincott Company.
Hutton, Lawrence. 1891. *Curiosities of the American Stage*. New York: Harper and Brothers.
Jackson, Joseph. 1939. *Literary Landmarks of Philadelphia*. Philadelphia: David McKay Company.
James, Reese Davis. 2017. *Cradle of Culture, 1800–1810: The Philadelphia Stage*. Philadelphia: University of Pennsylvania Press.
James, Reese Davis, and William B. Wood. 1932. *Old Drury of Philadelphia: A History of the Philadelphia Stage, 1800–1835, including the diary or daily account book of William Burke Wood, co-manager with William Warren of the Chestnut Street Theatre, familiarly known as Old Drury*. Issued also as Thesis (PhD)—University of Pennsylvania. http://www.degruyter.com/doc/cover/9781512818413.jpg.
James, Reese Davis. 1968. *Old Drury of Philadelphia: A History of the Philadelphia Stage, 1800–1835*. New York: Greenwood Press.
Lane, Roger. 1991. *William Dorsey's Philadelphia and Ours: On the Past and Future of the Black City in America*. New York: Oxford University Press.
Lewis, Michael J. 2021. *Philadelphia Builds: Essays on Architecture*. Philadelphia: Paul Dry Books.
Lippincott, Horace Mather. 1917. *Early Philadelphia: Its People, Life and Progress*. Philadelphia: J. B. Lippincott.

Marion, John Francis. 1984. *Within These Walls: A History of the Academy of Music in Philadelphia*. Philadelphia: Restoration Office, Academy of Music.

Mease, James, and Thomas Porter. 1831. *Picture of Philadelphia: Giving an account of its origin, increase and improvements in arts, sciences, manufactures, commerce and revenue: with a compendious view of its societies, literary, benevolent, patriotic and religious: Embracing the public buildings, the House of Refuge, prison, new penitentiary, widows' and orphans' asylum, Fair Mount Water Works, &c*. Philadelphia: E. L. Carey & A. Hart. https://archive.org/details/pictureofphilade31meas.

Philadelphia and Popular Philadelphians. 1891. Philadelphia: The North American.

Philadelphia Architects and Buildings (website). The Athenaeum of Philadelphia, 2024. https://www.philadelphiabuildings.org/pab/

Pollock, Thomas Clark. 2017. *The Philadelphia Theatre in the Eighteenth Century: Together with the Day Book of the Same Period*. Philadelphia: University of Pennsylvania Press. http://www.degruyter.com/doc/cover/9781512818413.jpg.

Quinn, Arthur Hobson. 1923. *A History of the American Drama: From the Beginning to the Civil War*. New York: Harper & Brothers.

Schmitz, Peter. 2021–24. *Adventures in Theater History: Philadelphia* (podcast and blog). www.aithpodcast.com/

Shinn, Earl. 1875. *A Century After: Picturesque Glimpses of Philadelphia and Pennsylvania, including Fairmount, the Wissahickon, and other romantic localities, with the cities and landscapes of the state. A pictorial representation of scenery, architecture, life, manners, and character*. Philadelphia: Allen, Lane & Scott and J. W. Lauderbach.

Simon, Roger D. 2017. *Philadelphia: A Brief History*. Pennsylvania Historical Association.

Stine, Richard D. 1951. "The Philadelphia Theater, 1682–1829; Its Growth as a Cultural Institution." PhD Dissertation, University of Pennsylvania.

Tanner, Henry Schenck. 1847. *A new picture of Philadelphia, or, The Stranger's Guide to the city and adjoining districts ... with a plan of the city and its environs*. New York: Published at the Map and Geographical Establishment.

The Stranger's Guide in Philadelphia and its Environs: Including Laurel Hill, Woodlands, Monument, Odd Fellows and Glenwood Cemeteries: With illustrations. 1852. Philadelphia: Lindsay and Blakiston.

Watson, John F., and Willis P. Hazard. 1905. *Annals of Philadelphia, and Pennsylvania, in the Olden Time: Being a collection of memoirs, anecdotes, and incidents of the city and its inhabitants, and of the earliest settlements of the island part of Pennsylvania*. Philadelphia: Leary, Stuart & Co.

Weigley, Russell Frank, Nicholas B. Wainwright, and Edwin Wolf. 1982. *Philadelphia: A 300 Year History*. New York: W. W. Norton.

Wemyss, Francis Courtney. 1968. *Chronology of the American Stage, from 1752 to 1852*. New York: B. Blom.

Wilson, Arthur Herman. 1935. *A History of the Philadelphia Theatre, 1835 to 1855*. Philadelphia: University of Pennsylvania Press.

Other sources used for this book

Alford, Terry. 2015. *Fortune's Fool: The Life of John Wilkes Booth*. New York: Oxford University Press.

Alger, William Rounseville. 1877. *Life of Edwin Forrest, the American Tragedian*. Philadelphia: J. B. Lippincott & Co.

Alpert, Hollis. 1964. *The Barrymores*. New York: Dial Press.

Anadolu-Okur, Nilgun. 1997. *Contemporary African American Theater: Afrocentricity in the works of Larry Neal, Amiri Baraka, and Charles Fuller*. New York: Garland Publishing, Inc.

Bailey, Pearl. 1968. *The Raw Pearl*. New York: Harcourt, Brace & World.
Bank, Rosemarie, K., "Louisa Lane Drew at the Arch Street Theatre: Repertory and Actor Training in Nineteenth-Century Philadelphia," *Theatre Studies* 24/25 (1977–1978/1978–1979): 37–46.
Barrymore, Ethel. 1968. *Memories, an Autobiography*. New York: Harper.
Barrymore, Lionel, and Cameron Shipp. 1951. *We Barrymores*. New York: Appleton-Century-Crofts.
Beamish, Ann. 2020. "Rational entertainment and instructive amusement: Philadelphia's nineteenth-century urban pleasure gardens and the emergence of nightlife." *Studies in the History of Gardens & Designed Landscapes*, 2020–01, Vol. 40 (1):14–42.
Beauvallet, Léon. 1856. *Rachel et le Nouveau-Monde: promenade aux États-Unis et aux Antilles*. Paris: Alexandre Cadot. https://gallica.bnf.fr/ark:/12148/bpt6k111677m.pdf.
Beauvallet, Léon. 1856. *Rachel and the New world. A trip to the United States and Cuba* (translated from the French). New York: Dix, Edwards & Co.
Bellion, Wendy. "Here Trust Your Eyes": Vision and Illusion at the Chestnut Street Theatre." *Early American Literature*, 51 (2) (March 2016):333–365. Chapel Hill: University of North Carolina Press.
Benes, Peter. 2016. *For a Short Time Only: Itinerants and the Resurgence of Popular Culture in Early America*. University of Massachusetts Press.
Bernard, John and William Bayle Bernard. 1832. *Retrospections of the Stage*. Boston: Carter and Hendee.
Biddle, Francis. 2017. *William Penn*. New Word City, Inc.
Bissinger, Tom. 2013. *The Fun House: Memory, Magic and Mayhem*. Bloomington, IN: Xlibris.
Bogar, Thomas R. 2006. *American Presidents Attend the Theatre: The Playgoing Experiences of Each Chief Executive*. Jefferson, NC: McFarland & Company, Inc.
Bowman, Kathleen Ann. 1989. "Of Stars and Standards: Actress-Managers of Philadelphia and New York: 1855–1880." PhD, Theatre, University of Illinois at Champaign-Urbana.
Branden, Barbara. 1986. *The Passion of Ayn Rand*. Garden City, NY: Doubleday.
Brook, Peter. 1968. *The Empty Space: A Book About the Theatre: Deadly, Holy, Rough, Immediate*. New York: Atheneum.
Brooks, Lynn Matluck. 2011. *John Durang: Man of the American Stage*. Amherst, NY: Cambria Press.
Browder, Laura. 2009. *Her Best Shot: Women and Guns in America*. Chapel Hill: UNC Press Books.
Brownstein, Rachel M. 1993. *Tragic Muse: Rachel of the Comédie-Française*. New York: A. A. Knopf.
Burns, Jennifer. 2009. *Goddess of the Market: Ayn Rand and the American Right*. New York: Oxford University Press.
Butler, Isaac. 2020. *The Method: How the Twentieth Century Learned to Act*. New York: Bloomsbury Publishing.
Calloway, Colin G. 2021. *The Chiefs Now in This City*. New York: Oxford University Press.
Calloway, Colin G. July 2021. "Urban Encounters," *History Today*. Issue 7, 66–75.
Centlivre, Susanna. 1749. *A Bold Stroke for a Wife: A Comedy*. London: J. Hodges and J. Osborn.
Cliff, Nigel. 2007. *The Shakespeare Riots: Revenge, Drama, and Death in Nineteenth Century America*. New York: Random House.
Clinton, Catherine. 2000. *Fanny Kemble's Civil Wars*. New York: Simon & Schuster.
Cooper, John. "Oscar Wilde in America," Documentary Archive, 2023. https://oscarwildeinamerica.org/.
David, Deirdre. 2007. *Fanny Kemble: A Performed Life*. Philadelphia: University of Pennsylvania Press.
Deford, Frank. 1975. *Big Bill Tilden: The Triumphs and the Tragedy*. New York: Simon and Schuster.
de Onis, Luis, *Memoir Upon the Negotiations Between Spain and the United States of America*. Madrid, 1820. Translated from the Spanish by Tobias Watkins, Washington, DC, 1821.
Drew, John. 1922. *My Years Upon the Stage*, New York: E. P. Dutton & Co.
Drew, Louisa. 1899. *Autobiographical Sketch of Mrs. John Drew*. New York: Charles Scribner's Sons.
DuComb, Christian. 2017. *Haunted City: Three Centuries of Racial Impersonation in Philadelphia*. Ann Arbor: University of Michigan Press.

Dunlap, William. 1813. *Memoirs of the Life of George Frederick Cooke, late of the Theatre Royal, Covent Garden Composed principally from journals and other authentic documents, left by Mr. Cooke, and the personal knowledge of the writer.* 2 vols. New York: D. Longworth.

Durang, John, and Alan S. Downer. 1966. *The memoir of John Durang: American actor, 1785–1816.* The Historical Society of York County and the American Society of Theatre Research, by University of Pittsburgh Press.

Ellman, Richard. 1988. *Oscar Wilde.* New York: Vintage Books.

Fennell, James. 1814. *An Apology for the Life of James Fennell.* Philadelphia: Moses Thomas.

Ferguson, Marcia. 2001. "Blanka and Jiri Zizka at the Wilma Theater in Philadelphia, 1997–2000: From the Underground to the Avenue." PhD Dissertation, Theatre, The City University of New York.

Friel, Brian. 1996. *Plays One: Philadelphia, Here I Come! The Freedom of the City, Living Quarters, Aristocrats, Faith Healer, and Translations.* London: Faber and Faber.

Furnas, J. C. 1982. *Fanny Kemble: Leading Lady of the Nineteenth Century Stage.* New York: The Dial Press.

Gagliardi, Paul. 2024. *All Play and No Work: American Work Ideals and the Comic Plays of the Federal Theatre Project.* Philadelphia: Temple University Press.

Gibbs, Jenna M. 2014. *Performing the Temple of Liberty: Slavery, Theater, and Popular Culture in London and Philadelphia, 1760–1850.* Baltimore: Johns Hopkins University Press.

Geiter, Mary K. 2000. *William Penn.* New York: Longman.

Gibbs, Henry. 1947. *Affectionately Yours, Fanny: Fanny Kemble and the Theatre.* New York: Jarrolds.

Gold, Arthur and Robert Fizdale. 1991. *The Divine Sarah: A Life of Sarah Bernhardt.* New York: Knopf.

Gottfried, Martin. 2003. *Arthur Miller: His Life and Work.* Cambridge, MA: Da Capo Press.

Gough, Monica, ed. 1990. *Fanny Kemble: Journal of a Young Actress.* New York: Columbia University Press.

Government of the Edwin Forrest Home. *History with list of officers and directors from its beginning: the will of Edwin Forrest and act of incorporation.* 1931. Special Collections Research Center, Temple University Library, Philadelphia.

Griffis, William Elliot. 1903. *John Chambers: Servant of Christ and Master of Hearts and His Ministry in Philadelphia.* Ithaca, NY: Andrus & Church.

Harding, Anneliese. 1994. *John Lewis Krimmel: Genre Artist of the Early Republic.* Winterthur, DE: Winterthur Publications.

Hare, Arnold. 1980. *George Frederick Cooke: The Actor and The Man.* London: The Society for Theatre Research.

Harrison, Gabriel. 1889. *Edwin Forrest: the Actor and the Man: Critical and Reminiscent.* Brooklyn, NY: Press of Brooklyn Eagle Book Printing Department.

Harry, Lou. 1995. *Strange Philadelphia: Stories from the City of Brotherly Love.* Philadelphia: Temple University Press.

Hayes, Margaret Calder. 1977. *Three Alexander Calders.* Middlebury, VT: Paul S. Erickson.

Heller, Anne Conover. 2009. *Ayn Rand and the World She Made.* New York: Nan A. Talese.

Hill, Errol and James V. Hatch. 2003. *A History of African American Theatre.* New York: Cambridge University Press.

Houchin, John H. "The Struggle for Virtue: Professional Theatre in 18th Century Philadelphia." *Theatre History Studies*, Vol. 19 (January 1999): 167–188.

Jando, Dominique. 2018. *Philip Astley & The Horsemen Who Invented the Circus.* Circopedia.

Jenkins, Rebecca. 2005. *Fanny Kemble: A Reluctant Celebrity.* New York: Simon & Schuster.

Johnson, Odai. 2017. *London in a Box: Englishness and Theatre in Revolutionary America.* Iowa City: University of Iowa Press.

Jones, Eugene H. 1988. *Native Americans as Shown on the Stage: 1753–1916.* Metuchen, NJ: The Scarecrow Press, Inc.

Kammen, Michael. 1996. *The Lively Arts: Gilbert Seldes and the Transformation of Cultural Criticism in the United States*. New York: Oxford University Press.
Kazan, Elia. 1988. *A Life*. New York: Alfred A. Knopf.
Keels, Thomas H. 2017. *Sesqui!: Greed, Graft, and the Forgotten World's Fair of 1926*. Philadelphia: Temple University Press.
Keels, Thomas. 2010. *Wicked Philadelphia: Sin in the City of Brotherly Love*. Charleston: History Press.
Kemble, Fanny ["Frances Anne Butler"]. 1835. *Journal*. Philadelphia: Carey, Lea & Blanchard. http://www.aspresolver.com/aspresolver.asp?NWLD;S757.
Kemble, Frances Anne [Fanny]. 1835. *Journal*, vols. I & II. London: J. Murray.
Kozuko, Matthew. Oct 2006. "The Shakspere Society of Philadelphia," *Borrowers and Lenders*. Athens, Vol. II, Issue 2.
Latham, Robert and William Matthews, eds. 1995. *The Diary of Samuel Pepys, Vol. III, 1662*. Berkeley: University of California Press.
Laufe, Abe. 1978. *The Wicked Stage: A History of Theater Censorship and Harassment in the United States*. New York: Frederick Ungar Publishing Co.
Little, Stuart W. 1974. *Enter Joseph Papp: In Search of a New American Theater*. New York: Coward, McCann & Geoghegan, Inc.
MacLaughlin, Whit. 2006. "Towards a Comprehensive Media Meteorology." *Live Movies: A Field Guide to New Media for the Performing Arts*, 55–67. Department of Art and Visual Technology, George Mason University.
Mandelbaum, Ken. 1991. *Not Since Carrie: Forty Years of Broadway Musical Flops*. New York: St. Martin's Press.
Marx, Groucho, 1959. *Groucho and Me*. New York: Random House.
Masters, Patricia Anne. 2007. *The Philadelphia Mummers: Building Community Through Play*. Philadelphia: Temple University Press.
McKenney, Thomas Lorraine and James Hall. 1838. *History of the Indian Tribes of North America*. J.T. Bowen Philadelphia: Frederick Greenough.
Merrill, Lisa. 1999. *When Romeo was a Woman: Charlotte Cushman and her circle of female spectators*. Ann Arbor: University of Michigan Press.
Mielziner, Jo. 1965. *Designing for the Theatre*. New York: Atheneum.
Molloy, Joseph J. 1897. *The Life and Adventures of Edmund Kean, Tragedian, 1787–1833*. London: Downey & Company.
Moody, Richard. 1960. *Edwin Forrest, First Star of the American Stage*. New York: Knopf.
Morris, Edmund. 1979. *The Rise of Theodore Roosevelt*. New York: Coward, McCann & Geoghegan.
Mostel, Kate, and Madeline Gilford. 1978. *170 Years of Show Business*. New York: Random House.
Murphy, Brenda. 1995. *Death of a Salesman*. New York: Cambridge University Press.
Murray, Ken. 1976. *The Body Merchant: The Story of Earl Carroll*. Pasadena: Ward Ritchie Press.
Oberholtzer, Ellis Paxson. 1908. *The Book of the Pageant*. Philadelphia: G. W. Jacobs & Company. https://lccn.loc.gov/08029301.
O'Keefe, John. 1784. *The Young Quaker; a comedy. As it is performed at the Theatre Royal in Smoke Alley, with great applause*. Dublin, 1784. https://archive.org/details/bim_eighteenth-century_the-young-quaker-a-come_okeeffe-john_1784.
Parish, James Robert. 2005. *Katharine Hepburn: The Untold Story*. New York: Advocate Books.
Peirce, William Shannon. April 1875. "The Relative Morals of City and Country," *The Penn Monthly*, Vol. VI, No. 64.
Penn, William. 1743. *No Cross, No Crown*, Eighth Edition. Leeds: James Lister. https://archive.org/details/nocrossnocrown00penn.

Peters, Margot. 1990. *The House of Barrymore*. New York: Alfred A. Knopf.

Picon, Molly and Jean Bergantini Grillo. 1980. *Molly: An Autobiography of Molly Picon*. New York: Simon & Schuster.

Plays and Players Theatre Dossier. 2011. PA Graduate Program in Historic Preservation, University of Pennsylvania School of Design Preservation Studio. Collection of University of Pennsylvania Library.

Pritner, Calvin Lee. 1967. "A Theatre and its Audience." *The Pennsylvania Magazine of History and Biography*, January, 72–79.

Rabe, David. 1993. *The Vietnam Plays*. New York: Grove Press.

Rees, James. 1874. *The Life of Edwin Forrest*. Philadelphia: T. B. Peterson & Brothers.

Robertson, Lanie. 1989. *Lady Day at Emerson's Bar and Grill*. New York: Samuel French.

Robeson, Susan. 1981. *The Whole World in his Hands: A Pictorial Biography of Paul Robeson*. Secaucus, NJ: Citadel Press.

Ryan, Carrie. 2000. "Translating The Invention of Love: The Journey from Page to Stage for Tom Stoppard's Latest Play." *Journal of Modern Literature*, Vol. 24, No. 2, 197–204. https://doi.org/10.1353/jml.2000.0043.

Ryan, James Emmett. 2009. "Staging Quakerism in American Theatre and Films," *Quaker Studies*, Vol. 14 (1) (March 2014): 57–71.

Sachs, Sid. 2020. *Notes on the Underground*. Published on the occasion of the exhibition "Invisible City: Philadelphia and the Vernacular Avant-garde," January 21–April 4, 2020. Curated by Sid Sachs/Organized by the Rosenwald-Wolf Gallery at the University of the Arts.

Sagolla, Lisa Jo. 2003. *The Girl Who Fell Down: A Biography of Joan McCracken*. Boston: Northeastern University.

Samuels, Peggy and Harold Samuels. 1995. *Remembering the Maine*. Washington, DC: Smithsonian Institution Press.

Sayer, Otto, ed. 1926. *"The Miracle" Edition: Max Reinhardt and His Theatre*. New York: Brentano's.

Sciabarra, Anthony. 2013. *Ayn Rand, the Russian Radical*. University Park, PA: The Pennsylvania State University Press.

Sculthorpe, Derek. 2018. *The Life and Times of Sydney Greenstreet*. Albany, GA: BearManor Media.

Sheean, Vincent. 1956. *Oscar Hammerstein I, The Life and Exploits of an Impresario*. New York: Simon & Schuster.

Siebert, Brian. 2015. *What The Eye Hears: A History of Tap Dancing*. New York: Farrar, Straus and Giroux.

Skeel, Sharon. 2020. *Catherine Littlefield: A Life in Dance*. New York: Oxford University Press.

Skinner, Cornelia Otis. 1967. *Madame Sarah*. Boston: Houghton Mifflin.

Spell, J. R. 1936. "An Illustrious Spaniard in Philadelphia, Valentín de Foronda." *Hispanic Review*, Vol. 4, No. 2, 136–40. *JSTOR*, https://doi.org/10.2307/469481.

Spoto, Donald. 2009. *High Society: The Life of Grace Kelly*. New York: Harmony Books.

Spoto, Donald. 1985. *The Kindness of Strangers: The Life of Tennessee Williams*. New York: Ballantine Books.

Stagg, Jerry. 1968. *The Brothers Shubert*. New York: Random House.

Stolp, Dorothy. 1953. "Mrs. John Drew, American Actress and Manager, 1820–1897." PhD. dissertation, Louisiana State University.

Svoboda, Marina and William Whisenhunt. 2008. *A Russian Paints America: The Travels of Pavel P. Svin'in, 1811–1813*. Montreal: McGill-Queen's University Press.

Swindall, Lindsay. 2013. *Paul Robeson, A Life in Activism and Art*. Lanham, MD: Rowman & Littlefield Publishers.

Taylor, Ivan E. 1997. *Samuel Pepys*. Boston: Twayne Publishers.

Tomars, Adolph S. 2020. *The First Oscar Hammerstein and New York's Golden Age of Theater and Music*. Jefferson, NC: McFarland & Company.

Turan, Kenneth and Joseph Papp. 2009. *Free for all: Joe Papp, the Public, and the Greatest Theater Story Ever Told.* New York: Doubleday.
Turner, Mary M. 1990. *Forgotten Leading Ladies of the American Theatre,* McFarland & Company, Inc.
Van Vechten, Carl. 1920. "Oscar Hammerstein: An Epitaph," *In the Garrett.* New York: Alfred A. Knopf.
Ward, Steve. 2023. *Opulence & Ostentation: Building the Circus.* Philadelphia: Modern Vaudeville Press.
Webb, Dorothy Lewis Beck. 1970. "The Early History of the Arch Street Theatre: 1828–1834." PhD, Speech-Theatre, Indiana University.
Wemyss, Francis. 1846. *Twenty-six Years of the Life of an Actor and Manager: interspersed with sketches, anecdotes, and opinions of the professional merits of the most celebrated actors and actresses of our day.* New York: Burgess, Stringer & Co.
Wesker, Arnold. 1999. *The Birth of Shylock & the Death of Zero Mostel.* New York: Fromm International.
Wilmeth, Don B. 1980. *George Frederick Cooke, Machiavel of the Stage.* Contributions in Drama and Theatre Studies, No. 2. Westport, CT: Greenwood Press.
Winter, William. 1915. "Matilda Heron," in *Vagrant Memories: Being Further Recollections of Other Days.* New York: George Dolan Co.
Wojczuk, Tara. 2020. *Lady Romeo: The Radical and Revolutionary Life of Charlotte Cushman, America's First Celebrity.* New York: Simon & Schuster.
Wood, William B. 1855. *Personal Recollections of the Stage, Embracing Notices of Actors, Authors, and Auditors, During a Period of Forty Years.* Philadelphia: H. C. Baird.
Woolcott, John R. 1971. "Philadelphia's Chestnut Street Theatre: A Plan and Elevation." *Journal of the Society of Architectural Historians,* 1971–10, Vol. 30 (3): 209–218.
Wright, Constance. 1972. *Fanny Kemble and the Lovely Land.* New York: Dodd Mead & Company.

Notes and Sources

Sources for each chapter are listed below. Interviews, newspapers and magazine articles, websites, videos, and podcasts that are not already listed in the Bibliography are cited in full. I have made additional notes and comments on certain sources and citations. Useful general sources for the chapter's topic are noted as well. See the Bibliography for complete citations for all books and journal articles.

All websites and URL addresses listed here (or in the Bibliography) were accessed and available to the public as of March 2024. All such online material referenced here pertains to documents or websites as they stood at that date. Any subsequent changes or alterations to information or documents are the responsibility of the databases on which they were accessed.

Quotations (obtained under the principle of "fair use") from published books, plays, and journal articles are noted in the text of the chapter and attributed to their authors. Copyrighted material that was quoted at length has been noted above, in Permissions. If I have made use of material that I myself have previously published online or shared in podcast episodes (under my own copyright), that is noted as well. Any unintended errors in the citations, or omissions of attribution and/or permissions, will be corrected in subsequent editions.

Part One: Only in Philadelphia

Durang's Hornpipe

Brooks, Lynn Matluck, *John Durang: Man of the American Stage*, pp. 1–32, 47–48. This book is the definitive scholarly account of Durang's life and career in the context of early American theater.

Durang, John and Alan S. Downer, ed., *The Memoir of John Durang, American Actor*, pp. 16–19, 21, 127. Durang set down his memories in his own hand sometime after 1816 and made several watercolors to illustrate them. According to historian Alan Downer, Durang clearly meant the book for eventual publication, but this project was never completed, and he died in 1822. The manuscript stayed in possession of his son Charles, who mined it for the early entries in his own "History of the Philadelphia Stage from 1752 to 1854," published serially in the *Philadelphia Journal* during the 1850s. Charles Durang died in 1870, and the whereabouts of his father's manuscript remained unclear until 1940, when it showed up in the collection of a Philadelphia book dealer. It was purchased by the York Historical Society in 1945, in whose collection it remains. Some scholars had access to the document during the 1950s, but it was not widely known until its publication in 1966.

"The Exhibition at the Theatre" (ad), *Dunlap and Claypoole's American Daily Advertiser* [as *The Daily Packet*], April 9, 1785, p. 1. Durang's first show could have been as early as January, though Lynn Matluck thinks it likely took place in early March.

"Harmony-Hall Theatre" (ad), *Dunlap and Claypoole's American Daily Advertiser*, November 10, 1789, p. 3. This ad shows that Durang himself performed his hornpipe during a performance of *The Wapping Landlady*.

"The Humours of a Wapping Landlady," print. Collection of The British Museum. https://www.britishmuseum.org/collection/object/P_1862-0614-1587. Durang borrowed heavily from this image for his own watercolor. The dancer is similarly posed, with a cane behind his back.

Even the slats on the floor are reproduced. The woman in the red dress in the framed picture may represent the "landlady."

Miller, "1776–1876: John Durang and the Dawn of American Theatrical Dance." In this article, Miller notes that the steps that Durang used for his hornpipe, which were later set down by his son Charles, "suggests that Durang was influenced by native African-American dance as well as the French ballet. Sissone, entrechats, and glissade are specific movements from the classical ballet, while buckle down, shuffle, pigeon wing, and others suggest steps common to the then-contemporary African-American dance vocabulary."

"Philadelphia, June 6." *Dunlap and Claypoole's American Daily Advertiser*, June 6, 1785, p. 3. The show described in this article seems to have been basically the same entertainment the company was offering all that winter and spring, with some additions and improvements along the way.

"Theatre. A Lecture" (ad), *The Pennsylvania Journal, or Weekly Advertiser*, January 29, 1785, p. 1. This seems to be the first occasion that Durang performed his hornpipe with the Hallam company, which—as we note later in the book—could not legally bill its performances as "plays." There are numerous other examples of advertisements for his Hornpipe dance being performed with Hallam's troupe for the next seven months.

36 Indian Chiefs and Warriors at the Olympic

(Note: Much of the material for this chapter was originally presented in my podcast, *Adventures in Theater: Philadelphia*, as part of Episode 7, "Two Painting at the Met.")

Calloway, "Urban Encounters," pp. 66–75.

Calloway, *The Chiefs Now In This City*. This entire book is useful to this topic. Visits of Native Americans to Philadelphia are discussed throughout—though admittedly there is not a specific discussion of Krimmel's painting.

"Exhibition of Indian Tribal Ceremonies at the Olympic Theater, Philadelphia," attributed to John Lewis Krimmel (1786–1821), Collection of the Metropolitan Museum of Art, New York, Accession Number: 42.95.28. https://www.metmuseum.org/art/collection/search/12717.

"For One Night Only: Olympic Theatre," *Poulson's American Daily Advertiser*, Philadelphia, September 3, 1812, p. 2.

Harding, John, *Lewis Krimmel: Genre Artist of the Early Republic*, pp. 39, 72, 244. Harding refers to the painting as "Indian Council." There is no discussion about the work in the context of a theatrical performance.

Jones, *Native Americans as Shown on the Stage: 1753–1916*.

McKenney, Thomas Lorraine, and James Hall, *History of the Indian Tribes of North America*. Philadelphia, 1838.

Quinn, *A History of American Drama*, pp. 203–245.

Svoboda, and Whisenhunt, *A Russian Paints America*, pp. 45–46. Subsequent scholarship has demonstrated that Pavel Svin'in did not "paint America" at all, but instead passed off a dozen or so of Krimmel's works as his own. The Russian's account of the evening at the Olympic—highly fanciful, but evidently with some basis in truth—is found on pp. 110–116 of this work.

Wood, *Personal Recollections of the Stage*, p. 86.

"A Young Gentleman of This City"

(Note: Some of the material for this chapter was originally presented in my podcast as part of Episode 13, "Forrest of Philadelphia, Part One.")

Alger, William Rounseville, *Life of Edwin Forrest, American Tragedian*. A source to be used with some caution. Written soon after Forrest's' death, under the supervision of the actor's close friend Titus Oakes, the book's style likely owes a great deal to the assistance of the author's cousin, Horatio Alger.
Cliff, Nigel, *The Shakespeare Riots*, pp. 19–23.
Davis, *America's Longest Run*, pp. 39–80.
Durang, Charles, *History of the Philadelphia Stage, Between the Years 1749 and 1855*, Vol. 2, pp. 138–139 (Colenda Digital Repository, University of Pennsylvania Libraries. Images 85, 86).
Jackson, *Literary Landmarks of Philadelphia*, pp. 124–125.
Moody, *Edwin Forrest, First Star of the American Stage*, pp. 10–61. Though now over 60 years old, Moody's book remains the most complete scholarly examination of Forrest's life and career. More recent publications tend to focus on either the Astor Place Riots or on the extended and bitter divorce trial from his wife Catherine Sinclair. I would suggest that another book is long overdue. It is perhaps worth mentioning that Edwin's brother William also became an actor, and indeed managed the Arch Street Theatre in Philadelphia for a brief period, but suddenly died in 1834. Their mother and three sisters lived in Philadelphia for many years, supported by Edwin. The family are all buried together (except for Lorman) in Old Saint Paul's Episcopal Church Burial Ground on Third Street. There are no descendants of the family left in Philadelphia. As Moody points out, he was the only one of his five sibling to even marry, and that tuned out to be quite an unhappy story. There are, however, a number of modern plays that feature Edwin Forrest as a character, including Richard Nelson's *Two Shakespearean Actors* (1990).
Rees, James, *The Life of Edwin Forrest*, pp. 39–65.
Wood, *Personal Recollections of the Stage*, pp. 250–252, 320.

Miss Philadelphia of 1896

"A Play That Is Our Very Own," *Philadelphia Times*, April 26, 1896, p. 16.
"At the Playhouses," *Philadelphia Inquirer*, April 5, 1896, p. 18.
"Chestnut Street Opera House," *Mount Holly News*, May 16, 1896, p. 2.
"Finale, Act 1 of 'Miss Philadelphia,'" *Philadelphia Inquirer*, May 10, 1896, p. 12.
"Fun Behind the Scenes," *Philadelphia Inquirer*, April 26, 1896, p. 18.
"Park—'Miss Philadelphia,'" *Philadelphia Inquirer*, April 26, 1896, p. 20.
"Philadelphia on the Stage," *Philadelphia Times*, April 12, 1896, p. 14.
"Philadelphia Scenes and Churches," *Philadelphia Times*, March 29, 1896, p. 14.
"Ready to be Played: Edgar Smith's New Burlesque in Shape for the First Night," *Philadelphia Inquirer*, April 12, 1896, p. 20.
"Sweetheart, I Love None But You," Supplement to the *Philadelphia Press*, Collection of the New York Historical Society.
"Theatrical Gossip: A New Act in Miss Philadelphia Not Repeated," *Philadelphia Inquirer*, October 12, 1896, p. 9.
"The Playhouses," *Philadelphia Inquirer*, March 29, 1896, p. 18.

"Three Cheers for Captain Sigsbee!"

"Captain Sigsbee Was Given A Tremendous Ovation," *Philadelphia Inquirer*, April 21, 1898, p. 7.
Morris, Edmund, *The Rise of Theodore Roosevelt*, pp. 593–616. I cannot tell you how pleased I am to include this quote from Morris, whose excellent biography of T. R. I first bought and read as a teenager. "The nation whooped to war" always struck me as a great line, and I am delighted to incorporate it here.
Samuels, Peggy and Harold Samuels, *Remembering the Maine*, pp. 219–232.
"Sigsbee at the Theatre," *Philadelphia Times*, April 21, 1898, p. 7.

Freedom at the Sesqui and The Miracle at the Met

"A Lesson in Intelligent Publicity," *Philadelphia Inquirer*, November 5, 1926, p. 10.
"An Open Letter to the People of Philadelphia and the Vicinity," *Philadelphia Inquirer*, November 1, 1926, p. 13.
"Freedom Pageant Lauded," William Smith Goldenberg, *Philadelphia Inquirer*, July 3, 1926.
"Freedom Produced: Burnside Spectacle Given In Municipal Stadium Last Night," *Philadelphia Inquirer*, July 4, 1926, p. 59.
"Great Throng at Sesqui Fete," *Kansas City Star*, July 4, 1926, p. 5.
Keels, Thomas H., *Sesqui!*, pp. 160–163. The entirety of this delightful book is essential reading for anyone wanting to know the story of the ill-fated 1926 Philadelphia World's Fair.
Sayer, Otto, ed., *"The Miracle" Edition: Max Reinhardt and His Theatre*.
"The Coming of Great Religious Play, 'The Miracle,'" *Philadelphia Inquirer*, October 3, 1916, p. 103.
"'The Miracle' Is Seen by Stanley Music Club," *Philadelphia Inquirer*, November 1, 1926, p. 3.
"When All Superlatives Fail," Pierre de Rohan, *Camden Courier-Post*, October 5, 1926, p. 18.

Shakspere in the Parkway

Alexander Stirling Calder—Artist (4/24/1930), *Shakespeare Memorial, Logan Square—1930*. [Photographic Prints]. Retrieved from https://libwww.freelibrary.org/digital/item/63680.
Hayes, Margaret Calder, *Three Alexander Calders*, pp. 162–169.
Pannapacker, William, "Literary Societies" in *The Encyclopedia of Greater Philadelphia* (website), Rutgers University, 2013. https://philadelphiaencyclopedia.org/essays/literary-societies/.
"Shakespeare Memorial (1926)," Association for Public Art (website). https://www.associationforpublicart.org/artwork/shakespeare-memorial/.
"Shakespeare Will Be Honored Here," *Philadelphia Inquirer*, April 16, 1916, p. 5.
"Temporary Roadway Ready Soon as Step to Vine St.-Expressway Link," C. Allen Keith, *Philadelphia Inquirer*, June 14, 1954, p. 19.
"Urge Statue of Bard," *Philadelphia Inquirer*, April 25, 1922, p. 7.

Shakespeare's Birthday at the Edwin Forrest Home

"Actor's Estate Hosts Party Honoring Bard," Ruth Seltzer, *Philadelphia Inquirer*, April 27, 1967, p. 25.
"Former Stage Stars Attend House Party," *Philadelphia Inquirer*, September 25, 1909, p. 13.
Government of the Edwin Forrest Home: history with list of officers and directors from its beginning: the will of Edwin Forrest and act of incorporation, 1931. Temple University Library, Special Collections Research Center.
Harris, Harry, "Legitimate: Edwin Forrest Home in Phila. Broadens Its Admissions Policy," *Variety*, May 26, 1982, Vol. 307, Issue 4, p. 88.
"Helen Hayes Changes Her Lines," William B. Collins, *Philadelphia Inquirer*, April 28, 1980, p. 14.
Moody, *Edwin Forrest*, pp. 392–393.
"New Edwin Forrest Home dedicated and opened today," *Philadelphia Evening Bulletin*, September 27, 1927. George D. McDowell Philadelphia Evening Bulletin Photographs, Temple University Library, Special Collections Research Center.
"Wife Left Fortune of Theater Man," *Philadelphia Inquirer*, February 11, 1949, p. 46.

Won't You Come Home, Pearl Bailey?

Bailey, Pearl, *The Raw Pearl*.
"Pearl Struts in With Saucy Dolly," Charles Petzold, *Philadelphia Daily News*, February 24, 1970, p. 33.
"Sell-Out Crowd Says Hello to Dolly," William Collins, *Philadelphia Inquirer*, February 24, 1970, p. 14.

"The Essence of Pearl Bailey," Karl Stark, *Philadelphia Inquirer*, August 20, 1990, p. 31.
"Vocalist From Phila.," *Philadelphia Inquirer*, October 13, 1945, p. 10.

The Show Rescued by a Helicopter

"An Uneven Finale for Playhouse in the Park," Jonathan Takiff, *Philadelphia Daily News*, September 12, 1974, p. 90.
"Cages is Offbeat and Stimulating," William B. Collins, *Philadelphia Inquirer*, September 14, 1974, p. 4.
"Could Playhouse Show Go On? Time Had to Tell," Stuart D. Bykovsky, *Philadelphia Daily News*, September 11, 1974, p. 22.
"Nehemiah Persoff: Going from Sinister to Soup to Nuts," Al Haas, *Philadelphia Inquirer*, September 18, 1974, p. 7B.

Philadelphia '76

"'1776' To Open in Park," *Philadelphia Inquirer*, May 23, 1976, p. 169.
"All of the area becomes a stage for Bicen plays," Al Haas, *Philadelphia Inquirer*, May 2, 1976, p. 115.
Eggert-Crowe, Madison and Scott Gabriel Knowles, "Bicentennial (1976)," *Encyclopedia of Greater Philadelphia* (website), Rutgers University, 2013. https://philadelphiaencyclopedia.org/essays/bicentennial-1976/.
"Musical '1776' will be staged nightly on mall despite losses," John Corr, *Philadelphia Inquirer*, July 11, 1976, p. 19.
"The Rigging Goes Up" and "New Playhouse Unfolds in Phila," photos by John C. Benene, *Philadelphia Inquirer*, May 5, 1976, p. 1 (both Philadelphia and New Jersey/Metro editions).

The Return of Lady Day

"After 80 Years, Philly Theatre Still A-Changing," Stephan Fatsis for the Associated Press. *The Journal News*, White Plains, NY, December 1, 1987, p. 17.
"Billie Holiday Fled Phila. Raid," *Philadelphia Inquirer*, May 20, 1947, p. 3.
"Holiday in Philadelphia," Leonard W. Boasberg, *Philadelphia Inquirer*, December 1, 1992, pp. 47, 51.
"Lady Day," *Philadelphia Daily News*, May 8, 1984, p. 34.
"'Lady Day' recreates Billie Holiday performance at a Philly jazz bar," *Philadelphia Inquirer*, April 6, 2023, p. B7.
"Lanie Robertson is finally dramatic enough," Frank Rossi, *Philadelphia Inquirer Magazine*, December 21, 1986, pp. 18–21.
"Playwright had his 'Day,'" Douglas J. Keating, *Philadelphia Inquirer*, June 5, 1987, p. 31.
Robertson, *Lady Day at Emerson's Bar & Grill*, pp. 12, 19.

Part Two: The Wicked Stage

William Penn Sees a Play

Biddle, Francis, *William Penn*.
Geiter, Mary K., *William Penn*.
Latham, Robert and William Matthews, eds., *The Diary of Samuel Pepys, Volume III, 1662*.
Frame of the Government of Pennsylvania, The Avalon Project: Documents in Law, History and Diplomacy, Yale Law School Library. https://avalon.law.yale.edu/17th_century/pa04.asp.
Taylor, Ivan E., *Samuel Pepys*.

The Friends of Virtue

Lippincott, *Early Philadelphia*, pp. 113–115.
Ryan, James Emmett (2010), "Staging Quakerism in American Theatre and Film," *Quaker Studies*: Vol. 14, Issue 1, Article 3.
O'Keefe, *The young Quaker; a comedy. As it is performed at the Theatre Royal in Smoke Alley, with great applause*. Dublin, 1784
Centlivre, Susanna, *A Bold Stroke for a Wife: A Comedy*. J. Hodges and J. Osborne, London, 1749.
"Forgotten Actors: Determined Opposition to Stage Plays in This City," *Philadelphia Times*, November 14, 1886, p. 9.
Pollock, Thomas Clark, *The Philadelphia Theatre in the Eighteenth Century*, Doctoral Thesis, University of Pennsylvania, 1933.

Theater Is Illegal in Philadelphia

Dunlap, *A History of the American Theatre*, pp. 55–58, 74–76.
Houchin, John, H., "The Struggle for Virtue: Professional Theatre in 18th Century Philadelphia."
Jable, J. Thomas, "Pennsylvania 1776: The Theater," *The Daily Item*, Sunbury, PA, January 21, 1976, p. 6.
Lippincott, *Early Philadelphia*, pp. 117–118.
Matluck, *John Durang*, pp. 14–20.
"To the Friends of the Drama," *Dunlap and Claypoole's American Daily Advertiser*, Philadelphia, PA, February 21, 1784, p. 3.

The Moral Structure of the Academy of Music

Charter and Prospectus of the Opera House, or American Academy of Music, Chrissy and Markely, printers, Philadelphia, 1852.
History and Description of the Opera House, or American Academy of Music, G. Andre & Co., Philadelphia, 1857, https://archive.org/details/historydescripti00phil/page/n4/mode/1up?view=theater.
Lewis, Michael J., *Philadelphia Builds*, pp. 81–97.
Marion, *Within These Walls*, pp. 14–49.

"Let Us Live to See the Theatres All Deserted"

Carlyle, Dennis, "Chambers-Wylie, Limestone Legacy On Broad Street," *Hidden City Philadelphia* (website), June 16, 2014. https://hiddencityphila.org/2014/06/south-broad-streets-limestone-legacy-lives-on/.
Griffis, William Elliot, *John Chambers: Servant of Christ and Master of Hearts and His Ministry in Philadelphia*.
Peirce, William Shannon, "The Relative Morals of City and Country," *The Penn Monthly*, April 1875, Vol. VI, No. 64.
"Philadelphia and Suburbs: The Theatrical Life," *Philadelphia Inquirer*, June 7, 1875, p. 2.
"The Row Officials," *Philadelphia Times*, June 7, 1875, p. 4.

The Battle of Salome in the Opera War

(Note: Some of the material for this chapter was originally presented in my podcast as part of Episode 47, "Hammerstein's Opera House, Part Two.")

"500 Pastors War on Salome," *Pittston Gazette* (PA), February 9, 1909.
"Brilliant Throng Greets Salome After Week of Battle," *Philadelphia Inquirer*, February 12, 1909, p. 1.
"Hammerstein Threatens to Withdraw Stars," *Philadelphia Inquirer*, January 1, 1909, p. 1.
Laufe, Abe, *The Wicked Stage*, pp. 28–29.

McClung, Rob, "The Rise, Fall, and Revival of North Broad's Opera Palace," *Hidden City Philadelphia* (website), June 14, 2018. https://hiddencityphila.org/2018/06/the-rise-fall-revival-of-north-broads-opera-palace/.
"Pulpit Fight on Opera Continues," *Philadelphia Inquirer*, February 8, 1909.
Sheean, Vincent, *Oscar Hammerstein I*, pp. 248–258.
"Stop 'Salome' Cry to Mayor," *Camden Morning Post* (NJ), February 9, 1909, p. 8.
"Want Salome Prevented by Police Power," *Philadelphia Inquirer*, February 10, 1909, p. 1.
"Want 'Salome' Suppressed," *New York Times*, February 9, 1909, p. 2.

Let My People Come on South Street

"Cabarets, art, and the LCB," Dorothy Storck, *Philadelphia Inquirer*, May 23, 1979, p. 17. (Most of the best quotes about the LCB hearings are from this article.)
"Let My People Do What?," Julia Lawlor, *Philadelphia Inquirer*, October 21, 1977, p. 29.
"On Stage by Stuart D. Bykovsky," *Philadelphia Daily News*, March 17, 1978, p. 42.
"The Music Man's Saga," Jonathan Takiff, *Philadelphia Daily News*, June 27, 1973, p. 35.
"'This is not a dirty show,' he said," Jack Lloyd, *Philadelphia Inquirer*, October 16, 1977, p. 117.
"Where do all the trendies meet? (Guess!)," Beth Gillin, *Philadelphia Inquirer*, May 30, 1986, p. 91.

Hugh Hefner in Old City

"A little trim suits the Fringe Festival just fine," Douglas J. Keating, *Philadelphia Inquirer*, August 26, 2011, pp. 141, 156.
"Fringe Benefits," Sono Motoyama, *Philadelphia Daily News*, August 30, 2001, pp. 41–43.
"James Bondage," Alexis Soloski, *The Village Voice*, New York, June 9, 1998, p. 165.
MacLaughlin, Whit. 2006. "Towards a Comprehensive Media Meteorology," pp. 55–67.
"The Place is the Thing," Ellis Lotozo, *Philadelphia Inquirer*, August 30, 2001, pp. 33, 36.
"Ticket sales up for this year's Fringe," Ellis Lotozo, *Philadelphia Inquirer*, September 18, 2001, p. 38.
Whit MacLaughlin interview with author, February 18, 2024. All quotes in the chapter not specifically taken from his 2006 article in *Live Movies* are from this interview.

Part Three: Playhouses

The Mysterious Case of the Stolen Spikes at the Old Theatre

"America's First Theatre," *The Theatre*, July 1912, Vol. XVI, No. 137. p. 16.
"Ten Pounds Reward. A Burglary," *Dunlap and Claypoole's American Daily Advertiser*, December 14, 1772.
"Theatre. A New Comic Opera," *Dunlap and Claypoole's American Daily Advertiser*, December 14, 1772.
"Theatre. By Authority" (ad), *Dunlap and Claypoole's American Daily Advertiser*, October 26, 1772.

The New Theatre on Chestnut Street

Bellion, Wendy, "Here Trust Your Eyes," pp. 333–365.
James, Reese Davis, *Cradle of Culture*, pp. 36–125.
James, Reese Davis, *Old Drury of Philadelphia*, pp. 1–20.
Mease, James, *The Picture of Philadelphia*, pp. 328–332.
"Nightlife in Philadelphia—an Oyster Barrow in front of the Chestnut Street Theater," attributed to John Lewis Krimmel, Collection of the Metropolitan Museum of Art, New York, Accession Number: 42.95.18. https://www.metmuseum.org/art/collection/search/12739.

Quinn, Arthur Hobson. *A History of American Drama*, pp. 136–162.
Wolcott, John, R., "Philadelphia's Chestnut Street Theatre: A Plan and Elevation," pp. 209–218.

Ricketts' Circus, Benedict Arnold, and the Death of Major Andre

(Note: Some of the material for this chapter was originally presented in my podcast as part of Episode 6, "Ricketts' Circus in the Capital City, Part Four.")

Baston, Kim, "Transatlantic Journeys: John Bill Ricketts and the Edinburgh Equestrian Circus," *Popular Entertainment Studies*, 2013, Vol. 4, Issue 2, pp. 5–28.
Greenwood, Isaac J., *The Circus: Its Origins and Growth prior to 1835*.
Jando, Dominique, *Philip Astley and the Horsemen Who Invented the Circus*.
Kuntz, Andrew, "At the Circus: Astley, Ricketts and Durang," https://www.ibiblio.org/fiddlers/circus.htm.
Moy, *John Bill Ricketts' Circus: 1793–1800*.
Poppiti, *A History of Equestrian Drama in the United States*, pp. 1–37.
"Rickett's Circus … The Ring and the Stage," *Aurora General Advertiser*, February 6, 1799, p. 3.
"Ricketts' Circus … Pantomime, Called the Defection of General Arnold," *Aurora General Advertiser*, February 9, 1799, p. 3.

The Spanish Consul and the New French Circus on Walnut Street

(Note: Some of the material for this chapter was originally presented in my podcast as part of Episode 9, "Chaos Comes to Walnut Street.")

Davis, *America's Longest Run*, pp. 23–35.
de Onis, Luis, *Memoir Upon the Negotiations Between Spain and the United States of America*, Madrid, 1820. Translated from the Spanish by Tobias Watkins, Washington, DC, 1821.
Diario de Madrid, del Martes 14 de Octubre de 1806, pp. 447–450. (Digitized by Biblioteca Nacional de España.)
Dominique, Denis, "Premier Cirque Olympique des frères Franconi," *Circus Parade* (website), June 16, 2018. https://www.circus-parade.com/2018/06/16/premier-cirque-olympique-des-freres-franconi/.
Dunlap, *History of the American Theatre*, pp. 277–399.
Spell, J. R., "An Illustrious Spaniard in Philadelphia, Valentín de Foronda," *Hispanic Review*, Vol. 4, No. 2, 1936, pp. 136–140. *JSTOR*, https://doi.org/10.2307/469481.

Farewell to Old Drury

Durang, *History of the Philadelphia Stage*, Vol. 6, pp. 418–419 (Penn Libraries, Colenda Digital Repository (images 362 and 367).
"M. Thomas & Sons, Auc'rs," *Philadelphia Public Ledger*, May 2, 1855, p. 4.
Marion, *Within These Walls*, pp. 14–49.
"Theatricals," *United States Gazette*, September 21, 1827, p. 4.
Wemyss, *Twenty-six Years of the Life of an Actor and Manager*, p. 163.

Mrs. John Drew's Arch Street Theatre

(Note: Some of the material for this chapter was originally presented in my podcast as part of Episode 20, "The Duchess of Arch Street, Part Two.")

Drew, Louisa, *Autobiographical Sketch of Mrs. John Drew*, pp. 106–110. This memoir is remarkable in its unhelpful brevity and lack of revealing detail. It was composed very late in her life, and Mrs. Drew was very protective of her family and private affairs. A copy of the Drew family bible, with its annotations about births, marriages and deaths, is in the Theater Collection in the Rare Books Department of the Free Library of Philadelphia.

"For the National Gazette," *Philadelphia Inquirer*, August 17, 1830, p. 1.

Glazer, *Philadelphia Theaters: A Pictorial Architectural History*, p. xv.

Glazer, *Philadelphia Theatres, A-Z*, pp. 61–62.

Peters, Margo, *The House of Barrymore*.

Stolp, "Mrs. John Drew, American Actress and Manager, 1820–1897," pp. 274–281, 323–324.

"The Apollo," *United States Gazette*, March 9, 1830, p. 4.

Turner, *Forgotten Leading Ladies of the American Theatre*, pp. 86–101.

"William Penn's Treaty with the Indians, 1682, Relief Sculpture," *Architect of the Capitol* (website), https://admin.aoc.gov/explore-capitol-campus/art/william-penns-treaty-indians-1682-relief-sculpture.

Opening Night at Hammerstein's Opera House

(Note: Some of the material for this chapter was originally presented in my podcast as part of Episode 47, "Hammerstein's Opera House, Part One.'")

"Beauties of Society Will Throng to Brand-New Opera House," *Philadelphia Inquirer*, November 17, 1908, p 1.

Glazer, *Philadelphia Theatres: A Pictorial Architectural History*, pp. 6–7.

Marion, *Within These Walls*, pp. 146–169.

McClung, Rob, "The Rise, Fall, and Revival of North Broad's Opera Palace," *Hidden City Philadelphia* (website), https://hiddencityphila.org/2018/06/the-rise-fall-revival-of-north-broads-opera-palace/.

Sheean, Vincent, *Oscar Hammerstein I, The Life and Exploits of an Impresario*.

Tomars, Adolph S., *The First Oscar Hammerstein and New York's Golden Age of Theater and Music*.

Van Vechten, Carl, "Oscar Hammerstein: An Epitaph," *In The Garrett*, Alfred A. Knopf, 1920, pp. 234–259.

"Workmen in Wild All-Day Riot Besiege Future Opera House Site," *Philadelphia Inquirer*, April 2, 1908, p. 2.

The Adventures of Chlora on Delancey Street

(Note: Some of the material for this chapter was originally presented in my podcast as part of Episode 66, "The Newest Oldest Biggest Little Theater.")

"A Week of Promise for First Nighters," *Philadelphia Inquirer*, March 2, 1913, p. 39.

"Little Theatre Makes Its Bow," *Philadelphia Inquirer*, March 4, 1913, p. 11.

"New Little Theatre," *New York Tribune*, March 4, 1913, p. 9.

"Opening of the Little Theatre," *Philadelphia Inquirer*, March 2, 1913, p. 39.

"Philadelphia's Little Theatre," Herman L. Dieck, *The Theatre*, August 1913, Vol. 18, No. 150, pp. 61, 107.

"Plays and Players Theatre," in Glazer, *Philadelphia Theatres, A–Z*, p. 190.

Plays and Players Theatre Dossier, 2011, PA Graduate Program in Historic Preservation, University of Pennsylvania School of Design Preservation Studio. Collection of University of Pennsylvania Library.

"This Woman Built a Theatre to Prove Her Theories," *New York Times*, June 22, 1913, p. 45.

Snake Hips at the Lincoln

Finkel, Ken, "Burning it up at the Lincoln: From 'Minnie the Moocher' to Hitler in Effigy," *The PhillyHistory Blog* (website), April 16, 2017, https://blog.phillyhistory.org/index.php/2017/04/burning-it-up-at-the-lincoln-from-mini-the-moocher-to-hitler-in-effigy/.

"Influx of Sepia Stage Stars To Philly Makes Quaker City The Mecca Of Negro Performers," Lou Garcia, *Philadelphia Tribune*, January 21, 1932, p. 7.

"Lincoln Theatre" (ad), *Philadelphia Tribune*, January 7, 1932, p. 6.

"Reviews," Lou Garcia, *Philadelphia Tribune*, January 4, 1932, p. 6.

Siebert, Brian, *What The Eye Hears: A History of Tap Dancing*, Farrar, Straus and Giroux, 2015, p. 179.

"Snakehips At Lincoln," *Philadelphia Tribune*, January 7, 1932, p. 6.

The Invention of the Wilma

Ferguson, Marcia, *Blanka and Jiri Zizka at the Wilma Theater in Philadelphia*.

"For Stoppard, a Play Must Be Just That, A Play," Robin Pogrebin, *New York Times*, March 18, 2001.

"'Invention' Lifts Playwright's Art to New Levels," Leo Irwin, *Wilmington News-Journal*, February 20, 2000.

Ryan, Carrie, "Translating The Invention of Love."

"Stoppard's Invention of Love at the Wilma," Douglas J. Keating, *Philadelphia Inquirer*, February 18, 2000.

"Struggles at an end, the new Wilma opens," Douglas J. Keating, *Philadelphia Inquirer*, December 29, 1996.

The Arden in Old City

"A Dream of a Theatre," Douglas J. Keating, *Philadelphia Inquirer*, April 5, 1998.

"Arden passes test with Major Barbara," Robert Baxter, *Camden Courier-Post*, October 5, 1995.

"Arden Theatre: 30 Years Old, and a force that helped Old Cit happen," John Timpane, *Philadelphia Inquirer*, September 27, 2017.

"Arden's Dream is Joyous," Robert Baxter, *Camden Courier-Post*, April 10, 1998.

"New F. Otto Haas Stage is an exquisitely simple setting for plays," Thomas Ferrick, Jr., *Philadelphia Inquirer*, April 5, 1998.

"The Arden Christens a New Stage," Clifford R. Ridley, *Philadelphia Inquirer*, April 9, 1998.

"The Arden Theatre Gets a New Home in Old City," Douglas J. Keating, *Philadelphia Inquirer*, March 16, 1995.

A Great Day on South Broad Street

"A New Venue, A New Season," Robert Baxter, *Camden Courier-Post*, October 23, 2007.

"New Digs With the Same Old Feel," Peter Dobrin, *Philadelphia Inquirer*, October 21, 2007.

"Turning a Page," Sally Friedman, *Doylestown Public Intelligencer*, October 19, 2007.

Interview with Sara Garonzik, March 14, 2024.

Part Four: Local Heroes

Edwin Forrest Plays Richelieu

Davis, *America's Longest Run*, pp. 70–71, 78–79.

Durang, Charles, *History of the Philadelphia Stage, Between the Years 1749 and 1855*, Vol. 4, p. 167. (Colenda Digital Repository, University of Pennsylvania Libraries. Image 307.)
"Edwin Forrest as Richelieu," *Philadelphia Inquirer*, February 3, 1863, p. 3.
Harrison, Gabriel, *Edwin Forrest, the actor and the man*, p. 201.
Moody, *Edwin Forrest, First Star of the American Stage*, pp. 187–190, 376–387.
"Mr. Forrest as Richelieu," *Charleston Mercury*, September 19, 1939, p. 2.
Rees, James, *The Life of Edwin Forrest*, pp. 184–185.
Wemyss, *Twenty-six Years of the Life of an Actor and Manager*, p. 320.

The Heron Takes Wing

(Note: Much of the material for this chapter was originally presented in my podcast as part of Episode 33, "Life and Death in the Theater: More 19th Century Stories.")

Hutton, Lawrence, *Curiosities of the American Stage*, pp. 83–84.
"Matilda Heron's Funeral," *New York Times*, March 12, 1877, p. 8.
Turney, Wayne S., "Matilda Heron (1830–77), America's Definitive Camille," *A Glimpse of Theatre History* (website).
Winter, William, "Matilda Heron," in *Vagrant Memories*, pp. 59–72.

The Little Tycoon

"A Comic Opera's Fate," *New York Times*, January 19, 1886, p. 8.
"A New Comic Opera: First Production of 'The Little Tycoon' at the Temple Theatre," *Philadelphia Times*, January 5, 1886.
"Ladies Without Escorts," *Philadelphia Times*, March 30, 1886, p. 3.
"Life in New York City: A PIECE called the Little Tycoon," *Brooklyn Daily Eagle*, April 4, 1886, p. 11.
"My Valet and I," *Buffalo News*, April 3, 1886, p. 7.
"The Comic Operas," *Philadelphia Times*, January 9, 1886, p. 2.
"The Little Tycoon," *New York Times*, April 5, 1886, p. 5.
"The Little Tycoon," *Philadelphia Times*, January 24, 1886, p. 6.
"The One Hundredth Performance," *Philadelphia Inquirer*, March 29, 1886, p. 3.
"Various Entertainments," *Philadelphia Times*, February 9, 1886, p. 3.

May Manning Lillie, Quaker Cowgirl

Browder, Laura, *Her Best Shot*, p. 85.
Enns, Chris, "Wild Woman Wednesday: May Manning Lillie," *Cowgirl Magazine* (website), August 3, 2016, https://www.cowgirlmagazine.com/wild-woman-wednesday-may-manning-lillie/.
"Gentlemen's Driving Park" (ad), *Philadelphia Times*, July 1, 1888, p. 13.
"Mary Emma Mae Manning Lillie," *Find a Grave* (website), https://www.findagrave.com/memorial/19858685/mary-emma-lillie.
"Mary Emma Manning Lille 'Mae Lillie,'" *National Cowgirl Museum and Hall of Fame* (website), https://www.cowgirl.net/portfolios/mary-emma-manning-lillie-may-lillie/.
"Pawnee Bill's Big Wild West Show Draws a Large Crowd," *Philadelphia Times*, July 3, 1888, p. 3.
"Route of the Wild West Parade," *Philadelphia Times*, July 2, 1888, p. 2.
"The Wild West," *Philadelphia Inquirer*, July 15, 1884, p. 2.
"The Wild West Shows," *Philadelphia Times*, July 1, 1888, p. 6.
"Wild West Show Attached," *Philadelphia Times*, August 28, 1888, p. 4.

NOTES AND SOURCES • 285

Blythe Spirit, or All Them Barrymores

Alpert, Hollis, *The Barrymores*—the question of Maurice's first use of the Barrymore name is found on pp. 12–13. The story of the gift of a red apple is on p. 44. The entire book is highly recommended for a wealth of Barrymore anecdotes too numerous to include in this chapter.

"A New Fitch Comedy," *Philadelphia Inquirer*, January 8, 1901, p. 3.

Barrymore, Ethel, *Memories: An Autobiography*, pp. 115–119. (The quote from the Philadelphia audience member—"You Drews is all good actors"—comes from this source. In other sources it is reported as "You Drews *are* all good actors," but I trust Ethel's memory on this, and anyway the former version is much more typical of Philadelphia-speak.)

Barrymore, Lionel, *We Barrymores*, pp. 15–41. Lionel has interesting insights into the Drew and Barrymore families in the early chapters of his autobiography, written in 1951. He stated incorrectly that his father took the name "Barrymore" because it was his own mother's maiden name (it was actually Chamberlayne). The story about Maurice seeing the name of William Barrymore on a poster appears likely to being the correct one. Indeed, if you find the name "Barrymore" in Philadelphia theater listings from the 1830s, it is likely to be that very same William Barrymore, who was otherwise unrelated to the family that was to make his name famous.

"Barrymores at the Garrick," *Philadelphia Inquirer*, March 6, 1906, p. 4.

Davis, *America's Longest Run*, p. 189.

Peters, Margot, *The House of Barrymore*, see pp. 9–45 for a an excellent summation of the family history.

Imogene Coca in Manayunk

"Imogene Coca Captivates in Hit Broadway Revue," Mark Barron, *The Sun*, Baltimore, November 5, 1939, p. 54.

"Imogene Coca Realizes an Ambition," *Brooklyn Times-Union*, May 24, 1936, p. 11.

"Imogene Coca Star Mimic," *Philadelphia Inquirer*, March 1, 1940, p. 57.

Jablon, Philip, "Inside This Manayunk Supply House? A Movie Palace," *Hidden City Philadelphia* (website), July 16, 2012, https://hiddencityphila.org/2012/07/the-former-empress-theater-in-manayunk/.

"Legion Post Roused by Minister's Protest," *Philadelphia Inquirer*, December 22, 1919, p. 4.

"Mayor Plays Gallant, Bans Girl Scout Skit," *Philadelphia Inquirer*, November 10, 1936, p. 21.

"'New Faces' Gay Review At Forrest," *Philadelphia Inquirer*, November 10, 1936, p. 12.

"No Dramatic Roles for Imogene Coca," Virginia Irwin, *St. Louis Post-Dispatch*, October 11, 1946, p. 45. The story about the firecrackers being set off during her vaudeville tryout in Manayunk is found here.

One of the Kelly Boys

Gagliardi, *All Play and No Work*, pp. 41–45.

"George Kelly, Playwright, Dies, Won Pulitzer for 'Craig's Wife,'" Robert McG. Thomas Jr., *New York Times*, June 19, 1874, p. 48.

"George Kelly's Play Awarded Pulitzer Prize," *Philadelphia Inquirer*, May 4, 1926, pp. 1, 6.

Spoto, Donald, *High Society*, pp. 24–27.

"Sure, and It's Mrs. Kelly's Proud Day," Gene Cohn, *Chattanooga News*, May 15, 1926, p. 25.

Trav S. D. (Donald Travis Stewart), "George Kelly: The Quintessential Vaudeville Playwright," January 16, 2013, *Travalanche* (website), https://travsd.wordpress.com/2013/01/16/stars-of-vaudeville-571-george-kelly/https://travsd.wordpress.com/2013/01/16/stars-of-vaudeville-571-george-kelly/.

They All Want Something from Big Bill Tilden

"Big Bill Tilden Insists on Being a Regular Actor," *New York Daily News*, November 6, 1926, p. 54.
"Bill Tilden Easily Wins Two Matches," *Philadelphia Inquirer*, June 16, 1926, p. 6.
"Bill Tilden Races Through 11 Sets," *Boston Globe*, June 21, 1926, p. 9.
Deford, Frank, *Big Bill Tilden: The Triumphs and the Tragedy*, Simon and Schuster, 1975.
"Ichabod Makes Formal Debut With Disparagement of Show," *Camden Courier-Press*, June 26, 1926, p. 6.
"New Show for Walnut," *Philadelphia Inquirer*, June 6, 1926, p. 59.
"Tennis Star Going on Stage," *Philadelphia Inquirer*, November 18, 1926, p. 8.
"Tilden Pseudo-Tramp in a New Comedy," *New York Times*, October 13, 1926, p. 30.
"Walnut St. Theatre" (ad), *Philadelphia Inquirer*, June 20, 1926, p. 50.

"The Girl Who Falls Down"

"A Bit of Actual Americana," Linton Martin, *Philadelphia Inquirer*, September 17, 1944, p. 38.
"Bloomer Girls Musical Opens at the Forrest," Linton Martin, September 12, 1944, p. 12.
"Joan M'Cracken Succumbs at 38," *Philadelphia Daily News*, November 2, 1961, p. 2.
"Joan McCracken Is Dead at 38," *New York Times*, November 2, 1961, p. 7.
"Joan McCracken to Marry Actor," *Philadelphia Inquirer*, December 30, 1952, p. 32.
Sagolla, *The Girl Who Fell Down*, pp. 8–45.
Skeel, *Catherine Littlefield*, pp. 109–111, 135–136.
"To Dance in the Dell," *Philadelphia Inquirer*, June 16, 1935, p. 83.

Molly Gets Married

"A lady of Yiddish theater, victorious after 75 years," Al Haas, *Philadelphia Inquirer*, May 6, 1979, p. 229.
Elkin, Michael, "The Yiddish leprechaun that was Molly Picon," *The Jewish Exponent*, Philadelphia, Vol. 191 (16), April 17, 1992.
"New Role for Molly," Barbara Wilson, *Philadelphia Inquirer*, September 4, 1967, p. 119.
"Pages From a Performing Life: The Scrapbooks of Molly Picon," *American Jewish Historical Society* (website), https://ajhs.org/exhibitions-programs/exhibitions/pages-from-a-performing-life-the-scrapbooks-of-molly-picon/.
Picon, Molly and Jean Bergantini Grillo, *Molly: An Autobiography of Molly Picon*, pp. 9–33.
"Yiddish Musical Here," *Philadelphia Inquirer*, May 8, 1938, p. 57.

Charles Fuller's Inspirations

Anadolu-Okur, *Contemporary African American Theater*, pp. 127–168. This work also contains an excellent chapter (pp. 23–70) on the life and work of Larry Neal.
"Charles Fuller Not Angry; He Wants to Improve Us," William H. Collins, *Philadelphia Inquirer*, September 12, 1977, pp. 157, 161.
"Charles Fuller, Pulitzer Winner," Neil Genzlinger, *New York Times*, October 4, 2022.
"Charles H. Fuller Jr… . memorialized by a city that admired him," Valerie Russ, *Philadelphia Inquirer*, November 6, 2022, https://www.inquirer.com/news/charles-fuller-memorial-pulitzer-prize-20221106.html.
"Farblonjet at Walnut," *Philadelphia Inquirer*, October 29, 1957, p. 13.
"Fuller's Triumphs on the Stage," Nels Nelson, *Philadelphia Daily News*, January 21, 1982, pp. 25, 30.

Part Five: Visiting Stars

George Frederick Cooke

(Note: Some of the material for this chapter was originally presented in my podcast as part of Episode 10, "George Frederick Cooke Heads to Philadelphia.")

Bernard, John, *Retrospections of America*, pp. 364–374.
Bowers, "Shakespearean Celebrity in America: The Strange Performative Afterlife of George Frederick Cooke," pp. 27–50.
Dunlap, *History of the American Theatre*, pp. 384–393.
Dunlap, William, *Memoirs of the Life of George Frederick Cooke*.
Durang, Charles, *History of the Philadelphia Stage, Between the Years 1749 and 1855*, Vol. 1, pp. 87–88, 92–94. Arranged and illustrated by Thompson Westcott, 1868. (Colenda Digital Repository, University of Pennsylvania Libraries. Images 292, 293, 305, 310, 311)
Fennell, James, *An Apology for the Life of James Fennell*, pp. 393–397, 405–410.
Hare, Arnold, *George Frederick Cooke: The Actor and the Man*, pp. 185–189.
Johns, Christopher M. S., "Theater and Theory: Thomas Sully's 'George Frederick Cooke as Richard III.'" *Winterthur Portfolio*, Vol. 18, No. 1 (Spring, 1983), pp. 27–38. Published by University of Chicago Press.
Wilmeth, *George Frederick Cooke, Machiavel of the Stage*, pp. 259–286.
Wood, *Personal Recollections of the Stage*, pp. 89, 134–170.

Edmund Kean Takes a Bow

Durang, *History of the Philadelphia Stage*, Vol. 2, pp. 138–139, 151–153. (Colenda Digital Repository, University of Pennsylvania Libraries. Images 80, 85, 121, 122, 127)
Molloy, *The Life and Adventures of Edmund Kean*, pp. 273–280.

Fanny Kemble Makes a Fateful Debut

(Note: Some of the material for this chapter was originally presented in my podcast as part of Episode 17, "Fanny Kemble, Part One.")

Clinton, Catherine, *Fanny Kemble's Civil Wars*.
David, Dierdre, *Fanny Kemble: A Performed Life*.
Davis, *America's Longest Run*, pp. 67–69.
Durang, *History of the Philadelphia Stage*, Vol. 4, pp. 73–78. (Colenda Digital Repository, University of Pennsylvania Libraries. Images 31, 32, 37, 38, 43, 44)
Furnas, J. C., *Fanny Kemble: Leading Lady of the Nineteenth Century Stage*.
Gibbs, Henry, *Affectionately Yours, Fanny*.
Gough, Monica (editor), *Fanny Kemble: Journal of a Young Actress*.
Jackson, *Literary Landmarks of Philadelphia*, pp. 197–201.
Jenkins, Rebecca, *Fanny Kemble: A Reluctant Celebrity*, pp. 356–375.
Kemble, Frances Anne (Fanny), *Journal, vols I & II*, London: J. Murray, 1835.
Wood, *Personal Recollections of the Stage*, p. 369.
Wright, Constance, *Fanny Kemble and the Lovely Land*.

Rachel Gets a Cold Reception

Beauvallet, *Rachel et le Nouveau-Monde*, "La Cité de Quakers," pp. 220–230.
Beauvallet, *Rachel and the New world*, "The Quaker City," pp. 279–293. In all quotations from Beauvallet, I have attempted to improve the quality of this rather rough translation, based on his original French text.
Brownstein, *Tragic Muse*, pp. 203–209. Brownstein rather skips over Rachel's visit to Philadelphia.
Davis, *America's Longest Run*, pp. 109–110.
Leff, Lisa Moses, "Rachel (Eliza Rachel Félix)," *The Shalvi/Hyman Encyclopedia of Jewish Women*, on Jewish Women's Archive (website), https://jwa.org/encyclopedia/article/rachel-eliza-rachel-felix.
"Rachel in Philadelphia," *Philadelphia Public Ledger*, November 12, 1855, p. 5, column 1.
"Walnut Street Theatre—Notice," *Philadelphia Public Ledger*, November 21, p. 3, column 5.

Bunthorne in the Quaker City

"Aestheticism," *Philadelphia Inquirer*, January 18, 1888, p. 8.
"Amusements, Music, &c—'Patience,' Lyceum Theatre," *Philadelphia Inquirer*, November 22, 1881, p. 3.
"'Carncross' 11th Street Opera House, the Family Resort" (ad), *Philadelphia Times*, February 5, 1882, p. 5.
"Concordia Operette Theatre" (ad), *Philadelphia Times*, January 8, 1882, p. 5.
Ellman, *Oscar Wilde*, pp. 166–174.
"Events in Society," *Philadelphia Times*, January 1, 1888, p. 2.
"The Aesthete Entertained," *Philadelphia Times*, January 19, 1882, p 1.
"The Aesthete's Lecture," *Philadelphia Times*, January 18, 1888, p. 2.

Sarah Bernhardt and the Mummers

"Bernhardt and Coquelin as Reichstadt and Flambeau in Rostand's Latest Drama," *Philadelphia Times*, January 1, 1901, p. 6.
DuComb, *Haunted City*, p. 6.
"First Day of the New Century," *Philadelphia Public Ledger*, January 2, 1901 (cited in DuComb, *Haunted City*, p. 152).
Gold and Fizdale, *The Divine Sarah*, pp. 287–289.
Masters, *The Philadelphia Mummers*, pp. 1–41.
Skinner, *Madame Sarah*, pp. 264–271.

Katharine Hepburn's Philadelphia Story

"Katharine Hepburn Stars in 'Philadelphia Story,'" Linton Martin, *Philadelphia Inquirer*, p. 13.
Kolendo, Joanna, "Philadelphia Story (The)," *The Encyclopedia of Greater Philadelphia* (website), Rutgers University, 2016, https://philadelphiaencyclopedia.org/essays/philadelphia-story-the/.
Parish, *Katharine Hepburn*, pp. 54–62, 190–195. (The quote about Hepburn's Bryn Mawr College freshman theatre experience is from this source, on page 57.)
"Theater was not always a waltz for her," and "Ah, Hepburn is a delight this time out," William B. Collins, *Philadelphia Inquirer*, October 23, 1981, p. 87.

Paul Robeson's Hammer

(Note: Some of the material for this chapter was originally presented in my podcast as part of Episode 35, "The Paul Robeson House.")

"Giving Life to a Legend," Linton Martin, *Philadelphia Inquirer,* December 17, 1939, p. 65.
"John Henry Bears Down Kinda Heavy on Singin' Paul Robeson," Burns Mantle, *New York Daily News,* January 12, 1940, p. 105.
"Paul Robeson Finds Basic Folk Music Melody Same," *Lancaster Sunday News Magazine,* December 31, 1939, p. 21.
"Paul Robeson Scores in Play's New Opening, *Wilmington Morning News,* December 12, 1939, p. 2.
"Paul Robeson Stars in Othello," Linton Martin, *Philadelphia Inquirer,* October 5, 1943, p. 26.
"Paul Robeson Stars in role of 'Othello,'" *Philadelphia Inquirer,* August 18, 1942, p. 15.
"Paul Robeson to Play Self," *Philadelphia Inquirer,* December 3, 1939, p. 75.
"Paul Robeson Will Appear in 'Othello' in Princeton," *Central New Jersey News,* August 16, 1942, p. 21.
"Robeson Gives 'Superb' Performance as Othello," *Philadelphia Tribune,* October 19, 1943, p. 15.
"Robeson Guest at Reception," *Philadelphia Tribune,* October 16, 1943, p. 2.
Swindall, *Paul Robeson, A Life in Activism and Art,* pp. 92–93.

Peter Brook Finds the Empty Space

(Note: Some of the material for this chapter was originally presented in my podcast as part of Episode 54, "Theatre of the Living Arts: A Beginning.")

Brook, Peter, *The Empty Space,* Atheneum, New York, 1968, p. 22.
"Brook's 'Dream' Triumphs Where his 'Lear' Failed," William B. Collins, *Philadelphia Inquirer,* April 25, 1971, p. 97.
"Majestic King Lear at Shubert," Jerry Gaghan, *Philadelphia Daily News,* May 12, 1964, p. 65.
"Scofield Great in King Lear," Henry Murdock, *Philadelphia Inquirer,* May 12, 1964, p. 11.

Part Six: Disputes, Deaths, and Disasters

Kean's Riot

Durang, *History of the Philadelphia Stage,* Vol. 2, p. 154. (Colenda Digital Repository, University of Pennsylvania Libraries, Image 133)
Molloy, *The Life and Adventures of Edmund Kean,* pp. 280–285.
"Theatre," *The United States Gazette,* January 20, 1826, p. 1.
"Walnut Street Theatre. Mr. Kean's Benefit" (ad), *Philadelphia Inquirer,* April 18, 1821, p. 3.

Charlotte Cushman Sends Too Many Flowers

(Note: Some of the material for this chapter was originally presented in my podcast as part of Episode 25, "The Charlotte Cushman Club.")

"American Theatre: Walnut Street" (ad), *Philadelphia Public Ledger,* September 21, 1842, p. 3.
Bradford, Gamaliel, "Charlotte Cushman," *The North American Review,* vol. 221, no. 827, 1925, pp. 689–700, jstor.org/stable/25113432."Charlotte Cushman, an American Star," *Shakespeare and Beyond,* Folger Shakespeare Library (website), July 22, 2016, https://www.folger.edu/blogs/shakespeare-and-beyond/charlotte-cushman-an-american-star/
"Charlotte Cushman: When Romeo Was a Woman," Folger Shakespeare Library, Shakespeare Unlimited (podcast).
Davis, *America's Longest Run,* pp. 85–87.

"Frances Anne (Fanny) Kemble Butler," *Archival Gossip* (website), https://www.archivalgossip.com/collection/items/show/51.
Merrill, Lisa, *When Romeo was a Woman*, pp. 69–74.
Wojczuk, Tara, *Lady Romeo*, pp. 79–89, 98–99.

The Marble Heart of John Wilkes Booth

"Addressing Abe," Joe Clark, *Philadelphia Daily News*, April 11, 2000, p. 34. This article contains the details of Lincoln's body at a North Philadelphia funeral home.
Alford, Terry, *Fortune's Fool*, pp. 135–137, 140–141.
Bank, "Louisa Lane Drew at the Arch Street Theatre," pp. 37–46.
Davis, *America's Longest Run*, pp. 144–145, 207.
"John Wilkes Booth: The Philadelphia Connection," Philadelphia in the Civil War, Part 2, *LaSalle Digital Connections* (website), March 13, 2013.
"Lincoln's Assassin Once Had Adoring Phila Fans," Edward Collimore, *Philadelphia Inquirer*, March 2, 2013, pp. 1, 2. (Published online as "John Wilkes Booth honed his acting career at Philadelphia's Arch Street Theatre," *Philadelphia Inquirer*, March 13, 2013, https://www.inquirer.com/philly/news/local/20130303_John_Wilkes_Booth_honed_his_acting_while_at_Philadelphia_s_Arch_Street_Theatre.html.)
"Meeting of the Theatrical Profession," *Philadelphja Inquirer*, April 22, 1865, p. 3.
"Mrs. John Drew's Arch Street Theatre" (ad), *Philadelphia Inquirer*, March 3, 1863, p. 2.
Mrs. Jno. Drew's Arch Street Theatre Marble Heart playbill, 1863 [starring John Wilkes Booth]. Historical Society of Pennsylvania, Playbill Collection (#3131).

The Death of Annie Kemp Bowler, the Original Stalacta

(Note: A previous version of this chapter originally appeared as my own essay about Annie Kemp Bowler for the Friends of Mount Moriah Cemetery website. https://friendsofmountmoriahcemetery.org/about/notable-burials/annie-kemp-bowler/)

"American Theatricals," *The Era* (London), March 10, 1861, p. 12.
"Amusements, Music, &c. Richings English Opera," *Philadelphia Inquirer*, September 3, 1869, p. 2.
"English Opera Company," *The Staffordshire Sentinel*, etc., July 18, 1863, p. 5.
"Musical and Dramatic: The City Amusements," *Philadelphia Evening Telegraph*, September 6, 1869, p. 8.
"Musical and Dramatic: Il Trovatore," *Philadelphia Evening Telegraph*, September 9, 1869, p. 5.
"Obituary: Sudden Death of Annie Kemp, Popular Actress," *Philadelphia Times*, August 22, 1876, p. 1.
"Prince of Wales Theatre. British Operatic Association," *Birmingham Daily Post*, May 17, 1863, p. 3.
"St. George's Hall. Grand Concert. Mad'lle Adelina Patti" (ad), *Liverpool Mercury*, April 6, 1863, p. 6.
"Theatre Royal, Nottingham" (ad), *The Guardian Journal*, September 19, 1863, p. 1.
"The Drama in America," *The Era* (London), September 17, 1876, p. 5.

The Temple Theatre Catches Fire

(Note: A portion of the material for this chapter was originally presented in my podcast as part of Episode 12, "Stages of Fire.")

"A Collection of Human Curiosities" and "Ninth and Arch Dime Museum" (ad), *Philadelphia Times*, March 11, 1888, p. 9.
"A Comic Opera's Fate," *New York Times*, December 30, 1886, p. 8.
"Burning of the Temple Theatre" (Illustration), *Harper's Weekly*, January 1, 1887, Vol. 31 Issue 1568, p. 24.

"Fireman Gibson Buried," *Philadelphia Inquirer*, January 4, 1887, p. 2.
"The Temple Theatre Fire," *Philadelphia Inquirer*, December 31, 1886, p. 2.

The Fall of Apollo

"Activities of the Day in Real Estate," *Philadelphia Inquirer*, June 19, 1936, p. 22.
"Another Landmark Disappears," Henry T. Murdock, *Philadelphia Evening Public Ledger*, June 26, 1936, p. 24.
"Century-Old Theatre to Form Parking Lot," *Camden Courier-Press*, June 19, 1936, p. 11.
"Demolishing Arch St. Theatre," *Philadelphia Inquirer*, June 28, 1936, p. 58.

Curtain Time, Minus Zero

"Banned Papa Goldberg Dies of Sleeping Pills," *Philadelphia Inquirer*, September 2, 1955, p. 5.
"Mostel Cremated at Secret Site," *The Ottawa Journal*, September 10, 1977, p. 5.
Mostel, Kate, 170 Years of Show Business, pp. 117, 171–175.
"N.Y. Actor-Producer Is Found Dead in Hotel" (Associated Press), *Miami News*, September 2, 1955, p. 1.
"Prizewinning Actor Mostel Dies at 62," *Philadelphia Daily News*, September 9, 1977, p. 3.
"Shubert sees the light despite dark theater," *Philadelphia Inquirer*, September 8, 1937, p. 38.
Trav S. D. (Donald Travis Stewart), "The Life and Martyrdom of Philip Loeb," *Travalanche* (website), March 28, 2020, https://travsd.wordpress.com/2020/03/28/the-life-and-martyrdom-of-philip-loeb/.
"Update: Filling out the record," *Philadelphia Inquirer*, September 10, 1977, p. 10.
"Wesker: 'Like Losing One of the Family,'" Al Haas, *Philadelphia Inquirer*, September 10, 1977, p. 12.
Wesker, Arnold, "Off to Philadelphia in the Morning," *The Birth of Shylock and The Death of Zero Mostel*, pp, 177– 211.
"Young Philadelphian Makes Stage Debut in New York Tonight," *Philadelphia Evening Public Ledger*, April 29, 1916, p. 7.
"Zero Mostel, famed comedian and actor, dies of heart attack here," William B. Collins, *Philadelphia Inquirer*, September 9, 1977, p. 1.

Zsa Zsa Gabor Gets Fired

"Curtains for Zsa Zsa a Break for Terry," *Philadelphia Daily News*, June 7, 1983, p. 4.
"Fired from show, actress denies accusations" (Knight-Ridder), *Tampa Tribune*, June 8, 1983, p. 95.
"Gabor Rebuke," Gene Seymour, *Philadelphia Daily News*, April 12, 1985, p. 4.
"Handicapped leave play after Gabor complains," *Philadelphia Inquirer*, June 2, 1983, p. 1.
"It's Always Something: Zsa Zsa's Troubles Didn't Begin in Phila." (UPI), *Scrantonian Tribune*, June 11, 1983, p. 54.
Lawlor, Rob, "Zsa Zsa Gabor" (editorial cartoon), *Philadelphia Daily News*, June 3, 1983, p. 41.
"Standards," *Philadelphia Daily News*, June 3, 1983, p. 41.
"The Show Goes On," *Philadelphia Inquirer*, June 12, 1983, p. 3.
"Unhealthy Situation," Larry Fields, *Philadelphia Daily News*, June 16, 1983, p. 52.
"Update: They Finally Saw the Show," Clark DeLeon, *Philadelphia Inquirer*, June 22, 1983, p. 14.
"Zsa Zsa's Back, Bigger Than Life," Nels Nelson, *Philadelphia Daily News*, May 25, 1983, p. 40.
"Zsa Zsa gets the hook," *New York Daily News*, June 3, 1983, p. 4.
"Zsa Zsa: 'I Was Treated Like Dirt Here," Jennifer Preston and Bill Reinecke, *Philadelphia Daily News*, June 3, 1983, p. 30.
"Zsa Zsa note," John Corr, *Philadelphia Inquirer*, June 23, 1983, p. 76.
"Zsa Zsa Shown the Stage Door," *Philadelphia Daily News*, June 3, 1983, p. 3.

Part Seven: The Tryout Town

The Marx Brothers Stay for the Summer
"As a mark of respect and deep affection for our late President" (ad), *Philadelphia Inquirer*, August 9, 1923, p. 16.
Davis, *America's Longest Run*, pp. 217–219.
"I'll Say She Is," *Philadelphia Inquirer*, June 5, 1923, p. 12.
"Is She a Phila. Favorite?" (ad), *Philadelphia Inquirer*, August 27, 1923, p. 14.
Marx, Groucho, *Groucho and Me*, p. 162.
"Now in its 3rd month" (ad), *Philadelphia Inquirer*, August 5, 1923, p. 49.
"Sounds Much Like a Motor Knock," Groucho Marx, *Philadelphia Inquirer*, August 26, 1923, p. 47.
Uhlin, Mikhail, "I'll Say She Is!" *Marxology* (website), https://marxology.marx-brothers.org/story.htm.
"Walnut," *Philadelphia Inquirer*, June 3, 1923, p. 91.

Mrs. Penfield Backs Fioretta
"Earl Carroll's 'Fioretta' Opens," R. P. H., *Baltimore Evening Sun*, January 1, 1929, p. 25.
"Fannie Brice is quitting 'Fioretta,'" *New York Daily News*, April 15, 1929, p. 29.
Murray, Ken, *The Body Merchant*, pp. 148–157.
"New York Theatres: What the Critics Said of 'Fioretta,'" *Yonkers Herald-Statesman*, January 5, 1929, p. 6.

Lysistrata—Modern Abdominal Merriment
"Acclaimed from the Acropolis" (ad), *Philadelphia Inquirer*, May 4, 1930.
"Aristophanes Play is Sprightly Acted," Brooks Atkinson, *New York Times*, April 29, 1930.
"Aristophanes Has a Hit!" (ad), *Philadelphia Inquirer*, May 11, 1930.
Kammen, *The Lively Arts*, pp. 162–164.
"Lysistrata Given Great Production," I. F., *Camden Evening Press*, April 29, 1930, p. 6.
Sculthorpe, *The Life and Times of Sydney Greenstreet*, pp. 100–101.
Young, Stark. 1930. "The Philadelphia Lysistrata." *The New Republic* LXII (806): 352–353.

Ayn Rand Writes a Play
Branden, *The Passion of Ayn Rand*, pp. 117–125. The description and quotations from the Philadelphia tryout period of *The Night of January 16th* are primarily from this source.
Burns, Jennifer, *Goddess of the Market: Ayn Rand and the American Right*, Oxford University Press, 2009.
Heller, *Ayn Rand and the World She Made*, pp. 75–76.
"Murder Play Trial Clicks at Chestnut," James M. O'Neill, *Camden Courier-Press*, September 10, 1935, p. 4.
"Night of January 16, in Which Members of the Audience Serve as Jury," Brooks Atkinson, *New York Times*, September 17, 1935, p. 26.
"Novel Crime Play Opens at Chestnut," L[inton] M[artin], *Philadelphia Inquirer*, September 10, 1935, p. 5, column 1.
"Patrons to Serve as Jurors in Play," *Philadelphia Inquirer*, September 5, 1935, p. 6.
"Peppy Al Woods Began Many Broadway Quips," *Philadelphia Inquirer*, September 10, 1925, p. 5, column 2.
Sciabarra, Anthony, *Ayn Rand, the Russian Radical*, The Pennsylvania State University Press, 2013.

Brando on Walnut Street

Butler, *The Method*, pp. 226–233.
Kazan, *A Life*, pp. 342–346. Kazan does not explicitly mention the tryout period in Philadelphia.
Spoto, *The Kindness of Strangers*, pp. 136–137.
"'Streetcar Named Desire' Is Strong Dramatic Meat," Linton Martin, *Philadelphia Inquirer*, November 23, 1947, p. 67.
"'Streetcar Named Desire' Opens at Walnut," Edwin H. Schloss, *Philadelphia Inquirer*, November 18, 1947, p. 37.

World Premiere of Death of a Salesman

"Academy of Music: Philadelphia Orchestra" (ads), *Philadelphia Inquirer*, January 22, 1949, p. 19, and January 28, 1949, p. 43.
"Backstage: Lee J. Cobb Escaped Young Roles," Marion Kelly, *Philadelphia Inquirer*, January 23, 1949, pp. 74, 80. In this article Marion Kelly states she interviewed Cobb in New York before the company arrived in Philadelphia. The actor admits to experiencing insomnia due to his work on the play, and that he was looking for ways to inject "additional realism" into the role. (An additional brief item about Cobb's efforts to get tickets for a friend was printed in Frank Brookhouser's column in the *Inquirer* on Friday, February 4, 1949, p. 15.)
"'Death of a Salesman' on Locust's Stage," Edwin H. Schloss, *Philadelphia Inquirer*, January 24, 1949, p. 11.
Gottfried, *Arthur Miller: His Life and Work*. Gottfried's version, pp. 143–145, correctly notes the company arrived in Philadelphia on Tuesday the 18th. However, he is a bit unclear about how the next few days progressed, and understandably he repeats Miller's version of the story about going to hear Beethoven at the Academy of Music.: "Miller leaned forward in the upper box and whispered to Cobb, 'Now this is the last ten minutes of the play'" (p. 144). However, to his great credit, Gottfried does incorporate additional fascinating stories and memories from both Mildred Dunnock and Alan Hewitt about the tryout weeks in Philadelphia into his narrative, which the two actors related at a Dramatist's Guild panel about *Salesman* in March 1981.
"Higher Call," *The New Yorker*, March 26, 1949, p. 21. The magazine interviewed Lee J. Cobb shortly during the monumental success of the Broadway run of the play. He discussed his career, his love for flying planes, his own father, and the initial reaction to reading the script—but not the tryout weeks at the Locust Street Theatre. It is interesting to note that Cobb and his wife were married in Philadelphia in 1940.
Kazan, *A Life*, pp. 359–362. Kazan does not dwell much on *Salesman*'s Philadelphia tryout run in his own book—but says that he thought Cobb's performances there were his best in the role. He does not mention attending the concert with Miller and Cobb.
"Lee J. Cobb Stars in New Drama by Arthur Miller," *Camden Courier-Press*, January 24, 1929, p. 20.
Mielziner, *Designing for the Theatre*, pp. 46–62. Mielziner's account of the creative team's preparations for *Salesman*'s debut is the most detailed of all those available. He stated that there were two initial days of lighting instrument installation and set load-in for *Salesman* at the Locust, done by local stagehands and his assistants. Since the previous show playing at the Locust (*The Shop at Sly Corner*, starring Boris Karloff) ended its run on Saturday the 15th, that would mean this work took place on Sunday the 16th and Monday the 17th. Mielziner also stated he did not arrive to supervise preparations until Tuesday the 18th, that Wednesday the 19th was "all mine," and the actors did not arrive until Thursday the 20th. But the designer also related that he and his technicians often worked through the night, and that he was getting very little sleep that week. Perhaps this accounts

for his own errors in memory about the actors' arrival. Theater historian Brenda Murphy also notices the discrepancy in dates in the designer's account, and that Mielziner incorrectly placed the opening night on Monday the 24th, not Saturday the 22nd.

Miller, Arthur, *Timebends*, pp. 186–191. Contains the much-quoted account by Miller about the concert at the Academy of Music and the stunned silence in the audience at the end of *Salesman*'s first public performance. It is essential that we note that this book is a *memoir*, however, and it would be wrong to hold the great man to account for any errors of fact. In his Introduction to *Timebends*, he clearly states: "This book is not an attempt at history."

"Milstein and Phila. Orchestra Heard by Capacity Audience," Linton Martin, *Philadelphia Inquirer*, January 22, 1949, p. 19. This review in Saturday's paper makes it clear that the orchestra did not play Beethoven the day before.

Murphy, *Death of a Salesman*, pp. 56–57. This is an excellent book about the entirety of *Salesman*'s creation and critical reception. But I would suggest that her account of the production's tryout weeks in Philadelphia needs some correction. Murphy writes that the set was being installed at the Locust by Friday the 14th, which cannot be correct, as the theater was still occupied by a previous show (see above). She also repeats Miller's story about Beethoven's *Seventh Symphony*, and she places the Philadelphia Orchestra's concert on Saturday afternoon—neither of which corresponds to Philadelphia newspaper ads and reviews from that weekend. The quote from the *Evening Bulletin*'s review was taken from this book.

"Playing the Salesman" (podcast), Christopher Bigsby, BBC Sounds, February 11, 2006, https://www.bbc.co.uk/sounds/play/b0076wzk. This is the source of the Miller quote "imaginings torn from the web of forgetting."

~~Something Wild in the Country~~ *Orpheus Descending*

"'Orpheus Descending' at Walnut," Henry Murdock, *Philadelphia Inquirer*, March 6, 1957, p. 26.

"Orpheus Descending" (ad), *Philadelphia Inquirer*, March 8, 1957, p. 28. Screen: 'Fugitive Kind'," Bosley Crowther, *New York Times*, April 15, 1960, p. 13.

"Screening TV: 'Wide World' Ranges Wide, But Disappoints," Harry Harris, *Philadelphia Inquirer*, March 4, 1957, p. 18.

Spoto, Donald, *The Kindness of Strangers*, pp. 236–238, 265.

"The Producers Theatre Presents: Something Wild In The Country" (framed poster), Collection of Walnut Street Theatre, Philadelphia.

"Theater Activities: Tennessee Williams' Drama To Bow," Barbara L. Wilson, *Philadelphia Inquirer*, March 3, 1957, p. 96.

"The Fugitive Kind," *Old Yorker —film notes* (website), January 8, 2016. https://oldyorkeronline.com/the-fugitive-kind/ (The quotes about the movie and Marlon Brando are from this source.)

Philadelphia, Here I Come!

"Black Dot Marks the Location of the Walnut," Photo from the *Philadelphia Evening Bulletin*, George C. McDowell Collection, Temple University Library.

Friel, Brian, *Plays One: Philadelphia, Here I Come!* In 1996, on the 30th anniversary of its arrival in the city of its title, the play was staged again at the Walnut Street Theatre with Philadelphia actors in the cast.

"Historic Photo Gallery: 1965," Walnut Street Theatre (website), **https://www.walnutstreettheatre.org/about/gallery/?ch=7&id=16.**

"Merrick Stages Import From Ireland," Henry T. Murdock, *Philadelphia Inquirer*, January 18, 1966, p. 13.

"'Philadelphia, Here I Come!' Arrives," Jerry Gaghan, *Philadelphia Daily News*, January 18, 1966, p. 46.

The King and Oy

"'Chu Chem' Folds Saturday Night," *Philadelphia Inquirer*, November 18, 1966, p. 18.
"Chu Chem Ticket Holders" (ad), *Philadelphia Inquirer*, November 21, 1966, p. 20.
Mandelbaum, Ken, *Not Since Carrie*, pp. 38–40.
"Molly Picon Quits 'Chu Chem' Role," Jerry Gaghan, *Philadelphia Daily News*, November 11, 1966, p. 43.
"Musical 'Chu Chem' Premieres at Locust," Jerry Gaghan, *Philadelphia Daily News*, November 16, 1966, p. 44.
Picon, Molly and Jean Bergantini Grillo, *Molly*, pp. 247–252.

Muhammad Ali vs. Big Time Buck White

"Big Time Buck White Opens Here—Was Hit in New York," *Philadelphia Tribune*, April 1, 1969, p. 18.
"Buck White—Muhammad Ali—We Came in Chains," *Daily Motion* (website), https://www.dailymotion.com/video/x4r5su.
"Clay Wins Decision in Big Musical," Jack Gaver (UPI), *Philadelphia Daily News*, December 3, 1969, p. 35.
"Informality Sets Tone of 'Big Time Buck White,'" Henry T. Murdock, *Philadelphia Inquirer*, April 4, 1969, p. 4.
"Isn't Life Dreamy?: Big Time Gets Writers Nod," *Philadelphia Tribune*, April 15, 1969, p. 17.
"Muhammad Ali Spars in W. Phila. Street," Tom Fox, *Philadelphia Daily News*, May 1, 1969, p. 4.
"Star of Hit Play: Dick Williams is Soft-Spoken Actor with Very Loud Message," *Philadelphia Tribune*, April 26, 1969, p. 23.
"That's Show Business," Barbara L. Wilson, *Philadelphia Inquirer*, May 9, 1969, p. 22.

The Line of Least Existence—Last Days of the TLA

Bissinger, *The Fun House*, pp. 106–108.
"Danny DeVito on David Blaine's Magic Show, Musical with Judd Hirsch & Working with His Daughter Lucy," *Jimmy Kimmel Live*, January 17, 2023, YouTube.
Drexler, Rachel, Unpublished script for *The Line of Least Existence*, Archives of the Historical Society of Pennsylvania, 1970.
"'Least Existence' Premieres at TLA," Charles Petzold, *Philadelphia Daily News*, January 28, 1970, p. 35.
"'Line of Least Existence': a poor excuse for a musical," Leslie Reidel, *Philadelphia After Dark*, February 4–11. (Clipping in TLA archives, Pennsylvania Historical Society.)
"Oral history interview with Rosalyn Drexler, 2017 May 17–June 2," Archives of American Art (website). https://www.aaa.si.edu/collections/interviews/oral-history-interview-rosalyn-drexler-17499.
"Reflections on South Street" *Issu* (website), *QVNA Magazine* (November/December 2018), https://issuu.com/qvna/docs/qvna_november_2018/s/22561."Rock Musical Makes World Debut," William H. Collins, *Philadelphia Inquirer*, January 28, 1970, p. 20.
"Rosalyn Drexler: Out of ring and onto stage," Barbara L. Wilson, *Philadelphia Inquirer*, January 25, 1970, p. 79.
Sachs, *Notes on the Underground*, pp. 267–270.
"Theater of the Living Bizarre: Can They Get It For You Wholesome?" *Camden Courier-Post*, February 16, 1970, p. 13.
"Theater Steams Along Through Sea of Debt," William Collins, *Philadelphia Inquirer*, May 10, 1970, p. 93.

"View From The Bleachers At TLA Play: Rock, Nudes, and a $50,000 Play," Walter F. Naedele, *Philadelphia Evening Bulletin*, January 25, 1970, section 5, p. 3.

Auntie Mame Leaves Early

"At the Shubert: 'Mame' Musical Appears Winner," Elain Jubanyin, *Camden Courier-Press*, April 5, 1966, p. 23.
"At the Shubert: 'Mame' Opens to Applause of Full House," Henry T. Murdock, *Philadelphia Inquirer*, April 5, 1966, p. 27.
"'Mame' Cakewalks onto Shubert Stage," Gerry Gaghan, *Philadelphia Daily News*, April 5, 1966, p. 34.
"Lansbury is Bringing Back Mame," William H. Collins, *Philadelphia Inquirer*, July 3, 1983, p. 71.
"'Mame' Has Been Around, but Wears It Well," Nels Nelson, *Philadelphia Daily News*, July 8, 1983, p. 47.
"Phila resists the charms of Liz, Dick, and Mame," William H. Collins, *Philadelphia Inquirer*, July 11, 1983, p. 24.

Part Eight: The Manning Street Theatre

(Note: The investigation of this topic involved extensive personal interviews and email communications with many of the subjects of the narrative for Part Eight. Therefore, the format of citation for Sources and Notes is different in this section of the book. Instead of listing books and articles alphabetically as previously done, I have instead provided a brief selection from the relevant text and then noted the exact source for the quotation or information.)

All citations marked "clipping" are in the Theater Collection of the Free Library of Philadelphia's Rare Book Department, which has an extensive file of archival material on the Manning Street Theatre. Other archives can be found in the Special Collections Research Center of Temple University Library. Transcripts and copies of interviews and emails are in my personal collection.

Hamlet in the Rafters

"*A cafe theater*"—"A Mixture of Theatre and Coffee," Ernest Schier, *Philadelphia Evening Bulletin*, March 25, 1969, p. 26F (clipping).
"*The Midway*"—"Icandy, part II: The Swinging 60s and Beyond," blog post by Bob Skiba on thegayborhoodguru.wordpress.com, dated August 5, 2012. Accessed June 12, 2019.
"*Writing a few small checks*"—Interview with Stuart Firestein, August 6, 2018.
"*With a thick, for real pony tail*"—Schier, "A Mixture of Theatre and Coffee."
"*Doc Watson's Bar*"—Interview with Patrick Cronin, August 15, 2018.
"*Valyric Hall*"—A church building is clearly shown on Philadelphia city survey maps dating back to the 1850s, but later the building became the Howard Hospital, run by Dr. Edwin C. Howard, a Harvard-educated Black physician. In 1890, it was remodeled into a church again by the carpenter F. P. Main for the Union A. M. E. Church congregation, which was moving from its original home nine blocks to the east. See Roger Lane's *William Dorsey's Philadelphia and Ours*, p. 119. The building was demolished in the summer of 1974.
"*Adjacent nursing home*" and other details about renovations—Stuart Firestein interview.
"*120 large pillows*"—"Pillow Counters," *Philadelphia Evening Bulletin*, August 10, 1971 (clipping).
"*Young actors of the company*"—Manning Street Flier, "History," Free Library of Philadelphia Theater Collection.

"It was like a movie"—Email from Marlea Evans, August 30, 2018.
"Department of Licenses and Inspections"—"Lombard St. Theatre Can't Get OK to Open," *Philadelphia Evening Bulletin*, April 22, 1970 (clipping).
"Trouble with inspectors"—"Theater Reopens," Desmond Ryan, *Philadelphia Inquirer*, July 3, 1971, p. 6.
"Young and inexperienced"—Firestein interview.
"The first planned production"—"'Joe Egg' Now Tries South Street," by Ernest Schier, *Philadelphia Evening Bulletin*, May 26, 1970 (clipping).
"Ladies with cherries in their hats"—Evans email, August 30, 2018.
"Core company of local actors"—Kersey was the sole African-American member of the company during all its years on Lombard Street. He left the company before its transformation into the Manning Street Actors' Theatre in 1973. (Don Kersey email, August 26, 2018.)
"It was one of the moments"—Interview with John Connolly, October 19, 2018.
"Never turn down a job"—Interview with Joe Stinson, May 31, 2018.
"We were all just spellbound"—Firestein interview.
"This highly anti-establishment aspect"—Interview with Mary Kaye Bernardo, September 3, 2018.
"It is all enormously entertaining"—"Manning St. Stages 'Ubu Roi' as an Energetic, Amusing Farce," Walter Naedele, *Philadelphia Evening Bulletin*, October 12, 1972 (clipping).
"How to dress for your first Ubu banquet"—"First Naughty Play has Worn Very Well," Susan Walker, *WELCOMAT*, October 12, 1972, p. 17 (clipping, Free Library of Philadelphia Theater Collection).
"Area theatregoers"—"A 'Nightingale' Sings on Manning Street," *Evening Bulletin*, n.d. (clipping).
"$5000 grant"—Bernardo interview.
"There were some signs"—Connolly interview.
"We just got to a point"—Stinson interview.
"Women of Trachis" and *"additional complications"*—interviews with Firestein, Bernardo, Connolly, and Stinson.
"It wasn't what I wanted"—"Inmates Taking Over as Theater Undergoes Change in Leadership," Joe Adcock, *Philadelphia Evening Bulletin*, August 26, 1973, Section 5, p. 1 (clipping).
"I was probably exhausted"—Firestein interview.

The Two Joes

"Stinson would be the nominal artistic director"—Stinson interview.
"This core group of actors"—"Walnut Has Everything From Chamber Music to Dance," *Philadelphia Inquirer*, September 9, 1973, p. 82.
"Mentioning in several interviews"—Papp had recently made a public pronouncement that he wished to form a "National Theater" at Lincoln Center, which Jim Lambert recalls as the source of their idea to approach him. Lambert email, April 5, 2019.
"At the time he was everything" and *"Extra projects lying around"*—Stinson interview.
"No cash coming in"—Lambert email.
"Whatever money we could get"—Stinson interview.
"They each had one working drawer"—Lambert email.
"The days were incredibly busy"—Stinson interview.
"It was a fantastic time of life"—Martha Kearns interview, May 31, 2019.
"Twelve dollars each"—"Manning Street is Alive and Well and Living at 1520 Lombard Street," Richard Fuller, *The Metropolitan Magazine*, February 1974 (clipping).
"Sam, As in Beckett"—"Beckett and the Blobs," Shelley Sclan, *The Daily Pennsylvanian*, November 15, 1973.
"A pie fight!"—Interview with Jim Leitner, April 4, 2019.

298 • ADVENTURES IN THEATER HISTORY: PHILADELPHIA

"I'm upstairs rehearsing"—Stinson interview.
"I had just gotten a new used car"—Interview with Steve Stephenson, July 9, 2018.
"A new carpet"—Stinson interview.
"It was like the takeover of two jocks"—"Joseph Papp at the Zenith—Was It Boom or Bust?" Patricia Bosworth, *New York Times*, November 25, 1973, pp. 1, 21.
"I was deranged, man"—Quotations from Rabe's *The Orphan*, as published in *The Vietnam Plays: Volume Two*, Grove Press, 1993.
"A play Rabe had been developing"—Little, *Enter Joseph Papp*, pp. 240–244, 251–257.
"Abruptly canceled by the network"—For Rabe's own account of the circumstances of the original productions and his relationship with Joe Papp, see his Afterword to the *The Vietnam Plays: Volume Two*, pp. 181–197.
"Outrun his dramatic language"—"Stage: Rabe's 'The Orphan' Arrives," Clive Barnes, *The New York Times*, April 19, 1973, p. 51.
"C'mon gimme a break"—Quoted in Turan, *Free for All*, p. 333.
"Rabe had balked"—Turan, *Free for All*, p. 332.
"A new member of the faculty"—Email from Barnet Kellman, May 29, 2019.
"The objective"—Interview with Barnet Kellman, June 3, 2019.
"We make it or we blow it"—Papp to Work with Manning Street," Jonathan Takiff, *Philadelphia Daily News*, n.d. (clipping).

The Orphan

"In our little world of Philadelphia"—"Kevin Bacon interview for *The Following*: 'my career went down the toilet,'" by Jane Mulkerrins, *The Telegraph*, January 22, 2013.
"Bacon was enrolled in acting classes"—Email from Alkis Papoutsis, September 10, 2018.
"Reviews were mixed"—"Physicists: Loonies Among the Scientists," Bonnie Gordon, *The Drummer*, January 29, 1974 (clipping). "Durrenmatt's Jolly Voice of Doom," Joe Adcock, *Philadelphia Evening Bulletin*, January 29, 1974 (clipping).
"It was not at all certain the theater could stay open"—"Manning Street Actors Theatre to Produce Rabe's 'The Orphan,'" Ernest Schier, *Philadelphia Evening Bulletin*, February 5, 1974.
"Guys with binoculars"—Stinson interview. However, despite its Philadelphia success, *Tubstrip* subsequently failed to make a splash in New York, and its producer's hopes all went down the drain.
"A little bit of Buxtehude"—Jim Leitner, in his interview with me, was still amused by Bacon's delivery of this line from *The Orphan* fifty years later.
"Commitment is, I think, the right word"—"Manning Street is Alive and Well and Living at 1520 Lombard Street," Richard Fuller, *The Metropolitan Magazine*, February 1974 (clipping).
"Kellman had discovered"—Kellman, Barnet, "Production Casebook no. 24: David Rabe's 'The Orphan'—A Peripatetic Work in Progress." *TQ—Theatre Quarterly* 7 (1977), p. 88.
"Papp himself continued to check on its progress"—Some of the participants' memories differ on how often Papp was present in Philadelphia. Connolly and Stinson both recall Papp visiting during rehearsals, but Kellman is clear that Papp did not arrive until opening night.
"Back to New York with him"—According to Stinson, Papp had sent an additional $4,000 to support the ongoing costs of the show.
"Arm wrestling contests"—Stinson interview. "I woke up the next day and my shoulder was killing me," related Stinson.
"The actors were all young ... Rude and insensitive"—Turan, *Free for All*, p. 335–336.
"Papp immediately rejected Rabe's accusations"—Kellman interview.
"We got into a kind of a row"—Turan, *Free for All*, p. 336.
"David was crab-red in the face."—Turan, *Free for All*, p. 336.

"Rabe was determined to have this out alone"—Quotations from interviews with Connolly, Stinson, and Kellman, respectively. The story of the fight, as it was passed among the Manning Street company in later recollections, often included an assertion that one of the two men had thrown a punch; however, it seems that was not the case.

"Joe never saw the second act"—Kellman interview.

"It was because we both cared a lot"—Turan, *Free for All*, p. 336.

"Scheier particularly praised"—"A Lively Production of 'Orphan,'" Ernest Schier, *Philadelphia Evening Bulletin*, March 16, 1974 (clipping).

"The Orphan is undoubtedly"—"'Orphan'—Tradition takes a New Tack," *Philadelphia Daily News*, March 16, 1974 (clipping).

"Fails as a drama"—"Manning's 'Orphan' Makes A Statement But Is A Failure," William B. Collins, *Philadelphia Inquirer*, March 18, 1974, p. 4B.

"Operating budget for the '73–'74 season"—"Greater Philadelphia Cultural Alliance—Application for Membership." Document in the Special Collection Research Center, Temple University, Philadelphia.

Epilogues

Ghost Light

This chapter was originally published—in a somewhat different form—as a personal post on Facebook after news arrived about Lori Aghazarian's death in July of 2022. I am deeply grateful to her brother, Aram Aghazarian, and the rest of the Aghazarian family for their consent to share it here.

Love Unpunished

Rothenberg's notes are published in an article on the Pig Iron website: "*Love Unpunished*, 2021. Presented by FringeArts and Swarthmore College," *PigIron.org* (website). https://pigiron.org/productions/love-unpunished-2021.

Index

Academy of Music, Philadelphia, x, 58–61, 62, 63, 90, 94, 95, 107, 114, 164–165, 171, 185, 191, 194, 222, 225, 239–240
Academy of Music, New York, 59
Actors Order of Friendship, 192
Adler, Jacob, 195
Aghazarian, Lori, 262–263, 298
Albee, E. F., 96, 206
Ali, Muhammad, 233–235
American Company, *see* Hallam Company
Anthony, Mab, 224
Arch Street Theatre, ix, 15, 58, 91–93, 125, 142, 186–188, 192, 195–197, 276
Arden Theatre Company, 105–106, 107
Arnold, Benedict, 81–83
Arts Bank Theatre, x, 63, 108
Astor Place Riots, 58, 114, 276
Atkinson, Brooks, 213–214, 217

Bache, Sarah, 5
Bacon, Kevin, 254, 256, 259
Bailey, Bill ("Willie"), 34–36
Bailey, Pearl, 34–36
Bainter, Fay, 212, 213
Barber, Samuel, 223
Barry, Philip, 170
Barrymore, Ethel, 124–128, 285
Barrymore, Diana, 228
Barrymore, John ("Jack"), 93, 124–127
Barrymore, Lionel, 93, 124–127, 285
Beauvallet, Leon, 161–162, 287
Bel Geddes, Norman, 24, 212–213
Bernardo, Mary Kay, 242–244, 247
Bernhardt, Sarah, 167–169
Beury, Joseph, 206, 208
Bijou Theatre, Philadelphia, ix, 141–142
Bissinger, Tom, 236–238
Black Crook, The, 190–192
Bloomgarden, Kermit, 221, 224
Blythe, Georgiana Drew (Georgie Barrymore), 92–93, 125–126, 127
Blythe, Herbert (Maurice Barrymore), 125–127, 284, 285
Booth, Edwin, 30, 31, 92, 114, 186–189

Booth, John Wilkes, 186–189
Bowler, Annie Kemp, 190–192
Brando, Marlon, 218–219, 227, 228
Breschard, Jean-Baptiste, 85–88
Brice, Fanny, 209, 210
Brook, Peter, 175–177
Brooks, Lynn Matluck, 5, 274
Brotherton, George, C., 193–194
Bucks County Playhouse, 198
Bulwer-Lytton, Edward, 112, 114
Burns, Jennifer, 217
Burnside, R.H., 22–23
Butler, Pierce, 156–158, 183–184
Bykovsky, Stu, 38, 69

Calder, Alexander Milne, 17, 28
Calder, Alexander Stirling, 28–31
Calloway, Cab, 35–36, 37
Carncross' Minstrels, 164
Carroll, Earl, 209–211
Centlivre, Susanna, 50–51
Chambers, John (Rev.), 62–63
Chestnut Street Opera House (near 10th St.), ix, 17, 167, 170, 171, 216
Chestnut Street Theatre, first, *see* New Theatre
Chestnut Street Theatre, second (near 6th St.), ix, 14, 29, 58, 79–80, 161
Chestnut Street Theatre, third (near 13th St.), ix, 19, 29, 92, 113, 166, 188
City Line Dinner Theatre, ix, 220–204
Clarke, John Sleeper, 92, 186–189
Clurman, Harold, 227
Cobb, Lee J., 221–225, 292–293
Coca, Imogene, 129–130, 285
Coquelin, Benoît-Constant, 167–168
Collins, William, 36, 40–41, 177, 200, 201, 240
Connolly, John, 245, 246, *248*, 255, 256, 257, 259
Continental Theatre, x, 92
Cooke, George Frederick, 150–152, 154
Cooper, Thomas, 13
Cronin, Patrick, 244, 245
Cushman, Charlotte, 91, 160, 183–185

DeMille, Agnes, 139
De Rohan, Pierre, 23–24
Dietrich, Daniel, 242, 243
Dexter, John, 200
DeVito, Danny, 237, 238
Dime Museum (9th and Arch), ix, 164, 194
Drew, John (Jr.), 31, *91*, 92, 126, 127
Drew, John (Sr.), 92
Drew, Georgiana, (see Blythe, Georgiana)
Drew, Louisa Lane (Mrs. John Drew), 15, 31, 91–93, 105, 125, 128, 130–131, 186–187, 192, 282
Drew, Sidney, 93
Drexler, Rosalyn, 236–237
Douglass, David, 54, 77–78
D'Oyly Carte, Richard, 164, 166
Dunbar Theatre, *see* Lincoln Theatre
Dunlap, William, 56, 57, 151
Dunnock, Mildred, 221, 222–223, 293
Dunphy, Jack, 139, 140
Durang, Charles, 5, 13, 87, 90, 92, 94, 149, 151, 155–156, 180–182, 274
Durang, Christopher, 5
Durang, Edwin Forrest, 5
Durang, John, 2–5, 56, 78, 81–82, 141, 147, 274–275

Edwin Forrest Home, 32–33
Eleventh Street Opera House, 164
Empress Theatre, Manayunk, ix, 129, 130
Ensign, Doug, 244, 246
Erlanger Theatre, Philadelphia, ix, 172, 210, 231
Evans, Linda (later Marlea Evans), 243, 246, 256, *248*, 256
Eyre, Wilson, 30

Ferrer, José, 174, 231
Finkelstein, Stuart (later Stuart Firestein), 242–247, 259
Ford, Ken, 68, 244, 246
Forney, William B. (Rev.), 130
Foronda, Valentin de, 87–88
Forrest, Edwin, 10–15, 31, 33–34, 59, 91, 112–115, 141, 183, 185, 190, 196, 276
Forrest Theatre, first (Broad Street), ix, 129, 134

Forrest Theatre, second (Walnut Street), ix, 36, 130, 139, 171, 200, 201, 226, 240
Forrest, William, 11, 12, 276
Fosse, Bob, 140
Francine, Anne, 239, 240
Franklin, Benjamin, 5, 51, 57, 76, 106, 128
Frazier, Joe, 233, 235
Freedom Theatre, ix, 258
Friel, Brian, 229–230
Fuller, Charles, 144–147
Fuller, Richard, ix, 256
Furness, Horace Howard (Sr.), 31
Furness, Horace Howard (Jr.), 31, 213

Gabor, Zsa Zsa, 202–204
Gaghan, Jerry, 176, 230
Garden, Mary, 64–65, 135–136
Garonzik, Sara, xi, 108–109
Garret, Maureen, 246, 259
Garrick Theatre, Philadelphia, ix, 125
Gates, Joseph, 206
Gentlemen's Driving Park, ix, 121, 122–123
Gest, Morris, 23, 24, 26
Gevelot, Nicholas, 91, 92, 196
Gimbel, Bernard, 224
Gregory, Andre, 238, 242
Grendel's Lair, x, 67–70
Gross, Samuel, 166

Haas, Al, 200
Hagen, Uta, *172*, 174
Hallam Company, 3–4, 52–54, 55–57, 79–82, 275
Hallam, Lewis (Sr.), 52, 54
Hallam, Lewis (Jr.), 3–4, 56–57, 77
Hallam, Sarah, 54
Hammerstein, Oscar, 23, 26, 27, 64–66, 94–97
Havard, Bernard, *xi*, 105
Haviland, John, 91, 92
Hayes, Helen, 33
Headlong Dance Ensemble, 71
Hedgerow Theatre, 136, 170
Hedley, Robert, 107
Heflin, Van, 170
Hepburn, Katharine, 170–171
Heron, Matilda, 116–118
Hewitt, Alan, 222, 224, 293
Hirsch, Judd, 236, 238

Holiday, Billie, 42–44
Hopper, DeWolf, 22, 23
Howson, John, *163*, 166
Hulce, Tom, *254*, 255, 259
Hutton, Lawrence, 118

Irujo, Martinez de, 85–86, 87

Jay, Beulah, 98–100, 107, 132
Jefferson, Joseph, 31
Jefferson, Thomas, 7

Kalich, Jacob, 142–143
Kazan, Elia, 218–219, 221–225, 292, 293, 303
Kean, Charles, 112
Kean, Edmund, 13–14, 112, 153–154, 180–182
Kearns, Martha, 249–250
Keels, Thomas H., xi, 22–23, 277
Kellman, Barnett, 252–253, 255–258, 259, 298
Kelly, George E., ix, 131–132
Kelly, Grace, 133, 204
Kelly, John B., 131, 133
Kelly, Walter, 131
Kemble, Charles, 156, 156–157 *passim*, 184
Kemble, Fanny, 31, 155–158, 160, 183–184, 185
Kersey, Don, 244, 296
Kiralfy's Alhambra Palace, *x*, 192
Kogan, Jay, 244
Knapp, Dorothy, 209–211
Krimmel, John Lewis, 6, 8–9, 275, 281

Lambert, Jim, 248–250, 255, 297
Lansbury, Angela, 239–240
Lawrence, Lawrence Shubert (Sr.), 130
Lee, Eugene, 237
Leitner, Jim, 255, 258, 298
Lenya, Lotte, 224
Lewis, Michael J., 60
Lillie, Gordon ("Pawnee Bill"), 121–124
Lillie, May Manning, 121–124
Lincoln, Abraham, 43, 186–188
Lincoln Theatre, 101–102, 108
Littlefield Ballet, 138–139
Locust Street Theatre, x, 142, 173, 174, *175*, 198, 218, 220, 222, 224, 230, 231, 242, 246, 257, 293

Loeb, Philip, 198–199
Loggia, Robert, 227, 228

MacLaughlin, Whit, 71–74, 208
Macready, William Charles, 59, 91, 112, 114, 115, 185
Malden, Karl, 218
Manning Street Theatre, x, xv, 242–259, 295–298
Marion, John Francis, 96
Martin, Linton, 139, 173, 216, 219, 293
Marx Brothers, 198, 206–208
Marx, Groucho, 207–208
Mastbaum, Jules, 25, 27
McCracken, Joan, 138–139
McCullough, John, 31
Merriam Theatre, *see* Shubert Theatre
Merrill, Lisa, 184
Metropolitan Opera, New York, 23 *passim*, 94, 95
Metropolitan Opera House, Philadelphia, 23–27, as Philadelphia Opera House, ix, 23, 64–66, 99–102, 142
Mielziner, Jo, 219, 221, 222, 224, 293
Miller, Arthur, 132, 220–225, 230, 292–293
Modjeska, Helena, 117, 126
Moody, Richard, 33, 276
Moore, Terry, 204
Moss, Milton, 37–39
Mostel, Zero, 199, 200–201
Mummers, 17, 167–169
Murdoch, James, 31
Murdock, Henry, 175, 196, 239
Murphy, Brenda, 293
Murray, Ken, 210

Naedele, Walter, 246
National Showroom, ix, 72
National Theatre, *aka* New National Theatre (Chestnut & 8th), ix, 58, 90
National Theatre, *aka* Welch's Circus (Callowhill & 10th), ix, 190–192
National Theatre, New York, 112
Neal, Larry, ix, 144–146, 286
Nelson, Nels, 144, 146, 240
New Paradise Labs, xi, 71–74
New Theatre, ix, 5, 7–8, 11, 12, 76, 79–80, 81, 87, 89, 150–151, 153

Nolen, Terry, 105–106
Nolen, Amy Murphy, xi, 105–106
North, Alex, 221, 223

O'Keefe, John, 51, 80
Old American Company *see* Hallam Company
"Old Drury" *see* Chestnut Street Theatre, second
Old Theatre, Philadelphia (*aka* Southwark Theatre), 3, 5, 11, 55–57, 76–78
Olympic Theatre *see* Walnut Street Theatre
Onis, Luis, 87

Painted Bride Art Center, Callowhill Street, ix
Painted Bride Gallery, South Street, x, 43, 67
Papp, Gail Merrifield, 251, 256, 257
Papp, Joseph, 237, 248–253, 254–258, 297, 298
Papoutsis, Alkis, 252, 254, 255, 258
Park Theatre (Broad & Fairmount), ix, 15, 17
Park Theatre, New York, 153, 155, 183
Payne, John Howard, 11
Peale, Charles Wilson, 5
Peirce, William Shannon, 62–63
Penfield, Anne Weightman, 209–211
Penn, William
    as character in *Miss Philadelphia*, 15–17
    as young man, 46–48, 73
    as founder of Philadelphia, 48–49, 54, 73–74
    in statuary, 17, 28, 46, 91
People's Light & Theatre Company, 44
Pepin, Victor, 85–88
Persoff, Nehemiah, 37–39
Petzold, Charles, 237–238
Philadelphia Drama Guild, 224, 257
Philadelphia Fringe Festival (later FringeArts), ix, 71–73, 264
Philadelphia Orchestra, 108, 222–223, 225, 293
Philadelphia Theatre Company, xi, 44, 107–109
Philadelphia, Here I Come!, 229–230
Philadelphia Story, The, 170, 171
Picon, Molly, 141–142, 145–147, 231–232
Pig Iron Theatre Company, xi, 71, 264–265, 298
Pilmore, Joseph (Rev.), 10–11
Playhouse in the Park, ix, 37–39, 40

Plays & Players Theatre, x, xi, 68, 107, 108, 213
Plumsted, William, 52, 53
Plumsted's Warehouse, x, 52–54
Poole, Frederick (Rev.), 213
Porter, Charles, 11–12, 14
Posner, Aaron, 105–106
Prince Music Theatre (Chestnut St.), ix, 112, 264

Rabe, David, 248, 251–253, 256–258, 297, 298
Rachel (Elisa-Rachel Félix), 159–162
Rand, Ayn, 215–217
Rees, James, 90, 115, 159
Reinagle, Alexander, 79, 89
Reinhardt, Max, 24–25
Rice, Edward E., 19
Ricketts' Circus, ix, 81–83, 85, 86
Ricketts, John Bill, 81–83, 86
Ricketts, Francis, 81–83
Rizzo, Frank, 41, 246
Robertson, Lanie, 43–44
Robeson, Paul, 172–174
Rothenberg, Dan, xi, 265
Roy, Phil, 67–70
Royal Shakespeare Company, 175–177
Rush, William, 29
Ryan, Carrie, 104

Sagolla, Lisa Jo, 140
Saunders, Matt, 71, 72
Schoeffer, Eric, 71
Schloss, Edwin, 219, 224
Scheier, Ernest, 232, 242
Scott, George C., 224–225
Seldes, Gilbert, 212, 213
Sesqui-Centennial Stadium, ix, 21–23
Shakspere Society, the, 30–31
Shubert, Lee, 216
Shubert Organization, 171, 200, 234
Shubert Theatre (Broad St.), x, 108, 142, 175–177, 218, 239
Sigsbee, Charles Dwight, 18–20
Sinclair, Catherine Norton, 113, 276
Skulnik, Menashe, 142, 231–232
Society Hill Theatre, x, 54
Society Hill Playhouse, 244

INDEX • 305

Southwark Theatre, (see Old Theatre)
Spenser, Willard, 119, 120
Spoto, Donald, 133
Stapleton, Maureen, 227, 228
Stephenson, Steve, 251, 258
Stinson, Joseph, 245–247, *248*, 248–253, 255–258, 259, 298
Stokowski, Leopold, 25, 27
Story, Belle, 22–23
Stotesbury, Edward, 27
Stuccio, Nick, 71, 72
Sully, Rosalie, 184–185
Sully, Thomas, 152, 156, 185
Suzanne Roberts Theatre, x, 63, 107–108
Svin'in, Pavel, 8, 275
Swift, John, 12

Tabas, Daniel M., 204
Takiff, Jonathan, 28, 41
Tandy, Jessica, 218, 219
Temple Theatre (Chestnut Street), ix, 119–120, 193–194
Theatre Exile, 71
Theatre of the Living Arts, *aka* TLA, x, 67, 236–238, 242, 244, 256
Thomashefsky, Boris, 141, 142, 195
Thomashefsky, Mike, 141, 142
Tilden, William II, 134–137
Tivoli Gardens, Philadelphia, ix, 12
Tompkins, Floyd W. (Rev.), 64, 66
Tree, Ellen, 112, 160, 184
Tucker, Earl, 101–102

Walnut Street Theatre, Philadelphia, ix
  as "American Theatre," 112
  as "New Circus," 86
  as "Olympic Theatre," 6, 8, 11, 12
  as "Walnut Street Theatre," 12, 13, 19, 33, 43, 58, 68, *84*, 84–88, 91, 92, 105, 107, 114, 116, 117, 120, 132, 134, 135, 142, 145, 146, 153, 156, 159–162, 180–182, 183–185, 186, 187, 189, 206, 208, 212, 218–219, 224, 226–228, 230, 233–235, 246, 248, 257, *262*, 262–263
Wanamaker, John, 21
Washington, George, 55, 79, 80, 82
Warren, William, 12, 13, 14, 89, 180
Weill, Kurt, 224
Weise, Frank, 243
Wemyss, Francis, 89, 112, 113, 115
Wesker, Arnold, 200–201
Wheatley, William, 92, 114
White, Lemuel, 11
Whitehead, Robert, 228
Whitman, Walt, 166
Wignell, Thomas, 31, 57, 79–80, 89
Wilde, Oscar, 64, 104, 137, 163–166
Williams, Tennessee, 218–219, 226–227, 249
Wilma Theater, ix, x, xi, 42, 44, 63, 103–104, 107, 108, 258
Wilson, Alexander, 11
Wilson, Earl Jr., 68–69
Wilson, S. Davis (Mayor), 130
Winter, William, 117
Winters, Shelley, 37–38
Wood, William B., 7–9, 12, 13, 14, 31, 89, 91, 154, 180, 181
Woods, Al, 215–217

Zimmerman, J. Fred, 32–33
Zizka, Blanka, 44, *103*, 103–104
Zizka, Jiri, *103*, 103